AGAINST POLITICAL EQUALITY

THE PRINCETON-CHINA SERIES

Daniel A. Bell, Series Editor

The Princeton-China Series aims to publish the works of contemporary Chinese scholars in the humanities, social sciences, and related fields. The goal is to bring the work of these important thinkers to a wider audience, foster an understanding of China on its own terms, and create new opportunities for cultural cross-pollination.

Leadership and the Rise of Great Powers by Yan Xuetong

The Constitution of Ancient China by Su Li, edited by Zhang Yongle and Daniel A. Bell, translated by Edmund Ryden

Traditional Chinese Architecture by Fu Xinian, edited by Nancy Steinhardt, translated by Alexandra Harrer

Confucian Perfectionism: A Political Philosophy for Modern Times by Joseph Chan

A Confucian Constitutional Order: How China's Ancient Past Can Shape Its Political Future by Jiang Qing, edited by Daniel A. Bell and Ruiping Fan, translated by Edmund Ryden

Ancient Chinese Thought, Modern Chinese Power by Yan Xuetong, edited by Daniel A. Bell and Sun Zhe, translated by Edmund Ryden

Against Political Equality

THE CONFUCIAN CASE

TONGDONG BAI

PRINCETON UNIVERSITY PRESS
PRINCETON & OXFORD

Copyright © 2020 by Princeton University Press

Published by Princeton University Press
41 William Street, Princeton, New Jersey 08540
6 Oxford Street, Woodstock, Oxfordshire OX20 1TR

press.princeton.edu

LCCN 2019935933
ISBN 9780691195995
ISBN (e-book) 9780691197463

British Library Cataloging-in-Publication Data is available

Editorial: Rob Tempio and Matt Rohal
Production Editorial: Natalie Baan
Text and Jacket Design: Pamela Schnitter
Production: Erin Suydam and Brigid Ackerman
Publicity: Nathalie Levine and Julia Hall
Copyeditor: Cathryn Slovensky

Jacket art: Shutterstock

This book has been composed in Arno Pro

Printed on acid-free paper. ∞

Printed in the United States of America

10 9 8 7 6 5 4 3 2 1

To my grandma, my first teacher of Chinese traditions

CONTENTS

The History of This Book

On the basis of a few articles, in 2009 I published a book in Chinese with the title, *The New Mission of an Old State: The Comparative and Contemporary Relevance of Classical Confucian Political Philosophy* (Peking University Press). The main title is from the Chinese and Confucian classic *The Book of Odes* (诗经) and was originally meant to be a statement about the ever-renewing mission or mandate of the old state of Zhou. In this book, I tried to show how Confucianism, an "old state," is still relevant in the contemporary world (its new mission or mandate), hence the title. Soon after it was published, I started working on a revised English version of this book. I finished a first draft a few years ago and was asked to make a few manageable revisions by anonymous reviewers at Princeton University Press, which I thought I could finish in a month or so, by August 2012. Instead, it has taken me five more years to finish the "revisions." In addition to being distracted by all sorts of tasks, a main reason for this is that instead of making revisions, I drastically revised and expanded the original draft.

Upon reflection, I realize that the 2009 book is fundamentally "reactive." Its underlying rationale is that liberal democracy is dominant today, and so for Confucianism to be relevant to the contemporary world, it has to "react to" the challenges from liberal democracy. In that book, I offered a somewhat original approach, inspired by Rawls's later philosophy, in addressing the compatibility issue between Confucianism and liberal democracy. Although this approach is, I think, not as forced as the overseas New Confucians' approaches, the focus is still the compatibility between Confucianism and liberal democracy. But I did try to show that Confucianism has something critical and constructive to offer in our search for ideal political regimes, rather than being a mere "cheerleader" of liberal democracy. This constructive revision of liberal democracy is an earlier version of the Confucian hybrid regime I also propose in this book. In addition, I offered some cases of comparative studies in that book that seem to lack an organizing thread (other than being cases of comparative studies).

But around the time that I finished the first English draft, I developed a rather unorthodox thesis, which was already implicit in some of the comparative works in the 2009 book. The thesis is that the so-called Zhou-Qin (周秦) transition (also known as the Spring and Autumn and Warring States periods, or the SAWS, roughly from 770 BCE to 221 BCE [these periods are often also called "pre-Qin," although this term literally means before the founding of the Qin empire in 221 BCE]) that early Confucians such as Confucius and Mencius were facing is a transition to early modernity. It is a radical thesis, because the common perception is that the reason that China was defeated by the West and a Westernized Japan in the nineteenth and twentieth centuries was because the West had entered modernity while China had not. What I argue here is the opposite of that perception. That is, not only did China not lag behind in the modernization process (with regard to *early* modernity), but it actually entered (*early*) modernity almost two thousand years before the West did. Nevertheless, I think that if we follow the typical understanding of modernity, such as the Weberian one, which considers rational bureaucracy the key to a modern state, my thesis is easy to defend. Even if there is something unique about Western modernity that China failed to develop before the nearly fatal encounter with the West in the nineteenth century, there are enough commensurable conditions between early modern Europe and China during the Zhou-Qin transition, and if we take a closer look at these conditions, my theory will appear rather obvious.

Similar political situations lead to similar problems, and since some of these problems still persist in the contemporary age, we should try to understand Confucian solutions, compare them with liberal democratic ones, and then say which solutions are more effective for today's world, instead of dismissing Confucian solutions as premodern and fundamentally obsolete. In short, what I am doing in this book is to first try to understand early Confucian solutions for "modern" problems in their own terms, update them to the contemporary world, and then compare them with liberal democratic solutions. In my book *China: The Political Philosophy of the Middle Kingdom* (2012b), based on the premise of China's early modernity, I offered a survey of the early Confucian, Daoist, and Legalist solutions for confronting the problems of "modernity" and compared and contrasted them with one another and with the solutions offered by Western modern thinkers. This book is a more detailed and scholarly version that focuses on the Confucian answers.

Put very simply, the shared modern conditions between the Zhou-Qin transition in China and the European transition to early modernity is the emergence of a large, populous, well-connected, mobile, and plebeianized society of strangers. Under these conditions, the premodern, feudal institutional answers that were once applicable to a small, close-knit, nobility-based society of acquaintances no longer worked, and three key political issues needed to be answered anew: What gives the right for some to rule, and how are these people selected (the legitimacy issue)? How can a political entity be bonded together (the issue of identity)? How are entity–entity relations (i.e., international relations) to be handled?

In this book, I have attempted to show how early Confucians answered these questions and how answers to these questions can be developed from some early Confucian ideas. I have also offered institutionalized and updated versions of these answers and have pointed out their somewhat unique features. Finally, I argue how these institutionalized and updated answers may offer better alternatives to domestic and global governance than the mainstream liberal democratic models.

The Structure of This Book

In chapter 1, I first question the (less and less) dominant idea that liberal democracy is considered to be the culmination of history in terms of political models, and I then argue that we should still search for better political alternatives that address the political problems that the world is facing. I suggest that perhaps Confucianism can offer such alternatives. But Confucianism is a very long tradition, and there are competing interpretations of it; thus I specify what I mean by "Confucianism," and what approach I take to interpret the selected (early) Confucian texts. The approach I take is philosophical, so I need to defend why—and also explain how—we can read these early Confucian texts philosophically. In this attempt, I look at the world in which the early Confucians lived, and I argue that the problems they faced resemble those in European early modernity.

In chapter 2, I focus on the early Confucian answers to the issue of political legitimacy and the selection of rulers. On the one hand, I show how early Confucians more or less embraced the ideas of equality, upward mobility, and accountability. On the other hand, they had reservations about the democratic idea of "by the people," or self-governance. Their political ideal was a hybrid between popular participation and intervention by the elites or, more properly, by the meritocrats.

In chapter 3, I explore the problems with the democratic institution of "one person, one vote" and why the corrections from within liberal democracy are inadequate. I offer an updated institutional proposal based on the early Confucian ideas introduced in chapter 2 and show how this Confucian hybrid regime, which combines democratic elements with meritocratic elements, can better address the problems of the one person, one vote system than "internal" corrections.

In chapter 4, I answer anticipated challenges to the theory that the Confucian hybrid regime is a better alternative when addressing the problems of democracy. But even if I could answer these possible challenges, some may still argue that even if the Confucian model brings good governance, or better governance than the democratic model, we should still reject it because it violates the sacred democratic idea of equality and self-governance. To address this challenge, I further argue that the Confucian conception of equality is not as different from the liberal democratic understanding as it first appears, and there are merits to the Confucian reservation of some radical version of equality.

The next issue of "modernity" we need to face is how to develop a bond in a society of strangers. In chapter 5, I argue that the early Confucian ideas of humaneness and compassion may have been meant to, or can be used to, address this issue. I also give an account of the Confucian cultivation of the universal moral sentiment of compassion. In particular, I show how the institution of family plays a crucial role in this cultivation. Moreover, I argue that even when it is developed to embrace the whole world, the Confucian idea of compassion is still hierarchical. That is, the Confucian ideal here is to develop universal but unequal care.

Crucial to the Confucian answer to the issue of bonding among strangers is the need to expand the universal seed of compassion outward. But when we do this, we inevitably encounter conflicts between one's care for those closer to us and one's care for those distant from us, or the conflicts between the private and the public, which I explore in chapter 6. To solve this, the early Confucians proposed what I call a "continuum and harmony model" between the private and the public, which is challenged by thinkers such as Han Fei Zi. In Plato's *Republic*, an apparently opposite solution is offered. By comparing and contrasting these two solutions, I hope to defend the merits of the Confucian solution. Then, applying the Confucian idea of continuity and harmony between the private and the public to contemporary issues, I offer a criticism of the contemporary liberal evasion of virtue that is premised on a sharp divide between the private and the public, and a Confucian argument for gender equality in public affairs.

After the conceptual analysis of the early Confucian ideas of universal and hierarchical care, in chapter 7 I illustrate how it can be used, along with the early Confucian distinction between *yi* (夷) and *xia* (夏), to develop what I call the "Confucian new tian xia model" of state identity and international relations. I then show how this model is superior to both certain versions of the nation-state model and the cosmopolitan model. I also demonstrate how this model can offer a real possibility for China to rise peacefully, and how it can address some urgent issues of ethnic identity within China, which can also be used to shed light on similar issues in other countries.

A difficult issue in global governance is the issue of war, or interventions in general. In chapter 8, on the basis of the general model illustrated in chapter 7, I first offer a more "conservative," "isolationist" version of international intervention based on Confucius's ideas and then move to a more "aggressive" version by Mencius. The overarching principle of early Confucian theory of international intervention is "humane responsibility overrides sovereignty," and I compare this with two mainstream models of intervention, one based on the principle of "human rights override sovereignty" and the other based on the "Responsibility to Protect" doctrine. At the end of this chapter, I also confront problems with the Mencian theory of just war.

So far, I have tried to offer Confucian alternatives to mainstream liberal democratic models. To be clear, what I am offering in this book is a revision, not a complete rejection, of the liberal democratic models. In particular, I think the "liberal" part of liberal democracy should be largely preserved. The issue then becomes how Confucianism can be made compatible with the liberal part of liberal democracy, in particular, rights and the rule of law. This is the main issue that chapter 9 intends to address. First, I offer a critical evaluation of the four camps on the issue of compatibility between Confucianism and liberal democracy (as well as rights). I then argue that for liberal democracy to be compatible with different doctrines and political conceptions, Confucianism included, we need to make rights freestanding, free from metaphysical ideas such as the Kantian idea of autonomy. Using this (revised) later Rawlsian maneuver, I then show how Confucianism can be made compatible with the rights regime. To illustrate general strategies that I have developed in this chapter to make Confucianism compatible with rights, I show how Confucianism can endorse a certain version of animal rights. A crucial concept used here is, again, the Confucian universal and hierarchical care model, especially when it is expanded to include animals as its object. This goes one step further than the expansion of care to include all human beings in the world, which is critical to the Confucian new tian xia model of state identity and global governance. In the end, I return to the issue that is partially treated in chapter 6, the issue of how the promotion of certain virtues by the state is not in conflict with liberalism.

In the postscript, I use ideas and mechanisms that were introduced in the previous chapters to offer some preliminary treatments of two pressing issues of our time: environmental issues (including climate change) and technological challenges. I then discuss the difficulties with putting the Confucian proposals offered in this book into practice, even if these proposals are indeed superior, as I have argued.

Liberal democratic theorists also see the problems with the present liberal democratic order. But domestically, many of them propose solutions that promote "true" equality and "real" self-governance. The Confucian hybrid regime that I propose is premised on the conviction that "true" equality is fundamentally evasive, and what we should look for is not "true equality," which is a hopeless project, but a kind of "inequality" that benefits the worst-off the most. On global governance, the model that I propose is also hierarchical or unequal, in contrast to the egalitarian ideal that is presupposed by the cosmopolitan model, and the idea of all states being equal that is presupposed by the nation-state model. Moreover, the Confucian new tian xia model and some other Confucian proposals made in this book are based on the Confucian ideal of universal but unequal care. This unequal care or "partiality," I argue, can be a good foundation for better political models than the present ones. In short, contrary to the general egalitarian critique of the present liberal democratic order, what I am proposing in this book is a defense of various inequality-based models (hence the main title). These models preserve some forms of equality and merely give up the unrealistic ideal of radical equality. Put differently, there is a growing trend in the real world, where democratic components threaten liberal ones, as we can see in the rise of illiberal democracy in the developing world, and the rise of populist politics in Europe and in the United States, which also leads to an encroachment on liberties.[1] This trend suggests that there are fundamental conflicts between liberalism and democracy, and in the real world, the solution is to suppress liberalism. Some liberal democratic thinkers and practitioners still try to preserve both the liberal and the democratic components of liberal democracy, and the aforementioned "left-wing" or egalitarian solution is to save liberal democracy by strengthening equality. But maybe it is time to recognize the unbridgeable discrepancy between the liberal and the democratic (as well as the egalitarian), and a true liberal should try to protect the liberal components from the threat of the democratic and egalitarian components. My solution, then, is to save liberalism by putting Confucianism-inspired limits on democracy and equality.

1. My criticism of the democratic element of liberal democracy was initially developed in the first decade of this century, and the main ideas haven't changed in this book. Curiously, when I delivered lectures that were related to my criticism of democracy in much of the past decade, I could only refer to George W. Bush or Sarah Palin. But now, the real-world references are plenty—George W. Bush looks like a statesman when compared to Donald Trump! So it is unfortunate that it has taken a few more years for me to finish this book, because I missed the opportunity to say, "I told you so." But it may also be a blessing: what I am arguing, especially the critique of the one-person, one-vote concept, may sound less radical or "crazy" and more acceptable to my readers.

ACKNOWLEDGMENTS

IT HAS TAKEN ME MANY YEARS to finish this book, and there are so many
people who have helped me along this long journey. Therefore, there is simply
no way I can thank them all, if I don't wish to end up writing a book-length
section of acknowledgments. I give special thanks to those who helped me
with this or that idea in the main body of this book, and here I will offer an
overview of how I have been helped along the way.

I was interested in Western philosophy before I went to college. Preparing
myself to do serious philosophy was one of the reasons that I chose physics as
my major. While studying at Peking University, reading Feng Youlan's (aka
Fung Yu-lan [冯友兰]) works and sitting in some Chinese philosophy classes
helped me to discover Chinese philosophy. Although Dr. Feng passed away
almost right after I entered Peking University, most of my teachers of Chinese
philosophy there studied with him, and in this way, I felt I studied with him as
well. I then read works by other scholars on Chinese philosophy, for example,
by Professor Tu Weiming. During my studies at Boston University, my main
exposure to Chinese philosophy came from the Confucianism seminars that
he directed at Harvard, and I also witnessed and was inspired by his devotion
to promoting Confucianism in the world. I owe my initiation into Chinese
philosophy to them.

After getting a master's degree in philosophy of science from Peking University, I came to Boston University to pursue my doctoral degree in philosophy. Two professors there have had the greatest impact on my philosophical
outlook and my works in Chinese political philosophy. I learned antimetaphys-
ics from the late Burton Dreben, and his Wittgensteinian version of Rawls's
later works also gave me great insight into how to deal with the compatibility
issue between liberal democracy and Confucianism. His defense of Rawlsian
pluralism and liberal democracy has also left a deep mark on my own political
philosophy. The other major philosophical influence on me has been Professor
Stanley Rosen, who seems to be the polar opposite of Dreben. For example,
Rosen claimed to be an ordinary-language metaphysician, and being a former
student of Leo Strauss, he is often considered a conservative by association,
whereas Dreben was a close friend of John Rawls, a philosophical symbol of

American liberalism. The apparent tensions and (in my view) the profound similarities between them offered me a great opportunity to philosophize. Indeed, in spite of their differences, they both gave great care to the "Great Books," although their choices of Great Books were rather different. Their care and their hermeneutic method in general inspired my own close reading of the Great Books (in Chinese philosophy). Rosen also shaped my own take on the history of Western political philosophy, and his obsession with the issue of antiquity versus modernity, which is sometimes phrased as the issue of the few versus the many, has also led to my own reflections on this issue, and has been instrumental in formulating my radical thesis on China's early modernity. In him I also found a kindred elitist—or dare I say Nietzschean?—spirit, which, I hope, will become obvious and maybe notorious in this book.

For a few reasons, I still decided to write a doctoral dissertation on issues in the philosophy of physics (the philosophy of quantum mechanics, to be precise, about which I learned a great deal from my thesis advisor, Professor John Stachel). After getting a job at Xavier University in Cincinnati, I finally switched to political philosophy and Chinese philosophy. I could do this only because the philosophy department there, under the leadership of the former chair and late professor Robert Rethy, was extremely nurturing. It didn't force tenure-track faculty members to publish, and it indulged and supported them to pursue their own academic interests. Without this environment, I wouldn't have dared to make the switch, or survived it, given the fact that during the first few years, I couldn't publish much in this new field. Rethy's and some of my colleagues' care for the Great Books also inspired me, and I learned a great deal from them. I have to say that my years at Xavier were my second graduate school, without which I wouldn't have been able to write this book. Put another way, in the American system, I ended up doing a German-style "habilitation" at Xavier (with job security, in contrast to the brutal German system today).

Many of the conferences I attended also helped me to better formulate my ideas. I couldn't name them all, but I would like to mention two small-scale conferences: "The Midwest Conference on East Asian Thought" (later "The Midwest Conference on Chinese Thought") and "Southeast China Roundtable." In these settings, in contrast to the big "marketplace," such as the APA meetings, a limited number of scholars could truly come to know one another and one another's works, which was very helpful to me, then a newcomer to the field.

On the basis of a few published articles, most of which are in English, I started working on a manuscript in Chinese that later became the 2009 book. In this process, a few talks I gave in China at the Uni-Rule Institute (天则研究所), Peking University, Renmin University, Tsinghua University, Beijing Normal University, Capital Normal University, and, in particular, a weeklong lecture series at Wuhan University helped me formulate my ideas. I am deeply grateful to those who invited me and offered me critical comments in these situations. Their critical inputs and friendly support made the publication of the 2009 book possible. For its publication, I would also like to thank my editor, Wang Ligang (王立刚), who has a keen eye on scholarship and is willing to devote himself to helping other scholars.

After the 2009 book was published, I received numerous comments through conferences, lectures, teaching, and private exchanges. I can't even list them here, due to the limit of space. There are also those whose ideas may have influenced my thinking, but I haven't yet had a chance to make a record. I am sorry for this broad-stroke mentioning, and I am grateful to all those who have helped me in the drastic revision of the 2009 book.

The School of Philosophy at Fudan University, which I joined in the spring of 2010, also offered a great nurturing environment. In particular, Professor Sun Xiangchen (孙向晨), who later became the dean of the school, and Dr. Hu Huazhong (胡华忠), who was the party secretary at the school, helped me greatly with the transition from the United States to China. But there were also other responsibilities I took on there, including overseeing a master and visiting student program in Chinese philosophy, with courses taught in English. Professor Thomas Pogge suggested that I take a fellowship in the United States, which made me realize that I needed to take a year off to finish this book. In the next year, Sun and the School of Philosophy encouraged me to take a year of absence, and thanks to a tip from Professor Mathias Risse of Harvard's Kennedy School (who became a friend in our shared efforts to promote comparative political theories), I applied for a position as a faculty-in-residence at Harvard's Edmond J. Safra Center for Ethics. When I was awarded the fellowship, it turned out that it was newly cosponsored by the Berggruen Center for Culture + Philosophy. The title of my fellowship became "Berggruen Fellow at Harvard's Edmond J. Safra Center for Ethics." The supportive environment at the center and this year of "freedom" were crucial for me in finally completing this book, and I am deeply grateful to my department, Harvard's Edmond J. Safra Center for Ethics (under Danielle Allen's leadership), and the Berggruen Institute for their support. Indeed, I admire Nicolas Berggruen for his serious attempt to promote deep thinking in a cross-cultural manner, and am honored to be a (small) part of this endeavor.

As I mentioned, it has taken far longer to finish the "revisions" than I had promised, so I would like to thank my editor, Rob Tempio, for his patience and his help. I would also like to thank others at the press, including Matt Rohal (editor), Natalie Baan (production editor), Cathy Slovensky (copyeditor), Theresa Liu (copywriter), and a few others who have facilitated the production of this book and offered very good advice and suggestions along the way. Their professionalism and care are deeply appreciated. I would also like to thank Justin Tiwald, Stephen Angle, Jane Mansbridge, Carlin Romano, and Melissa Williams for their input on the book's title. The extremely encouraging and generous words, as well as the good revision suggestions, by the two anonymous reviewers are also deeply appreciated.

Throughout my years of thinking about the issue of the contemporary relevance of Confucianism, two people have helped me the most. One is Daniel Bell. Many of my "own" ideas were first inspired by his, such as the idea of the hybrid regime. He has a talent of offering original perspectives on so many issues. Although I don't always agree with him on his readings of Confucianism, China, the West, or politics, I always find his ideas provocative, giving new directions for my own thinking. In spite of the "contrarian" bent that he often shows publicly, especially when he challenges some Western orthodoxies, he is an extremely kind person who has helped me in so many ways. It feels like he is a big brother of mine—in the Confucian sense, and not in the 1984 sense. Indeed, he is a true Confucian, perhaps much truer than I am.

The other person who has helped my thinking greatly and consistently is Dr. Qian Jiang (钱江). If Daniel Bell plays the role of the big brother who takes care of his younger brother (i.e., me), Qian Jiang is like a naughty little brother who always creates troubles for his elders. As I argue in this book, my version of Confucianism is one that can resist the challenge of Han Fei Zi, and, in reality, Qian Jiang is my Han Fei Zi, who has always revealed my over-rosy reading of this or that and has pushed me to be "tough" on my version of Confucianism. Both Daniel's and Jiang's encyclopedic knowledge and deep appreciation of history, politics, and philosophy are always instrumental in my own thinking.

This book is dedicated to my grandma. She was barely literate but was my first teacher of Confucianism and Chinese culture. Through her, and through the extended family (my mom, an aunt I was very close to, and so on) that centered around her (as stars centering around the North Star), I didn't learn but felt the spirit of Confucianism and Chinese culture. They are the source of my own love of the Chinese traditions. Ironically, in my own effort to defend family-oriented Confucianism, I have often had to sacrifice time I could have spent with my family. I am grateful to my parents for their indulgence of a workaholic son, and Ms. Liu Hongyu (刘虹瑜) for supporting me and helping me to raise our children, Alexander Yuchen Bai (白与尘) and Athena Yuge Bai (白与歌), to whom I am also grateful because they give me immense happiness and broaden the meaning of my own life, although, as it is often said, I would have finished the book earlier if not for them, of which I have no regret.

Some chapters in this book are based on published articles of mine, although most of them have been revised to a great extent. I thank the original publishers for allowing me to use them in this book. These include: chapter 1, Bai (2011 and 2014b); chapters 2–4, Bai (2008a, 2013b, and 2015b); chapter 5, Bai (2014a); chapter 6, Bai (2008b); chapter 7, Bai (2015a); chapter 8, Bai (2013a); chapter 9, Bai (2005 and 2009a); and the postscript, Bai (2015c and 2017).

NOTES ON ABBREVIATIONS, KEY TERMS, AND TRANSLATIONS

THERE ARE TWO COMMON SYSTEMS of romanizing Chinese, the Wade-Giles and the Pinyin systems. This book mostly uses the latter but occasionally uses the former, when, for example, the Wade-Giles system is used in an author's name, in the title of a book or paper in a published work, or in a quotation from another author. In all the Chinese terms that contain more than one Chinese character, I put a space in between the characters, while many other authors don't. For example, I use "Lao Zi," *tian xia,* and *jun zi,* instead of "Laozi," *tianxia,* and *junzi.* My reasoning is that, for example, in the name "Lao Zi," "Lao" is allegedly the name of the legendary person while "Zi" means "master." In English, we write "Master Lao" and not "Masterlao" or "Laomaster."

Two numbers separated by a period (".") are used to refer to passages in the *Analects,* and two numbers separated by either capital letter "A" or capital letter "B" are used to refer to passages in the *Mencius.* These numbering systems function similarly to the Stephanus Numbers in quoting Plato, helping readers to track down the passages in these two texts, but they are not as standardized as the Stephanus Numbers. The systems I am using in this book are identical to those used in D. C. Lau (2000 and 2003).

Unless otherwise noted, all translations of the *Analects,* the *Mencius,* and the *Lao Zi* are mine; I have consulted with a few translations that are listed in the references (especially Wing-Tsit Chan 1969 and D. C. Lau 2000 and 2003). All translations of *The Doctrine of the Mean* and *The Great Learning* are mine; I have consulted with Wing-Tsit Chan (1969). The English translation of Plato's *Republic* used in this book is from Bloom (1991).

There are many translations of the crucial Confucian concept of *ren* (仁). I think "benevolence" is a good translation that catches the meaning of *ren* well. But in this book, I will use the term "humaneness" and its variants to translate *ren,* for "humaneness" also means benevolence and kindness, and it nicely catches the subtle allusion of the Chinese term *ren* to human beings in that *ren* sounds exactly the same as *ren* (人 human).

The Chinese term *tian xia* (天下) means literally "under Heaven," which can mean all that is under Heaven, that is, the world or all people who are under Heaven, that is, the entire human race. I will use "the world" or "the people" to translate *tian xia* when its meanings are clear. I will use the transliteration *tian xia* when it doesn't clearly refer to either the world or the people.

The Chinese term *jun zi* (君子) literally and originally means a member of the nobility. But as happened to many terms like this, early Confucians reinterpreted it, ridding the term of the meaning associated with feudal hierarchy and turning it into something purely meritocratic. In the *Analects*, this term could be used in one, the other, or both meanings. I will use the transliteration *jun zi* when the double meaning is intended, and use the phrase (morally) "exemplary person" to translate this term when it clearly does not allude to nobility in the feudal sense.

AGAINST POLITICAL EQUALITY

1

Why Confucianism?
Which Confucianism?

Has History Ended? Message from a Rising China

In 1992 Francis Fukuyama famously announced that we are at the end of history because liberal democracy is the "final form of human government," and the "end point of mankind's ideological evolution" (1992, xi)—that is, the development of human political history ends with the best possible regime, a goal every state should strive for. More than twenty-seven years after this hopeful declaration, liberal democracies seem to be losing, not winning, ground. One important cause for this appearance is the rise of China and the (apparent and relative) fall of the "West" (Japan included), and the fact that China seems to have reached this position by not following the Western models. Domestically, the Chinese regime is not liberal democratic. In the area of international relations, China adopts the idea of absolute sovereignty and follows the nation-state model, which is in conflict with the Western ideal that human rights override sovereignty.

One may argue that China cannot continue to rise by doing what it has been doing, and it should eventually follow the liberal democratic models. But as mentioned, Western models have encountered their own problems. Domestically, newly democratized countries are often plagued with ethnic violence, and developed liberal democracies also fail to face up to many challenges, such as the recent financial crisis, the growing inequality that has something to do with globalization, and advancements in technologies, and, as a result, the rise of populism from both the Left and the Right. The election of Donald Trump as the forty-fifth American president is only the most recent and the most striking example *so far*. Internationally, it is ironic that the sovereign-state and nation-state models that China so firmly embraces also come from the West. But the nation-state model is a root cause of the ethnical conflicts in China and in many other countries. Internationally, it has caused

1

two world wars, which were in fact started by Western nation-states and a Westernized Japan. If China adopted this model, the logical conclusion would be that it would follow the path of Germany and Japan before and during the two world wars, because rising nation-states are destined to demand more from the rest of the world and thus to challenge the existing world order with any means necessary. It is no wonder that the rest of the world is worried about the rise of China, in spite of the fact that the Chinese government keeps asserting that the rise of China is peaceful, and the Chinese government that upholds the nation-state model has itself to blame for this worry.

In response, there are cosmopolitan attempts to transcend nation-states, but they, too, are increasingly questioned. A more aggressive form of the cosmopolitan attempt is guided by the idea that human rights override sovereignty, and it leads Western countries to intervene with some human rights violations and crude oppressions and mass killings. But recent interventions, such as with Iraq and Libya, seem to create new and even more miseries than they are intended to eliminate. Moreover, to make things right is so demanding on Western countries that oftentimes they can only pay lip service to the principle that human rights override sovereignty, which makes the rest of the world suspect that their true intention is nothing but a disguised pursuit of their national interests, and thus leads to skepticism and cynicism.

A less aggressive form of cosmopolitanism, such as the formation of the European Union and the creation of a world market, doesn't seem to do too well either, for it leads to serious domestic problems, such as the aforementioned rising economic inequality and the apparently incurable political instability that is caused by the failure to assimilate a large group of people with different cultures and religions. Examples are abundant: the trouble of maintaining the European Union because of the European sovereign debt crisis (PIIGS); in France, the problem with a large and economically depressed minority that is nevertheless culturally distinct and almost impossible to assimilate; the refugee crisis both within a state and among European states; Brexit; and again, the election of Trump, who partly ran on an isolationist and mercantilist ground.

However, the failure of present liberal democratic models doesn't mean the success of the "China models," if there are such models to begin with.[1] On the

---

1. Those who are selling China models should think about the curious fate of Erza Vogel's *Japan as Number 1: Lessons for America* (1979), popular during the height of Japan's apparently unstoppable rise to economic dominance. But I doubt that anyone would take this book seriously anymore, other than for the sake of looking for clues of Japan's three-decades-long stagnation. Vogel himself is now known in China for his recent biography of Deng Xiaoping, the Chinese politician who kick-started China's apparently unstoppable rise to economic dominance.

domestic front, politically, the violation of rights and the lack of the rule of law in China are disturbing, to say the least. Economically, many Chinese politicians and scholars are pushing the Chinese economy to become more "liberal" and market-oriented, that is, more "Western," rather than holding on to some "China models." Internationally, a nationalist China will pose a threat to the rest of the world as well as to itself. Therefore, it seems that all the contemporary political models and discourses are not very adequate in dealing with the pressing political problems today, and to address these problems, we should reject the myth that history has already "ended," recognize the problems with present models, and explore new political possibilities and models with an open mind.

Put another way, if there were no crises in liberal democratic models, and if China had not been so successful in the past few decades, few would bother to read anything related to China, this book included, even if it were intrinsically valuable. But the Chinese regime in the real world has its own problems. Now that there is more interest in things related to China, maybe a philosopher like me should take a "free ride" with the rise of China and attempt to offer a message that the rise of China should offer, instead of what it does offer, or what is offered by various China commentators.

In this book, then, I try to show the problems with some of the existing political models. But instead of proposing China models that are based on the present Chinese regime and politics, I show a different kind of China model that may have contributed to the stellar performance of China, not so much in the past few decades but in the past two thousand years or more. More importantly, I show that the political models that are based on early Confucian ideas may, in theory, better address various political problems of today than other existing models. Of course, this doesn't mean that these Confucian models can address all the pressing political problems; rather, it is just that they can handle some of these problems better than other models. The ideal regime, then, would be a mixture of these Confucian models and some other political models. But for this mixture to be possible, it needs to be shown that the Confucian models can be compatible with these other models. If this mixture is possible, and if this ideal regime would indeed be better at addressing the pressing problems of today's politics, it would be a blessing for both China and the rest of the world.

Which Confucianism?

Confucianism is a long tradition, a big tent, under which many diverse thinkers and ideas fall. From Confucius on, the Confucian tradition has been updated, revised, and even revolutionized itself, oftentimes under the banner of going back to the true Confucian tradition. The defender of "true"

Confucianism is often nothing but the defender of *his/her* Confucianism, which, in the eye of other Confucian thinkers, is nothing but heresy. It is ridiculous, or at least presumptuous, to say "we Confucians think this or that." "Confucianism" is a term that has resulted from family resemblance—we need to remember that over generations, members belonging to the same family tree can look quite different! I am not saying that we can't pinpoint certain shared ideas among a group of Confucian thinkers, but it is quite challenging to define and defend these characteristics. In this chapter, I take an easy way out by specifying and clarifying what kind of Confucianism I utilize in this book (which is not to deny other readings of it).

Because of the diversity among different Confucian thinkers and texts, it is prudent to focus on one or two particular thinkers or texts. At the same time, it is desirable that the thinkers and texts we use are widely considered Confucian, so that we won't be accused of digging up some obscure and controversially "Confucian" thinker(s) for the purpose of showing the merits of Confucianism. A safe approach, then, is to go to its roots, that is, to the early founders of what was later known as "Confucianism," for almost no one would challenge how Confucian these founders were, and their ideas set the foundation for later developments and are thus very representative of certain characteristics of Confucianism, although not necessarily in a comprehensive manner.

There is another benefit when using these early thinkers: they are closer to the root of political problems and thus tend to address these problems directly rather than through metaphysical jargons and obscure references to early predecessors. This makes their ideas accessible to those who are not experts on Chinese philosophy but are interested in political problems shared by people with different cultures, religions, or metaphysical doctrines.

Therefore, in this book, I focus on two early founding Confucian thinkers, Confucius and Mencius, or, more precisely, the Confucius in the *Analects* and the Mencius in the *Mencius*, as well as the other two of the "Four Books," the *Zhong Yong* (中庸) (commonly translated as *The Doctrine of the Mean*) and *The Great Learning* (大学). There is little need to explain why Confucius is included in our discussions. As for Mencius, he was always considered an important early Confucian thinker, and since the Song dynasty, he has been considered second only to Confucius in terms of importance among the Confucians.[2] The other two texts of the Four Books are also often closely related to the ideas of Confucius and Mencius in the *Analects* and in the *Mencius*, re-

2. Another important early Confucian thinker is Xun Zi. But his status as a perfectly Confucian thinker was challenged by some Neo-Confucians, among others. More importantly, his views are often in conflict with those of Mencius's. It is difficult to offer a coherent picture of "Confucianism" if we wish to include both Mencius and Xun Zi in this book, and wish to do

spectively, and have been considered key Confucian texts, or two of the four essential Confucian texts since the Song dynasty. In this book, then, unless otherwise specified, the term "Confucianism" and its variations mean the ideas of Confucius and Mencius (with supplemental materials from the other two texts of the Four Books), especially when their ideas can be considered to be compatible with each other, or to be possible interpretations and elaborations of each other. When there are significant differences, I will use "Confucius's ideas" and "Mencius's ideas" to mark the distinctions.

The Philosophical Approach to Early Confucianism

One may wonder why we should still bother to read Confucius and Mencius, two thinkers who lived more than two thousand years ago in a region and a society so different from ours, and among a people also very different from us. One may even assert that their ideas cannot be relevant to today's world. Especially among the Chinese intellectual historians, sinologists, and sociologists of "ancient" China, ideas of these early thinkers are taken as ideologies, something like "items in a museum," that is, like some dead objects that are not freed from the time, space, and people from which they were produced.[3] I don't deny the possibility that these ideas can be studied this way; I merely deny that they can *only* be studied this way. Obviously, we could "ask" what Confucius and Mencius would say about democracy and human rights if they were alive today, or what they would say about the idea of promoting the public (good) by suppressing (almost) everything private, as suggested in Plato's *Republic*. This is what a philosophical reader of Plato or Kant does to these Western philosophers all the time.

The twentieth-century Chinese philosopher Feng Youlan (冯友兰; also spelled as Fung Yu-lan) introduced a distinction that nicely captures what was discussed above. He distinguished between two approaches of studying and teaching Chinese thought: a faithful reading (照着讲), that is, studying Chinese thought as it was originally; and a continuous reading (接着讲), that is, studying it against an ever-changing context and taking it as a continuing and living tradition (1999, 200). As is said in the Confucian canon the *Book of Odes*, "Zhou is an old state, but its mandate/mission is ever renewing"

---

justice to their sophisticated ideas at the same time. This is why Xun Zi won't be mentioned much in this book, and this doesn't in any way deny his significance to Confucianism.

3. Here I borrow the phrase from the sinologist Joseph Levenson, who claimed that Confucianism in the past hundred or more years has gone through the process of "museumization" (1968, 160).

(周虽旧邦其命维新).[4] The latter approach sees Chinese thought as a living tradition, and believes ideas of thinkers such as Confucius and Mencius have lives of their own.[5]

To be clear, the distinction between the more empirical and the more philosophical approaches is a matter of degree. To insist on the purity of the empirical approach presupposes two metaphysical tenets: first, the original author has a definite and objective idea in his or her mind; and second, the empirical researchers can somehow have access to this idea.[6] But these tenets have been seriously challenged by Ludwig Wittgenstein, W.V.O. Quine, and other philosophers. On the other hand, to insist on the purity of a philosophical approach may lead to a frivolous reading of the original author (although this reading could be interesting in its own right). As a philosopher, I have adopted the "continuous reading" or a more philosophical approach to early Confucianism, while trying to do some justice to it in its original context.

However, the philosophical approach to Chinese thought has been under attack or just ignored by many. To take Chinese thought as a philosophy—in the way I illustrated above—is to acknowledge its universal dimension and its continuing relevance. Attributing the defeat of China by Western and Westernized Japanese powers to traditional Chinese thought, many scholars of Chinese thought and history only study Chinese traditions to show what is wrong with them, or at best study them as dead objects in a museum, famously expressed by the slogan of "sort out the old things of the [Chinese] nation" (整理国故). After the communist revolution, especially under Mao Zedong, this trend of not taking Chinese thought as a living tradition was reinforced by the fact that only Marxism was taken as a living and viable philosophy. All this leads to the curious phenomenon that many empirical researchers of traditional China are simultaneously staunch antitraditionalists—Hu Shi (胡适) and Fu Sinian (傅斯年) being two representatives and influential figures in this group, whose influence still remains in today's academia of greater China

4. 诗经・大雅・文王

5. For a similar attitude toward how to approach Confucianism in the contemporary world, see J. Chan (1999, 213).

6. This is almost like an internalized version of the cave in Plato's *Republic*, and it is, not surprisingly, similar to what the Platonist Gottlob Frege called "sense" or "thought" (while he used "idea" to refer to the more subjective aspect of thinking) (Beaney 1997, 184–85nG; see also 154 and 156nE). That is, other people can never fully understand the idea of the original author and are thus doomed in the realm of appearances, the "cave," while only the author himself or herself (and, miraculously, the empirical researchers) has access to the idea (or the Idea) in his or her mind.

(mainland China, Hong Kong, and Taiwan), and among scholars from other parts of the world who are educated or influenced by people from Greater China. For these antitraditionalists, Chinese thought, especially Confucianism, is something particular to the Chinese and is thus a culture, an outdated one that has to be replaced in order for China to become a "better"—that is, Western—state. All these factors have led to the exile of Chinese thought from the philosophical world.

Ironically, there are some so-called cultural conservatives—those who are sympathetic to Chinese traditions—who also insist that Confucianism is the root of Chinese culture, and thus China needs to adopt a different polity from the West's, which, they believe, is rooted in Christianity.[7] In spite of their assertive attitude toward things traditionally Chinese, they are actually adopting the language of those who deny their contemporary relevance.

More importantly, the alleged "fundamentalist" attitude is actually a betrayal of the Confucian "fundamentals," or the consensus of early Confucian thinkers. That is, Confucius and Mencius never thought that they were developing ideas only for peoples from the states of Lu and Zou (Confucius's and Mencius's home states, respectively), but for all the *xia* (夏) people. The term *xia*, or *hua xia* (华夏), is now used in reference to the Chinese, but in early Confucian classics, it was used as the opposite of "barbarians." That is, it means "the civilized" and is not referring to a particular race or people.[8] Confucius even expressed the confidence of turning barbarians into xia if he or some Confucian gentleman moved to a barbaric place (*Analects* 9.14).

Different from the antitraditionalists who actively attack Chinese thought as a philosophy, another trend is simply to ignore the philosophical dimension of Chinese thought. This has something to do with the hubris of Western supremacy. That is, for many, if not most, Western philosophers (those who are doing Western philosophy but who are not necessarily Westerners), philosophy is Western philosophy. In Europe and North America, few mainstream philosophy departments offer courses in Chinese philosophy, and even fewer

7. See, for example, the contribution of contemporary Confucian thinker Jiang Qing (蒋庆) in Fan, Bell, and Hong (2012, part 1, 27–98). A more moderate view on this issue is that "philosophy" is a Western category, and it is then deeply problematic to put Confucianism under this category. Rather, it should be studied as the traditional *jing xue* (经学) (Confucian canonical studies) scholars did. But I argue later in this chapter that if we take a broader understanding of "philosophy," it is at least possible that we study Confucianism as a philosophy.

8. See, for example, Mencius's claim that someone from the state of Chu, often considered a barbaric state, became a xia person because of his devotion to the Confucian classics, whereas someone from the state of Song, often considered a xia state, degenerated into a barbarian by abandoning Confucian teachings (*Mencius* 3A4).

faculty members are specialized in Chinese philosophy. Worse still, few philosophy faculty members consider Chinese philosophy as an important subfield to strengthen a philosophy department.[9] As a result, many researchers of Chinese thought are in the field of sinology, and their own disciplinary bias against the philosophical approach to traditional Chinese texts and the impression that they give to philosophers reinforce the neglect of the philosophical dimension of Chinese thought, constituting a vicious cycle.

Yet another reason to deny the significance of the philosophical approach to Chinese thought is the evasion and rejection of philosophy in general. One reason for this rejection is science-worship. Many twentieth-century nonphilosophical researchers of Chinese thought—again, the aforementioned Hu Shi and Fu Sinian being two influential figures in this group—take this position. For them, the archaeological, historical, social, and linguistic approaches to Chinese thought, being "scientific," offer the "objective" and absolute truth about it, whereas the philosophical approach to it is nonscientific, speculative, subjective, and arbitrary. It is curious to note that the assertive tone among many nonphilosophical scholars of Chinese thought (in this and previous centuries) who have an overblown sense of the objectivity of their research is perhaps more difficult to find among those who are doing real "hard-core" (natural) sciences.[10]

This is not the place to explore an adequate answer to this scientism-based antiphilosophy attitude, but let me just make the following points: First, the belief in the objectivity of empirical studies is often rooted in the fact-value distinction, but this distinction is itself a value, or laden with values. Second, with a strong worship of modern natural sciences, some empirical researchers of traditional China seem to believe in the objectivity (understood as authority-giving and truth-giving) of their studies. But as discussed earlier, this belief is based on an internalized version of the cave metaphor, which is shown to be problematic by many contemporary philosophers. Third, if we understand how modern natural sciences are conducted, we should know the issue of the so-called underdetermination thesis. That is, logic and empirical facts alone don't seem to determine the truth of one theory over a competing theory. If even "hard" sciences are underdeterminate, how much "objectivity"

9. In a recent online poll on the ranking of specialties in terms of their importance to a strong (Anglo-American?) PhD program in philosophy, "history of non-Western Philosophy" was voted the twenty-sixth among the twenty-seven specialties considered. See http://warpweft andway.com/we-are-not-last/.

10. This group of people admires the stunning achievements of modern natural sciences, and not doing these sciences firsthand, they then turn this admiration into science-worship. See Bai (2009c) for an example and further discussions.

and "truth" can we expect from "soft" sciences such as history and linguistics? Unfortunately, this sophisticated understanding of natural sciences often fails to reach the worshippers of natural sciences.

Another reason to reject philosophy completely is apparently the opposite of the worship of science: the rejection of philosophy as the search for truth and the denial of objectivity. Out of this rejection and denial, some relativists and postmodernists embrace Chinese thought as a "discourse," a trendy and "new agey" one at that. Sometimes, the science-worship with a narrow field of empirical studies and the postmodernist attitude toward philosophy can even be strange bedfellows, for dogmatism and relativism are often two sides of the same coin. The issue with relativism and postmodernism is also too complicated to be handled here, but let me just say that I reject this postmodernist attitude toward Chinese thought.

All these trends—from the radically antitraditional attitude that demotes Chinese philosophy into the rank of a particular culture, to neglecting the philosophical dimension of Chinese thought, and to the rejection of philosophy in general—contribute to the dominance of the sinological approach to Chinese thought. I have offered some criticisms of these trends, but they are not comprehensive. Although I am disturbed by the dominance of the sinological approach to Chinese thought, I am not denying the significance of this approach. Rather, I only call for modesty from these empirical researchers and charity toward the philosophical approach to Chinese thought, early Confucianism included.

Can Early Confucian Texts Be Read Philosophically?

If we decide to take the philosophical approach to early Confucianism,[11] an immediate obstacle is that early Confucian classics don't look like Western philosophical texts, which explains why people who are familiar with Western philosophy reject the idea that these texts are philosophical texts. The *Analects*, for example, appears to be a random collection of conversations and lacks systematic argumentation.[12] This argument against studying early Confucian texts philosophically presupposes that philosophy is rooted in arguments. But has this presupposition been argued for?

11. For a detailed and systematic treatment of the issue of whether there is Chinese philosophy, see Bai (2014b).

12. For example, the scholar of Chinese philosophy Bryan van Norden argues that the *Analects* should not be taken as a philosophical text because it lacks the kind of systematicity a philosophical text must have (2002b, 230–31).

Indeed, to say whether something is a philosophy or not, we have to define what philosophy is and draw a sharp line between philosophy and non-philosophy. Twentieth-century philosophers of science try to draw a sharp line, or to have a consensus on this line, between science and non-science—a line that seems to be obvious and easily drawn—but they have failed. Should this failure tell us anything, it should tell us of the difficulty, if not the impossibility, of making a demarcation between philosophy and non-philosophy.

If, however, we wish to answer the question of whether early Confucian texts can be read philosophically, we must first define what philosophy is. In the following, I take a constructive approach in defining philosophy and examine whether early Confucian Chinese texts can be considered philosophical texts on the basis of this definition. Those who don't accept my definition are free to define philosophy in their own way and offer their own examinations.

Although it is my own definition, it is not purely arbitrary. On the one hand, the definition of philosophy should not be so broad as to include what is usually not considered a philosophy; on the other, it should not be so narrow as to use a particular branch of philosophy (e.g., analytic philosophy) as the only legitimate way of doing philosophy. Obviously, to achieve such a balance is an art and not a science.

With all these cautionary notes, here is my definition (which was already alluded to earlier in this chapter): Philosophy is a systematic reflection on "philosophical problems" (to be defined separately).[13] Philosophy should be fundamentally reflective. This means that it shouldn't merely consist in social customs and one's own habits but in reflections on them. These reflections are also open to further "higher-order" reflections, which will lead us to make these reflections a coherent whole. This is why philosophy should be systematic reflections,[14] the object of which are "philosophical problems," that is, problems that transcend a certain time, space, and people; the problems that human beings have to face but cannot solve once and for all. If the problems are restricted to a certain time, space, and people, they are problems of history, area studies, geography, sociology, anthropology, and so on, but not of philosophy. If the problems can be solved, they are problems of modern sciences and thus should "emigrate" out of the philosophical realm.

With philosophy so defined, some may still reject the philosophical approach to early Confucian texts, because, as mentioned earlier, argumentation

13. As we will see, this definition is close to Feng Youlan's definition of philosophy as "systematic, reflective thinking on life" (1966, 2).

14. By "systematic," I don't mean to say that a philosophy should offer a comprehensive treatment of all philosophical problems. Rather, what I mean by it is that there should be coherence among one's reflections, thus making them a system or a coherent whole.

seems to be lacking in these texts. But this is to confuse systematic reflection with argumentation. For argument's sake, however, let's suppose that argumentation is an important form of expressing systematic reflections, and let's see if there is argumentation in the *Analects*.

In the *Analects* 17.21, there is a discussion between Confucius and a pupil (Zai Wo 宰我) over the "three-year mourning" ritual. This ritual should be a code of conduct from the ritual system of the old regime, and if Confucius were merely an unreflective follower of the old, this discussion would end pretty quickly ("This is how it has been done—end of question!"). But in this passage, both sides offered arguments that do not rely on custom and authority. Of course, compared to the discussion in 17.21, many conversations in the *Analects* are very brief and apparently cannot be considered as argumentations. For example, in the *Analects* 14.34, when asked about his thoughts on the idea of repaying a heinous deed with kindness, Confucius answered, "What do you repay a kind deed with?" Although extremely short, this answer concisely and incisively shows the problem with the idea of "repaying a heinous deed with kindness": this idea sounds very noble and forgiving, but the tolerance of evil deeds is actually an injustice done to the virtuous people in the world.

Generally speaking, the apparent lack of argumentation in some traditional Chinese texts doesn't mean that they don't contain argumentation. Rather, they may have simply skipped many argumentation steps and offered instead an "argumentation sketch," or the key and most difficult steps in an argumentation. In fact, even in works of physics and mathematics that are known for their rigor, argumentation steps are often skipped, and the failure of a reader to understand them is often not a sign of the lack of rigor of the works in question but the lack of the reader's competence in becoming a good physicist or mathematician. As Friedrich Nietzsche put it in his discussion of the beauty of the aphoristic style, "In the mountains the shortest way is from peak to peak: but for that one must have long legs. Aphorisms should be peaks—and those who are addressed, tall and lofty" (1954, 40 [part 1, sec. 7, "On Reading and Writing"]).

But why an argumentation sketch? The reasons are to save time or simply to be realistic (a rigorous proof in an axiomatic system can be impossibly long), to show off, from an "aristocratic pride" that despises the plain and the common, and so on. But there is also a philosophically relevant reason for it: every complicated problem may demand countless steps of argumentation if we want truly rigorous argumentation, but the readers may be distracted by and lost in all the trivial arguments. An argumentation sketch, then, may be advantageous in that it offers readers the big picture with important signposts, and a qualified reader can fill in the missing steps. This incisiveness, and the ability to see and show the big picture, I believe, is what makes the great think-ers—whether great philosophers or great scientists—great.

In short, an argumentation sketch may be able to inspire and lead us in our reflections. We can take one step further by acknowledging that there may be other ways—for example, the aphoristic and even mystical style exemplified in the *Lao Zi* and to some extent Nietzsche's writings—to express (the au-thor's) and inspire (the readers') reflections than argumentation (argumenta-tion sketch included). This style has its benefits, especially if what is to be expressed has some form of internal tension, or if what is to be said is ineffable in a way. This is the issue underlying the problem of writing in Plato's *Phae-drus*, the problem of speaking about the unspeakable Dao in the *Lao Zi*, the problem of how to express oneself without being trapped in one's words in the *Zhuang Zi*, and the problem of how to assert nothingness in Buddhism.

Therefore, reflections can be found in traditional Chinese texts. But it can-not be denied that they often look scattered and unsystematic in contrast to treatises, the common form of Western philosophical writings. One important reason, as the Chinese historian Qian Mu (钱穆) has pointed out, is that from the so-called Spring and Autumn period (which began around 770 BC) on, the Chinese intellectual elite had the opportunity to become part of the ruling elite, which was sharply different from the situations in medieval Europe (2005a, 21).[15] In contrast to thinkers in medieval and even early modern Eu-rope, the Chinese intellectual elite in the past had far better access to the upper echelons in politics. As a result, they could put their political thoughts and theories into practice, and had little need (and leisure) to formulate them in the form of treatises detached from practice. In fact, the early modern Euro-pean thinker Jean-Jacques Rousseau made a claim that supports Qian Mu's account. He wrote in the opening paragraphs of *On the Social Contract*, "I shall be asked if I am a prince or a legislator, to write on politics. I answer that I am neither, and that is why I do so. If I were a prince or a legislator, I should not waste time in saying what wants doing; I should do it, or hold my peace" (1978, 46). In contrast, many political writers in Chinese history were in the center of politics, and it was already the case during the SAWS.

Of course, this defense only explains why the writings of many Chinese political writers are different from those in the Western tradition, and suggests that if given the opportunity (or, more accurately put, the lack of opportunity

---

15. Feng Youlan also claimed, "from a [traditional] Chinese philosopher's point of view, to write books so as to disseminate one's ideas is the worst luck [for the philosopher], and has to be the last resort" (2000, 7; my translation). The reason Feng offered is the traditional Chinese philosophers' belief in "sageliness within, and kingliness without," but I think that Qian Mu's explanation makes more sense than Feng's.

in real-world politics), these Chinese writers could have written works that bear more resemblance in style to the writings in the Western tradition. But the apparent lack of a system in traditional Chinese texts doesn't mean that there is no hidden system in these texts. Feng Youlan expressed a similar view, claiming that there are two kinds of systems, the formal and the real, and the lack of a formal system in Chinese philosophical texts doesn't mean the lack of a real system (2000, 10).[16]

How to Read Early Confucian Texts Philosophically

Early Confucian (and Chinese) classics can be read philosophically, if philosophy is understood as I suggested above. This understanding of philosophy then implies certain methods of reading these texts. It requires us to clarify and enrich the argumentation in these texts by making up the missing steps, and to tease out the hidden systems in these texts, always with their contemporary relevance in mind and with a sensibility to their original contexts simultaneously.

To apply these methods to traditional texts, the first thing we need to do is to discover the apparent discrepancies and even contradictions within an argument and among different arguments in the same text or by the same author. After actively making these discoveries, however, we should not do what an analytically minded thinker of classical Chinese texts tends to do, such as claiming that the author failed to see the contradictions, he didn't know logic, and so on. Rather, we should apply the principle of respect and charity to the reading of these texts, for since ancient Greece or pre-Qin China, there haven't been many great thinkers in human history (which is why we call them "great thinkers"). If we can easily find apparent confusion and contradictions in their works, a reasonable guess is not that they didn't think clearly but that we didn't; that is, we failed to appreciate the depth of these most profound thinkers in human history due to our own limited intellectual capacity or being confined to our own context. In this sense, to respect "authority" (great thinkers and their texts) is to think critically and to criticize and transcend the authority of today (our own prejudices and close-mindedness). Therefore, after discovering the discrepancies, we should try to see if we can make up the missing steps, or reconstruct hidden coherence between apparently contradictory arguments.

Indeed, when reading classics, what immediately makes sense to us may be of little worth, and what seems to be confusing and even contradictory at first

16. According to Zheng Jiadong (郑家栋), similar distinctions were made by Wang Guowei (王国维), Hu Shi (胡适), and Cai Yuanpei (蔡元培) before Feng's (Zheng 2004, 8).

sight may have been the most interesting part of the classics ("I study it because it is absurd," to revise an expression attributed to the theologian Tertullian). We should give them the most attention and care, utilizing the methods from the traditional Chinese commentary tradition or, more generally, the philosophical hermeneutics, and combining rigorous analysis with a lively imagination, in order to discover the hidden and deeper meanings of the classics.

The key to my hermeneutic method is the principle of holism. That is, we should try, as best as we can, to take a philosophical classic or classics by the same author as a whole that expresses a coherent system of thought. But this holistic approach has been challenged. In the West, for example, it is often argued that different parts within the same dialogue and different Platonic dialogues were written by Plato over a period of time, and they don't represent a coherent thought system but show development and even changes in Plato's philosophy. In China, the integrity of classical texts has been even more seriously challenged by the aforementioned worshippers of science, for example, the Chinese *gu shi bian* (analysis of ancient history; 古史辨) school of the early twentieth century and its contemporary followers, such as Li Ling (李零).[17] On early Confucian texts, in their controversial book *The Original Analects*, for example, E. Bruce Brooks and A. Taeko Brooks also offer one of the most radical challenges to the holist understanding of the *Analects* (2001).

One common challenge to the holism of reading a classical text is that it was actually written by different authors and thus couldn't be read as offering a coherent message. An important proof often cited for the claim of multiple authorship is stylistic discrepancies in a text, the thought being that these different phrases and styles were developed over a period of time and couldn't be mastered by the alleged author. However, can we really ascertain that these styles and phrases only came after the alleged author? Even if they did, how often do these "new" styles and phrases occur in the text? If they didn't occur often, why shouldn't we take a moderate stance, claiming that there are problems with these places where these phrases and styles occur but not doubting the overall authenticity and integrity of the text? Moreover, considering the fact that many of the classics were lost and rediscovered, or were transcribed through many hands, isn't it a reasonable guess that these discrepancies may have been introduced by the transcribers, and, although these transcribers used later styles and phrases, they nevertheless didn't change the content of

17. Although it has roots in the Chinese traditions (I thank Stephen Angle for reminding me of this point), this skeptical attitude toward the Chinese classics may have been strengthened by the worship of modern science.

the classics, or, even if they did make some changes, we can nevertheless discern them and eliminate them?[18]

Generally speaking, some historians and linguists seem to have a very strong faith in the "hardness" of the evidence and logic they employ. I suspect that this not-so-scientific attitude toward empirical (historical and linguistic) evidence and logical analysis results from a worship of the natural sciences. As mentioned earlier in this chapter, this "faith" is philosophically naive and is quite alien to how many natural scientists understand science. If we realize that there is an underdetermination by experience and logic even in the "hardest" science such as physics, we should see that the underdetermination by linguistic and historical evidence and logic in the studies of classics should be much harder to eliminate.

To be clear, I am not in any way denying the worth of historical or linguistic studies of the classical texts but am only calling for a more cautious (and truly scientific) attitude toward their findings. More importantly, I am calling for tolerance of a philosophical hermeneutics that is based on the principle of holism, if the evidence against the integrity of a classical text is not conclusive (i.e., beyond a *reasonable* doubt).

Moreover, even if a classic is proven to have had multiple authors, it could be the case that these authors tried to offer a coherent system of thought. Even if this were shown not to be the case, as long as the text in question was considered a whole in the history of thought, and was treated accordingly by some great thinkers (e.g., Wang Bi's [王弼] commentaries on the *Lao Zi* [1991], or Zhu Xi's [朱熹] commentaries on the *Analects*), it is still meaningful to apply the principle of holism to this text in order to understand the coherent thought that was not intended by the original author(s) but has been adopted by some later thinkers.

Indeed, the principle of holism is often challenged on a much "softer" ground than the linguistic evidence mentioned above. The speculations that a text has multiple authors or an author changes his or her views over time are often introduced to solve the apparent discrepancies within a text or among texts that are commonly believed to be by the same author. To use these speculations to object to the principle of holism seems to be a circular argument: a coherent reading cannot be given to some texts because they have different authors or the author has changed his or her mind, and the text(s) have different authors and the author has changed his or her mind because a coherent reading is not yet given to the text(s). Of course, sometimes, there

18. For a solid case study along this line of argument, see section 1 of Han (2008), in which he offers interesting criticisms of the skepticism of the integrity and wholeness of the *Zhuang Zi*.

are independent evidences for these speculations, but as we have seen, they are likely to be inconclusive.[19]

Philosophically speaking, to resolve the apparent discrepancies by resorting to multiple authorship and the change of the author's mind is rather cheap. If a book could only be dissected into simple, disconnected, or even contradictory ideas and doctrines, it wouldn't be philosophically interesting. If we couldn't resolve a conflict in the classics with our philosophical hermeneutics, but there is no independent hard evidence to suggest multiple authorship or the change of the author's mind, we should honestly acknowledge the fact that we don't know how to understand the text in question.[20]

Drawing together all the above considerations, I think that the principle of holism can be applied to the *Analects* and the *Mencius*, the texts that will be the focus of this book, as well as other classical texts such as the *Lao Zi* and the Platonic dialogues. But I do not suggest that this principle can be applied to every classical text, especially those that have always been reasonably believed to have multiple authors with no shared intentions, and thus have rarely

19. I am not saying that an author never changes his or her mind. In the *Analects* 2.4, for example, Confucius described what characterized him at different ages, and these different characteristics implied a possible change of his thought with regard to certain matters.

20. What I am defending here is a philosophical approach to the classics against a dogmatic and assertive attitude by some "classicists." However, the doubts of the authenticity and integrity of the classics might be neglected by many scholars in contemporary China. If this is the case, perhaps such doubts, if used properly, can be a healthy balance in the above context. The philosophical approach I defend here is similar to that of Han Linhe (韩林合), although there are also some differences (2008). For example, I think that different principles in his approach, for instance, the completeness principle (完全性原则), the systematicity principle (系统性原则), and the coherence principle (一致性原则), are the expressions of one and the same principle, the principle of holism. Although presented differently, he and I share similar doubts about the dogmatic stance often associated with the "classicist" approach, and his principle of creative reading (创新性原则) is in line with my call for a reconstruction of a hidden system of argumentation. However, my reconstructive reading is more "conservative" than his creative reading. That is, based on the principle of respect (Han also has a similar idea), although I don't pre-eliminate the possibility that classical authors fail to think through some issues, I will only consider this possibility as the very last resort. Although I acknowledge the fact that my approach is philosophical and is not necessarily faithful to the original intention of the classical authors, I don't exclude the possibility that my reading is merely teasing out the hidden meaning that the classical author was aware of or even planted in the text intentionally, or the possibility that my reading is what the author would have said in the new context. Moreover, in a conference in which he and I presented our approaches to the classics, Han expressed the view that there is no philosophy in (traditional) China, which is what I have been arguing against in this chapter.

been treated as coherent texts.[21] One might argue that the principle of respect suggests an attitude of disrespect toward more recent challenges to the classics. This may well be the case. But this attitude of "disrespect" is also based on a similar commonsensical consideration. That is, recent challenges have not themselves been thoroughly challenged by various thinkers over time and are likely not as reliable as those that have been tested by time. Moreover, encouraged by an emulation of the perceived scientific method, contemporary scholars seem to value new ideas more than preserving the traditional ones. Understanding this zeal also lends reasonable doubt to the doubts (challenges) by contemporary thinkers. The emphasis on the respect for traditions can serve as a counterbalance against a progressive view of the history of ideas and against the fetish of the novel.

But the philosophical approach to Chinese classics that is rooted in elucidation and systematization has been criticized by some, because, according to these critics, this approach would ruin the beauty of Chinese philosophy. For example, after explaining Feng Youlan's philosophical approach to Chinese classics, which bear many similarities to what I have offered, the contemporary Chinese intellectual historian Zheng Jiadong (郑家栋) criticizes this approach. According to him, "elucidation and systematization" have become essential to "modernizing" Chinese philosophy, and Feng Youlan thinks that the brevity with which ideas in traditional Chinese texts are expressed demands that scholars studying Chinese philosophy in a modern sense make up the omitted steps of argumentation in these texts through logical procedure. Feng's contribution lies in this elucidation and systematization effort, but here also lies a heavy price. For example, Feng's consistent attempt to use Western philosophical concepts to interpret ideas in the *Lao Zi* diminishes the wisdom in this book, turning it into fourth-rate metaphysics or worse (Zheng 2004, 8). Zheng also criticizes the trend that, under Feng's influence, many contemporary scholars of Chinese philosophy focus their attention on the ontology and metaphysics of Chinese philosophy (ibid.). Indeed, according to those who hold attitudes even more radical than Zheng's, Chinese philosophy is a way of life that emphasizes moral cultivation and personal enlightenment, and Chinese philosophy can only be understood by Chinese who use original and unique Chinese concepts.

The latter position is a form of mysticism about Chinese philosophy, and it may eventually fall into the trap of private language, or a form of radical relativism. That is, we can ask a believer in this position how he or she can know what that unique thing called Chinese philosophy is: Does he or she somehow get

21. I thank Paul Goldin and Stephen Angle for reminding me of the limit of the principle of holism.

into the mind of the traditional Chinese thinkers and see the truth of their ideas? If the answer is no, he or she may have to accept the conclusion that he or she is trapped in his or her own mind. Indeed, this person may eventually be forced to admit that his or her thought at a particular moment can only be understood by him or her at that particular moment, a linguistic version of the strange claim that one cannot even step into the same river twice! Moreover, as mentioned earlier, if a thought belongs only to China or the Chinese, it is a subject for anthropology or sociology, not for philosophy.

Of the view that Chinese philosophy is a way of life, as Chinese philosophy scholar Franklin Perkins has shown (2012), there is such a tradition in Western philosophy as well. Moreover, this claim actually mistakes some particular readings of some particular schools as the whole of Chinese philosophy, and it is clearly false: the pre-Qin Chinese philosopher Han Fei Zi's philosophy, for example, has little to do with a way of life, as this phrase is usually understood. Moreover, the concern with life can be integrated into my understanding of philosophy: philosophy consists in systematic reflections concerning philosophical problems—that is, problems that can transcend a certain time, space, and people; problems that human beings have to face but can't solve once and for all—and one of the aspirations of these reflections is to lead human beings to a good life. All I am insisting on here is that having systematic reflections is a necessary condition of philosophy.

Zheng's objection to this view is that the elucidation and systematization effort tends to turn Chinese thought into fourth-rate Western philosophy. I, too, think that to force Chinese philosophy into some particular conceptual system of Western philosophy is very problematic. According to my understanding of philosophy, the commensurability between different philosophies comes from their shared problems. Therefore, we should start with these problems and not be lost in the conceptual systems that are meant to address these problems. More directly on the above objection, I think that some elucidation and systematization efforts have indeed failed, and there should be a broader understanding of elucidation and systematization rather than, for example, taking the form of a treatise or a narrow form of argumentation embodied in early analytic philosophy as the sole legitimate form of philosophical expressions. But as long as we don't choose silence or telepathy, we will have to convey our ideas through words, even if what is to be said is "ineffable." After all, the *Lao Zi* doesn't stop right after the first line that reads, "the Dao that can be spoken of is not the eternal Dao," and many commentators on this text have tried to elucidate the ineffable Dao.[22] Elucidation and systematiza-

22. To be clear, it is not just the contemporary or Western readers who fail to see through this apparent contradictory action. For example, the Tang poet and intellectual Bai Juyi (白居

tion are inevitable as long as we philosophize. The failure of a particular attempt to do so doesn't mean the failure of such an attempt in general.[23] If we are doomed to fail, then what we are facing is not philosophy.

We also cannot claim that elucidation and systematization are alien to the Chinese traditions, because these are precisely what some commentaries in traditional China are meant to achieve, and thus these attempts are internal to Chinese thought and not a result of reactions to Western philosophy.[24] In this sense, the reader is simultaneously the interpreter and the coauthor of the classics.

Early Confucianism as a Modern Political Philosophy

The Progressive View of Philosophy and Its Problems

Some people may still deny the contemporary relevance of early Confucianism even if they acknowledge the fact that it is a philosophy and its texts can be read philosophically.[25] They may argue that the early Confucian thinkers belong to the childhood of philosophy, and their ideas are thus outdated, even if we study them with the "continuous" reading or philosophical approach, that is, "asking" their views on this or that political matter of today. But this claim presupposes a progressive view of philosophy, according to which philosophy is progressing over time toward the ultimate truth. This view may have also been influenced by the envy-turned-worship of the stunning achievements of modern natural sciences.

This is not the place to adequately criticize this progressive view, and let me just clarify my own position on this matter. According to my definition of

易) expressed his perplexity in a poem, "Reading the *Lao Zi*" (读老子): "Those who speak don't know, and those who know don't speak; this I have heard from Lao Zi. But if we say that Lao Zi is someone who knows, why did he himself write a book of 5,000 characters?" (言者不知知者默, 此语吾闻于老君。若道老君是知者, 缘何自著五千文?). This poem can be found in *Quan Tang Shi* (全唐诗), vol. 455, no. 1. There are many printings of *Quan Tang Shi*, and the reference in one of the printings is Peng (1960, vol. 14, 5150).

23. Stephen Angle deals with some similar objections to taking Chinese thought as a philosophy, and some of his responses are similar to mine (2012, 7–9).

24. To categorize the subject matters into philosophy, religion, and so on may have come from the West, especially the "modern" (nineteenth century onward) Western university system. Traditional Chinese learning is perhaps not categorized the same way. But this doesn't mean that in the latter we can't carve out a set of studies that correspond to philosophy as we understand it in the (modern) Western categorization.

25. This section only offers an outline of the modern and political nature of early Confucian philosophy. For more detailed discussions, see Bai (2014a and 2014b).

philosophy, philosophical problems belong to a repertoire of problems that we have to deal with in our "lifeworld(s)" over time but cannot solve once and for all. If so, we can no longer dismiss a philosopher just because he or she comes to the world stage early.

But one can object to this nonprogressive, comparative approach with regard to the depth of philosophical thinking by arguing that how philosophical problems are expressed, given the change of time, locale, and presenter, may have changed and been changing. My response to this objection is that in spite of the changes, at least some philosophical problems nevertheless retain "family resemblance" or commensurability to each other in spite of the differences of time, space, and person. The family resemblance may have been rooted in the family resemblance of our lifeworld(s).

Although the problems may have different contextual features, and their solutions are thus also different, we can decontextualize the reasoning from one context and recontextualize it in another, doing an "abstract translation" of reasoning, making the reasoning from the first context internal to the philosophical reflections in the new context. The possibility of abstract translation presupposes some form of commensurability. An analogy to the abstract translation in the world of physics is the adoption of the conceptual system of theoretical mechanics by electromagnetism and even quantum mechanics. In theoretical mechanics, formulas and theorems in mechanics are written in an abstract manner, and the conceptual system is later used in electromagnetic theories and even quantum mechanics when the symbols in the system are given new meanings. Of course, the abstract translation in philosophy is less rigorous than in physics, and whether it works (or not) depends upon, well, whether it works.

In short, what matters to the philosophical significance of a philosopher doesn't have to have anything to do with whether he or she comes to the world stage earlier or later, but with how deep and profound he or she is, especially with regard to the aspects of our world that are not fundamentally different from those of Plato's or Confucius's times.

What aspects of our world haven't changed much since the times of Plato or Confucius? For example, our human nature, or, using a less metaphysics-sounding term, the dominant tendencies among human beings, including our cognitive capacities, our rationality or the lack of it, and so on, haven't changed much, perhaps since the time when human beings were merely hunter-gatherers. Early thinkers' observations based on this kind of human nature, then, may still remain very much relevant today. But in spite of my above criticism of the progressive view, I acknowledge the fact that some other aspects of human beings' lifeworlds may have changed greatly. For example, the power and ubiquity of modern finance may be unique to our world, and early thinkers' treatments of economy without taking modern finance into account may be obsolete, or at least need to be significantly updated.[26] Generally, it may be argued that Plato and Confucius lived in the age of antiquity, while we live in the age of modernity, or even postmodernity. But first we have to specify what aspects in modernity are fundamentally or at least significantly different from antiquity. In the aspects in which there are no great differences between antiquity and modernity, ideas of ancient thinkers would remain relevant, or their relevance would depend on their depth and not on when these ideas were first introduced. Finally, although few would challenge the idea that Plato belonged to antiquity, I argue in the following that "ancient" Confucian thinkers were actually already faced with a modern or modernizing world, or at least their world bore more resemblance to the world of modernity than to Plato's world or the medieval European world. In this sense, early Confucian (and Chinese) philosophy is more comparable to the modern Western philosophy that came into being almost two thousand years later than to its Western contemporary, classical Western philosophy.[27]

To be clear, earlier in this chapter I defended the contemporary relevance of early Confucianism by arguing that there are certain human problems that transcend time, and in the previous paragraph I argue that there may have been problems that belong to modernity only. That is, there are human problems that are eternal or shared between the world of antiquity and that of modernity. But there are also problems particular to one of the two worlds, problems that are expressed differently in these worlds, or problems that demand different solutions due to differences between ancient and modern conditions. These problems and their solutions still transcend space, a people, and time; it is only that they are not eternal but conditioned on, for example, modernity. This is like the division between classical mechanics and quantum mechanics: there are fundamental gaps between them, but they also have shared commonalities.

The Zhou-Qin Transition as an Early Modernization

Now, let us take a look at the world early Confucians lived in. As mentioned earlier in this chapter, early Confucians lived in the pre-Qin period or the

26. I thank Qian Jiang for pointing this out to me.

27. Many twentieth-century Chinese thinkers have argued that traditional Chinese philosophy is comparable to classical or medieval Western philosophy, and depending on whether one has a progressive or regressive view of the development of philosophy, one can try to "modernize" Chinese philosophy or try to use this "premodern" philosophy to criticize modernity (for an example of the former, see Feng 2001, 1:307; for an example of the latter, see M. Liu 1996, 898–956). In addition to the problems with the progressive and regressive views, I think that their shared premise—that traditional Chinese philosophy is premodern—is wrong.

SAWS. This is a transitional period also known as the Zhou-Qin transition (周秦之变). The political structure before this transition, the regime of West-ern Zhou, is "feudalistic." Whether "feudalism" (and the terms associated with it) is applicable to the regimes of Western Zhou China and even medieval Europe is a controversial issue.[28] But for the lack of a better and more conve-nient term, I will use "feudalism" to label these regimes. Acknowledging the differences between the regimes in medieval Europe and in Western Zhou China, I use the term "feudalism" to refer to a regime with the features that will be discussed below and that I believe are shared by these regimes.

First, let us look at the feudal regime of Western Zhou China. The original intention of the founding fathers of Western Zhou was to control a vast and hostile land and the political entities on this land, many of which still pled allegiance to Shang or didn't plead allegiance to Zhou after the surprising de-feat of the powerful Shang empire by the small state of Zhou, and the policy is described as "enfeoffing the [king's] relatives, and using them to protect the Zhou [king]" (Zuo Commentaries [左传 · 僖公二十四年]). Thus, these feudal states were strategically established by the Zhou founding fathers in the re-gions that were not well controlled by the Zhou state, and often in a group of three or so feudal states that could come to one another's defense. This is a colonial and expansionist policy.[29] After these feudal states expanded by en-croaching upon the areas of the "barbarians" ("barbarians" are defined as those who refused to submit to the Zhou political order), their rulers did the same as the kings did, enfeoffing their own relatives and ministers. In the en-tire empire, the king ruled over feudal lords one level lower than him, greater lords over lesser lords, and so on. On each level, it was one master ruling over a limited number of subjects (while one's subject's subject was not one's sub-ject), making it possible for the master to rule through personal influence, blood relations, contracts between rulers and their subjects, and noble codes of conduct. Thus, a large empire was divided into small and close-knit com-munities through this pyramid-like structure (with the king at the very top), and rulers of each level had much autonomy from their lords one level higher. Only the nobility by pedigree were qualified as rulers of various ranks.

But this feudalistic structure collapsed during the SAWS.[30] The allegiance of lower lords to higher ones was broken down, and it was a world of war of all against all. The Zhou king was eventually eliminated, and the "fittest" few

28. See Brown (1974), Reynolds (1994), and F. Li (2005 and 2008) for more detailed discus-sions. I thank Keith Knapp for bringing up this issue with me.

29. See Qian Mu (1996), 57; and F. Li (2005).

30. F. Li (2005) has a detailed analysis of the fall of the Western Zhou empire, especially the flaws internal to its regime.

survived. During the Warring States period (475 BCE to 221 BCE), there were seven strong states (and some minor ones, most of which were on their way to elimination), and each of the seven strong states was on a similar scale as the Western Zhou empire in terms of the size and the population.[31] But the political pyramid that was crucial to the Zhou rulers for running a large empire was not available to the kings of these strong and de facto sovereign states anymore, because, in the war of all against all, most of the lower lords (and the Zhou king) and the feudal political structure were eliminated. Therefore, crucial political issues needed to be answered again.

In politics, there are three crucial issues (maybe more) that always need to be answered. First, every political entity needs to find a bond, a banner, or an identity with which it can form a unity. Second, if the entity has to be run through a political order, who should be in charge of maintaining the order? If it is through a group of people, how can members of this group be selected and what is the legitimacy of the selection procedure? Third, what is the mechanism to deal with entity–entity relations?

Under the Western Zhou regime, all these questions were well addressed through surprisingly simple ways. It is claimed in the *Zuo Commentaries*, which should represent how the feudal order was commonly perceived at that time, that "the important affairs of the state lie in sacrificial ceremonies and wars" (左传 • 成公十三年). In these and other feudal ceremonies, a community of a limited number of nobles gathered to sacrifice, hunt, and eat together. The leader of the ceremonies, a nobleman of higher rank, would sometimes show off his military and economic force. All these practices would reinforce the bond among the nobles. In these ceremonies, homage was paid to the founding ancestors and Heaven, reinforcing the noble pedigree and the legitimacy of the feudal order that was built on it. The implicit line in these ceremonies is the following: "My great-grandfather founded the whole empire because he had the mandate of Heaven, and you were a feudal lord because your great-grandfather was a delegate who derived his legitimacy from my great-grandfather's. Therefore, you need to obey me. If you don't, look at my armies and weaponry on display here." When there were quarrels (and even wars) among feudal states, the lord of a higher rank would be the arbiter (and the Zhou king was the ultimate arbiter). The term for "war" (戎) has a special connotation, for it originally meant a branch of barbarians. To them, the Zhou feudal order didn't apply, and only naked force was applicable.

---

31. It is understandable that each of the states could have a population comparable with that of the Zhou empire if we consider the natural population growth. But even with regard to the territory, because many barbarian "pockets" were now annihilated and under control of one or another of these states, many of the states had a size comparable to the Zhou empire as well.

But the collapse of nobility-based feudalism means that the solutions to the three fundamental political problems stopped working. It is obvious that the legitimacy of the ruling class became a problem, for the legitimacy of the feudal order ultimately derives from the king and Heaven. With the king gone, many nobles eliminated, and many usurpers seizing power, one couldn't claim legitimacy by referring to one's pedigree or to Heaven. On the issue of social and political bonds, as mentioned earlier, what emerged, especially during the Warring States period, were a few large and populous states in which the kings had to deal with thousands of strangers without the nobility-based delegatory system available to them anymore. In politics, size matters. What was effective at bonding a small community (kinship, codes of conduct among nobles, personal contract through rituals, a shared sense of the Good, etc.) couldn't bond a large society of strangers together, unless oppressive force was used constantly. That is, without oppression, plurality of values is inevitable, which is recognized by some modern European political thinkers and pre-Qin thinkers such as Han Fei Zi.[32] Finally, without an overlord and without lesser lords beneath them, within each state, the centralization of power emerged, and each state became independent from other states. The relations among these de facto sovereign states were similar to international relations as we understand this term today.

Now it should become obvious that the transition these Chinese states experienced during the SAWS has some similarities to the European transition from the Middle Ages to Western modernity, and early modern European thinkers and politicians were also faced with political issues similar to those faced by Chinese thinkers and politicians during the SAWS, which was about two thousand years before European modernity. I am not saying that the transition China experienced during the SAWS is exactly the same as the European transition to early modernity. There were ancient Greek and Roman civilizations before the Middle Ages, and these heritages were not available to the Chinese during the SAWS and throughout much of traditional China.[33]

While the Western Zhou version of feudalism was based on a design from the top and was constructed from top to bottom, the European one was a result of the struggles and compromises among various elements from the bot-

32. For how some Western liberal thinkers understood the relations between pluralism and the size of the community, see Zhou (2007 and 2008a). For Han Fei Zi's view of the plurality of values, see Bai (2011). To be clear, I am not saying that Han Fei Zi was a liberal thinker, but that he understood the above inevitability of plurality of values in a large society, as a liberal thinker would.

33. By "traditional China," I mean China before its violent encounter with the modern West in the late nineteenth century.

tom up, and not a result of a conscious design from the top.[34] Through a *zong fa* (宗法) system, different nobility lines were clearly delineated, even if they ultimately came from the same ancestry, in the Western Zhou system. For example, the ruler of the feudal state of Lu would never, through inheritance or bequest, became a lord under the ruler of the state of Qi; his successors were always chosen from his children and, at worst, from his siblings or his siblings' children within the state of Lu, but never from a noble family outside of the state. In contrast, such phenomena were not rare in the European feudal system. In short, the European feudal system was much "messier" than the one in Western Zhou. Moreover, although it is not the case that Western Zhou China was organized through kinship, and medieval Europe was organized by contracts, as it is often stated, contracts and agreements in Western Zhou China were often between a nobleman of a superior rank and that of an inferior rank, while those in Europe, due to the disorganization of the feudal structure, were often between two equals or two noblemen, one of whom didn't clearly outrank the other. All this could make Europeans more resistant to a centralizing tendency during the transition to modernity than the Chinese.[35]

There was no secular throne in medieval Europe that enjoyed the status of overlordship as high, long-standing, and stable as was the office of the Western Zhou king, and there was also the papacy, which prevented the secular ruler from having unified political power. Besides, the Age of Discovery that accompanied the European transition to early modernity also offered the Europeans territorial expansions, colonialism, and emigrations that dwarfed those during the SAWS. There were more "warring states" with a total size of land significantly larger in Europe than in China during the SAWS, which made the unification and dominance by one state and one kind of regime more difficult in Europe than in China.[36] Different from the Chinese experience, the European "warring states" did not manage to achieve the kind of unity that the Chinese states achieved, although they did manage to wage two world wars, among many other smaller-scale wars.

All these distinctions may have contributed to the different paths the Chinese and Europeans took while facing similar issues. In particular, consti-

34. Qian Mu pointed out this profound distinction in Qian (2005b, 1–3).

35. The fact that a system is disorganized is not necessarily always a bad thing. The messiness of the European system may have been a contributing factor for the emergence of competing political regimes in modern Europe, which in turn was crucial for the emergence of constitutionalism in the United Kingdom and a few other states (such as Denmark), a great contribution of Europe to human civilization.

36. This may also have contributed to the accidental emergence and development of constitutionalism in some corners of Europe.

tutional monarchy first emerged in England, which paved the way for the dominant political regime today, constitutional democracy or liberal democracy. Industrial revolutions also appeared first in England, which pushed modernity to its next level, a "modernity 2.0" that eluded traditional China. The distinctive features of modernity 2.0 and their significance to political issues will be further discussed in later chapters of this book (e.g., in chapter 5). But let me be clear on one issue here: the term "early modernity" can be misleading, because to enter early modernity doesn't necessarily guarantee the transition to late, industrialized modernity.

There are other ideas that are commonly believed to be unique to European modernity, such as equality, freedom, market economy, and secularization. But they may have also occurred, perhaps in slightly different forms, in China during the SAWS, and they can be explained by the deeper structural changes (from nobility-based close-knit feudal societies to centralized, plebeianized, and large states) that are common to Chinese and European early modernity. For example, when nobility vanished, all people would naturally be born equal and have more freedom to choose what they wished to do, including moving to a different location. Land would be freely sold in the market, which would lead to the emergence of a land-based market economy. As for secularization, it could be a side effect of what was peculiar to Europe: the separation and the struggle between the throne and the papacy.

Whether these differences are real or not, all I need here is for readers to acknowledge that there were profoundly similar problems in the Chinese and European transitions to "modernity," especially the three fundamental political issues that were brought about anew by the dawn of modernity, under the "modern" conditions of large, populous, well-connected, mobile, and plebeianized states of strangers.

These similarities may also lead us to reflect upon the nature of modernity, but that is not the focus of this book. In this chapter, I am attempting to show that liberal democracy, nation-states, and other models that have been developed in the West may have been answers to the issues that arose in the transition to "modernity," and that these issues, whatever they were called (modern or not), were also faced by pre-Qin thinkers, early Confucians included. If so, we should investigate early Confucians' answers to these issues and their merits relative to those offered by the West, and then and only then can we come to a conclusion about where the history regarding politics should end.

To argue for the similarities between the Zhou-Qin transition and the European transition to early modernity is controversial, to say the least. But there is a growing minority who shares this view with me, or explicitly or implicitly supports my view. To give a few examples, the American scholar and diplomat Richard Walker noted quite early the clear parallels between China during the

SAWS and modern Europe (1953, xi). The American sinologist and scholar of Chinese thought Herrlee Creel also pointed out the similarities between modern (Western) centralized bureaucratic administrations and Chinese ones in the early Han dynasty (Creel 1970a, 3; and Creel 1970b, 124), the latter of which was a result of the Zhou-Qin transition. Kenneth Waltz (1979, 329–30), Bin Wong (1997, 101), and Charles Tilly (1998, 7) all noticed the similarities between early modern European and traditional Chinese regimes. In recent literature, Tin-bor Hui argues for the similarities between the international environment in early modern Europe and that in Warring States China, and she also explains why China was eventually unified while Europe was not (2005). Francis Fukuyama also clearly states that the state of Qin, which unified China at the end of the SAWS, was politically modern (2011, 125–26).

Again, whether the Zhou-Qin transition is an early modernization or not is a controversial issue. But what I think is not controversial but a historical fact is that during this transition, the feudal order and many political and social features associated with it disappeared; a large, well-connected, plebeianized, and mobile society of strangers emerged. These changes led to the demand for new political orders. The changes and the demands are common to the Zhou-Qin transition and the European transition to early modernity. These claims are not or should not be controversial. What is controversial is whether these changes are modernization or not. Fortunately, as we will see in the following chapters, my discussions of the contemporary relevance of Confucian political philosophy only depend on what I consider the noncontroversial part.

In Contrast to the New Confucian and Moral Metaphysical Readings

The above understanding of early Confucianism is in sharp contrast to the mainstream understanding today—a representative of the latter is the twentieth-century "overseas New Confucians" (海外新儒家). Most scholars today believe that traditional Confucianism is an "ancient" thought system or tradition that is primarily concerned with moral metaphysical issues. Even if we put the issue of antiquity versus modernity aside, my claim that early Confucianism was primarily a political philosophy is still quite different from the mainstream understanding. But early imperial historians also primarily understood pre-Qin philosophy as a political philosophy (Sima 1981, 358). According to the contemporary historian Yu Ying-shih (余英时), even Song-Ming Neo-Confucianism, which is more commonly considered primarily a moral metaphysics, had a political dimension that has been ignored by contemporary scholars (Yu 2004).

Then why is there such a widespread misunderstanding of the nature of early Confucianism? Perhaps the common belief in the total failure of traditional Chinese politics and the notion that liberal democracy is the end of history in terms of political models (Fukuyama 1992) explains why scholars ignore the political aspect of traditional Chinese philosophy, early Confucianism included. If there is nothing good about traditional Chinese politics (often dubbed as "authoritarian" and even "feudalistic," which is often simply interpreted as "outdated"), and we have already discovered the best political model, then why should we bother to look at the political dimension of traditional Chinese philosophy, other than as a curious item in a museum?

Moreover, this understanding of Confucianism is not only historically incorrect, but it is far less promising than reading Confucianism primarily as a political philosophy. On the one hand, this understanding ignores the rich resources of traditional Chinese political thoughts and practices that may critically and constructively contribute to our reflections on the issue of the best political regime. On the other hand, taking Confucianism as a moral metaphysics severely limits the scope of its applicability in the age of pluralism, in which a comprehensive doctrine, moral metaphysics included, can never be shared by the majority of people without oppression, while a political conception can.[37]

Due to the dominant moral metaphysical reading of Confucianism, one may prefer Neo-Confucianism, which, under the influence of the introduction of Buddhism to China, appears to be more metaphysical than pre-Qin Confucianism, and twentieth-century New Confucianism to an early, less metaphysical form of Confucianism. As a result, attempts have been made to read moral metaphysics into early Confucianism, thus "refining" the latter. It is true that in contrast to the metaphysicalization of later Confucianism, early Confucianism is less metaphysical—or can be more easily read "ametaphysically," as a political conception—than later Confucianism, which is why I prefer early Confucianism to the later versions of Confucianism.[38] This less meta-

37. For a detailed criticism of the moral metaphysical reading of Confucianism, see Bai (2010b).

38. To say this means that we have to define "metaphysics," which is beyond the scope of this chapter. In my defense of the legitimate status of Confucianism as a philosophy, I argue that early Confucians did offer justifications for their claims, and in order to avoid infinite justification ascent, a final grounding has to be given somewhere. If justification-offering and the existence of some ultimate grounding are considered a metaphysical activity—in many usages, "metaphysics" is meant to be something much thicker than this—then early Confucians are metaphysical. However, even so, their "metaphysics" is a very thin one in that its justifications are conducted with a kind of "ordinary language metaphysics"—it sticks to some widely shared ordinary reasoning, language, and lifeworld, and thus can be endorsed by many who hold different thick metaphysical doctrines. I thank Huang Xiang (黄翔) and Lin Mingzhao (林明照) for pushing me to clarify this. The criticism of (thick) metaphysics and the appreciation of or-

physical, "thin" version of Confucianism can be endorsed by Confucians of competing schools, and even by people of different comprehensive doctrines. Thus, for example, not only is the dialogical format of the *Analects* not a problem when we approach it philosophically, it also has its merits, because this format can more easily take context (such as who the interlocutors are) into consideration and deal with the dialectical tensions of reality, and is thus less subjected to being taken as a set of comprehensive doctrines and even dogmas than the treatises.

To understand early Confucianism primarily as a political philosophy, then, entails the perspectives I take. It means, for example, that when I deal with the famous Mencian position of the original goodness of human nature, I won't resort to some moral metaphysics, as scholars today tend to do, but I will use its political root or function as the ultimate explanation. In fact, Confucius was silent on whether human beings are by nature good or bad. Mencius's and Xun Zi's followers have been arguing about this issue for ages, and it seems to be another metaphysical debate that can only be determined by who can thump the table harder. But all of them would probably agree that human beings need to be good and can be good, and this thin understanding of human "nature" can enjoy greater universality among people with different comprehensive doctrines. In this sense, Confucius's evasion of this issue seems to be so much wiser, and I will follow his lead on this matter.

Conservative versus Progressive Readings of Confucianism

To take the three political issues brought about anew by modernity as the central issues to early Confucians, we can still argue whether their position is fundamentally conservative, reformist, or even revolutionary. Facing these problems, early Confucians could argue for solving them by "returning" to "small states with few people" (小国寡民), as the *Lao Zi* and Jean-Jacques Rousseau suggested (Bai 2009b), or to the Western Zhou feudal system. Some pre-Qin Confucian texts seem to suggest a return to the "old regime." Early critics, such as Han Fei Zi, also suggested that this conservative proposal was the Confucian position. The debate on whether Confucians are conservative or not has been going on in the following centuries, embodied, for example, in the debates between *gu wen jing xue* (古文经学) and *jin wen jing xue* (今文经学) in the Han dynasties. Even today, philosophers who are sympathetic to Confucianism, such as Zhang Xianglong (张祥龙), still propose the construction of a

---

dinary language metaphysics are inspired by my two great teachers, the late Burton Dreben and Stanley Rosen, to whom I am forever grateful.

"Confucian reservation" (儒家保护区), in which a small group of people can practice what Confucianism dictates.

This reading of Confucianism as a conservative doctrine is not totally base-less, but this is not the place for me to criticize this reading adequately. Rather, what I can do is to be explicit about the reading that I propose. In my view, early Confucians were revolutionaries with a conservative facade. According to this "progressive" reading, they tried to solve issues of modernity not by rejecting modernity but by embracing it, although some of their locutions seem to resonate with those widely used in the "good old days," and they were not as resolute as thinkers from some other schools.[39] Moreover, not accept-ing early Confucianism as a moral metaphysics, I also reject the reading that early Confucians tried to solve political issues by improving on people's mor-als alone. Rather, the premise of my reading is that they apprehended the po-litical concerns as primary and the ethical ones as secondary, a byproduct of their political concerns. They were concerned with reconstructing a political order and were thus open to the idea of institutional design, even though they themselves didn't discuss it in detail. To take a continuous reading of early Confucianism by asking about which political institutions they would have in mind, especially in today's political reality, as I try to do in this book, wouldn't be alien to Confucianism.

In other words, this kind of Confucianism can answer challenges from thinkers such as Han Fei Zi. Han Fei Zi, a brilliant political philosopher who was allegedly educated by Xun Zi (a very important early Confucian thinker), waged a powerful attack on Confucianism. In his reading, Confucians were trying to restore the old regime, in which the world was ruled by virtue (virtu-ous subjects and rulers) and by rituals, but they failed to realize that the world in which this kind of governance was applicable was gone for good. In "mod-ern times," institutions and the rule of law are what are effective.[40] In my view, by not answering Han Fei Zi's challenges in a positive and constructive man-ner, Confucianism could not even remain relevant during the Han dynasties,

39. For example, Yuri Pines argues that it is the Mohists and later the Legalists who were the first to embrace the idea of meritocracy fully and openly (2013). But in the following chapters, especially in chapter 2, I see meritocracy as a key idea to Mencius. To say so depends on how seriously or unseriously the reader interprets certain passages of a text. Although how to read a text is not totally arbitrary, there is a certain flexibility involved. What I can do is to be explicit about my general approach (the progressive reading) and about which claims I take seriously or not.

40. To be clear, Han Fei Zi's understanding of the rule of law is both different from the kind of rule of law we have in today's liberal democracies and from the so-called rule by law that is often used to describe an authoritarian way of governing. For a general discussion of Han Fei Zi's insights on his times, see Bai (2011).

let alone today. Confucianism has survived precisely because it has faced up to these challenges.

In short, my version of Confucianism is progressive or forward-looking, embracing the reality of modernity and open to the idea of institutional design and the rule of law. I am not rejecting the possibility of other ways of reading Confucianism; I only wish to be explicit about my own position.

2

Confucianism on Political Legitimacy

FOR THE PEOPLE, OF THE PEOPLE, BUT NOT BY THE PEOPLE

Confucian Equality

As discussed in chapter 1, the world in which early Confucians lived was one in which the old regime was disappearing and a new political order was not yet established. One of the crucial issues in establishing this new order was to consider who should rule; that is, what gives legitimacy to those who rule and how are they selected? In this and in chapters 3 and 4, I will investigate early Confucians' answer to this issue, how it can be reconstructed into a viable model applicable to the contemporary world, and why it is superior to the present democratic model in dealing with various political issues. In all these endeavors, I will mostly use materials from the *Mencius*, while using the *Analects* and other texts as supplements and points of contrast. There are some differences between Mencius's and Confucius's answers to the above issue, and in order to offer a coherent picture, it is good to focus on Mencius's answers. Moreover, Mencius lived in a period in which the old regime had almost completely collapsed, and his theory was more adapted to a "modern" world and more easily adaptable to today's world than Confucius's.

As we discovered in chapter 1, the Western Zhou "feudal" regime collapsed during the SAWS, as did nobility by pedigree and the legitimacy of the nobility as members of the ruling class of various ranks. Most people were now born to be equal. From this perspective, the idea of equality, which is considered so essential to (Western) modernity, may have been an epiphenomenon that accompanied the collapse of nobility-based feudalism, and is thus not unique to Western modernity. What distinguished all these "modern" thinkers (pre-Qin Chinese thinkers and modern European thinkers) on the issue of equality is what they did with it.

Interestingly, almost no prominent school from the Pre-Qin era argued for a return to the feudal hierarchy and nobility by birth. Pre-Qin Confucians were no exception, and in spite of their "conservative" reputation, they embraced equality. For example, Confucius, a mere commoner, was said to be the first private teacher, publicly offering lessons of statecraft to anyone who came to him with an eagerness to learn, whereas in feudal times, both teaching and learning statecraft were solely privileges of the nobles. This was a daring move that challenged the foundation of feudal hierarchy. In the *Analects*, Confucius claimed that even if someone only had a meager present for him, he had never denied instruction to him (7.7). At another place, he made his point more clearly by saying that "I educate everyone without [taking into account] categories"; by "categories," presumably, he meant distinctions that were based on class, wealth, and where the learners were from (15.39).

Nevertheless, nowhere in the *Analects* did Confucius claim that everyone is equal. The idea that everyone should be educated doesn't have to presuppose that everyone is equal, but it can be based on a minimum premise or a very limited sense of equality that either everyone should have some education or we cannot predetermine who is educable and to what level one can be educated until we actually educate him or her. Mencius (as well as Xun Zi), however, went a step further by claiming that every human being is educable and has the same potential to become a sage, morality-wise if not wisdom-wise. In the *Mencius* 2A6, he claimed that everyone has a compassionate heart, which is essential for anyone to be human. In 7A4, he further claimed that everything necessary for one's moral development is already in oneself. That is, in terms of potential, human beings are all equal. In this sense, "the sage and I are of the same kind" (6A7). The only difference between a sage and a common person is that the former never ignores his original goodness and cares to cultivate it to its fullest, an effort that everyone can make (4B12, 6A8, 6A11, 6A12, 6A18, 6A19, and 6A20). In 6B2, he made the most explicit claim of the equality of all: when asked if it was the case that everyone could become a Yao and a Shun, two sage rulers that often serve as the ideal ruler and the ideal human being in a Confucian text, Mencius said yes. Indeed, in spite of his famous denial of the innate goodness of human beings, Xun Zi, too, claimed that anyone on the street could become a Yu, another legendary sage ruler and ideal human being (chap. 23 of the *Xun Zi*; for a partial English translation, see W. Chan 1969, 133).[1]

---

1. There are some subtle but significant differences among these three early Confucians. As already shown, Confucius didn't embrace equality as fully as Mencius and Xun Zi. Although both of the latter two embraced equality, the ideals that Mencius liked to use were Yao and Shun, whereas Xun Zi talked about Yu much more frequently than Mencius did. Yu was said to give

Confucian View of Political Legitimacy:
Of the People, for the People . . .

If, according to early Confucians, especially Mencius and Xun Zi, we are all equal in terms of our moral potential, and everyone is able to become a sage ruler, then should there still be a ruling class, and if there is, what gives legitimacy to its rule? On the legitimacy issue, again, early Confucians didn't advocate a return to the old regime, the legitimacy of which ultimately existed in some sort of divine right of the king, but tried to offer a new source of political legitimacy. They firmly believed that the legitimacy of the government resided in service to the people, that members of the ruling class should be selected on this basis, and that the government should be held accountable to the service offered. In this sense, their answer resonates with the one offered by some modern European thinkers who also faced the issue of political legitimacy, which was brought about anew after the collapse of the medieval regimes.

According to a quasi-historical and quasi-state-of-nature account presented by Mencius, which was obviously intended to describe the ideal government and thus was meant to be normative, what the sage ruler Yao and his ministers did was to drive away the beasts and control the flood that threatened people's lives, to make the natural conditions suitable for farming and other productive activities, and then to teach people farming and other life skills (3A4). That is, the ideal government should first be responsible for the material well-being of its people by offering securities and basic goods and (technical) education to them. This sounds exactly like how many modern and contemporary Western thinkers, more than two thousand years after Mencius, understand the government's responsibilities and has become the mainstream understanding of the duty of democratic governments today.[2] For example, the late modern European thinker Jeremy Bentham defines the common good as nothing but

---

the throne to his son, instead of a nonrelative who was the most virtuous and wise. This might have been a reflection of Xun Zi's own embrace of hereditary monarchy with an increasingly centralized power, which became the norm during his time. On how to realize people's moral potential, Mencius emphasized inner moral development, whereas Xun Zi emphasized the regulative and corrective function of *li* (礼), often translated as "rituals," which for him needed to be institutionalized. In contrast, Confucius seemed to pay attention to both the internal and external means of moral development.

2. According to Samuel Fleischacker, it was not until the eighteenth century when the idea that "everyone should have their basic needs satisfied" was introduced (2004, 2 and 53–79). But as Elizabeth Perry points out, he completely overlooks the Confucian tradition (Perry 2008, 39), which, as we see here, introduced this idea much earlier than Western thinkers did.

the sum of individuals' material interests (1948, 1–3). But Mencius didn't stop there; he went on to say that when the people

> have a full belly and warm clothes on their backs they almost degenerate to the level of beasts if they are allowed to lead idle lives, without education and discipline. This gave the sage king further cause for concern, and so he appointed Xie as the minister of education whose duty was to teach the people human relationships: love between father and son, duty between ruler and subject, distinction between husband and wife, precedence of the old over the young, and trust between friends. (3A4)

Thus, according to Mencius, it is these social or communal relationships, taught by the government, that make people human. For him, "human" is not only a biological concept but also a moral and social one. A human being in the biological sense, or as an individual entity free of available social relationships,[3] is not a human being. This resonates with his idea that the potential of developing oneself to possess the four basic virtues (humanity, righteousness, observation of rites, and wisdom), each of which is defined in terms of social relations, is what distinguishes humans from beasts (2A6 and 4B19). Therefore, a government, if it is considered a government of humans, has to make sure its people possess these basic moral virtues.[4]

Mencius's understanding of the government as a necessary good, whose duty includes taking care of the moral well-being of the people, seems to be different from the contemporary mainstream democratic understanding of the role of the government. His understanding of human beings is also different from the individualist understanding that a human being is human because of some inner worth, independent of social relations. I discuss these differences and their implications throughout this book, and let me just say for now that this understanding of the role of government doesn't necessarily lead to the kind of oppression that cannot be accepted by liberalism.[5]

Mencius's understanding that it is certain basic morals that make us human is often accused of being overly moralistic, ignoring the material conditions of human life. But this is a false accusation. For he argued that, although in terms of what makes us human, certain morals come first, in terms of governmental

---

3. Clearly, for example, the relationship with a wife is not and should not be available to a little boy.

4. Many traditional societies and classical philosophers (e.g., Aristotle) also adopted the idea that "human being" is not only a biological but also a sociopolitical concept; but what is distinctively Mencian is the special emphasis on the role of government in the moral inculcation of its people.

5. For a detailed discussion of the compatibility between early Confucianism and liberalism, as well as the rule of law, see chapter 9.

duties, to offer security and basic material goods should be primary. In the passage from 3A4 of the *Mencius* that was discussed earlier, we can clearly see that Mencius's ideal government is one that takes care of people's material interests first. The reason for this, according to another passage of the *Mencius*, is that the moral well-being of the common people depends upon their material well-being, or the satisfaction of their material interests:

> Only a member of the scholar-officials (*shi* 士)[6] can have a constant [or "stable"] heart in spite of a lack of constant means of support [or "properties"]. The people, on the other hand, will not have constant hearts if they are without constant means. Lacking constant hearts, they will go astray and fall into excesses, stopping at nothing. To punish them after they have fallen foul of the law is to set a trap for the people. (1A7; see also 3A3)

One implication of this belief is that if people commit crimes due to the lack of economic stability, the government should be held accountable, meaning that the government should be punished for the crimes of necessity. But at the same time, Mencius believed that everyone could be good if he or she chose to be, and thus the criminal was accountable for his or her criminal deeds (although some leniency could be applied in this case).[7] In this sense, Mencius's position is a combination of the American Left (blaming the crime of the poor on their economic status) and the American Right (blaming the crime of the poor on their own character). On the issue of morality and the satisfaction of material needs, the above passage clearly suggests that the material well-being of the people should be a priority in governmental policies, which makes him not as far from how the role of the government is understood in present democratic regimes as it appears to be.

A passage in the *Analects* expressed something similar to the idea that service to the people should always come first (12.9). More importantly, it suggested that when, in a bad year, a ruler didn't have enough revenue, counterintuitively, the policy was to lower the tax, not to increase it, the reason being that, "When the people have sufficient, who is there to share your [the ruler's] insufficiency? When the people have insufficient, who is there to share your sufficiency?" (12.9).[8] This reasoning can be interpreted as merely stating the

6. The term *shi* (士) referred to an official in the feudal system who was of noble pedigree, and later, thanks to the early Confucian reinterpretation of the old system, referred to Confucian intellectuals and scholar officials among other variations. In the *Analects* 15.2, Confucius also stated that the masses couldn't maintain virtues while poor, but the exemplary people could.

7. This resonates partly with Mencius's comment that one is wrong if he wrongs the superior for not giving him a share of some luxurious enjoyment, and one is also wrong if, being the superior to the masses, one doesn't share the joy with them (1B4).

8. This is offered by You Ruo (有若), who, in the *Analects*, seems to enjoy an authoritative status close to Confucius's.

Confucian idea of government's duty to its people, and can also be interpreted as something similar to today's fiscal conservative's argument: to lower taxes in a bad year may put more into people's pockets, which will trigger more production and consumption, which will eventually increase the government's revenue. The validity of the latter interpretation aside, in traditional China, Confucians tend to favor low tax and the policy of "storing the wealth in the people" (藏富于民). This might explain why in today's China some economically "liberal" thinkers (e.g., followers of Friedrich Hayek) are simultaneously "conservatives" or "traditionalists" in the sense of being advocates of Confucianism.[9]

So on the one hand, Confucians consider government, which is responsible for the well-being of the people, a necessary good. This Confucian position aligns with the idea of a welfare state and opposes the libertarian position on government. On the other hand, Confucians also favor a free market–style policy, which aligns them with the libertarian position and not with those who support the idea of a welfare state. Their position then offers an interesting comparison and contrast to both today's Left and Right with regard to economic policies.[10]

Following these Confucian ideas, we can also imagine that Confucians can easily endorse the contemporary political philosopher John Rawls's famous "difference principle," which is intended to take care of the worst-off in an effective and economically viable manner (1971, 60–62 and 78–83; 1996, 5–7). One important difference between Rawls and Mencius, however, is how they each define the worst-off group. For Mencius, the government should give consideration to both those who are materially deprived and those who are deprived of key social relations, like widows, orphans, and so on (1B5). Rawls, however, doesn't say much about the latter group. Put in contemporary American political terms, Mencius's considerations are a combination of the concerns of both progressive liberals and social conservatives in that he would be concerned with both sources of middle-class anxiety, one caused by (staggering) wages and the other caused by the threat to the traditional two-parent family structure, as the political commentator David Brooks put it (2008).[11]

9. The contemporary Chinese economist Sheng Hong (盛洪), public intellectual Yao Zhongqiu (姚中秋) aka Qiu Feng (秋风), and the late Zhou Dewei (周德伟), a Chinese economist who went to Taiwan after the communist takeover of the mainland, are good examples of this.

10. Of course, it is debatable whether Confucians would still hold on to such a policy in an industrialized world, and whether this policy was viable then and is viable now.

11. To be clear, the family structure during early Confucians' times was not necessarily one man and one woman, and thus the Confucian concern is really about a stable family structure, be it two-parent or multiple-parent families.

With the governmental duties so specified, then, for Mencius, members of the ruling class should be selected on this basis, and they should be held accountable accordingly. In the *Mencius* 5A5, in a discussion with a student (Wan Zhang [万章]) on how the sage ruler Shun was given the throne by his predecessor, the sage ruler Yao, Mencius pointed out, "the son of Heaven [the ruler of the known world] cannot give the world [tian xia (天下)] to another," but can only "recommend a man to Heaven." It is Heaven that gave the world to Shun. But "Heaven does not speak but reveals itself through its acts and deeds," and the ultimate source of this revelation comes from the people; that is, "Heaven sees with the eyes of its people; Heaven hears with the ears of its people."

One may challenge this humanistic reading of Mencius's Heaven by pointing out that in this passage, the candidate also had to be accepted by the gods. But the only criterion for the gods' acceptance was that when the candidate was in charge of sacrifices, the gods enjoyed them, which seems to be merely a formal requirement,[12] and in spirit it is not much different from the necessity of performing well in the American presidential inauguration ceremony.[13] Moreover, according to Mencius, even the altars to the gods can be replaced if the gods fail to fulfill their duties to the people! In the *Mencius* 7B14, he claimed,

> The people are of supreme importance; the altars to the gods of earth and grain come next; last comes the ruler. . . . When the sacrificial animals are sleek, the offerings are clean, and the sacrifices are observed at due times, and yet floods and droughts come, then the altars should be replaced.

Although Mencius greatly reduced the transcendent aspect of Heaven and the gods, from the passages quoted above we can see that he didn't abandon the appeal to Heaven and the gods completely. Through the collapse of the feudal order, people were "disenchanted" with the divine (Heaven-given) right of the Zhou king, and Mencius reinterpreted Heaven's will and grounded it in the will of the people. But he didn't give up the language of Heaven's will completely because, as we can speculate, he may have wished to strengthen the new source of legitimacy (the satisfaction of the people) with the appeal

---

12. For how do we know if gods enjoyed them or not, other than observing whether the sacrificial rituals are well performed or not?

13. For example, the newly elected president has to be sworn in by the chief justice, and these two people have to recite the oath correctly, the importance of which was highlighted by the incident when President Obama, in his first inauguration, had to be sworn in twice by Chief Justice Roberts because of a mistake made in the oath in the first round; in his second inauguration, the two men practiced before this apparently simple performance took place (Jacobs 2013).

to the divine. This is a move similar to such early modern European thinkers as John Locke, who, in his *First Treatise of Government*, deconstructed the old divine right of the king, but in his *Second Treatise of Government* anointed his new account of political legitimacy with "natural" rights that are guaranteed by God. This is a deft move that combines the disenchantment of the old legitimacy with the reenchantment with the new legitimacy, which is perhaps a wiser move than the one made by those during the process of the transition from the old source of legitimacy to the new one, which was to get rid of enchantment (the appeal to something divine and sacred) completely.[14]

Now, if the legitimacy of the top leaders of the state (and even the gods) is ultimately determined by service to the people, the legitimacy of other members of the ruling class should also be so determined. In the *Mencius* 1B7, Mencius argued that when a ruler needed to decide which candidate was suitable or unsuitable for an office, and which official should be demoted or even punished with death, either the consensus of those in his innermost circle or that of the ministers was not enough, and only that of the people would be enough for the ruler to have the case investigated in order to make a decision.[15] Thus, in the case of punishing an official with death, "It is the people who put him to death. Only by acting in this manner can one be father and mother to the people."[16]

14. Thus, secularization, which is often taken as a feature of modernity, may have been a consequence of the collapse of the old order, or a normative attempt to reinforce this collapse. It doesn't necessarily mean every source of the sacred was secularized, and the process of "secularization" could be connected with a new process of sacredization. If this is the case, to understand modernization completely as a secularizing process may be misleading. Of course, in the European setting, the conflict between church and state added additional tension to secularization in the European embrace of modernity.

15. At the beginning of this passage, Mencius said, "when promoting the wise, if there is no other choice, the ruler of a state has to put the lowly above those of high ranks, and put the distant above the close [relatives or confidants]. How can the ruler not be very cautious [when making such decisions]?" This can be interpreted as Mencius's conservativeness in the sense that he still wished to preserve feudalism in which only the king's relatives and noblemen could serve the office, and he only called for the rejection of it in special circumstances. But as I said in chapter 1, my progressive reading of the *Mencius* sees this claim by Mencius as a general cautionary stance rather than an unwillingness to reject the feudal order.

16. Some might object that "the people" in 1B7 should be translated literally as "the men in the capital" (国人). They should not be seen as the same as the common people, because they were originally believed to be superior to the people in the "wild" (野人). But in passage 15.28 of the *Analects*, Confucius already made a similar claim: "Be sure to investigate the case if someone (or something) is disliked by the people; be sure to investigate the case if someone (or something) is liked by the people." He used the generic word for "the people" or "the masses" (众) in this passage, and it is hard to imagine that the more egalitarian Mencius would limit the

Therefore, the legitimacy of every member of the ruling class is determined by service to the people. Moreover, the government should be held accountable accordingly. We already saw in the aforementioned passages that ministers and even the gods can be demoted or replaced for failing to serve the people. The top leaders of a state are not exceptions. In the *Mencius* 1B6, Mencius said to King Xuan of Qi,

> "Suppose that one of Your Majesty's ministers were to entrust his wife and children to the care of a friend, while he himself went into Chu [another state] to travel, and that, upon his return, his friend had let his wife and children suffer from cold and hunger, then what should he do about it?"
>
> The king said, "Break with his friend."

After discussing another hypothetical case, Mencius asked,

> "If the whole realm within the four borders [of your kingdom] is ill-governed, what should be done about it?"
>
> The king looked to his right and left, and spoke of some other matters. (1B6)

Clearly, the answer should be that a ruler who fails to serve the people in a disastrous manner should also be removed, and the ridicule of King Xuan of Qi is plainly obvious.

In a later passage, the king mentioned in the above passage asked Mencius, perhaps in an attempt to get even with him,

> "Is it true that Tang [a lord under King Jie] banished Jie [the last king of the Xia dynasty who was said to be a tyrant] and King Wu marched against Zhou [the last king of the Shang dynasty, who was also said to be a tyrant and was killed by King Wu who was a feudal lord under King Zhou]?"
>
> "It is so recorded," answered Mencius.
>
> "Is regicide permissible?"
>
> "He who mutilates humaneness is a mutilator; he who cripples righteousness is a crippler. A man who is both a mutilator and a crippler is a lone fellow [secluded from and abandoned by the people]. I have heard of killing the lone fellow Zhou but have not heard of any regicide." (1B8)

---

scope of the people in a similar claim. In his classic commentary on this passage of Mencius, the Eastern Han Confucian "classicist" (经学家) Zhao Qi (赵岐) used the *Analects* 15.28 to interpret the message in the *Mencius* 1B7 (Jiao 1986, 85). Besides, in the *Mencius* 5A5, he used the term *min* (民), which literally means "the people." Historically, the distinction between the men in the capital and the men in the wild was disappearing in Confucius's and Mencius's times. Based upon all these considerations, it is reasonable to conclude that "the men in the capital" refers to the common people in general.

Thus, if a ruler is not only incompetent but tyrannical, a violent removal and even killing him is justified.

It is important to note that in this passage, Mencius carefully distinguished between regicide and killing a lone fellow. In doing so, he tried to separate the tyrant from his office, and suggested that it is the tyrant, and not the office, that can be removed. It is comparable to the idea that in the American government, a bad president can be impeached, but the office of the presidency cannot be eliminated. This is a sign of Mencius's attempt to strike a middle way between revolution and caution (conservatism), a recurring theme in the *Mencius* and the *Analects*.

In sum, Mencius clearly held the idea that government is for the people, and more importantly, this is not an empty claim, because the government has to be held accountable to this essential role. In other words, Mencius embraced two ideas often seen as essential to a democratic regime. Indeed, he may have been the first thinker, or among the first group of thinkers, who developed the idea that government is for the people, and the idea of accountability.

As for another crucial component of a democratic regime in which the state is of the people, there may be more controversies regarding how to characterize Mencius's stance. That the state is of the people apparently means that the ultimate owner of the state is the people. If we read passage 5A5 literally, it is really Heaven who is the owner of all under Heaven (the people and the world). But John Locke, a modern European thinker who is considered crucial to the development of democratic ideas, in his discussion of people's property rights (i.e., the justification for people or the state to own a piece of land) in the *Second Treatise of Government*, also seems to say that God is the ultimate owner of everything in the world (see, e.g., sections 25 and 26 in Locke 1986, 19–20). But we can interpret Locke's claim as merely asserting God's *nominal* ownership, and this is not to deny the real ownership of the people. Similarly, as I argued earlier, Mencius eventually claimed that Heaven sees and hears through the eyes and ears of the people, and we can interpret this as Mencius's tacit acknowledgment of people's real ownership of a state. Indeed, in 5A5, he said, after Heaven revealed its acceptance of Shun (the candidate for the son of Heaven) through the gods' enjoyment of the sacrifices, and after people revealed their acceptance of Shun by being content with the political order offered by his governance, "Heaven gave it [the world (tian xia) or the position of the ruler of the world] to him; people gave it to him." The fact that people can give the world to a ruler—and the fact that although Heaven also has a share of giving the world to the ruler it sees and hears through people—supports the idea that for Mencius, people are the de facto owners of the state.

An often-quoted statement from another early Chinese classic, *Lv Shi Chun Qiu* (呂氏春秋), "All under Heaven are not of one person, but are of all the

people under Heaven" expresses more explicitly the idea of people's ownership of the world, let alone a state (Gao 1986, 6; 呂氏春秋・貴公). This classic
is not generally considered purely Confucian, but this statement is often considered Confucian or Mencian and to be in line with what is less explicitly
expressed in other Confucian classics.[17]

We have to make it clear, however, that even if we could interpret Mencius's idea as endorsing people's real and ultimate ownership of the state, we
would have to distinguish this from the idea of popular sovereignty, if popular
sovereignty has to be expressed through one person, one vote. As we will see,
Mencius has reservations about popular sovereignty so construed. For Mencius, although people own the state, they don't run it on their own. Rather,
their delegates will do it on their behalf. But if we identify people's ownership
with one person, one vote, then the democratic idea "of the people" wouldn't
be different from the democratic idea "by the people," or at least "by the
people" should become a necessary condition of "of the people." But one can
own something and yet ask others to run it for him or her. The action of asking others to run it or taking it back doesn't have to be decided directly by the
owner himself or herself but through certain procedures. Moreover, these
procedures are not necessarily established or actively endorsed by the owner
(consider, e.g., when the owner owns something through inheritance), although he or she has to accept it *somehow*, but not necessarily through one
person, one vote. Therefore, unless we interpret a special reading of the idea
"of the people" or "sovereignty," we can argue that Mencius would also endorse the democratic idea that people are the sovereign of the state. Or we
can acknowledge that Mencius wouldn't endorse the idea of "of the people,"
but this is because we make "by the people" an essential part of "of the people." In this case, then, it is more meaningful to discuss Mencius's reservations
regarding the democratic position on the issue of whether the state is by the
people or not.[18]

---

17. See, for example, R. Li (2016, 6). It is interesting to note that after quoting this line, Li
uses precisely 5A5 of the *Mencius* to elaborate on the meaning of this line.

18. Jeffrey Green also distinguishes between sovereignty and self-legislation or autonomous
decision making (2011, 204–11). Critical of representative democracy, he proposes an alternative: plebiscitary democracy. It "conceives of popular sovereignty as the rule of a principle:
specifically the principle of candor. That is to say, the plebiscitarian understands the People as
realizing its sovereignty to the extent leaders and other high officials are compelled to appear
in public under conditions they do not control" (ibid., 207). Contrary to my claim here, Joseph
Chan argues that early Confucians rejected the idea of people's (and a single ruler's) ownership
of the state (2013b, 28–29 and 213–32). I have no problem with his arguments against the ruler's
ownership of the state. Of people's ownership, although I may not agree with him on some
details, I find his interpretation of the Confucian claim *tian xia wei gong* convincing (ibid., 225–

. . . But Not by the People

So far, in spite of the subtle differences between some liberal democratic ideas and Mencius's, Mencius sounds awfully democratic: he embraced equality and argued that the government is for the people and (in a sense) of the people and should be held accountable to the satisfaction of people's needs, although the needs to be satisfied in Mencius's theory are broader than mere material needs, which are the only needs that, according to the mainstream understanding of democratic accountability, the government should satisfy. More importantly, whether people are satisfied or not had to be decided by the people, according to the aforementioned motto that Heaven hears and sees through the ears and eyes of the people. This decision, if we update Mencius's theory, can be expressed through one person, one vote. Many contemporary Confucian sympathizers thus argue that Confucianism is fully compatible with democracy. Indeed, they believe that some of the aforementioned passages actually mean that people have a right to revolt, and the government is by the people as well. With these three elements (of the people, for the people, and by the people), Mencius would be considered a protodemocrat.

---

27), a claim I didn't use at all to support my idea of people's ownership. He also argues that the aforementioned statement from *Lv Shi Chun Qiu* should not be interpreted as the idea of people's ownership. I find his argument coherent and see that it can be considered as an alternative to my interpretation. My argument for people's ownership, which is based on the *Mencius* 5A5, can also be interpreted differently. That is, what Heaven and the people give to the next son of Heaven is the authority to govern, or in Chan's terminology, "imperium." In spite of the apparently opposite conclusions about people's ownership, I believe that Chan and I share the same substantive understanding. We both argue that Confucians reject the idea of people's natural right of self-governing, or people as the sole and ultimate source of political decision making (my argument for this is in the paragraphs that follow). So, even if my interpretation that Confucians could accept the idea of people's ownership of the state ("of the people") is correct, the ownership, as we have seen, is rather limited and qualified. Chan also argues that there are layers of meanings of ownership (ibid., 216), but he may respond to me by saying that this limited understanding is too stretched to be nonempty (ibid., 218). My response to his apparently opposite claim is as follows. First, as I have argued in this section, ownership is often stretched or qualified (Locke and Green). Second, Chan's rejection of the ownership idea is mostly based on the rejection of popular sovereignty, which is understood as the idea that people are the sole and ultimate source of political decision making. In this sense, "of the people" and "by the people" collapse into the same thing. I can accept this "collapse," and then argue that Confucians only accept the idea of "for the people" but not "of/by the people." If we wish to say that there is something about "of the people" that is independent of "by the people," then we may have to accept a rather qualified understanding of people's ownership, which is my position in this section. I thank Reviewer #2 for pushing me to address Chan's apparently different understanding of the ownership issue.

A careful reading, however, reveals the fact that although we could make a case for Mencius's endorsement of the idea "of the people," by no means did he endorse the idea "by the people."[19]

In the two passages quoted earlier in this section (1B6 and 1B8), although advocating the idea of removing a grossly incompetent and even tyrannical ruler, Mencius never said that it was the people who had the right to do the removal. In 5A5, it was Yao, the previous ruler, who recommended Shun to Heaven and its ears and eyes (i.e., the people), and it took the people twenty-eight years to form a reasoned judgment on Shun the candidate. The necessity of people spending a substantial amount of time with a candidate who is given a significant position to demonstrate his abilities is supported by another passage in the Mencius, where he argued that although a candidate (Yi [益]) recommended by another "son of Heaven" (the sage ruler Yu) was wise and virtuous, he only served for seven years before the former ruler died, and thus people didn't know him well and chose another wise and virtuous person (Qi [启]), who happened to be a son of the deceased ruler, and whose ability was presumably far better appreciated by the people (5A6).[20]

In the aforementioned passage 1B7, where Mencius discussed how to promote and demote a minister, if he had been a democrat, he would have said that when people made a judgment, an action should be taken according to it. But as we saw, the ruler had to have the case investigated before an action was taken. Again, the people's voice can only be one factor, but cannot be the sole determining factor, in contrast to the case of democracy.

Mencius's reservation of the principle "by the people" is very explicit in 3A4. A former follower of Confucianism decided to "convert" to an egalitarian school. According to this school, human beings could and should be self-sufficient and independent, and if everyone worked to satisfy his or her own needs, there wouldn't be any exploitations and wars, thus returning the chaotic world during the Warring States period back to order. In particular, the ideal ruler should work in the fields like his subjects, and not tax his people, which this school considered an exploitation. Addressing this teaching, Mencius famously maintained,

19. See Tiwald (2008) for a similar criticism of the overly "democratic" reading of Mencius.

20. In this passage, Mencius was trying to answer a challenge from the same pupil who asked him about what makes a ruler legitimate in 5A5. The challenge is that if the throne should be passed to the wisest and most virtuous, why did Yu, the sage ruler after Shun, give his throne to a son of his? Indeed, since this incident, unless in a violent removal, the throne had always been passed from a father to a son (or a brother) all the way to Mencius's time. The explanation Mencius offered in this passage about why the son was chosen over another candidate (the son was more virtuous and/or happened to have the opportunity to demonstrate his capacities) sounds ad hoc, to say the least. Still, it seems that he was sincere about the time needed for a candidate to demonstrate his moral, intellectual, and political capacities to the people.

There are affairs of great people, and there are affairs of small people. . . . There are those who use their minds and there are those who use their muscles. The former rule; the latter are ruled. Those who rule are supported by those who are ruled. This is a principle accepted by the whole world. (3A4)

The reasons for this distinction are the following. First, as he argued earlier in 3A4, there has to be a division of labor among people, because one person cannot produce everything that he or she needs in his or her life. This is also why we human beings are social to the core, and it is deeply problematic that the teaching of the egalitarian school, the idea of self-sufficiency in particular, implicitly rejects the need of society.

Second, it is not that the job of ruling a country and that of a laborer are merely different, but that the former is superior to the latter. This can be implied from Mencius's general teachings in other parts of the *Mencius* (which are discussed in detail in chapter 5 of this book). According to these teachings, one is not born to be a human but needs to learn to become a human. If one can develop his or her distinctively human nature (compassion and wisdom that helps to apply his or her compassion to all) more fully than others, he or she is more human, or a greater human being than others. In particular, the job of ruling (i.e., helping all human beings under one's rule) is the deepest expression of compassion and demands wisdom, two elements essential for us to be human, and thus rulers have to be great human beings, or, put more precisely, only great human beings can become rulers. In contrast, laboring with one's muscles for one's own or a close circle's needs is not fundamentally different from animals' activities, and those who can and are only willing to do this fail to develop their humanhood. Therefore, given his normative understanding of "human," the terms "great people" (great human beings) and "small people" are descriptive.

Third, Mencius argued in 3A4 that since the job of the "great people" or rulers, which is focused on how to promote the material and moral well-being of the "small people" or the common people, is time-consuming and demanding, they do not have time and energy to do any menial tasks. From this argument of Mencius's, we can infer that those whose time and energy is consumed by daily labor, which renders them unable to pay any serious attention to political matters, cannot undertake the task of ruling a state.

The laborers Mencius talks about are the farmers and artisans, and in an agrarian society, they are the ones who mostly work for their own living. With the spirit of the continuous or philosophical reading, we should not take Mencius's distinction between those who labor with their minds and those who labor with their muscles literally, and should understand that the key distinction for Mencius is whether one works for oneself and those close to oneself or for the people. Indeed, in 3A4 and elsewhere, the sage ruler Yu is described as someone who had to go through a lot of physical pain in his endeavor to control the flood and help the people, and in spite of his laboring with his muscles, he belongs to those who "labor with their minds." In contrast, in today's setting (the industrialized and information age), it is reasonable to include in the group of those who "labor with their muscles" many of today's "white-collar" professionals, such as scientists, engineers, doctors, financiers, teachers, and so on—that is, those whom José Ortega y Gasset called "learned ignorami," because many of them are consumed by their daily work and may have limited knowledge about public affairs or anything outside of their narrow specializations (1932, 108–12).

The conclusion from the above analyses seems to be that Mencius would be strongly against any democratic participation in political matters, let alone the full and equal participation embodied by one person, one vote, because it is impossible for the working class to make sound political decisions, and their judgments are either based on narrow and immediate self-interest and bias or are misdirected by demagogues.

On the inequality among human beings and the suspicion of common people's capacity of making sound political decisions, Confucius's view was even more "politically incorrect" than Mencius's. As mentioned at the beginning of this chapter, he never acknowledged that human beings are equal in terms of their moral potentials, as Mencius and Xun Zi did. For him, "human beings are similar in nature, but apart by habituations," and immediately following this, he claimed that "only the most wise and the most stupid cannot be moved" (*Analects* 17.2 and 17.3). Even worse, in his view, the uneducable include not only the most stupid but many more. He warned that "you can acquaint those above the average with higher things, but you cannot acquaint those below the average with them" (*Analects* 6.21). Rather, the masses "can be made to follow, but not to know" (*Analects* 8.9).[21]

Confucius's attitude toward political decision making is equally "elitist." According to the *Analects*, a fundamental task of governing is to get the names right (13.3), meaning the ruler, subject, father, and son must do what their names (titles or roles) dictate (12.11). When one doesn't hold an office, one shouldn't plan its policies (8.14 and 14.26). With regard to the consultation role, the people's voice can and should come into play when selecting members of the ruling class, but its role is not decisive. In the *Analects* 15.28, Confucius said, "be sure to investigate the case if someone is disliked by the mul-

---

21. Some Neo-Confucians and other Confucian scholars have tried to "whitewash" these apparently elitist messages (see Y. Huang 2008 for some examples), but I suspect that they are reading their own more egalitarian views into Confucius.

titude; be sure to investigate the case if someone is liked by the multitude." On another occasion, he went even further by claiming that it is better for someone to be liked by the good people in a village and disliked by the bad people in the village than being liked (or disliked) indiscriminately by all in the village (13.24). Perhaps to find out by whom and on what basis a person is liked or disliked is what the superiors in 15.28 need to investigate, and this idea resonates with Mencius's idea of the involvement of the morally and intellectually superior in the decision-making process.

The Confucian Middle Way: Between Equality and Hierarchy, and between Mobility and Stability

Then, how to reconcile the early Confucians' embrace of equality with their defense of hierarchy, and how to reconcile their idea that the legitimacy of the state lies in service to the people, with the idea that it is not the people alone who make the final political decisions?

On the issue of equality, the case for Confucius is relatively easy, for he never said that human beings are equal. Equal education at the beginning may have been intended to reveal different capacities among humans, and after the discovery, different kinds of education should be given to different people according to their capacities.

For Mencius, the problem is trickier. He explicitly stated that we are all equal in that we have the potential to become the ideal human being (the sage ruler), and the difference between a sage ruler and a common person is the effort that they have made. But why do common people fail to make the effort? Is this inborn or also a product of social conditions that we can correct, so that the common people can realize their potential fully? Mencius didn't seem to offer further answers, but it seems that he firmly believed that in reality, those who develop their moral and intellectual capacities are always few in number.

Although we are not clear about Mencius's ultimate ground for the hierarchy among people in reality, however, what we can be sure of is that this hierarchy cannot be determined at birth, and he would consider it unjust if this hierarchy resulted from the failure of governmental policies. As we saw earlier in this chapter, Mencius explicitly argued that the government should be responsible for the material and spiritual well-being of its people. This means that the government should provide food, shelter, education, and, in today's context, basic health care to all. That is, the government is responsible for offering a level playing field. But for reasons unspecified (which may have been contingent and beyond human control), in spite of the equal opportunities offered by the government and the equal potential of all people, in reality, people differ, and the majority of the people will fail to develop their potential adequately. We have to consider this a basic assumption in Mencius's theory (and Confucius's theory), a fact of life in his view.

Then, on the one hand, we have to promote mobility in a level playing field so that those who can excel in reality do excel. On the other hand, in reality, the majority will fail to develop their capacities to a satisfactory degree ("satisfactory" in the sense that one can make an informed decision that also takes other people's interests into account), and thus too much mobility will lead to bad governance, and even chaos. The tension here is in fact similar to that in Plato's *Republic*. It is proposed in this text that at the beginning, education should be open to everyone, even women, which was quite unconventional at that time (456c–57c). But the equality in opportunity is aimed at producing the best and brightest for the ruling class through enlarging the candidate pool, and this education is not an open-ended commitment. Thus, after the wise and virtuous rulers are chosen—with little explanation, Socrates claims later in this dialogue that they are the smallest in number (428d–29a)[22]—in the *Republic* he proposes to tell a noble lie to all, and part of it is to convince people of the following: the rulers are not chosen based on how they have performed through education and various tests (indeed, education did not even happen but was a dream); rather, the rulers are chosen based on what metal they were born with (414b–15d). After the noble lie is told, the masses have to obey the rulers willingly, and justice is equal to each class doing its own job. In particular, the masses should not try to do the job of the rulers (430c–34d). In spite of the awkwardness of this noble lie, Socrates's underlying consideration may have been to maintain stability and order while promoting mobility at the same time, a reasonable political concern. This is his way to strike a middle ground between equality and hierarchy, mobility and order, a concern shared by early Confucians and perhaps by many other political thinkers.

But there are some crucial differences between Socrates and early Confucians. First, the virtues that are considered essential to a ruler are different between these two groups (which I will discuss in more detail in chapters 5 and 6). Second, more related to the topic of this chapter, after the noble lie is told, the masses are basically left out in the rest of the *Republic*, and the noble lie imposes a fixed and sharp line between those who can have further education and participate in political decision making and those who can't. In contrast, the Confucian line is not fixed, and the masses can always lift themselves up to the higher echelon of politics. Moreover, although the masses cannot understand the Confucian way, in order to make them follow it, some basic

22. Throughout this book, "Socrates" refers to the character in different Platonic dialogues and is not necessarily related to the historical Socrates.

education is still needed, and this education is continuous with the education of "the best and the brightest." A very good illustration is offered in a passage in the *Zhong Yong* (中庸):

> The Way of the exemplary person [jun zi] is everywhere yet hidden. Man and wife of simple intelligence can know it, and yet in its utmost reaches, there is something that even the sage does not know. Man and wife of no moral character can put it into practice, and yet in its utmost reaches there is something that even the sage is not able to put into practice. . . . The Way of the exemplary person has its simple beginnings in [the relations between] man and wife, but in its utmost reaches, it is clearly seen in Heaven and Earth. (chap. 12)

Now, let us come back to the question raised at the beginning of this section: How can the tension between the idea that the legitimacy of the state lies in service to the people and the Confucian suspicion of the moral and political capacities of the masses be reconciled? First, as it becomes clear in the *Mencius* 3A4 and some other aforementioned passages, Mencius maintained that only those who have basic moral education can be considered human beings. Thus, the people who are considered critical in determining political legitimacy of a government must already have this education, and they cannot be some asocial individuals, as they were presupposed to be in some social-contract theories. Second, not only do they have to have a certain education, but they are to be consulted only in matters in which they are capable of making sound judgments. This idea is implied by the statement in 5A5, "[people were consulted only after] Shun assisted Yao for twenty-eight years." That is, through twenty-eight years of good work, Shun sufficiently displayed his all-around abilities, so that people could truly know him.

However, for Mencius, all human beings are equal in the sense that they all have the potential to become "rulers" or active members in political decision making, and the state is then responsible for making each citizen such a member. This role of the state is twofold. First, the government should offer education and other necessary means for each individual to develop himself or herself fully in a moral and intellectual sense. Second, if a citizen develops himself or herself adequately, the state should offer conditions necessary for his or her participation in politics. That is, the government should make it possible for this citizen to be freed from his or her daily work, so that he or she may have time and energy to think about public affairs. The government should also make sure that this citizen can have access to information relevant to public affairs, and should encourage open, comprehensive, and in-depth discussions of political matters. An obvious means to achieve these goals is to protect freedom of speech and openness of political matters that are aimed at good governance, and to offer material conditions (such as holidays for political discussions) so as not to render freedom of speech and open access to politics empty.

In sum, the lack of capacities of making sound political decisions by the masses cannot result from the failure of the state to secure basic goods, education, and other necessary conditions for people to make sound political decisions, and it has to be the result of a basic fact of human life. That is, in spite of all these governmental efforts that are demanded by them, and in spite of their beliefs that human beings are all potentially equal (Mencius and Xun Zi) or close to being equal (Confucius), early Confucians also took it as a fact of life that the majority of the people cannot actually obtain the capacity necessary to make sound political decisions and participate fully in politics.

Therefore, according to Mencius, on the one hand, the state is for the people, and it can even be argued that people are the real owner and sovereign of the state. Moreover, from some of the passages in the *Mencius* that have been quoted, we can see that for Mencius, people do have the capacity to decide whether they are satisfied with the services by the government or not. Thus, whether people are satisfied with the government has to be determined by the people, which can be through the mechanism of popular voting (and can be used as another Confucian ground for justifying freedom of speech). On the other hand, Mencius also argued that in reality, no matter how much effort the government has made, the masses are doomed to lack the capacity of making sound political decisions. It is worth emphasizing here the subtlety of Mencius's position. According to him, the masses are capable of deciding on whether they are satisfied with the government, but they are not capable of deciding which policies have made or will make them satisfied. This position has to be considered a basic observation that Mencius has about human beings, and a basic premise of his political theory. Then, it has to be the few, the Confucian "great people," who have the capacity to make sound political decisions and thus should be given the power to do so.

Although Mencius clearly had no clue about democracy, in the spirit of a continuous or philosophical reading, we can ask a "Mencian" how to recontextualize and institutionalize his or her considerations in today's world. As we saw, an ideal Mencian regime has to have both "democratic" and meritocratic elements, and it is of the people, for the people, and by the (morally and intellectually competent) people. Therefore, apparently, an ideal Mencian regime is different from a democratic regime that is of the people, for the people, and by the people.[23]

23. On the aforementioned issue of the right of rebellion, Mencius's position is that people's dissatisfaction justifies rebellion but doesn't justify *their* right of rebellion. Rather, the rebellion needs to be led by some "great people," when they are available.

In chapter 3, I show that there are some fundamental problems with contemporary democracy, especially the ideology beneath the one person, one vote system and the inevitable consequences of it. Then I show how the "internal" solutions are inadequate. Next, I construct a Confucian hybrid regime that is based on Mencius's ideas discussed in this and the previous sections, and show how it can address the problems with democracy more adequately than present liberal democratic regimes. That is, I show in chapter 3 that the Mencian reservation of one person, one vote is actually a good thing about Confucianism.[24]

24. My interpretation of the Confucian position "for the people, but not by the people" is very close to Joseph Chan's "service conception of political authority" (he introduces this idea in 2013b, 30 while the discussion occurs in many places in this book). Sungmoon Kim, among others, has criticized Chan's idea (2014, 60–64 and 2017). I can only offer some simple responses here, given the limit of space and the focus of my own discussion. One of Kim's criticisms is that contemporary Confucian accounts of perfectionist meritocracy cannot answer the challenge of pluralism (2014, 61–62), but he acknowledges that Chan's conception is "least susceptible to this charge" (ibid., 62n79). My position is not, or at least not explicitly, based on any form of perfectionism. Indeed, as I have argued in this book, my Confucian proposals are built on the fact of pluralism. Although I criticize mainstream liberalism for its retreat to values too thin to hold liberalism, the moral values I consider necessary are also thin enough to accommodate pluralism. Another criticism of Kim's is that the Confucian meritocracy is presumptuous and paternalistic (ibid., 63), and my response is, yes, it is presumptuous from the perspective of a believer in popular sovereignty. But maybe, as I have argued, the problem is that people and the believers in people are too presumptuous about people's political capacities. I also argue that the Confucian regime I am defending in this book is somewhat paternalistic, but being paternalistic is not necessarily a bad thing. Kim also asks how we can have "both ancient Confucian aristocracy and modern representative democracy . . . without developing an internal contradiction" (2017, 10), and why a Confucian meritocratic thinker would still wish to preserve democracy (to some extent) (ibid., 12). As I have shown in this book, there can be a reconciliation, although the Confucian reading and defense of one person, one vote is not based on popular sovereignty. Reconciliation becomes contradictory only if we understand one person, one vote as an expression of popular sovereignty and self-governance. Kim also argues that Chan's uses of various concepts are different from how they are used by those who first introduced them, including the service conception by Joseph Raz (ibid., 3–4), the definition of democracy by David Beetham (ibid., 8–9), and the idea of a fallback mechanism (ibid., 5–8), which I will also use in chapter 9 of this book. He may well be right in all this, but it is not a serious challenge if what we are trying to do here is not to stay faithful to those who first introduced these ideas. I thank Reviewer #2 for asking me to compare my understanding with Chan's service conception and to address Kim's challenges.

3

A Confucian Hybrid Regime as an Answer to Democratic Problems

Four Problems with Democracy

In this chapter, I first illustrate four problems with democracy, especially the institution of one person, one vote. Then I discuss democratic solutions for these problems and show why they are inadequate. Finally, I argue that a Confucian hybrid regime that is based on the ideas discussed in chapter 2 can address these problems more adequately.

As mentioned in chapter 1, in spite of the common belief in the end of history (Fukuyama 1992), democratic countries have continued to encounter many problems. Facing these challenges, the more informed tend to appeal to the famous retort allegedly made by Winston Churchill: "Democracy is the worst form of government, except for all those other forms that have been tried from time to time."[1] Clever as it seems, merely using this claim to defend democracy may be a sign of our intellectual laziness, because empirical and theoretical supports for this claim are wanting. Empirically, in controlling corruption, making sound long-term economic policies, decreasing ethnic violence, and choosing leaders that are competent and who represent the true will of the people, democratic states, especially in the developing world, don't always or don't clearly do better than nondemocracies.[2]

1. House of Commons speech, 1947, WikiQuote, http://en.wikiquote.org/wiki/Winston _Churchill.

2. For some examples, see Kaplan (1997) and Zakaria (2003). Many academic studies have also been conducted on the relations between democracy and growth, democracy and corruption, and democracy and ethnic violence (I thank the late political scientist Shi Tianjian [史天健] for bringing my attention to some of these). For example, the political scientist Jonathan Krieckhaus has shown that democracy had a negative effect on economic growth in the 1960s and should have had a negative effect in Latin America (although it had a positive effect on growth in the 1980s and should have had a positive effect in Africa) (2004 and 2006). Daniel

Theoretically, the first issue we need to address is: What is democracy, or what makes a state democratic? A dominant belief among Western politicians and Chinese prodemocracy intellectuals is that what is essential to democracy is the institution of "one person, one vote." Some may also believe that market economy—"one dollar, one vote"—is what represents this institution on the economic level.[3] This is why, for many people, the establishment of one person, one vote and market economy is considered essential for a state to be democratic.

One can argue that one person, one vote is merely one possible embodiment of some more general democratic elements, such as representation and accountability. Moreover, the kind of democracy that has been developed in the West and has become a model for the rest of the world is really a "package" and should be properly called "*liberal* democracy," which is different from merely "counting heads." The liberal part of liberal democracy includes the rule of law, the protection of basic rights and liberties that are supported by social and political institutions, and perhaps some other elements.[4] In the package of liberal democracy, I believe that the liberal or constitutional part is the relatively nonproblematic element, while what is often popularly considered essential to democracy, the institution of one person, one vote, is precisely the source of many problems with contemporary democracies.

Four Problems with One Person, One Vote

To be specific, there are four theoretical problems with the institution of one person, one vote.[5] First, the contemporary mainstream ideology behind one

---

Treisman (2000) shows that the perceived corruption is influenced by many factors, and whether a country is democratic or not is only one of them. Moreover, with regard to the effect of democracy on perceived corruption, a country has to have been democratic for *decades* in order for democracy to have had a significant but *relatively small* effect on perceived corruption. Steven I. Wilkinson (2005) offers a complicated picture of the relations between democracy and ethnic violence in India, while Daniel Bell (2006) shows that, oftentimes, democratization leads to an increase of ethnic violence. A more comprehensive account and explanation of the connection between democracy and ethnic cleansing is offered by Michael Mann (2005).

3. In fact, the economist Milton Friedman even argues that economic freedom, achievable only in a market economy, "is simply a requisite for political freedom. By enabling people to cooperate with one another without coercion or central direction, it reduces the area over which political power is exercised" (Friedman and Friedman 1980, 2–3).

4. For the other elements, see, for example, some of Rawls's corrections of democracy that will be discussed in the next section.

5. More sophisticated democratic theorists (e.g., Pettit 2013 and Macedo 2013) may acknowledge the following problems, but argue that there are "meritocratic" checks and balances of the

person, one vote, especially in the United States, is the belief in the power of the people, and, by implication, the suspicion of the power of the elite and even the power of the government.[6] The belief in the power of the people and the suspicion of the elite and the government lead to, for example, some peculiar American phenomena. These phenomena include, first, a critical factor of "electability" of a candidate, that is, whether he or she is likable, is one of "us," and is someone who can come to visit us in our living rooms. In the 2004 presidential campaign, a "masterpiece" by the Bush team was to successfully label his opponent John Kerry as a member of the East Coast elite. Those who supported Bush believed in this propaganda, while those who were against him were convinced that Bush was a redneck, like so many of his supporters. However, the truth is that the Bush family also came from the East Coast, and his family is actually far more established than Kerry's. Bush and Kerry both went to Yale and attended the same secret (read as "elitist") club. Moreover, what many Americans don't know is that Bush had higher GPAs than Kerry in college.[7] The cover-up of Bush's background and the attack on Kerry may have been the result of a political culture that is anti-intellectual and antielitist. Second, American politicians often claim to be outsiders of the government in order to get elected into the government, and that their role in the government is to get rid of it. When a ruling branch of a government consists of "simple folks" who despise government (i.e., themselves),[8] it is hard to imagine that this branch will turn out to be respected, even by the people who put them there. This is probably why

> the US Congress—in principle, the most representative of political institutions—scores at the bottom of most surveys asking Americans which institutions they most respect whereas the Supreme Court, the armed forces, and the Federal Reserve system (all appointed rather than elected bodies) score highest. (Zakaria 2003, 248)

Daniel Bell quotes this passage and uses it to support his Confucian model, which is partly based on the rule of the wise and virtuous, and demands respect for government (2006, 289n34).

---

problems with one person, one vote in real-world democracies. I will discuss these remedies in chapter 4.

6. American democracy, at its founding, contained far more "elitist" or meritocratic elements than it does today. See Macedo (2013).

7. There are a few reports on this. See, for example, Benedetto (2005).

8. I put "simple folks" in quotation marks because the members of Congress are not really simple folks.

One may object to the above criticism by arguing that this is about real-world, nonideal forms of democracy and is perhaps peculiar to the American regime. But the underlying ideology is quite common, if not universal, among democracies, although how strong or unchecked by other ideologies differs from one country to another. The European democracies may not be as anti-establishment as the American one, although the recent rise of right-wing political powers in Western Europe seems to cast doubt on this "European exceptionalism."

Second, in a globalized and increasingly complex world, a state's policies often have significant effects on the nonvoters, including future (and past) generations and foreigners, and should take their interests into consideration. But the institution of one person, one vote lacks effective mechanisms to do so. For example, democracy may have difficulties in dealing with issues of budget deficit (i.e., spending future generations' and foreigners' money for the present voters), environmental issues (i.e., spending future generations' and foreigners' resources for the present voters), proper treatment of resident aliens (e.g., legal domestic helpers and illegal immigrants),[9] and foreign aid or other issues involving the interests of foreigners. One telling example in the United States (and likely in other developed democratic countries as well) is that those interest groups that are concerned with the interests of American workers, such as unions and Democrats that are supported by these unions, often favor protectionist policies that hurt the interests of poor workers in other countries.[10]

Third, even among the current living adults of a state, the interests of the vocal and powerful tend to trump the interests of the silent (or silenced) and the powerless, and this silencing effect can be triggered, reinforced, or legitimatized through the institution of one person, one vote. This is one reason for

9. Bell argues that there is an interesting phenomenon in Singapore and Hong Kong that shows democracy is bad for foreign domestic helpers, whereas "bureaucratic" elites can do more for their interests (2006, 281–322).

10. One example is the World Trade Organization (WTO) lawsuits and bans on products made in China by the American government, under various excuses (the most ironic of which is that Chinese factories fail to treat their workers properly). A recent case is the Obama administration's filing a WTO lawsuit that is clearly intended to cater to American voters in the "industrial battleground" in the 2012 presidential campaign (Landler 2012). A curious twist now is that right-wing politicians such as Donald Trump and Marine Le Pen have stolen the typical radical left-wing rhetoric against globalization and added a nationalist flavor to it. Because the nationalist rhetoric of anti-immigration is not easily available to the left-wing politicians, this contributes to the rise of this new breed of right-wing politicians and the crisis of pro–domestic workers left-wing parties.

the ethnic problems in democracies, especially the newly democratized ones, because the latter haven't yet fully developed the functional rule of law and the protection of liberties.

Fourth, even with regard to their own interests, it is questionable whether voters alone can be the best judges of what those interests are and how to satisfy them. As many political observers—from both a more popular and anecdotal perspective and a more scholarly perspective—have pointed out, the appalling political ignorance of the (American) general public is a well-established fact over "the six decades of modern public opinion research" (Ackerman and Fishkin 2004, 34).[11]

Climate Change: A Perfect Storm

A combination of these problems is at the root of some other political failures in and challenges to democratic regimes. One example is foreign policy. Foreign policy often needs expertise, patient and often painful dialogues, and long-term planning. But in a popular democracy such as the American one, as Henry Kissinger argues, foreign policy is often driven by the public mood, and this mood is in turn swayed by what is on TV, but not determined by what is important in international affairs. Another influence on foreign policies is domestic politics that has nothing to do with diplomacy. Oftentimes, a congressperson or an official who is in favor of a foreign policy has to promise to support a domestic item to get the support of another congressperson or official. These factors are obviously in conflict with the needs of good diplomatic policies (Kissinger 2001, 77).

An even "better" challenge to the institution of one person, one vote is the issue of climate change. Let me first make a distinction. Climate change is an environmental issue. But for the developing countries, the concern with environmental issues is more focused on pollution, whereas climate change (greenhouse gases and global warming) is more of a central issue for those in the developed world. In developing countries, the neglect of the pollution problem is often a result of governmental corruption, the influence of big businesses, and the tradeoff between development and pollution. People in these countries are not necessarily rational, even if pollution is clearly bad. Nonetheless, pollution is still a "clear and present danger" that is often localized (both

---

11. For a more detailed account, see Ackerman and Fishkin (2005). A more recent scholarly account on this issue is Caplan (2008). There are also numerous popular accounts of the lack of basic political knowledge among Americans. See, for example, Kristof (2008). I don't think that there is much controversy over voters' ignorance, but it can be debated whether this ignorance matters in political decision making. For a very good summary of the debates over this issue, see Elstein (2015, 186–89).

in terms of those who pollute and those who suffer from the pollution). For example, citizens of Beijing and Delhi can clearly see and breathe in the smog almost every day, and the source of the pollution is often nearby. Although it has its limits, a democratic regime can respond, more or less adequately, to a localized "clear and present" danger better than to other kinds of danger.

In contrast, climate change and global warming is almost a "perfect storm" to the institution of one person, one vote. First, climate change doesn't pose a clear and present danger or an immediate threat to most human beings. Its effects tend to be long-term, which means that its effects are barely visible in the short term. But as I argued earlier in this section, voters are not even necessarily rational about their short-term material interests, let along long-term ones. In particular, people from poor countries have more immediate problems to solve, such as food, health care, and visible pollutions, and they would ignore the issue of climate change as a rich man's problem. With their immediate needs satisfied, people from rich countries may pay more attention to long-term issues, but they, too, have a lot of short-term issues to deal with (such as unemployment and wage stagnation, which have become an ever more serious issue in the developed world),[12] are not very motivated by long-term issues due to their lack of immediacy ("in the long term, we will all be dead"), and may have different long-term issues to be concerned with (which is partly due to the uncertainty of the long term). To make matters worse, the impact of climate change can be so long-term that those who have to suffer from it can be those who are not old enough to vote, or even those who haven't yet been born. Indeed, those who are not yet born may never be born due to the present voters' choice of inaction with regard to climate change.[13]

Second, the contributors to climate change are the many, and those who suffer from it tend to be the few. If they live in the same democratic country, the interest of the many (to sustain their way of life without paying any immediate price) can easily override the interest of the few (to ask the many to make some slight sacrifice so that the few can avoid far greater suffering). If the suffering few are concentrated in one country, for example, Bangladesh, a lowland country that doesn't have good infrastructure to protect itself from the rising sea level, they have no political influence over the many from other countries under the democratic framework because they don't even have any

12. To be clear, the idea that environmental concerns would decline during economic downturns is quite intuitive and often mentioned, but it has been challenged by some research. See, for example, Mildenberger and Leiserowitz (2017).

13. On a more abstract level, as Derek Parfit shows in the so-called nonidentity problem, a policy of depleting resources, for example, may be bad for no one (1987, 351–456; in particular, 361–64). I thank Frances Kamm for bringing my attention to the relevance of this problem on the issue of climate change.

votes in those countries. The few may eventually have to "adapt," or resign themselves to this misfortune.[14]

Of course, we can try to "nudge" voters to become sensitive to the long-term threat and the threat that is not directly targeted at them. But if the voters are at best responding to issues related to their immediate material interests, the clear and present danger, any effective "nudging" has to be "inflammatory," disproportionately blowing up the danger posed by climate change. This nudging then becomes a work of demagoguery and thus violates some basic principles of liberal democracy. When its inflaming rhetoric is exposed, it can contribute to the denial of climate change. It can also be directly used by the climate change deniers for their cause, turning the battle into one between two groups of demagogues. Therefore, as long as the evaluation of the capacities of voters in this section stands, any nudging within a liberal democratic framework is self-defeating at best and destructive at worst.

Nonmeritocratic Solutions and Their Fundamental Limit

Many liberal and democratic thinkers also understand the aforementioned problems with democracy, and have offered various answers to these problems. On the first problem, the problem of the belief in the power of the people and the suspicion of the elite, an obvious answer is a call for a proper respect for reason, people with reason, and the government. The respect for those with reason doesn't necessarily mean the negation of equality. People can still be equal in many ways, because equality is a rather broad concept. One way to develop respect for the government is through civic education that emphasizes the idea that government is a necessary good and not a necessary evil, or even an unnecessary evil. Popular elections should be understood as selecting the most competent and worthy, and not as the punishment of the bad.[15] In contrast, the understanding that elections are to punish the bad may have contributed to the destructive culture of smear campaigns, which are aimed not at showing "I am a good candidate" but at showing that "the other candidate is bad." These revisions can be endorsed by some liberal and democratic thinkers without contradicting their fundamental tenets (I will come back to the compatibility between the Confucian reading of elections and democracy in chapter 9).

A cause of the first three of the four problems of democracy, suspicion of and even hostility toward the elite, neglect of the interests of nonvoters, and neglect of the interests of the minority and powerless voters (but not the fourth problem, the irrationality of voters), is an immoral and radical version of indi-

14. For a telling example, see Norgaard (2011).
15. See Chan (2013) for more discussion of this issue.

vidualism that is believed by some to be the sacred ideology of democracy. According to this individualism, we are and should be free and equal individuals who care for nothing but our self-interests ("self" understood as an atom- or monad-like individual). We become citizens under a government by conceding part of our freedom to this government because we would be better off than we would be in the natural state of affairs, where our interests are in constant jeopardy from other selfish individuals (hence, the government is considered a necessary evil) or because we are deceived to think so (hence, the government is considered an unnecessary evil). As long as we don't violate the regulations by the government, which are considered necessary in this tradeoff, we should assert our self-interests as much as we like. As mentioned, "self" here is understood as an atom- or monad-like individual, and thus self-interests are narrowly defined. The interests of the ancestors or descendants of current voters and foreigners are not part of these self-interests. To say that self-interests are narrowly defined doesn't mean that they only include immediate material interests. They can also include articles of faith that are sacred to the individual. As a result, for example, there are so-called issue-voters in American democracy. They vote based on their predetermined articles of faith (on abortion, gun rights, etc.), which doesn't allow them to be open to fair discussion with others. Democracy then degenerates into a form of war of might, the outcome of which depends upon which side is mightier in terms of the number of votes, and democratic stability is but a modus vivendi.

Perhaps seeing this selfish and radical version of individualism as a cause of the first three of the four problems of democracy, John Rawls, for example, challenges the view that one person, one vote is nothing but counting heads, and argues that, for voting to be justifiable, the voting entity has to consider the common good or the interests of other entities, rather than merely its own narrowly defined private interests.[16] We can see this attempt of Rawls from his concept of "reasonable," as well as the related concepts of public reason and reciprocity, which are crucial to his understanding of liberal democracy in his later philosophy. On the concept of "reasonable," Rawls writes,

> Citizens are reasonable when, viewing one another as free and equal in a system of social cooperation over generations, they are prepared to offer one another fair terms of social cooperation ... and they agree to act on those terms, even at the cost of their own interests in particular situations, provided that others also accept those terms. (1996, xliv)[17]

16. A few other liberal thinkers also argue that certain virtues are necessary to a desirable form of democracy. See, for example, Brennan (2012) and Macedo (1991).

17. An almost identical passage can be found in Rawls (1999a, 136), and a similar passage can be found in Rawls (1996, 49). See also Rawls (1999a, 86–88 and 177–78).

On the contrary, if one votes purely on the basis of one's "comprehensive doctrine" (e.g., religious dogmas) and accepts the failure of pushing through his or her agenda by the majority of votes only as a convenient truce waiting to be broken by any means possible, for Rawls, the stability so achieved is a modus vivendi and is not stability for the right reasons (1996, xxxix–xliii and 146–50; and 1999a, 149–50 and 168–69). In short, according to Rawls, liberal democracy requires that each voter vote not merely on private interests, including both material and doctrinal, but on a conception of common good. Thus, Rawls's requirement of voters to be reasonable is a moral one, although it is "thin" enough not to violate tolerance of plural values in a liberal society.

But how to achieve this? How to make people moral as required by Rawls and by the need to address the first three of the four problems of democracy? To achieve this "civil friendship," Rawls appeals to education and habituation ("moral learning"), which are conducted through social and political institutions arranged by liberal democracy (1999a, 137; 15 and 44–45), through families (ibid., 157), and through international and domestic political and cultural environments (ibid., 27n23, 102–3, and 112–13). He also pins his hope on the role of statesmen (ibid., 97–103 and 112).

The question, then, is whether these corrections will be effective and adequate. If the majority of voters are able to be reasonable in a Rawlsian sense, they may be able to pay attention to the interests of nonvoters and powerless voters. But if reasonable voters do not constitute a majority, the first three of the four problems of democracy will remain. Unfortunately, it seems that we cannot realistically expect the reasonable people to form a majority. In fact, Rawls himself offers an argument for this impossibility under the institution of one person, one vote, which he attributes to the Hegelians, but never answers this challenge. He writes,

> whereas, so the [Hegelian] view goes, in a liberal society, where each citizen has one vote, citizens' interests tend to shrink and center on their private economic concerns to the detriment of the bonds of community, in a consultation hierarchy, when their group is so represented, the voting members of the various groups take into account the broader interests of political life. (1999a, 73)

One solution is to ask the unreasonable to yield authority to the reasonable and informed. But it doesn't seem to cross Rawls's mind, because he says little about nurturing respect for the reasonable and/or the government.

Of course, whether a majority of reasonable people can be formed is open to theoretical and empirical studies. But there is yet another—I consider most fatal—problem with democracy, which is the aforementioned fourth problem: voters' inability to understand their own interests. Indeed, if the majority of people cannot even be self-interested in a rational manner—being self-interested (rational) is often considered a basic fact of being human, or at least it is more natural to human beings than being concerned with others (reasonable)—it seems unlikely that the majority of people can be reasonable. Again, liberal and democratic thinkers such as Rawls acknowledge the irrationality of voters in the real world, but he contributes it to some defects of real-world democracies and considers these defects correctable within the framework of liberal democracy. He thinks that in a real—rather than formal—liberal democracy, citizens have to be informed. To achieve this, it is crucial that their basic needs be satisfied and they enjoy education, as well as the means necessary to be informed. For example, Rawls points out, "Hegel, Marxist, and socialist writers have been quite correct in making the objection" that "liberties taken alone" are "purely formal. . . . By themselves they are an impoverished form of liberalism, indeed not liberalism at all but libertarianism (VII:3).[18] The latter does not combine liberty and equality in the way liberalism does; it lacks the criterion of reciprocity and allows excessive social economic inequalities as judged by that criterion" (Rawls 1996, lviii; also see 1999a, 49–50).

To ensure a plural liberal democracy that is stable for the right reasons, Rawls proposes the following institutions: "a. Public financing of elections and ways of assuring the availability of public information on matters of policy"; "b. A certain fair equality of opportunity, especially in education and training"; "c. A decent distribution of income and wealth meeting the third condition of liberalism: all citizens must be assured the all-purpose means necessary for them to take intelligent and effective advantage of their basic freedoms"; "d. Society as employer of last resort" so that citizens can have a sense of long-term security and the opportunity of meaningful work and occupation, which are crucial to their self-respect and their sense of being a member of society; "e. Basic health care assured all citizens" (1996, lviii–lix). According to Rawls, failing to establish these institutions will lead to the sorry state of (American?) political reality. He writes,

> When politicians are beholden to their constituents for essential campaign funds, and a very unequal distribution of income and wealth obtains in the background culture, with the great wealth being in the control of corporate economic power, is it any wonder that congressional legislation is, in effect, written by lobbyists, and Congress becomes a bargaining chamber in which laws are bought and sold? (Rawls 1999a, 24n19)

It should become clear that, for Rawls, the desirable form of liberal democracy is a kind of deliberative democracy. In *The Law of Peoples*, he explicitly expresses this idea: "Here I am concerned only with a well-ordered

18. Based on this distinction, many so-called liberals in China are not really liberals, in Rawls's sense, but libertarians.

constitutional democracy . . . understood also as a deliberative democracy" (1999a, 138). Deliberative democracy

> recognizes that without widespread education in the basic aspects of constitutional democratic government for all citizens, and without a public informed about pressing problems, crucial political and social decisions simply cannot be made. Even should farsighted political leaders wish to make sound changes and reforms, they cannot convince a misinformed and cynical public to accept and follow them. (ibid., 139–40)

In addition to the above arrangements, obviously, freedom of speech and information, and other liberties are also necessary for people to get informed. As Rawls points out, measures such as public financing of elections need to be taken to ensure that public information on matters of policy is not distorted by the influence of money and the availability of public information in general, in addition to the formal protection of relevant liberties. Moreover, the public has to be given an opportunity to digest the information that is available. Otherwise, the availability of information will again become merely formal. For example, political scientists Bruce Ackerman and James Fishkin propose that there should be a new national holiday, Deliberation Day, when "registered voters would be called together in neighborhood meeting places . . . to discuss the central issues raised by the campaign. Each deliberator would be paid $150 for the day's work of citizenship" (2004, 34). Clearly, the days when voters cast their votes should also be national or state holidays.

However, I argue in the following that these measures—already drastic and radical against the political reality of today's democracies—are still not adequate. These liberal thinkers have a vision of liberal democracy that is at least in one aspect fundamentally republican. That is, in their ideal form of democracy, citizens need to be well informed and actively participatory, and have a form of civil friendship (Rawls 1999a, 137), although the degree of participation in their democracy may not be as extensive as it was in ancient republics such as Rome in the republican period and ancient Athens.

In spite of the differences of degree of participation between Athens and contemporary democracies, a look into Athenian democracy can help us to see why today's (weaker) republican form of democracy is doomed to fail.[19]

---

19. It should be noted, for example, that the ideal state discussed in Plato's *Republic* is very small (423b–c), and, in Plato's *Laws*, the number of landholders and defenders is said to be 5,040, a dubiously exact number (737e ff.). Even in such a tiny state (perhaps smaller than Athens), Plato seems to be suspicious of the desirability of democracy. So we can imagine his suspicion would only grow with regard to the desirability of democracy in today's societies, the size of which makes the adequate education of even those who have the potential of becoming

First, the success of Athenian democracy was built on slavery. That is, the use of slave labor contributed to the freedom from daily work that the Athenian citizens enjoyed—either directly or through rich patrons and the support of the city—and this freedom made it possible for them to fully participate in political matters. But even by using slaves, the adequacy of the political competence of Athenian citizens was still challenged by classical writers such as Plato and Aristophanes. So how likely is it that the common people in a modern democracy, who need to work hard to maintain their desired living standard—this is a basic fact of capitalism and perhaps all modern societies that rid themselves of the guilty leisure of slavery[20]—can participate in politics to the extent of acquiring the political competence necessary for a desirable form of liberal and deliberative democracy? It is true that, through mass education, the modern society produces much more educated, white-collar professionals. But as argued in chapter 2, what education gives them is a special "art" or craft, and they are so consumed by their daily work as to know little about public affairs or anything outside of their narrow specializations.

To make the problem worse, we need to understand that also crucial to the level of political participation in ancient Athens was the fact that Athens was small in size and in population compared to most of the contemporary democratic countries. According to many political thinkers, on the issue of what kind of regime a state can adopt, "size matters." Montesquieu offered one of the most powerful arguments for this view. According to him, it is necessary that a democracy be small. No medium-sized or large country can really be a democracy. The reasons he offered are the following:

> In a large republic [which includes both democracy and aristocracy], there are large fortunes, and consequently little moderation in spirits: the depositories are too large to put in the hands of a citizen; interests become particularized; at first a man feels he can be happy, great, glorious without his homeland; and soon, that he can be great only on the ruins of his homeland.

---

political leaders far more difficult, perhaps impossible. For argument's sake, let us put his suspicion aside and assume that Athenian democracy was largely successful, and see if its success can be translated into that of today's democracies.

20. In today's world, some oil-rich countries that sustain the leisurely and luxurious life of a class of oligarchs by exploiting migrant workers or by simply subjugating a majority of people (often of different ethnicities or faiths from the ruling class) are exceptions. Indeed, they are still premodern in spite of the fact that they exist in modern times because, as indicated in chapter 1, an essential feature of modernity is deep-rooted and comprehensive political and economic mobility. However we would like to categorize these states, it is obvious that the oligarchs in these countries are not republican citizens in the ancient Greek and Roman sense.

In a large republic, the common good is sacrificed to a thousand considerations; it is subordinated to exceptions; it depends upon accidents. In a
small one, the public good is better felt, better known, lies nearer to each
citizen; abuses are less extensive there and consequently less protected.
(1989, 124)[21]

In short, for Montesquieu, a large republic leads to large fortunes. This cor-
rupts the virtue necessary for a democracy. In particular, a person's interest
becomes detached from, or even in opposition to, the common good. Moreover, the common good becomes too sophisticated for the citizens of this state
to grasp.

One can argue that, for Montesquieu, a large state can be democratic in the
form of a federal republic (1989, 131–32). But what Montesquieu discussed is
something similar to the federation of ancient Greek states, a federation still
far smaller than most of today's democracies. Also different from Montesquieu's understanding, the central government of today's democracies is directly elected and has far greater power than what Montesquieu would allow.

One can also argue that the kind of democracy Montesquieu discussed is
not the same as the liberal democracy Rawls and others understand. This argument may be true, but this and the previous arguments do not affect the
force of Montesquieu's challenge. We can put it in today's language, challenging the likelihood for citizens to be informed in a large state that does not
allow the use of slave labor to free its citizens from their daily works. First, the
overwhelming material wealth in a large state may tempt people away from
the civil duties of being reasonable and informed citizens. This requirement
of citizens to be reasonable and informed is much more limited than what
Montesquieu considers the necessary virtue in a democracy (1989, 22–26),
but it is still very demanding. Second, corporations, especially in the age of
globalization, develop interests separate from and even in conflict with the
interests of their own states, be it democratic or otherwise—outsourcing is an
obvious example. Third, the common good in a large state is so complex that
it is beyond most people's willingness or ability to comprehend, and the majority is doomed to be uninformed. Related to this point, in a small state,
people are likely to be acquainted with political figures, whereas, in a large
state, the majority of the people cannot judge the quality of a politician
through long-term and close contact with him or her, as in the case of how
people observed Shun through his twenty-eight years of service (*Mencius*

21. Jean-Jacques Rousseau agreed with Montesquieu on this issue, and offered similar arguments. See his dedication "To the Republic of Geneva" in his *Discourse on the Origin and Foundations of Inequality among Men* (1964, 78–90) and chapters 3 and 4, book 3 of his *On the Social
Contract* (1978, 83–85).

5A5), but can only make a judgment of a politician by being influenced by all kinds of propaganda, which makes their opinion of the politician easily manipulatable. Indeed, generally speaking, it has become a common understanding of evolutionary and cognitive studies that our inborn cognitive capacities were formed through hundreds of thousands of years of evolutionary process where we lived in small bands, and they often fail us in the ever larger, complicated, and well-connected societies that have only "recently" emerged— "recently" on an evolutionary scale, especially when the majority of us fail to develop these capacities too much beyond the inborn level through education and other efforts, or don't have leisure and other conditions to apply the thinly developed cognitive capacities to complicated matters.

In an article by journalist Robert Kaplan (1997), he offers many examples of failed democracies in the modern and contemporary periods. His analysis of the reason for these failures is similar to Montesquieu's argument, although he presents this kind of argument in the context of modern and contemporary democracies. The solution Kaplan offers is a hybrid regime that combines democratic elements with paternalistic elements, which, as we will see, is similar to the hybrid regime that a Mencian would support.

In a recent article by political scientist Russell Hardin (2002), he discusses "three devastating theoretical claims" in postwar public choice theory made by Kenneth Arrow, Anthony Downs, and Mancur Olson that are "against the coherence of any democratic theory that is conceived as even minimally participatory, collectively consistent, and well-informed" (ibid., 212). Hardin develops these claims "by relating them and, in particular, by subjecting them to an economic theory of knowledge" (ibid., 213). Two crucial arguments he makes in this paper are: first, each person's vote doesn't really matter; and second, to be informed is rather demanding, perhaps much more so than we usually think. If we put these two arguments together, the implication is that if they are rational, voters will have, or should have, very little interest in voting, let alone in being informed. The first argument is partly a result of the fact that today's democracies—even on the scale of the state of New Hampshire, which has about a quarter of a million voters—are too large for one single vote to matter. This is because even if there is a one-vote difference after we count all the votes in a large state, "merely for practical reasons of the impossibility of counting votes accurately," we still cannot say for certain which side wins, and other means have to be used for us to make this judgment (ibid., 220).[22] To understand this point, we only need to be reminded of the fact that during

22. This impossibility may be a mathematical impossibility: the statistical error of counting a large number of votes is too significant for a one-vote difference to be considered meaningful in terms of determining the outcome. I thank Qian Jiang for pointing this out to me.

the Florida recount in the 2000 American presidential election, the controversy over the voting result had to be resolved by the Supreme Court, and the
tactical mistake of the Gore team to concede the race too early was also an
important factor that contributed to Gore losing. That is, in the case of the
difference by a few hundred votes against a voting populace on the level of a
million or more, a few hundred votes cease to matter. The second argument
also has something to do with the size of today's democracies, as their large-
ness makes the price of getting informed unbearably high. Thus, we can consider Hardin's thesis as being one more contemporary development of Montesquieu's. If all these thinkers and considerations are correct, then it is simply
impossible for the majority of voters to even come close to meeting the preconditions of meaningful democratic participation.

On a more sympathetic note, all the previous problems aside, some citizens
may prefer other obligations and interests—such as family obligations or scientific or artistic pursuits—to a time-consuming involvement in politics.
These citizens may choose to remain politically indifferent. This choice of remaining politically indifferent becomes increasingly sensible in a large state of
working people. Unlike the ancient republican form of democracy, a contemporary liberal democracy should let these voluntarily nonparticipating citizens
be. In fact, as Bell puts it, the Confucians or the "[East] Asian communitarians"
(2006, 335) justify the political indifference of the ordinary citizens by endorsing their devotion "to family and other 'local' obligations" with their political
participation kept at a minimum and "with political decision making left to an
educated, public-spirited elite" (ibid., 151). In fact, even an exemplary person
who is engaged in politics has to be released from his public service to observe
the three-year mourning period upon the death of his parents (*Analects* 17.21).[23]
This sympathetic attitude could also be approved by a stargazing Platonist who
wants to be left alone to study matters that he or she considers more interesting, if the state is entrusted to a competent elite (cf. 347d).[24] However, there
should also be a mechanism that prevents the indifferent or nonparticipating
citizens from having too much influence on political matters.

23. Of course, for a Confucian, to focus on family doesn't necessarily mean being politically
indifferent, or merely a negative liberty, that is, the liberty to be left out of the political and the
public. Family obligations are still political and thus related to the public. Of course, they are
not political in a purely active sense, although they can be turned active. See chapter 6 in this
book for more discussions.

24. By "Platonist," I mean someone who believes in the existence of a realm of the Good,
Beauty, and Truth. The pursuit of these eternal objects is the only thing worth doing, and the
world of appearances and the human body are only a hindrance to this pursuit. Given the complexity and subtlety of Plato's writings, I cannot assert that Plato is a Platonist.

In *Political Liberalism*, Rawls points out five facts of a democratic society, which lead to his consideration of the central problem: how a plural yet stable liberal democracy is possible (1996, xxvii, 36–38 and 58; also see 1989, 474–78). We can then add a sixth fact of modern democracy. To be clear, the "sixth fact" is a group of three related facts. Of this group of facts, the first one is that human beings have a tendency to fall back on their self-interest, which is encouraged by one person, one vote. The second "subfact" of the sixth fact is that some citizens choose to remain politically indifferent to many political matters. The third subfact is that modern democratic states are in general so large that it makes it impossible for the majority of the citizenry to be adequately informed about state affairs, however hard both the government and the individuals try. The causes of this impossibility are: due to the size of modern states and the noble rejection of slavery, to be informed is a burden that most citizens' intelligence, education, and willingness cannot bear; the population of modern states renders a single vote practically meaningless; and big corporations run free and wild, and their material wealth and power destroy the motive of the elite to devote themselves to the common good and distort information. The sixth fact seems to suggest that the Rawlsian liberal and deliberative democracy, or liberal and deliberative democracy in general (that is, not merely counting heads), in which every citizen participates in an equal manner and in the form of one person, one vote, is impossible in the modern world, where each state is simply too large and almost everyone has to work for a living.

The Confucian Hybrid Regime

The above problems with democracy and the "internal" solutions are, however, not meant to suggest the viability of authoritarianism. Surely an authoritarian government that can ignore the will of the people could do the right thing, for example, for the environment and the long-term interests of the citizens, and it may be very effective because it doesn't encounter as much resistance from the people as in a democracy. But if the government does what is damaging to the environment, it is also harder to stop it from doing so.

But do we have to choose between democracy and authoritarianism? My answer is no. In the following, I present a Confucian/Mencian form of ideal government that is based on the discussion of Mencius's ideas in chapter 2 of this book. As we will see, this regime can address the four problems of democracy (the suspicion of the elite, the neglect of the interests of nonvoters, the neglect of the interests of the minority, and the irrationality of voters) better than the current democratic regimes with all their possible internal, nonmeritocratic revisions can. To be clear, this regime embodies certain fundamental

Confucian/Mencian features and is meant to be an ideal type. This regime does not presuppose the social dominance of a "Confucian" culture in a narrow sense—a culture Chinese or East Asians have allegedly adopted—but it is meant to be universal, applicable to any state that satisfies the sixth fact listed in the previous section. This regime is also not meant to be an endorsement of any of the so-called China models of economic development and governance, if these models actually exist. Real regimes in China's past and present may have certain features of this regime, but the latter is never fully actualized in the real world. In the following, I offer a framework of this regime.

Some Moderate Revisions

First, the rule of law and human rights are endorsed and firmly established in this Confucian hybrid regime.[25] Second, as we can infer from the discussion of Mencius's ideas in chapter 2, in this regime, the government is considered responsible for the material and moral well-being of the people. It is responsible for making it possible that average citizens have their basic material, social, moral, political, and educational needs met. On the issue of material needs, economic inequality is contained, following Rawls's own difference principle (1971, 60–62 and 78–83). On the issue of education, in addition to theoretical and technical knowledge, the government is also responsible for offering citizens civic education. The goal of civic education is to make citizens understand the following: each citizen should have compassion for others and maintain proper relationships with them; the role of the government is to maintain the material and moral well-being of the people (moral well-being includes citizens' care for one another, their proper family relations, etc.); the politicians in the government should be those who are morally and intellectually superior (morally superior in the sense that they are willing to extend their care to all the people who are within their power to help); if the politicians are indeed morally and intellectually superior, they should be respected by the common people; and the right to participate in a certain political matter is inseparable from one's willingness to consider the common good and one's competence at making sound decisions on this matter. To satisfy the political needs of each citizen includes satisfying his or her need to participate in politics. Then, after the citizen is offered the above civic education, if a citizen is interested in and has potential for participating in politics, the government should offer all means necessary—for example, the freedom of speech and information that makes it possible for people to be informed,

---

25. In chapter 9, I discuss how Confucianism is compatible with the rule of law and rights.

place and time (e.g., "deliberation days") necessary for political discussions and voting, and so on.

Some democratic thinkers may accept the necessity to respect the government and the statesmen and stateswomen, but this respect is built into Confucianism, making the Confucian hybrid regime more firmly equipped for dealing with the first problem with democracy (suspicion of the elite). A fact noticed by many is that in America, politicians often pretend to know less than they actually do (e.g., think of the aforementioned fact of the Bush team portraying Bush as an average Joe and Kerry as an East Coast elitist), while in East Asia, perhaps with its Confucian influence, politicians often pretend to know more than they actually do—the first thing almost every Chinese politician does when getting to some higher office is to get an MA and a PhD degree from a university that wishes to prostitute itself to said official. Of course, pretending to know is not what we want, but at least pretending in the right direction may help give birth to the desired reality. We can reveal his or her lie if a leader fakes his or her educational background, thus encouraging other leaders to become truly learned. The faker himself or herself, after faking for a long time, may be forced to—and even sincerely identify himself or herself with—the beliefs he or she pretends to have.[26] But if, in a culture, to have knowledge and experience is considered a hindrance in regards to political qualifications, no hope is left for improvement.

The treatments with other problems of democracy by democratic thinkers are also heartily endorsed and earnestly promoted in this regime. Indeed, Confucian education may be more adequate than a democratic one because, as mentioned, democratic hope lies in a form of civil friendship, which becomes impossible when the population is large, while the Confucian education emphasizes care that is targeted at strangers.

And Their Limitations

As I argued in the previous section, these arrangements, even with further revisions in the Confucian hybrid regime, are not adequate. This leads to the third arrangement of this regime that departs from the "internal," nonmeritocratic solutions that today's democratic thinkers could easily endorse. As we can infer from the earlier discussion of Mencius's ideas, firmly asserting that service to the people offers legitimacy to a government, but understanding the

---

26. After condemning the "five hegemons" (wu ba [五霸]) "borrowing" benevolence or humanity (ren [仁]), that is, pretending to be a humane overlord intending to maintain peace among the fighting feudal lords, Mencius said, "but if a man borrows a thing for a long time and doesn't return it, how can one be sure that it will not become [truly] his?" (Mencius, 7A30).

fundamental limitations of the aforementioned arrangements to improve people's morals and informedness, a Mencian would be in favor of a hybrid regime that introduces and strengthens the role of the competent and morally superior people, the "meritocrats," in addition to the institution of one person, one vote. As we will see below, since the meritocrats are not beholden to popular votes as are popularly elected legislators, it is more likely that they will consider nonvoters' and minorities' interests, and voters' long-term and real interests, when there are conflicts between voters' and nonvoters' interests, majority and minority interests, and voters' short-term or apparent and long-term or real interests, and it is also more likely that they will maintain stable, long-term policies than the legislators who are directly subjected to the popular vote.

As a principle, a Mencian would think that the right of political participation in decision-making processes should be based on intellectual, moral, and political competence, and the sixth fact of a modern democratic society is that many citizens are not capable of making sound judgments on many political matters. Through civic education, hopefully these citizens would willingly stay away from the decision-making process on these political matters, if they could not quickly improve their competence on these matters. But we shouldn't pin our hope solely on their discretion, for education, being a "soft power," needs to be enforced by institutions and regulations, and it is more important in this case, because the goal of the above education is to educate the masses so that they will know that they are not "educated" enough to understand politics, which seems to be a self-contradictory and self-defeating endeavor, revealing the difficulty of this task. Therefore, we should have more institutional arrangements in place that help prevent incompetent citizens from having too much of a voice in political matters. Based on this consideration, the following arrangements are made in the Confucian hybrid regime.

"Democracy" on the Strictly Communal Level

We should see that a main reason for people not being informed is that modern states are often way too large for people to grasp. But on "strictly" communal and local matters, almost any local resident has better knowledge than officials in the distant central government.[27] Since the matters dealt with here are the daily affairs most relevant to residents, it is likely that they are willing to pay attention to them rather than staying indifferent. It is also likely that the private interests of local residents can be checked by local governments. Therefore, the preconditions for the sixth fact of a modern democratic society

27. See the discussion in the next paragraph on the meaning of " 'strictly' local."

(that makes citizens unable to make sound judgments on political issues) don't exist in a small community. This means that all residents should be allowed to participate in local affairs, elect local officials through one person, one vote, vote directly on important matters, and so on.

A difficult problem here is deciding which matters should be considered "strictly local." In a well-connected world, no local matters are strictly local. Thus, strictly local matters are merely those that have relatively little outside influence. With regard to local matters that have a relatively strong influence on the outside world, then, the votes from this community can only be one factor in the decision process, and arrangements (such as those that will be discussed later) need to be made to prevent local voters from doing things in a "NIMBY" (not in my backyard) or shortsighted way. Meanwhile, if certain national policies are closely affecting local affairs, and the populace can make sound judgments on them, people should be allowed to participate, and these matters can be decided by a referendum. A general problem entails knowing how large a community has to be in order for its complexity not to be beyond the comprehension of its people, and the answer to this problem is what will determine the size of the "local community." These questions need to be answered empirically and cannot be answered by armchair philosophers. But a philosopher can offer a general principle: how much democratic participation depends upon how likely the participants are able to make sound decisions that are based on public interests.[28]

Hybrid on Higher Levels

When we are dealing with matters beyond those of a small community, the preconditions for the sixth fact of modern democracy are met, meaning that

28. The treatment of local affairs in this regime is different from the village elections in today's China in that, first, village (local) elections should be free from interventions of higher officials; second, on this level, popularly elected government should be the only executive branch; third, basic liberties and rights should be effectively protected by law; fourth, there are popularly elected elements in governments and legislatures of higher levels, meaning that elections should not be restricted on the village or town levels; and fifth, certain national issues should be open to a referendum. None of these is satisfactorily done in today's China. Another challenge to local elections in China is that village elections in some parts of China have led to the monopoly and abuse of powers by powerful village clans or strongmen (I thank Zhang Qingxiong [张庆熊] for pointing this out to me). I suspect that the rule of law, protection of rights and liberties, and more democratic elements on every level of the government might eventually correct these abuses. But this is something that needs to be treated by political scientists and political philosophers.

it is likely that citizens are indifferent to many of these matters, and they lack the capacity for making sound judgments. We should then introduce arrangements to limit the influence of an uninformed and unreasonable popular will on policies. There are many ways to achieve this restriction. One way is by utilizing plural voting. For example, with regard to voting for higher levels of the legislature, each voter would have to take a class and participate in discussions, or take a test specially designed for this level, before he or she would be allowed to vote. Different weights may be given to their votes based on their performances in class or in the test, or based on their educational levels, social and political roles, and other relevant factors.

Another perhaps more practical and manageable arrangement is this: In present democracies, the legislature is often divided into two houses. In some democracies, for example, in the case of the US Congress, members of both houses are popularly elected. With regard to how they are elected, they only differ in terms of the districting and the length of their terms. In some others, members of one house are popularly elected, and members of the other are not. But the latter is marginalized politically. A good example of this is the upper house in the United Kingdom. In the Confucian hybrid regime, the legislature can be a bicameral structure. Members of the lower house are popularly elected. But the explicit aim of having such a house is not to give decision-making power to the people, as it is usually understood in present democracies, but to let the popular will be expressed, which, as we have seen in chapter 2 (under "The Confucian Middle Way"), is crucial to a Mencian ideal regime. Whether people are satisfied with the present administration, and whether they are better off or worse off than they were under the previous administration, have to be voiced by themselves. Members of the lower house are the mouthpieces of the people.

In addition to this branch of the legislature, whose role is already understood differently from the legislature in present democracies, in the Confucian hybrid regime, the other branch of the legislature is introduced. Let's call the former branch the lower house or the house of the people, and the latter the upper house or the meritocratic house, which consists of people with intellectual and moral merits.[29]

I can imagine three ways that are not mutually exclusive and can be complementary to one another when selecting members of the upper house. The

29. Obviously, in today's democracies, especially in today's American context, these names themselves would likely doom the latter branch to failure, because "people" is often taken as a good word by the people, while "meritocrats," from the original coinage of this term (Young 1958), has often been a word of ridicule. I use it because it expresses the intention of this branch, and I will leave it to the politically savvy to come up with a better name for it.

first one can be called a leveled model. Legislators of the lowest level, the "strictly local" level, are directly elected by the people of the corresponding local districts. These legislators should be free from specialized jobs (to the extent possible) and are exposed to policy making on a higher level. Thus, they are likely to be capable of understanding higher-level affairs that are beyond the grasp of the common people. They are then eligible for selecting or being selected for the upper house of the legislature one level higher. That is, legislators of both house(s) (on the lowest level, there is only one house, and on every higher level, there are two houses) are either candidates or electors (voters) for members of the upper house one level higher. This process is to be repeated until we get to the upper house of the legislature of the highest level. The job of all legislators should be full-time, maybe with the exception of legislators of the lowest level, who can work part-time as legislators and can maintain their close and daily interactions with their constituencies through their previous jobs.

In fact, traces of this leveled way of selection can be found in American political history. For example, at the earlier stage of the republic, American senators, and even the president, were not directly elected by the people but were voted in by state legislators or electors of the electoral colleges. It was intentionally designed this way by the American founding fathers, especially the Federalists, precisely for countering the uninformed and immoral popular will ("popular whim" might be a better term), identical to the aim of my design of the leveled way of selection.[30]

The second way of selecting members of the upper house (of various levels) is exam-based. For example, Bell offers the following model: Central to this model is "a bicameral legislature, with a democratically elected lower house and a 'Confucian' upper house composed of representatives selected on the basis of competitive examinations [later called the *Xianshiyuan*]" (2006, 267). When there is a conflict between these two houses,

> [t]he "Confucian" solution might be to strengthen the *Xianshiyuan*, for example, by means of a constitutional formula providing supermajorities in the upper house with the right to override majorities in the lower house. The Head of Government and important ministers could be chosen from the *Xianshiyuan*. Most significant legislation would emanate from the *Xianshiyuan*, with the lower house serving primarily as a check on its power. (ibid., 271)

One can question the practicality of Bell's model by making the following points. In traditional China, the *ke ju* (科舉) exams were used to select

30. See Macedo (2013) for a more detailed discussion.

officials,[31] and there was already a constant and constantly increasing pressure on this system caused by the increasing number of exam-takers fighting over a limited number of official positions. This happened when state-funded mass education was extremely limited.[32] Now there is far more extensive state-funded mass education, in China and elsewhere, meaning that there are far more qualified and aspiring students who might wish to take the exams, greatly outpacing the increase of the number of offices or legislative positions available. A look at how fiercely competitive the present Chinese civil service exams are in recent years can give us a vivid picture. The phenomenon of too many people trying to squeeze themselves into the few opportunities available can be a root cause of many social problems. But we can argue that the problem with traditional and today's China is that there is not an adequate number of channels that can divert the talent.[33] Moreover, as Elman suggests, the "losers" in these exams can become learned practitioners of other arts needed in a society (2013), which is not a bad "unintended consequence" (knowing this possible consequence, we should actually intend it to happen). That is, these exams can unintentionally or intentionally improve the "political intelligence" of the citizenry.

Nevertheless, when there are far more people taking exams than the number of positions available, the results can be extremely arbitrary. Not only are they deeply unfair, but the perceived unfairness can breed resentment and lead to the loss of respect for this institution. An alternative exam-based selection process can make the passing of exams an eligibility qualification for voting for the upper house or being a candidate of the upper house.[34] In the

31. This term is sometimes translated as the Chinese civil service exam system, but this translation is a bit misleading because those selected are often not merely civil servants but members of the ruling structure. Daniel Bell translates it as "public service examinations," which is better than "civil service examinations" (2015, 78).

32. See Elman (2013) for a more detailed description of the pressure and the reality of education in later traditional China.

33. See Qian (2005a, 156–57). Yuri Pines also argues that the Qin state's success in defeating other states and unifying China was partly due to maintaining multiple avenues of social and political advancement, and maintaining such an environment can make the system "fairer, more dynamic, and more adaptable," preventing ossification (2013, 191). Daniel Bell refers to this and argues that "[d]iversity of avenues of entrance would preserve the flexibility that is particularly important in today's fast-changing world" (2015, 133).

34. Considering the fact of specializations in the contemporary world, there can also be different tracks in the exams, the economics track, the political science track, the natural sciences track, and so on, which, although still requiring a general, liberal arts–style education, emphasize a particular expertise.

second scenario, the qualified candidate can then be selected on the basis of popular votes or votes by members of houses of one level lower.

Another possibility is for those who pass the exams to be sent to some sort of academy, where they could be exposed to further education and be involved in observing statecraft and writing policy proposals. They could also be appointed to local offices, thus obtaining some real-world political experience, which may prevent them from being merely book-smart. Then, a further selection could take place, either through exams or through voting. As I show later in this section, this way of selecting meritocrats has historical precedence in traditional China. More importantly, the request of practical training may be crucial to the exam-takers. Discussing the Confucian tradition of selecting Confucian advisors to rulers, Kenneth Winston makes an important distinction between the scholar-officials (士大夫) and mere scholar-teachers (2011). The latter, like the applied ethicists today, haven't held any decision-making positions. This lack of practical experience "can open a space for radical critique of existing policies, but also for ideological intransigence and useless abstraction" (ibid., 240). Put in Confucian terms, as I argue in chapter 6, to grasp Confucian moral principles, one needs to test them in the real world, which is full of conflicts of duties. The practice is a constituent part of grasping the principles. In the three ways of selecting meritocrats, the exam-based way is the only one that lacks a practical dimension, making it possible that those who excel at exams are merely book-smart. Thus, this fact makes it even more important for the exam-based way to include a practical-training element in it.

Clearly, administering exams in this exam-based way of selection is an important issue. One common objection to it is that exams don't seem to be good at testing one's morals. This objection is true but only partially so, for exams can direct exam-takers to study works in moral philosophy, thus improving their moral sophistication if not their morals. Exams can also direct people to study moral exemplars of the past, and this can have a positive effect on people's moral cultivation, especially if the studies of moral exemplars have been conducted since early childhood. To master materials for the exams demands not only intelligence but also some virtues, such as persistence and delayed gratification. This means that exams do test certain virtues, and these virtues are essential for good politicians, although the virtues tested are not as comprehensive as we wish. Moreover, although it should be acknowledged that exams in a narrow sense are targeted primarily for one's competence, the aforementioned institutions of political academy and real-world experiences can be a way to observe and to test candidates' moral and political character.

Another objection is that this kind of exam is based on a conception of the Good, and this conception is incompatible with pluralism, or a liberal defense of plural values. This is indeed a problem in countries such as Iran, where a theocratic element exists or even dominates in politics, and discriminates against people of different faiths or other comprehensive doctrines. Thus, exams in the Confucian hybrid regime have to be designed to test what lies in the "overlapping consensus," or some "good" qualities that reasonable citizens all believe a political decision maker should have, such as general or specific knowledge (e.g., economics), compassion or care for the people, ability to resist bribery, and so on. Having some of these desirable qualities, members of the upper house can differ on the specifics. For example, two people with expertise in economics can adopt theories of different schools of economics and can (and should) freely debate with each other.

Moreover, to guarantee fairness of exams, the rule of law and other institutions are clearly necessary. In spite of these arrangements, some may still doubt the possibility of fair examinations. They should be reminded of the fact that in traditional Chinese ke ju (科舉) examinations, China's current national college entrance exams, as well as exams such as the SATs or the difficult and comprehensive foreign service exams in the United States, although there are problems with them, as with any and every procedure in human society, there is a relatively fair and uncontroversial process of determining the content and the scores of the exams.[35]

Generally speaking, for those who doubt the practicality of the exam-based way of selection, the fact that ke ju and some earlier forms of exam-based selections were relatively successfully used to select members of the ruling class for a rather long period of time in traditional China may answer their doubt.[36] Indeed, these practices and their successes and failures are also rich resources for us to design exam-based selection models.[37] For example, as we have already seen, the ke ju system has some resonance with certain models in the

35. Philip J. Ivanhoe once suggested to me that the foreign service exams can be a possible form of the selection or qualification exams for the upper house. I thank him for this suggestion.

36. I am not saying that the regimes in traditional China were mixing meritocratic with democratic elements. I am not even saying that they were purely meritocratic. As Elman points out, the meritocratic elites in later imperial China never broke free of a system where emperors had the highest and ultimate authority. But he also maintains that a modern political system can be more compatible with meritocracy, with which I fully agree. Indeed, if we replace the office of the emperor with popular will, the games of dominance, checks and balances, and cooperation between emperors and Confucian elites in traditional China can be easily translated into lessons for our explorations of an ideal hybrid regime.

37. The late Chinese historian and philosopher Qian Mu (錢穆) offers many detailed, subtle, and insightful analyses of political arrangements in traditional China. See, for example, Qian (1996 and 2005a).

exam-based way of selection. In this way of selection, I have also suggested a more complicated model in which people are sent to an academy or local offices. The former resonates with the *han lin yuan* (翰林院) in later imperial China and the imperial college (*tai xue* [太学]) in early imperial China. As for practical training in local offices, which serves as a further testing ground in the complicated model, we can find historical resonance in the earlier imperial form of selection during the two Han dynasties (206 BCE to 220 CE): "recommending the filial and the uncorrupt" (*ju xiao lian* [举孝廉]). In this form of selection, promising students were first selected to the imperial college, then those who did well in studies and exams were sent to local governments. Those who did good works in their governmental jobs were eventually recommended for higher offices. Indeed, the intention of my proposal is to combine examinations with practical training, which can be understood as an attempt to combine the Song-style ke ju with the Han-style *ju xiao lian*.

Moreover, in the exam-based models, there are levels. We can find traces of this design in the traditional ke ju system as well. In this system, exam-takers could pass exams on various levels and thus have a chance to obtain titles of various levels, and there were official academies on different levels and formal and informal channels for those who passed the exams to hold offices or take up some practical duties. In short, in spite of our philosophical approach, the various experiments of selecting those with merits in traditional China show that our designs here are not purely armchair, idle, and overly idealized inventions.

The third way of selecting members of the upper houses of various levels is a quota system. There are local officials (county, municipality, state, etc.), industry leaders, scientists, retired military officers, organizers of local NGOs (nongovernmental organizations, such as environmental groups, groups for minority affairs, and unions), and so on, whose competence, experience, and morality have been tested in their services. These services may have been better proxies for "moral exams" than any exams on paper, which can be another answer to the question about how we can test people's morals. Let me offer three examples. First, in the United States, those who volunteer to serve in the military, have done so over a reasonably long period of time, have obtained college or even postgraduate degrees while in service, and have moved up the ladder of the ranks tend to have a good sense of service to the country, and are decent and of above-average intelligence, qualities important to a good politician. Second, scientists are trained to be objective and fact- and truth-oriented, a quality also significant to public service.[38] Third, it is likely that a governor

38. I thank Jane Mansbridge for making these points about the military people and the scientists to me in a conference on meritocracy.

of a state or a province who has served two terms, maintained an approval rating of 40 percent or higher, and has not been caught in any grave violation of his or her office (such as corruption) is someone with moral and intellectual capacities who could serve the public. We could designate a certain number of seats in the upper house for these people, and they could then be selected through elections by legislators one level lower, or by people of their organization or group in the corresponding district of the legislature; or they could be directly given a seat in the upper house (e.g., in the aforementioned case of a two-term governor).

The Chinese People's Political Consultative Conference in today's mainland China and the Functional Groups in the present legislature in Hong Kong have, on paper, tried to select members through a quota system similar to what I am proposing here. But to my knowledge, the institution in mainland China falls far short of the role of the upper house proposed in this chapter. For example, the members of this house are often not full-time legislators (in fact, they are not given the power of a legislator, and the right and power that is given to them on paper is never actualized); the rule of law and other liberties listed in this section (e.g., freedom of press) are not established; and so on.

To be clear, these three ways of selecting members of the upper houses of various levels are not mutually exclusive and can be combined. Indeed, the quota way of selection is likely to be merely a supplement to two other ways of selection. We can also propose that the candidates through the quota system, and the legislators who are one level lower be put together, and be open to elections either by the people or by themselves. In American Democratic National Conventions, superdelegates, including elected officials and party activists and officials, who can vote freely on their own, and delegates who need to vote on the basis of popular votes choose the presidential nominee together. This can be considered a real-life example of the aforementioned mixture. There can also be other arrangements that are intended to ensure members of the upper houses of various levels are not beholden to short-term considerations. For example, it can be required that they serve one (long) term only (a six-year or eight-year fixed term).

The next issue to consider is the functions of the upper house. In the case of a referendum, they can be entrusted with formulating propositions for people to vote on, as political activists Nicolas Berggruen and Nathan Gardels suggest (2013). The upper house and the lower house can be entrusted with the usual legislative matters, as well as with matters such as the selection and confirmation of Supreme Court justices, the prime minister, officeholders of various levels, and so on. The weights of the votes of the two houses should be specified, and the upper house should be given more weight with regard to issues that are concerned with nonvoters and long-term consideration, since, as I have argued, these issues are what the voting public tends not to be able to handle adequately, which is why this kind of upper house is introduced in this chapter.[39]

Differences from Representative Democracy

A clarification needs to be made. All these ways of selection, especially the leveled model, should be distinguished from a certain form or understanding of representative democracy. According to this understanding of representative democracy, legislators are to represent the people's will. In the Confucian hybrid regime, members of the lower houses are to represent the people's will. This is necessary to a Mencian because "Heaven sees with the eyes of its people; Heaven hears with the ears of its people" (*Mencius* 5A5), that is, whether people are satisfied with the state's policies has to be determined by the people, or, if the state is too large for people to voice their satisfaction directly, by their representatives. But this may be different from the "true" will of the people, the will the people should have, or, in Rousseau's terms, the "general will." In my design, those who enter the upper houses are capable of participating in policy making on a higher level, and by checks and balances between the lower and upper houses, hopefully political decisions would better represent the general will of the people. In spite of how we understand their roles in theory, however, in practice, if they are subjected to frequent elections by the people, members of the upper house may not be free from special interests, especially the immediate and narrow interests of their constituencies. This is what often happens in the US Congress, an obvious example being the various infamous earmarks or pork barrel projects in which congressmen or congresswomen allocate federal money to pet projects in their own districts. Oftentimes, these projects use federal money in the districts from which their legislators are best at bargaining with and manipulating other legislators through material interests and threats and not in districts that desperately need it. Therefore, in my proposal, the various ways of selecting members of the upper houses and other arrangements is to free politicians from the control of special interests.

Whatever the details of the designs of the upper house may be, it is clear that these arrangements of different branches of the legislature can be checks and balances to the popular will, and give more power to the relatively knowledgeable, experienced, and caring. It is a government of the people and for the people, but not purely by the people; rather, it is only partly by the people and partly by the competent people.

39. I thank Daniel Bell for making this suggestion to me.

Centralization versus Autonomy

On the communal level, democracy through direct and popular voting is still fully preserved in the Confucian hybrid regime. Many efforts by liberal and communitarian thinkers that are intended to improve on communal life can be happily accepted by this regime. Indeed, both in theory and in practice, many Confucian thinkers have also supported similar kinds of efforts. The mixing of meritocracy happens in governments on levels beyond the communal. For these governments, an important issue is how centralized they should be. Confucians have their preferences on this issue, although they are not closely related to the Confucian ideas discussed in chapter 2 and this chapter. But it does have something to do with the design of an ideal Confucian regime, so let me briefly comment on this here. Early Confucians were known to have a conservative side, and part of this conservatism is expressed through their apparent fondness or nostalgia of (their interpretations or even imaginations of) feudalism. As I argued in chapter 1, a key to feudalism is local autonomy. Mencius seems to support this idea.[40] But a key development after the collapse of feudalism, and an essential feature of postfeudal ("modern") states is centralized bureaucracy. As I suggested in chapter 1, if we adopt a "progressive" reading of Confucianism, one possibility is for us to accept centralized bureaucracy while simultaneously preserving some features of "feudalism," such as autonomy. A much later Confucian thinker, Gu Yanwu (顾炎武) (1613–82), discussing the tension between a centralized bureaucracy (the so-called *jun xian* [郡县] system) and feudalism, argued that there was no return to feudalism because it was a flawed system, although the centralized government that emerged after the Zhou-Qin transition had its problems as well.[41] The solution, according to him, lies in "making the feudal spirit reside in the *jun xian* system" (Gu 1983, 12). From his elaborations in the "First Treatise of the *Jun Xian* System" (ibid.), it should become clear that one implication of this synthesis is to combine the centralized bureaucracy with the autonomy of lower-level governments, so that the latter can enjoy more freedom to experiment with ways of taking care of their people. The same argument, after being adapted to today's realities, can still be used to defend some form of autonomy of lower-level governments.[42] This autonomy is good because it would allow different local governments to take into account the par-

40. For example, Mencius offered what he allegedly heard about the old feudal order and implicitly criticized the feudal lords in his time for deviating from it because it didn't serve their self-interests (5B2).

41. For a fuller discussion, see Gu's "Nine Treatises on the *Jun Xian* System" (郡县论九篇) (1983, 12–17).

42. Gu had his own designs about how to incorporate feudal spirit into a centralized bureau-

ticularities of their districts, and to experiment with different policies. The successful policies could then be emulated by other lower-level governments and be promoted by the higher-level governments. Such a system has adaptability and resilience.

A difficult issue concerns the size of the autonomous unit and what should remain autonomous. The Confucian defense of local autonomy can be used to support local communities that are small enough to have popular elections as the only way to select legislators and magistrates on the communal level. But it can also be used to defend autonomy on higher-level local governments because their autonomy can help the adjustment of policies to different contexts and the experimentation of different political models. For policy experimentations to be successful, oftentimes the size of the unit cannot be too small. For example, experimenting with technological advancements has to be supported by a suitable size of economy and population. The unit of autonomy in this regard has to be on municipal and even state (in the case of the United States) and provincial levels. Moreover, autonomy in the forms of localism and federalism is often used to justify unfair practices.[43] For example, some of the American Southern states used federalism or state autonomy to defend first slavery and then their segregation policies. In the United States, much of the funding for public schools comes from the local taxes of the school districts, which explains the inequality among different school districts. Clearly, issues such as these should not be left to local governments alone, whatever levels they are. There should be some centralized institutional and legal constraints (e.g., in the case of abolishing slavery and forbidding racial segregations) or centralized distribution of funding (e.g., in the case of funding for local public schools), while autonomy is allowed in other aspects to encourage policies tailored for particular local conditions, and innovations for other local governments to follow. It is hard to imagine that any moderate person would embrace centralization or localization only and reject a mixture of the two. The really difficult issue is to specify what should be left to local governments of various levels and what should be left to the centralized administrations. But it is beyond the scope of this book to examine this important issue.

To sum up, a more comprehensive arrangement of the Confucian ideal regime should be democracy on the communal level, some form of autonomy

---

cracy, and what I follow here includes some of his general considerations but not his particular designs.

43. The following discussion benefited from some spirited exchanges between Yuval Levin and Mathias Risse, when the former gave a speech, "The Pursuit of Solidarity in the Age of Trump," at Harvard on February 23, 2017.

in the communal and higher-level governments within a centralized system, and a hybrid regime on all levels of government but the communal one.[44]

44. Bell proposes a model that consists of democracy on the bottom, meritocracy on the top, and experiments (through some form of autonomy) in the middle (2015, 180–95). My discussion in this paragraph is partly inspired by his proposal. But there are some significant differences. In his model, the top-level government is purely meritocratic, although lower-level governments other than the bottom one can be hybrids. His proposal is based on what he observes as the model the contemporary Chinese regime has adopted, or an idealized version of it. Mine has nothing to do with the present China model and is rooted in some earlier Confucian considerations. He thinks that the kind of autonomy offered by American federalism wouldn't work as well as the middle-level experimentations in his China model, but I think that the former is a possible embodiment of the Confucian idea of "feudal" autonomy.

4

The Superiority of the Confucian Hybrid Regime Defended

Internal Challenges to the Superiority of the Confucian Hybrid Regime

In this chapter, I consider a few challenges to the desirability and superiority of the Confucian hybrid regime, especially the meritocratic elements in this regime that are apparently a significant departure from the present liberal democratic regimes (while the features of democracy on the communal level and some kind of autonomy in higher-level governments are not). Some people may object to this regime because it apparently violates what they take as principles of liberal democracy: the principle that the legitimacy of a government comes from popular votes and the principle of equality. This kind of objection is an "external" one because it considers some fundamental ideas of the Confucian hybrid regime problematic (which I answer in the next section). In this section, I look at some "internal" objections to this regime, such as it will lead to consequences that it considers bad within its own framework, it is not as good as it claims to be, or we don't have to go that far to achieve what is desired by the framer of the Confucian hybrid regime. By answering all these challenges, I hope to elaborate on the designs of this regime and the reasoning behind it, and to further show the superiority and the desirability of it.

Perpetuate the Powers That Be?

The first objection is that various uses of exams in the Confucian hybrid regime may become an excuse for the powers that be to exclude a certain group of people from politics (e.g., the exclusion of African Americans in American history), which will breed resentment in the disenfranchised and make them question the legitimacy of the state, and thus threaten the state's stability.[1] In comparison, an important function of democracy is precisely to give people a sense that the legitimacy of the state and the government lies in the approval by all, so that people will sincerely support the state and the government.[2] My answer to this objection is the following: as has already been shown, it is crucial to the Confucian hybrid regime that people be instilled, through civic education, with a sense of respect for moral and intellectual excellence and acceptance of the rule of the wise and virtuous so as to abdicate willingly their right to participate when they consider themselves incompetent. Chinese peasantry in the past and many Western voters before the age of populism and cynicism had respect for authority, and they didn't find it unacceptable that the experienced and knowledgeable had more authority. This fact shows the power of education and culture. In the Confucian hybrid regime, the meritocratic selections are open to everyone, and the rule of law has to be established to protect their fairness. More importantly, the government bears the responsibility of offering the necessary means for people to live a materially and morally flourishing life, to have a broad-spectrum education, and to have the resources to participate in politics. Thus, the fairness of exams is not merely formal and is clearly different from the disenfranchisement of African Americans or other poor and "lowly" people in history and can diminish the feeling of resentment.

A related objection is that the rule of the wise will make the people who are excluded from politics more and more incompetent, thus artificially perpetuating the distinction between the ruler and the ruled. This is also an argument for popular participation in democracy, and against (benign) paternalism. To understand this objection, let us take a look at John Stuart Mill's account of this problem. He warns of the danger of paternalism in his criticism of the idea that "if a good despot could be ensured, despotic monarchy would be the best form of government" (1958, 36).[3] According to Mill, even if we could find such a despot, and this good despot could take care of everything for the people (which is nearly impossible), his paternalistic actions would chain up the free agency of his subjects and thus perpetuate their incompetence. This

1. I wish to thank Daniel Bell and Qian Jiang for pointing out this problem to me.

2. This challenge is different from the challenge that the Confucian hybrid regime violates a democratic tenet of legitimacy, which is discussed in the next section. Here the issue is not about the violation of a "sacred" principle but about the consequences of this violation, which, if true, a Confucian would also find objectionable.

3. Mill's choice of words is rather curious. The "despotic monarchy" he refers to is what we usually call "benevolent absolutism" or "enlightened absolutism," and the despot he talks about is what we usually call a benevolent or enlightened monarch. He uses "despotism" and its variants perhaps in order to lead, through rhetoric, his readers to feel repelled by this kind of regime.

is like the situation where children never grow up when the parents are over-competent and overindulgent, trying to take care of everything. In contrast, popular participation offers the best civic education of the people, leading their vision to go beyond themselves (ibid., 36–55).

From the discussion of the sixth fact of modern democracy (that many citizens are not capable of making sound judgments on political matters), however, we should see that Mill's expectation of the educational function of popular elections may have been overly optimistic. On the contrary, through popular elections, the voting public tends to retreat to their narrow and often misguided private interests.

On Mill's critical note, I should first point out that Rawls offers a similar argument in his earlier work *A Theory of Justice*. He first defends plural voting (i.e., "persons with greater intelligence and education should have extra votes"), an arrangement different from one person, one vote and, interestingly, an idea Rawls (correctly) traces back to Mill:

> The political liberties are indeed subordinate to the other freedoms that, so to say, define the intrinsic good of the passengers [in a metaphor, Rawls compares the state with a ship and people with the passengers]. Admitting these assumptions, plural voting may be perfectly just. (1971, 233)

Immediately after making this argument, he criticizes this arrangement, and his criticism is similar to Mill's criticism of paternalism. He states that the participation of all citizens "lays the foundations for civic friendship and shapes the ethos of political culture" and "enhance[s] the self-esteem and the sense of political competence of the average citizen" (ibid., 234).

In response, we can see that in the Confucian hybrid regime, popular participation, and thus the educational and civil function of such a participation that is emphasized by Mill and Rawls, is still preserved. As we have seen, the local community of this regime is, to a very large extent, autonomous, and people of the community make political decisions or make them through their representatives. On higher levels, there are still popularly elected branches of the legislature, and it is just that the checks by meritocrats are added to the legislating and decision-making processes. More importantly, although Mencius and other early Confucians didn't discuss the educational and civilizing role of mass participation, a Confucian can nevertheless happily acknowledge this role and embrace it. Moreover, Confucians may even see the practical and psychological benefit of making people feel politically involved through mass participation in the age of democracy.[4] As Bell points out, even in today's

4. Based on some fieldwork in Indonesia, Benjamin Olken arrives at the following conclusion: although direct participation doesn't lead to policies significantly different from those

China, "the symbolic ritual of free and fair competitive elections—even if the people's views have minimal impact on actual policies"—has to be recognized (2006, 273). All these considerations give us additional reasons for the Confucian hybrid regime to preserve popular elections, although, at the same time, different from Rawls, Confucians are also concerned with the possibility that through this civilizing process, people may grow overly confident and thus lose respect for the wise and the virtuous.

Moreover, in the Confucian hybrid regime, certain merits are introduced as the basis for voting rights in the case of certain political matters or for membership or candidacy in the upper house of the legislature, but, as it has been emphasized a few times, the fairness of meritocratic selection has to be guaranteed by law, it must be open to the public, and the government has responsibility for offering any means necessary for citizens to be educated and to participate in politics. Even if people fail to pass or choose not to take the exams, the door will always be open when they change their minds or improve their competence. That is, unlike the paternalistic regime that is described and criticized by Mill, the Confucian hierarchy is not fixed. On the contrary, it encourages and is inseparable from upward mobility. As a famous line of a Chinese poem (exaggeratingly) says, "one can be a farmhand in the morning, but come to the emperor's court in the evening" (朝为田舍郎, 暮登天子堂).[5] This mobility, as discussed earlier, may also dispel possible resentment of the disenfranchised against the powerful elite. When discussing the ke ju system, which can be considered a forerunner of the selection mechanism we discuss here, the historian and philosopher Qian Mu (钱穆) argues, it "can fundamentally eradicate the social classes . . . [and] can cultivate people's interest in politics and strengthen their patriotism" (1996, 405–6). We can see here that these arrangements by the Confucians have an intention similar to that of popular

---

adopted without mass participation, people in the former situation feel far more satisfied with these policies (2008). One might dismiss democratic participation as cynical manipulation. But we shouldn't ignore the significance of democratic participation, even if it lies chiefly in psychological satisfaction. After all, for a Confucian, the goal of a good state is to win the hearts and the minds of the people, and a Confucian would be among the first to embrace the idea that happiness does not merely come from the satisfaction of material needs. I wish to thank Qian Jiang for pointing this out to me.

5. Of course, the picture portrayed through this line is perhaps too rosy (and maybe mobility across all kinds of human societies is very slow [Clark 2014]). Benjamin Elman shows in a paper that a peasant would rarely, and likely never, have a chance to move up the ladder all the way to the ruling elite (2013). But the apparent mobility offered hope to the peasant and other people of the lowest strata of the traditional Chinese society, and they could—perhaps over the efforts of a few generations—first move up to the level of propertied men (landlords and wealthy merchants) and go from there to the elite ruling class.

participation in a democratic regime, which encourages a sense of civil friend-ship, as, for example, defended by Mill. Indeed, in the same book, Mill intro-duced plural voting and other mechanisms that are also intended to provide checks and balances for uninformed voters (1958, 127–46). That is, the Confu-cian hybrid regime may be different from how democracy is practiced today, but it is not necessarily different from what Mill—and to some extent even Rawls—envisioned or would endorse. With real fairness and upward mobil-ity, the meritocratic elements can also nurture a sense of civil "friendship." To be precise, the citizens are not always equal, and their relations can be similar to those between teachers and students. Still, they have a sense of identity and solidarity that is similar to what civil friendship would result in, but in addition to this, there is also a sense of respect between them.

Generally speaking, as argued in chapter 1, the hierarchy by pedigree, which is characteristic of feudalism, collapsed very early in China, and Confucian and other Chinese schools of political thought emerged during and after this collapse. When we use English terms to translate ideas and concepts of these schools, it can be very misleading, which may be why English-speaking read-ers resist these ideas. Although Confucians embrace a form of hierarchy, we should always keep in mind that this hierarchy is built on mobility. Similarly, paternalism is also inseparable from this mobility. For the lack of a better term, I have been using "ruling class," but we have to remember that for Confucians, this class is not a class by birth, and although it refers to social and political status, one has to "earn" this status by the service offered to the people.[6]

In fact, the merits of the mobility-based hierarchy are also defended in eco-nomics and business studies.[7] Economic inequality has been perceived to be bad, having a larger role in the well-being of the citizens than, for example, average income. But a more profound question is, what type of income in-equality has a very negative effect on people? According to the tournament theory, income inequality can encourage competitors to move up, contribut-ing to the overall economic output. This is really similar to my defense of Confucian hierarchy. In a study done by Li Xuhong (a professor of business management) and others (manuscript), it is argued that achievable (mobility-based) inequality (it is called "achieved inequality" in their paper) is good for the well-being of the employees, while the ascribed (fixed and not mobility-based) inequality is bad. For us, this study suggests that mobility-based hier-archy really encourages people to move up, and the hierarchy is not perceived

6. It is true that in traditional China, the office of emperorship stayed hereditary within a particular dynasty, but it was not an institution Mencius and some other early Confucians would endorse. It was accepted more widely by later Confucians, not as an ideal but as a realistic compromise.

7. The following account is based on Li et al. (manuscript).

to be bad and may have a positive effect on the well-being of the people. In short, perhaps it is wrongheaded for people to attack inequality or hierarchy in general. Instead, they should attack immobile hierarchy.

Meritocracy as a Correction of Democracy?

As we have seen, the reason we need the upper house is because many citizens are not capable of making sound judgments on political matters (the sixth fact of modern democracy). One can argue that historically, the popular election system was introduced in order to prevent a small group of noblemen from controlling the political decision-making process and using public resources for their own gain. Mass participation was a good check for avoiding this situation. But a grave problem of today's democracies is that what was meant to be a correction of aristocracy has gone to the other extreme, and it has given too much voice to the blind popular will.[8] Therefore, we need to reintroduce the good aspects of aristocracy, that is, "aristocracy" in its original sense—rule by the excellent (in terms of both knowledge and certain morals, especially the virtue of caring for others)—and use it to check the excesses of democracy. This hybrid regime is intended to achieve a more desirable middle ground between premodern aristocracy and modern democracy, rather than pinning our hope for good governance on the conscience of members from either side.

8. As mentioned, those who favor popular election (unchecked by the rule of the meritocrats) may offer different diagnoses and treatments of these problems. For example, Thomas Pogge argues that a reason for the American protectionist policies is that American democracy is not a genuine democracy based on one person, one vote but on one dollar, one vote (a diagnosis similar to Rawls's). The American government recompenses a small portion of influential voters, for example, the big farmers, while harming both the majority of the domestic voters and people in other countries. This is a response Pogge gave to a question I asked in a discussion at Tsinghua University, Beijing, May 2005. See also Bell (2006, 162n35). Generally, one can argue that what happened in Western early modernity was that inherited nobility didn't entitle someone with political access anymore; rather, the acquisition of wealth replaced noble status as a qualification for political participation. That is, the problem with today's democracies is still the failure to give political access to all, or the failure of comprehensive representation. But if my account holds, then the treatments by these democratic thinkers are doomed to fail. The problem with modern and contemporary democracy is not that it has been a wealth-based meritocracy that openly or secretly excludes the poor and the working class, as democratic thinkers argue, but that it has been the wrong kind of meritocracy. The solution, then, is to introduce the right kind of meritocracy, mixed with democratic elements. I thank Michael Puett for helping me formulate the differences between a democratic solution and my solution to the problems of today's democracies.

But if there are so many problems with the popular will and popular participation, why don't we go with meritocracy all the way? As I have argued, for Mencius, the legitimacy of a regime comes from service to the people, and the level of satisfaction with this service has to be determined by the people. Underlying this idea and the Confucian embrace of meritocracy is the basic assumption of the capacities of the masses. Confucians seem to assume that the masses are competent enough to know whether they are satisfied with the regime and its policies or not, but they are not competent enough to make political decisions that will maintain or lead to a satisfying political environment. This is the theoretical basis for the Confucian hybrid regime. Moreover, as was argued earlier, popular participation is also instrumental to the political education of the masses, and to a sense of identity and civil friendship.

Now, if we accept the idea that pure meritocracy is not desirable, but to use meritocracy to check democracy is, we can still argue that in nondemocratic countries such as China, perhaps we should promote popular elections as a more effective practical means to achieving the desirable middle ground of checked democracy. But as the path of democratization has shown us, oftentimes, we cannot stop at the desirable middle, and we will slide helplessly and hopelessly to the extreme that we originally used merely as a corrective. Even if we put aside this possibly controversial empirical observation, democratic promoters should at least be aware of what the ideal state is.

The underlying assumption of meritocracy as a correction of democracy is that meritocrats make better decisions than the masses, but this can be questioned.[9] For example, one may refer us to the Iranian model. Today's Iran tries to combine democratic election with rule by the (religious) elite, but the success of this hybrid is questionable, to say the least. An obvious answer to this challenge is that the core merits in the Confucian hybrid regime are care for the people and the ability to put this care into successful policies, but the choice of the elite in Iran is based on religious expertise, which may be politically irrelevant.

Intuitively, people with the right kind of merits should make better political decisions, but we have to acknowledge the complexity of the real world. Therefore, whether this intuitive assumption is true or not is open to empirical studies, and there can also be different kinds of tinkering that can influence the role of meritocrats in politics. For example, one concern is that rule by the elite often falls victim to the interest of the elite class. To prevent this from happening, we hope that the moral education of the elite may play some role. More importantly, some institutional arrangements should be made. Foremost, we must establish a respectable and stable rule of law that regulates the

9. For a good account of this objection, see Elstein (2015, 186–90).

elite branch and use the house of the people to check the former branch, so as not to let the elite establish laws at their own will to benefit themselves or their associates. Another mechanism to prevent the elite from serving their own interests is that each branch has to have a significant number of members, so that it is hard for the elite to form a unified interest group. Indeed, as many researchers suggest, to produce better decisions and results, a diversity of opinions is crucial, perhaps even more important than expertise.[10] In the upper house of the Confucian hybrid regime, then, the condition of assuring that the number of members is large is also an attempt to guarantee the diversity of expert opinions.

But one can still argue that assuring diversity by having a large number of members in the upper house in the Confucian hybrid regime is still not enough. An element of the sixth fact of modern democracy is that the populace in a large state can easily be misled by interest groups. But however large the number of meritocrats in the upper house, it is still small in comparison with the people of a state. To mislead and to bribe a small circle of elites is practically even easier than misleading millions of people.[11] This could be the case, and I can only give an imperfect answer. We need empirical evidence for this claim, and, until we have it, we can at least hope that the ruling elite who are wiser, more experienced, more virtuous, and with better conditions (time, assistance, etc.) are less susceptible to misinformation than the populace.

Besides, even if the branch of the experienced and learned does not directly improve the quality of policy making, its existence can be taken as performing the function of civic education, thus indirectly improving the quality of policy making. That is, the existence of this branch makes people aware of the idea that political participation is not an inborn right but is based on competence and has moral requirements. It is a right to be earned. Mill and Rawls are correct to say that political participation offers opportunity for civic education. But when participating, common people are also helped by looking up to exemplary people and institutions that offer role models for participating in politics. As Confucius says, "Governing by virtue is like the north polar star, which remains in its place while all the other stars revolve around it" (*Analects* 2.1). The role of civic education by the upper house in the Confucian hybrid regime enriches the educational role of mass participation discussed by Mill and Rawls.[12] In short, as long as we don't hold a radically pessimistic attitude that denies any positive role of reason and morals in decision making, we should see that the upper house can improve government.

10. See Phillips (2014) for a review of these studies.

11. I wish to thank Qian Jiang for pointing out this problem to me.

12. Again, Mill himself acknowledged the significance of a role model in popular participation (1958, 127–146).

Sortition and Deliberative Voting as a Solution?

Another possible challenge is that even if all the problems that were discussed in chapter 3 are true and cannot be solved adequately through internal "tinkering," as liberal thinkers like Rawls would advocate, do we have to resort to the Confucian hybrid regime to address them? There is a growing amount of literature on deliberative voting, deliberative polling, and sortition that is built on some deliberative procedures, and their introduction is also meant to address the fundamental problems of today's mainstream representative democracy and democratic elections. To address these new and innovative mechanisms adequately is beyond the scope of this book, so in the following, I will only offer a general response to some basic ideas introduced by these mechanisms.

Historically, selection by lot was prevalent in ancient Athens, republican Rome, and the republics in the land that would become today's Italy. Conceptually, Montesquieu believed that "Voting by *lot* is in the nature of democracy; voting by *choice* is in the nature of aristocracy" (1989, 13). In this understanding, today's "democracies" should be properly called "aristocracies," while the selection of rulers in a true democracy should be through voting by lot. But a common feature of all these states is that they are small, and it seems to be difficult to envision how a large state may still practice this.

But in recent years, there are a few experiments that revive this democratic tradition of voting by lot, and there are even more scholarly discussions of them. For example, in 2004, 160 citizens from British Columbia, Canada, were randomly selected to form a citizens' assembly to deliberate on electoral reforms. The assembly lasted eleventh months, and in the first stage, these citizens learned about electoral systems from the experts. Later, there were similar citizens' assemblies in the Netherlands (2006) and in Ontario, Canada (2006–7).[13] In the wake of the 2008 financial crisis that devastated Iceland, a constitutional reform was considered. In 2011, 950 randomly selected citizens set up an agenda, and a constitutional assembly was formed by twenty-five members elected from a pool of 522 people, excluding politicians. In their effort to come up with a proposal of constitutional reform, they engaged the general public online.[14] In Ireland, a constitutional convention of one hundred people took place in 2011, and sixty-six members were randomly selected, while thirty-three were politicians recommended by political parties, with one chairperson nominated by the government.[15]

13. There are many scholarly works on these assemblies. See, for example, Warren and Pearse (2008) and Fournier et al. (2011). A good summary can be found in Hayward (2014).

14. I rely on Landemore (2016) for the Iceland case.

15. Renwick and Pilet (2016, 208–9).

In the revivals of the democratic tradition of voting by lot, problems with applying it to contemporary societies and with mainstream representative democracy through one person, one vote are addressed. Sortition can be done in a large state, but those who are selected don't know state affairs well, partly due to the size of the state. Through educational and deliberative processes, however, this issue can be dealt with. Another challenge I raised in chapter 3 is the lack of leisure for average voters, but selected citizens are provided with leisure and pay to look into the relevant matters. Deliberation and leisure together make it possible for these citizens to get informed, the lack of which is another challenge I've made to today's democracies. Selection by lot may also address the problem of money in politics. When representatives are elected through one person, one vote, through gerrymandering, they can become de facto permanent members of the legislature and thus become easy targets for interest groups. Sortition makes legislatures far more mobile than in representative democracy, and less likely for interest groups to influence.

But if we look at many of the experiments, we should see that they have features of the Confucian hybrid regime. In the British Columbia case, selected citizens need to be educated on the relevant matters by experts. In the case of Ireland, the assembly is really a mixed one, with thirty-three politicians involved. The assemblies' proposals can be subjected, and perhaps need to be subjected, to the evaluation of the government. But even with these meritocratic elements, the matters that are deliberated by these assemblies are mostly of a narrow range, such as certain constitutional matters. In real-world politics, however, there are many complicated matters that need to be handled regularly. This requires a standing chamber of legislators and decision makers. An important feature of the British Columbia case is that these citizens mostly spend just weekends on these matters. We can argue that in order for them to be able to deal with more complicated matters, we should give them an even longer education period and ask them to become full-time legislators. But according to deliberative theorists,[16] the lack of rotation is one of the major problems in representative democracy, and these citizens are not examined through public services, as most politicians are. Full-time positions can also be extremely demanding on the citizens involved, and they may not want to become full-time legislators, especially given the fact that they will retire after presumably many years of political service, which would make it difficult for them to go back to their previous lives. The problems that plague jury selection would likely plague the selection of citizen-legislators too.

Lying beneath all the above challenges is the fact that such a deliberative body is still implicitly republican. But the fact that most of us do not live in

16. See, for example, Landemore (2016).

small republics anymore makes the republican form of government difficult to actualize. There are other features of these experiments that are also deeply related to the (small) size of the state. For example, an important innovation in the Iceland case is that the selected citizens have regular exchanges with other citizens online. But obviously, this is only possible in Iceland, a country of approximately 330,000 people, the size of a large town in the United States or a (rather) small one in China.

Therefore, my general response to the challenge from sortition and deliberative voting is that it is a very nice revision of today's democracies. But these solutions are still fundamentally republican, and given the size of most of the states today, and the fact that people in liberal societies are often interested in and consumed by matters other than politics, that is, the sixth fact of modern states, these solutions are of limited value. A standing chamber of meritocrats, as suggested in chapter 3, is still necessary for addressing the sixth fact of modern states adequately. But in addition to using various deliberative mechanisms as supplements, we can incorporate some of their designs into the Confucian hybrid regime. For example, in this regime, members of the lower chamber are to represent the people, or the popular will. They can be selected by lot, and minimum deliberation is needed in this chamber because we wish to hear the "raw" voice of the people through these representatives. Their job can also be part-time, because they are not necessarily involved in the deliberation processes. Indeed, we may even turn the lower chamber into a polling system, through which we poll common people randomly on various matters that are to be decided. The discussion here is rather rudimentary, and my main point here is that the lower chamber of the Confucian hybrid regime can be open to some innovative design, such as selection through lottery.

Why Bother? Real-World Democracies Are Already Meritocratic

The above objections to the Confucian hybrid regime are to show that it creates new problems, such as disenfranchisement; it fails to hit the targets it desires (better political decisions); or there are other, more democratic alternatives (sortition). Others may be more willing to acknowledge the need of a hybrid regime, but they could argue that, for example, the real-world American regime is already a hybrid regime. In spite of its claim of being a democracy, the reality in the American regime is its rule of law and bureaucratic system, as well as other meritocratic institutions (the Supreme Court, the Federal Reserve, the military, etc.) play an important role, and one person, one vote doesn't really have as much influence as it appears to. Moreover, one person, one vote only gives people a sense of imagined equality, which can be seen from the disproportionately high number of rich and highly educated people in the US Congress. Therefore, although there are no explicit arrangements like those in the Confucian hybrid regime, the American legislature is a de facto meritocratic regime, making arrangements introduced in this regime unnecessary.

But first, those with merits in the branches of the American legislature may not possess the relevant kinds of merits. Second, and more importantly, this meritocracy is a hidden one, and it needs to "come out of the closet" and become a proud part of the political regime and culture. As Confucius said, "when the names are not right, what is said will not sound reasonable; when what is said does not sound reasonable, things [tasks] will not be accomplished" (*Analects* 13.3). If meritocracy is not a proud member of the political regime and culture, politicians tend to hide their meritocratic identities and cater to the popular will instead of doing what is right for the populace, in order to survive in a disingenuous meritocratic environment. If they dare to remain exposed in an antimeritocratic culture, they and the openly meritocratic institutions would be under constant suspicion, even under attack by the populace, and could only yield to the popular will or accept the fate of being marginalized.

As Stephen Macedo shows, the American regime during the founding of the republic was a hybrid regime that contained many meritocratic arrangements (2013). These arrangements, such as the election of the president by electors (who could vote on their own discretion rather than along the popular vote of the state, as is the case today), the election of senators by state legislators (which is precisely what the leveled model proposed in chapter 3), and so on, were put in there specifically for preventing the uninformed populace from having too much influence and harming people's true interests. Macedo maintains that the government is of the people and for the people, but he is hesitant about whether it is by the people. In this sense, the American regime at its early stage, especially with regard to the aspects mentioned above, can be considered an (imperfect) example of the Confucian hybrid regime. Again, the Confucian hybrid regime is not merely applicable to those who are ethnically Chinese or culturally Confucian ("Confucian" in a thick or narrow sense), and, indeed, the fact that the American regime at its founding can be considered a Confucian hybrid regime supports the universality of the latter, and it also shows that the design of the Confucian hybrid regime is not purely an armchair invention. However, as we have seen earlier, many of these meritocratic elements in the American regime have been eroded and eliminated, and a reason for this may have been that the open ideology is not in favor of meritocracy but in favor of equality—equality understood as being the opposite of meritocratic hierarchy. Thus, although the founding fathers, the Federalists in particular, and contemporary scholars such as Macedo think that meritocracy and democracy are not mutually exclusive, the meritocratic elements, if closeted, will end up being locked up permanently and thus dead for good. To avoid repeating this history, we should make the meritocratic elements explicit.[17]

Of course, one can still question the stability of the hybrid regime. For example, one can argue that the demand for political participation is a historical trend that cannot be averted, whether it is good or bad or the meritocratic element is exposed or not. The masses, which by definition outnumber the elite, will constantly tip the balance between the two branches of the legislature and eventually eliminate the meritocratic branch. If this is truly the case, we can only hope that repeated crises will change this trend, and that civic education may strengthen the meritocratic elements that are introduced after severe and repeated crises.

The "elitist" design of the Confucian hybrid regime is to give more power to the politically motivated, compassionate, and competent people, and check the influence on politics by those who are politically indifferent, narrow-minded, and incompetent. Some may ask why we cannot leave it to "natural selection" within a regime. Those concerned with politics naturally wish to push for their ideas. From American political reality, however, this hope seems to be overly optimistic, because "natural selection" often results in the rise of the extreme, such as the so-called issue-voters. On the surface, they are the opposite of the politically indifferent, but in reality, they adopt the same kind of attitude of political indifference and have the same kind of political ignorance as the openly politically indifferent and ignorant. The former are concerned with, and have a dogmatic conviction about, one issue, refuse to discuss it with others, and are indifferent to or ignorant of other issues. They actually offer a supporting example to the sixth fact of a modern democratic society.

Further Clarifications

It should be acknowledged that although the arguments in chapters 2, 3, and 4 are meant to be normative, many observations of democracy and the examples used here are based on American political reality. Whether this reality is peculiarly American or is worldwide can be debated. In particular, we need

17. As I mentioned, the American regime at its founding is an imperfect example of the Confucian hybrid regime. Clearly, slavery, gender inequalities, and the lack of suffrage in general are some of the major problems with the American regime at its founding, and they should be eliminated in the Confucian hybrid regime. Ironically, the fact that there are few meritocratic elements left in the present American regime may have had something to do with the efforts of eliminating these unjust arrangements. In their elimination, unfortunately, what was good in the original design of American democracy has also been eliminated, and has gained a reputation of being too toxic to be taken seriously.

to refer to political scientists for their theoretical and empirical studies of whether Western European and Japanese democracies suffer from the problems caused by the sixth fact of democracy, and if they do not, we will then have to ask where the sixth "fact" fails to be a fact.

As I have said repeatedly, I believe that the Confucian hybrid regime is applicable to all states. The account of it is not only theoretical but is also meant to be practical. However, whether the ideal can be realized depends on many particular factors, especially the mainstream culture of each state. In the United States, where most people take one person, one vote as something sacred and any challenge to it as simply outrageous,[18] the Confucian hybrid regime may only be established through skillful disguises, or only after repeated failures of democratic states and the establishment of a shining model of such a regime somewhere else first. But in emerging democracies and democratizing countries, there may be less resistance to a Confucian hybrid regime, especially when there is a tradition favoring meritocracy and democratic states are not as attractive as they would have been because of their repeated failures.[19] Of course, the failure of democracies doesn't necessarily lead to the embrace of a better regime, and history doesn't always advance in the way we consider right.

Although I have criticized liberal democracy, the design of the Confucian hybrid regime can actually help the democratization process of predemocratic countries. This is because a problem with recently democratized countries is that there are many populist governments among them. The chaos that these governments create not only makes their own citizens suffer but also makes people in predemocratic states resist democratization. For example, much of the political turmoil in Taiwan—and the turmoil in the United States and Western Europe—is often taken as a product of a populist government, and the lack of education and other conditions in today's China makes many who desire democracy think that it is not feasible. But the Confucian hybrid regime, especially its limited or restricted form of democracy, can help us to avoid these obstacles. Moreover, as I discuss in chapter 9, liberties (rights) and the rule of law are the gem of liberal democracy, while, as I have discussed in chapter 3, popular election needs revisions. People often believe that liberties

18. For example, a most powerful objection to Samuel Alito's nomination to the US Supreme Court is a ruling he made that *could be* interpreted as an *indirect* challenge to one person, one vote, "a cornerstone of American democracy" (Cohen [2006]; see also the *New York Times* editorial [2006]). Interestingly, some, if not all, who defended Alito didn't defend him by criticizing the idea of one person, one vote, but by claiming that Alito didn't really challenge this idea in his ruling (see, e.g., http://www.professorbainbridge.com/2006/01/what_the_ny_tim.html).

19. For the perception of democracy and meritocracy in East Asian countries and the rest of the world, see Shin (2013).

and the rule of law and popular election are inseparable, but this view is unverified either theoretically or empirically. If the two parts are distinct, a very simple summary of the above discussions in dealing with democratization is: embrace liberties and the rule of law but balance popular participation with meritocracy.

Incompatible with Liberal Democracy?

After answering challenges to the superiority of a Confucian hybrid regime when compared with liberal democracies, let me deal with the elephant in the room: the apparent conflict between the Confucian hybrid regime and liberal democracy. Liberal democracy has an almost sacred "end of history" status. Any apparent challenge to it and its basic principles is dismissed offhand. Unfortunately, the Confucian hybrid regime seems to violate two basic principles of liberal democracy, the principle of legitimacy of the state and the principle of equality. I will address this issue in this section.

Legitimacy through Popular Vote?

The issue of legitimacy has already been discussed in the previous section in the context of the more practical issue of resentment. In general, some may believe that the legitimacy of the government comes from being voted in by the people, but first we need to explore the legitimacy of this understanding. If we don't appeal to some a priori tenet, an easy answer seems to appeal to the contemporary consensus on the idea of legitimacy. But this sounds like a circular argument: to appeal to people's consensus to support popular votes (a form of consensus) as the legitimate foundation of a government. Moreover, people can be educated to think otherwise. Just because the above understanding of the legitimacy of government may have been the dominant view today doesn't mean that this should be and will always be the dominant view.

But for argument's sake, let me put the theoretical quibbles aside and accept the idea that the legitimacy of the government comes from the people. This idea doesn't necessarily mean that only direct voting by the people can confer legitimacy on the government. Many institutions in a democracy, such as the US Supreme Court, are not directly selected by the people. In a recent article, Philip Pettit distinguishes indicative representation from responsive or deputy representation. In the former, representers' attitudes are evidential of representees' attitudes, whereas in the latter, representees' attitudes causally determine representers' attitudes. Examples of the latter are members of the US Congress who are directly elected by their constituencies and beholden to interests of these constituencies, and examples of the former are US Supreme

Court justices. Although the justices are not directly elected by the people, they nevertheless represent the people's will. In my view, this distinction seems to have something to do with the distinction between the popular will and the general will. The meritocrats in the Confucian hybrid regime also represent the people's (general or true) will, even though they are not directly elected. If Pettit's argument that these two forms of representation are legitimate in a democracy holds, why can't we also consider the meritocratic element in the Confucian hybrid regime to be legitimate?

One can argue, as Pettit does in his paper, that those who appoint Supreme Court justices are elected by the populace, meaning that the legitimacy of the Supreme Court ultimately comes from the people. But as mentioned, in the meritocratic selections, popular elections often take place. In the leveled model, for example, legislators on the lowest level are elected directly and are eligible to vote for and to be a candidate of the upper houses of the legislature. Again, this was how US senators on the national level were elected at the founding of the American regime, and scholars such as Macedo consider it a legitimate way of selecting legislators in a democracy. In the exam-based models, exams serve as qualifications for either voters or candidates. The exams are open to all, and there can be a popular voting element in these models. In the third kind of models, retired governors or provincial leaders can also trace their legitimacy back to voting. Thus, the Confucian hybrid regime can be considered legitimate, even if we consider that voting by the public offers ultimate legitimacy to the government, as long as we don't equate this with direct elections by voters.

Confucian Equality Is Only in Conflict with a Particular Strand of Equality

Another issue with the Confucian hybrid regime is its apparent violation of equality and its advocacy for hierarchy. As we have seen in practice, a key difference between this regime and liberal democracy is that the former indirectly restricts one person, one vote and leads to some sort of political inequality. But is this restriction a violation of equality, and if it is, does it mean that the Confucian hybrid regime is incompatible with liberal democracy?

Equality is a complicated concept, and we have to specify "equality about what" and "equality to what degree." As I have argued in chapters 1 and 2, during the SAWS, China experienced the collapse of the nobility-based feudal regime. When nobility is gone for good, people are born to be equal. Early Confucians embraced this equality. To them, especially to Mencius and Xun Zi, all human beings have equal opportunity to become politically and morally superior human beings. But we can argue that they differ from *some*, but not all, modern European thinkers in that they deny that *in actuality*, all human beings are morally and politically equal, because being "human" is a process of becoming, and we become (learn to be) fully human, and are not born fully human. Nevertheless, as I argue in chapter 9, Confucians can endorse many rights and equality before the law. As I argued earlier, people's opinions also need to be heard through their own mouths. Confucians only deny the equal voice in the political decision-making process due to the *actual* differences among human beings with regard to their moral, political, and intellectual capacities. For Confucians, the right to govern is not an inborn right but a right that must be earned (and it is "earnable" by all). Their position is close to the concept of "equal opportunity," and is also close to what is argued in Plato's *Republic*, where to rule is a burden that should be left to the wise and virtuous.

With the Confucian understanding of equality clarified, we can now see that the idea of equality in the Confucian hybrid regime is only in conflict with one particular strand of the concept of equality in the liberal democratic tradition.[20] One of the first and very influential defenders of this concept of equality was Thomas Hobbes. In his *Leviathan*, he introduced a radical sense of liberty that justified equal rights for all human beings by birth, without any qualifications,[21] while in the early Confucian tradition, there are qualifications for people's "rights."[22] We can then add some Aristotelian or Kantian elements to this kind of equality and argue that all human beings should enjoy a fulfilling and flourishing life, and a life of self-respect. Finally, we can argue that this fulfillment and self-respect can only be actualized through equal voting, that is, one person, one vote. Confucianism as I interpret it is indeed in conflict with this reading of liberal democracy.

This reading is a mainstream understanding of the idea of equality in liberal democracy, and it rejects the challenge from the Confucian tradition, for the qualifications of one person, one vote in the Confucian hybrid regime comes from the consideration of good governance, but the above reading of equality puts equal respect through one person, one vote above good governance (and all other goods). Moreover, one can argue that especially in a developed country, we can afford to sacrifice good governance and economic development to some extent for the sake of making people feel more empowered and more

20. I thank Sun Xiangchen (孙向晨), Qian Yongxiang (钱永祥), and Daniel Brudney for pushing me to clarify the difference between the ideas of equality in the Confucian hybrid regime and in a "Hobbesian" liberal democratic tradition.

21. See, in particular, chapter 14 in Hobbes (1985, 189–201).

22. I thank Sun Xiangchen for sharing this distinction with me.

respectful toward themselves.[23] This makes prioritizing self-respect not as overly idealistic as it may sound to those who are primarily concerned with good governance.

Therefore, the above reading of equality can be coherent and even sensible. But it also becomes obvious that to arrive at this reading of equality, there are three assumptions, each of which can be rejected by someone who also holds some sense of equality: it doesn't have to be the case that all human beings should enjoy equal rights and liberties by birth; these rights and liberties don't have to be in the form of self-respect, autonomy, or self-fulfillment; and self-respect and self-fulfillment don't have to be actualized through one person, one vote. From a Confucian point of view, one can argue that this reading has invested too much in the modern idea of equality and is an unnecessary interpretation of what emerged from the collapse of nobility and from modernity.

But Still Compatible with Many Other Strands

In fact, the Confucian "moderate" embrace of equality is in line with how democracy and equality are understood by some other classical and modern Western thinkers. For example, after pointing out problems with contemporary democratic societies and offering the hybrid regime as a solution, the journalist and political commentator Robert Kaplan points out:

> According to Aristotle, "Whether the few or the many rule is accidental to oligarchy—the rich are few everywhere, the poor many."[24] The real difference, he [Aristotle] wrote, is that "oligarchy is to the advantage of the rich, democracy to the advantage of the poor." (1997, 80)

From this he argues that perhaps the hybrid regime he discusses is real democracy, while modern democracies have degenerated or will soon degenerate into de facto oligarchies. Similarly, we can say that if we follow Kaplan/Aristotle's understanding of democracy, the Confucian hybrid regime is real democracy.

As for equality, in the *Spirit of Laws*, for example, Montesquieu made it clear that equality that is essential to a democracy is equality through the law, and democracy is not only threatened by inequality but by extreme equality (chaps. 2–4, book 8 [1989], 112–15). He said,

23. This is an argument Brudney made during a private conversation.

24. Kaplan doesn't offer the source of this quotation. He may have been paraphrasing a passage in Aristotle's *Politics* (1279b30–80a5). In the *Politics*, Aristotle also gave many arguments that support a hybrid regime (see 1281b25–35).

the true spirit of equality... consists neither in making everyone command nor in making no one command, but in obeying and commanding
one's equals. It seems not to have no master but to have only one's equals
for masters.... The difference between the democracy that is regulated and
the one that is not is that, in the former, one is equal only as a citizen, and,
in the latter, one is also equal as a magistrate, senator, judge, father, husband, or master. (ibid., 114)

Therefore, we can see that the idea of equality for Montesquieu is also limited,
and there can be a hierarchy in political decision making. This understanding
of equality comes very close to the Confucian one.

One can argue that the kind of democracy Montesquieu considered is an
Athenian form of democracy, and his account doesn't apply to the kind of
democracy that is practiced today. But the Confucian position may not be too
much different from that of the American philosopher John Rawls, who is a
contemporary liberal thinker and a strong defender of equality. He famously
makes the principle of equality the first principle of justice. However, the first
principle reads, "each person is to have an equal right to the most extensive
basic liberty compatible with a similar liberty of others" (1971, 60), and political liberty, one of the basic liberties, means "the right to vote and to be eligible
for public office" (ibid., 61). But here Rawls doesn't make the claim that every
citizen's vote should be counted equally, or that popular voting is the sole and
ultimate ground of legitimacy.

Indeed, although, according to Rawls, reasonable citizens in a liberal democracy should view one another as free and equal, there is little mention that
one person, one vote is an expression of such an equality. Only in his discussion of the decent consultation hierarchy does Rawls seem to express the belief that one person, one vote is an essential element of liberal democracy
(1999a, 71). However, in the *Law of Peoples*, he explicitly excludes the "right"
to equal political participation from basic human rights, an exclusion noticed
and criticized by many.[25] This suggests that this right is not as important as
what he considers basic rights. In fact, as we see from his discussion of plural
voting in *A Theory of Justice*, he doesn't seem to think that the violation of one
person, one vote is in conflict with liberal democracy, although, as was mentioned earlier, he defends it (or some form of popular and equal involvement
in politics—he doesn't explicitly say that this involvement is in the form of
one person, one vote) on the ground that it encourages civil friendship, self-
respect, and competence (1971, 233–34).[26]

25. See Nickel (2006) and Buchanan (2000). For a defense of this exclusion, see Berstein
(2006).

26. Of course, one can argue that Rawls's principle of equality demands one person, one

Therefore, the meritocratic element in the Confucian hybrid regime is not even necessarily in conflict with Rawls's egalitarian stance, for in the former, citizens are free and equal in many ways, and even in terms of voting, people do participate, either directly through voting for the popular branch, indirectly through voting in the leveled model, or participating through equal access in the exam-based models. It is just that the Confucian hybrid regime rejects building political legitimacy solely on one person, one vote.

The Political Difference Principle and the Search for the Best Inequality

More importantly, Rawls may have good reasons to embrace the hybrid arrangements in the Confucian regime. As discussed in chapter 3, both the Confucian hybrid regime and Rawls believe that political participation presupposes proper education and political cognizance of the voters. For Rawls, however, although the uninformed and unreasonable citizens are bad citizens, their voting rights are not explicitly curtailed (by law or by other means).[27] The Confucian hybrid regime doesn't legally ban "bad citizens" from voting, but it does have mechanisms to reduce the influence of their votes. But with regard to these mechanisms that seem to be a form of political inequality, if we follow the rationale of Rawls's difference principle in *A Theory of Justice*, that economic inequality can be accepted if the least advantaged are benefited (1971, 75–83), why can't we have a difference principle in politics (I will call it the "political difference principle"): political or electoral inequality can be accepted if the least advantaged (from a material point of view) are benefited? If Rawls's difference principle doesn't disqualify him as an egalitarian thinker, why should the political difference principle make the Confucian hybrid regime incompatible with equality? Indeed, as we have seen, early Confucians emphasized equal potentials among all, and the morally and intellectually superior people in actuality could only justify their status by serving the common people, helping them to fully develop themselves and strive to become equals with the superior ones. This Confucian position can be

---

vote, and the ambivalent and even opposite claims Rawls makes elsewhere only reveal a contradiction in his thought. Rather, the principle of equality that is expressed through one person, one vote is his real position. (I thank Daniel Brudney for making this argument to me in a private conversation.) But the burden is with those who make this argument to justify the "contradictory" statements Rawls has made in his works.

27. I thank Brudney and David Elstein for making this point with me.

called egalitarianism-based elitism or "egalitarian meritocracy,"[28] "compassionate moral conservatism," or "compassionate elitism."

Let me elaborate on the Confucian considerations of the issue of equality. According to Mencius, extreme equality cannot be achieved, or can only be achieved at a cost too high for everyone in the society. We have already seen in chapter 2 that in the *Mencius* (3A4), he argued that there has to be a division of labor, and in the case of politics, the divisions are hierarchical. Toward the end of 3A4, Chen Liang (陈良), the main interlocutor with Mencius in this section, and a convert to some sort of egalitarian school of thought, tried one last defense of his master Xu Xing's (许行) teachings. He argued that if the price of the same quantity of goods is the same, deceptions will disappear, and you could send a child to buy things without being worried that he would be cheated on. This argument seems rather intuitive, because, for example, if an iPhone 6 is sold at the same price as a crappy low-end cell phone, who would still make the fake iPhone or try to cheat an innocent buyer, even a child, into buying one by pretending that it was authentic? Mencius answers,

> That things are unequal is a matter of fact. . . . If you rank them the same, it will bring confusion to the world. If a roughly finished shoe sells at the same price as a finely finished one, who would make the latter? Following the way of Master Xu is to lead each other to deception. How can one govern a state in this way?

If we think Chen Liang's argument is intuitive, Mencius's, then, is rather odd. But it is easy to imagine that using our example, if an iPhone 6 is sold at the same price as a crappy cell phone, no one would bother to make iPhone 6s anymore. Apparently this forced equality is bad for economic development, which is the argument typically made against communism and even socialism, although an egalitarian could question the merits of economic development. But Mencius further claimed that this would lead to deception, which is a more serious challenge, and is also a puzzling one. To understand this claim, we can imagine that if one is paid by the length of time one is at work, no matter how hard and skillful he or she does the job, the majority of the people, being self-interested, would try to be slackers while pretending to be working, which is deception and cheating. This is what allegedly happened in many real-world communist countries, especially during the Cultural Revolution in China, when an extreme egalitarian ideology required that everyone, no matter how hardworking or skillful, or what gender the person

28. A term I borrowed from Elstein's description of my position (2015, 171).

was, and so on, would be paid the same hourly wage. Therefore, according to Mencius, even if extreme equality is possible, the social and political cost (slow or no economic development and even deception) is so high, presumably higher and more uncorrectable than certain nonegalitarian societies, that few would like it.[29]

In fact, it can be argued that the radical egalitarianism during the Cultural Revolution was merely apparent and not real. Most Chinese people were indeed equal, or more precisely, equally poor. But the party elites enjoyed great privileges over the masses, making them "more equal" than the rest. So if inequality can only be eliminated at a high cost, or its apparent elimination will lead to another hidden inequality, the question that we should ask is not how to eliminate inequality but what kind of inequality is the best inequality. Of course, then we will have to ask, "Best for whom?" For Confucians, it should be the best for the common people with regard to their daily needs.[30] Let's consider two scenarios. In the United States, political and social inequality is considered deeply problematic. But economic inequality in the United States is more far-reaching than that in Japan and South Korea,[31] two countries where, perhaps thanks to some Confucian heritage, political and social equality is not deep-rooted, and the respect for seniors ("senior" in terms of positions in a company or the government) is still widespread. As in any political matter, the causes for this difference are myriad and complicated, but one possible explanation is this: If Confucians are correct in their understanding that we human beings are hierarchical in nature, that is, wishing to excel in comparison with others (in this regard, Confucians are in line with Nietzscheans), then it has to be expressed in one form or the other. In Japan and South Korea, the CEOs can satisfy their hierarchical desire with people's respect. In the United States, however, since everyone is considered equal, the CEOs

---

29. The deception in an egalitarian world leads to a race to the bottom (the greatest slacker wins), but in the hierarchical world, which firmly and really embraces mobility, it leads to a race to the top. The former, as was argued in this paragraph, also leads to slow and even no economic development. The cure of it seems to depend on turning each worker into a conscientious one. This is indeed what was tried but failed in real-world communist countries. One can argue that the deception in a competitive market economy, however, has been controlled through economic development and the rule of law. But it is possible that people can offer further defenses of egalitarianism. What is clear is that Mencius is not on the egalitarian side.

30. As I discussed earlier in this chapter, Li et al. (manuscript) advocate this kind of rationale in the field of economics and business studies. That is, instead of focusing on the question of eliminating equality, it urges us to pay attention to identifying and promoting good inequality and identifying and eliminating bad inequality.

31. One can refer to the Gini coefficients of these countries (see data from this website: http://en.wikipedia.org/wiki/List_of_countries_by_income_equality).

have to prove their superiority through other means. Since all other venues of hierarchy are largely suppressed because of the formal equality of all, the most convenient way is to show off through the most base and naked means, that is, money and material possessions.[32] Again, real-world affairs are complicated, and this explanation may not be true. But we can put these issues aside and consider two hypothetical scenarios: Which scenario is better, greater political and social equality with greater economic inequality or greater political and social inequality with greater economic equality?[33] For a Confucian, it is a good trade-off that by giving the competent people a higher political and social status, they share more of their wealth with the masses and try to help the masses economically. Indeed, it is almost like pulling a trick on the competent: to give them an almost empty title ("the great people" or "the morally exemplary people") in exchange for real goods for the "small people" or the masses.[34] Put in Rawlsian terms, to achieve what is desired in the (economic) difference principle, (a certain form) of political inequality may be necessary.

We can appreciate Confucian wisdom from another perspective. Friedrich Nietzsche offered some serious criticisms of equality.[35] According to him, the obsession with equality and the interests of the masses suppresses our "will to power" or, to put it more politically correct, our will to excel. This leads to the mediocracy of our modern times. But his solution, even if we could disassociate it from Nazism, is still quite oppressive, consisting in a master race subjugating the rest of humanity.[36] This oppression breeds resentment in the masses and plants the seed for political unrest. Perhaps what Nietzsche dreamed of is the age of nobility, including the classical Greek and Roman eras, where the Greek or Roman citizens were de facto nobles and dominated aliens and slaves. As I argued in chapter 1, the emergence of equality in Nietzsche's Europe may have been a natural consequence of the decline of nobility, which occurred in China during the Zhou-Qin transition (770 BCE to 221 BCE). Resonating with this emergence, early Confucians introduced the Confucian idea of equality (as we saw in chapter 2). At the same time, however,

---

32. Indeed, studies have shown that many people are willing to trade their income with what would give them status and self-esteem. See Li et al. (manuscript), Solnick and Hemenway (1998), and Sivanathan and Pettit (2010).

33. Apparently, Nordic countries offer a more thoroughly egalitarian model. But both political and economic inequalities still remain in these countries, and Confucians would again ask us to consider the best mixture of equalities and inequalities.

34. See Bell (2006, chap. 3, 38–55) for a similar discussion.

35. See, for example, Nietzsche (1994).

36. See, for example, his short essay "The Greek State" in Nietzsche (1994, 176–86).

they also tried to justify hierarchy. But the Confucian hierarchy is not hereditary but is the result of an equality-based, meritocratic competition. Early Confucians preserved some features of the disappearing nobility in this design. But through upward mobility, the Confucian hierarchy allows the possible resentment of the lowly to be vented by encouraging them to turn their resentment regarding their lowly status into a drive to strive for a higher status. This venting doesn't threaten the stability of the hierarchy and prevents a "slave revolt" from disrupting the status quo. Moreover, the Confucian emphasis on compassion, especially from superiors to inferiors, also helps diffuse the resentment of the lowly. It simultaneously allows the "great people" among us to express their will to power, but through compassion, the expression doesn't lead to domination and subjugation but to lifting up the masses. Thus, this Confucian equality- and mobility-based hierarchy addresses Nietzsche's legitimate concerns, and leads to stability without oppressing either the weak or the strong, as Nietzsche advocated or worried about.

A More Realistic Utopia

Now, let's go back to the central issue of this section, the compatibility between the Confucian hybrid regime and liberal democracy. I have already argued that the deviation of this regime from a Rawlsian liberal democracy may not be that great. In fact, there is yet another way to show how this regime makes sense in Rawlsian terms. If we follow Rawls's idea that there is an analogy between what is within a people and what is among different peoples, we see that this analogy actually breaks down in Rawls's later philosophy.[37] That is, in his theory, domestically, a liberal people consists of free and equal citizens, and its majority is reasonable. Internationally, however, he never asserts that well-ordered peoples—the only peoples that are reasonable—must be the majority. The well-ordered peoples actually possess a higher position than other peoples, and thus Rawls introduces a de facto hierarchy of peoples on the international level. In contrast, the Confucian hybrid regime carries out the analogy much more nicely. Its domestic hierarchy corresponds to the hierarchy of peoples: the informed and compassionate play a justifiably larger role in domestic politics, just as the well-ordered peoples play a justifiably larger role in international politics. Of course, the percentage of incompetent citizens over all the citizens of a state may be higher than the percentage of disorderly societies over the totality of all societies. To be clear, many cosmo-

37. For an argument concerning a different kind of breakdown between the domestic case discussed in *Political Liberalism* and the international case discussed in *The Law of Peoples*, and a more liberal solution for it, see Tan (2006, 88–91).

politan liberal thinkers also see the discrepancy between Rawls's domestic and international theories but argue instead that we should carry over his approach in A *Theory of Justice* to the international case.[38] I argue for a consistent approach in the opposite direction: to carry his approach to the international case over to the treatment of the domestic case.[39] Then where do we put Rawls's liberal people in the domestic case in my "backward" analogy? The liberal people and its corresponding international society of liberal peoples can be taken as a domestic ideal and an international ideal.

In addition to the above formal comparisons, from a more substantial perspective, the Confucian hybrid regime actually develops Rawls's ideas, deals with problems Rawls doesn't deal with, and offers more realistic solutions to the problems with which Rawls is concerned. As is implied by Rawls's third fact of a democratic society that "an enduring and secure democratic regime must be willingly and freely supported by at least a substantial majority of its politically active citizens" (1996, 38), his version of liberal democracy presupposes that at least a substantial majority of citizens have to be reasonable, and he doesn't discuss how to deal with the situation in which the unreasonable people may constitute the majority or a substantial minority in a society. He has a good reason to make this presupposition. That is, we have to solve the problem of stability first in the ideal situation in which the majority of a society consists of reasonable people who nevertheless hold conflicting and irreconcilable, comprehensive doctrines. Then and only then can we deal with the problem in a more realistic situation.[40] However, if we accept the fact that no real-world liberal democracy has a majority of reasonable and informed citizens, then liberal peoples as Rawls understands them simply don't exist. In contrast, the Confucian hybrid regime deals with the problem of the relations between reasonable and informed citizens and unreasonable, uninformed, or indifferent people. To be clear, my focus is not about Rawls's failure to offer a proof of the desirability of liberal democracy, as some people are concerned with.[41] Rather, my concern is that if, due to the sixth fact, this ideal of liberal

---

38. See, for example, Pogge (1994 and 2006), Buchanan (2000), and Tan (1998 and 2006).

39. As I argue in chapter 7, the Confucian international order is also hierarchical, resembling the hierarchical order within a state and resonating with the hierarchical order proposed by Rawls in *The Law of Peoples*. But the Confucian international hierarchy is not based on whether a state is well ordered in a Rawlsian sense but on its humaneness, just as the basis of Confucian hierarchy in the domestic case.

40. In *A Theory of Justice*, he offers a similar rationale for dealing with the problem of justice first and postponing the more pressing problem of injustice (Rawls 1971, 8–9).

41. On this alleged failure by Rawls, I share Burton Dreben's view, expressed in his response to someone who asked a question about the justification for liberal democracy (2003, 328–29). According to him, there are enough problems with a coherent conception of a constitutional

democracy is too utopian, can we have a regime that deals with this fact that is nevertheless in line with many of the Rawlsian ideals? I argue in this and the previous chapters that the Confucian hybrid regime fits the bill. Moreover, this regime tries to deal with many practical problems, such as maintaining Social Security (welfare for the people), international aid, and domestic and international human rights (which Rawls is deeply concerned with; 1997, 773). The difference between the Confucian hybrid regime and Rawls's ideal liberal democracy is that the former doesn't believe that these problems can be solved within the regime of the latter but needs the corrections offered by the Confucian hybrid regime.

In chapters 2–4, I first showed how early Confucians, Mencius in particular, answered the emerging "modern" question of how to select rulers and their legitimacy in a plebeianized society. I then showed how these answers could be institutionalized, especially against the contemporary setting, and why this Confucian regime is a viable regime that can address various issues of politics better than the regime of one person, one vote. If my arguments stand, we can see the vitality of Confucianism in the contemporary world. Moreover, as we have seen, the criticisms of one person, one vote, and the reasons for a hybrid regime, are not culturally specific—the Confucian hybrid regime is meant to be universal for all human societies that meet the sixth fact, not just the allegedly "Confucian" states. The corrections that Confucianism offers here are about the basic political structure and not merely some ethical "tinkering," such as educating the rulers and the citizenry, or an evasion and rejection of modern conditions through retreating to some "Confucian reservations." As I've stated numerous times, the Confucianism-based hybrid regime doesn't reject liberal democracy completely but can be viewed as a development of it. It preserves what is truly valuable in liberal democracy (constitutionalism, rule of law, protection of liberties and rights, etc.), and deals with the sixth fact of modern democracy, which other liberal democratic thinkers fail to deal with adequately. In *The Law of Peoples*, Rawls calls the regime he designs a "realistic utopia." To establish a realistic utopia is the difference between a political philosopher and a politician (the former being more utopian), and between a political philosopher and an idle dreamer (the former being more realistic). But from the point of view of the Confucian hybrid regime, Rawls fails to deal with some realistic factors that

---

liberal democracy, and to argue for or against its foundation (e.g., why it is better than totalitarianism) is not a worthy or fruitful enterprise. One can't reason with someone like Hitler, because reason has no bearing on this question. As Dreben suggests, perhaps the only choice when dealing with Hitler is to shoot him.

arise even in an ideal design. Therefore, using Rawls's terminology, we can say that the Confucian hybrid regime is a more realistic utopia than Rawls's design of liberal democracy.[42]

42. Of course, as Elstein challenges, if the hybrid regime doesn't lead to better governance, then the Confucian hybrid regime would prove to be an undesirable project (2015, 189).

5

Compassion as the New Social Glue in the Society of Strangers

Introducing Humaneness and Compassion

As discussed in chapter 1, because of the profound social and political changes during the SAWS, which resemble the European transition to early modernity, three fundamental political issues had to be answered anew. In chapters 2–4, I discussed how early Confucians answered the issues of the selection of political decision makers and the legitimacy of the selection, and how their answers can be institutionalized and remain relevant today. In this chapter, I discuss the key concept that early Confucians developed to address the issue of finding a new bond for an emerging "modern" society, the large and populous society of strangers, as well as the issue of state–state (international) relations. The main texts that I use in this discussion are the *Analects* and the *Mencius*.

As argued in chapter 1, another crucial issue regarding any political entity is discovering the bond that can unite the entity as one. In the Western Zhou dynasty (roughly 1150 BCE to 770 BCE), through a pyramid-like feudal structure, a large empire was divided into small and closely knit communities in which people could hardly move from one place to another, or from one rank to another. In such a society, especially among nobles, the effective social glue was *li* (礼), that is, rites and rituals that offered opportunities for nobles to bond and identify with one another and that regulated their behaviors toward one another. But a bond that presupposes a small, stable, and closely knit community of acquaintances doesn't work in a large and mobile society of strangers. A new way of bonding the people of a state together was desperately needed.

Humaneness by Confucius

Apparently, the solution Confucius offered was to restore the old world order by sticking to *li*.[1] But Confucius also stated quite explicitly in the *Analects* 9.3 that he was open to the change of one, but not another, code of conduct. So the question is: How do we decide on what code of conduct to change or not to change?

In a discussion between him and his pupils on the three-year mourning ritual, according to which one is required to resign from his office and abstain from luxuries, (certain?) sexual conduct, and entertainment for three years when a parent dies, Confucius indicated his criterion for reexamining and reconstructing *li*.

> Zai Wo [a pupil of Confucius's] asked, "The three-year mourning period is too long. If the jun zi stops practicing li for three years,[2] li will be in ruins . . . So one year is enough."
>
> The master said, "Eating your rice [which was considered a delicacy at that time] and wearing your brocade [fine clothes], would you feel at ease?"
>
> Zai Wo said, "Yes, I would."
>
> "If you feel at ease, then do it! The jun zi in mourning finds no relish in good food, no pleasure in music, and no easy feeling in his home, which is why he does not do it. If you feel at ease, then do it!"
>
> After Zai Wo left, the master said, "How inhumane [not *ren* 仁] Zai Wo is![3] A child ceases to be nursed by his parents only after he is three years old. Three years' mourning is observed throughout the world [tian xia]. Was Zai Wo not loved by his parents for three years?!" (*Analects* 17.21)

A few observations can be made on this passage. First, Zai Wo realized that observing the particular code of the three-year mourning period was detrimental to preserving the feudal codes of conduct in general, and he proposed changing this code in order to preserve *li*. Thus, he was a conservative reformer. Second, if Confucius were a conservative, even a fundamentalist, who would only wish to stick to *li*, he would simply reject Zai Wo's moderate proposal. If Confucius were a conservative reformer, he would embrace it. But

1. See, for example, the *Analects* 3.14 and 7.1, in which Confucius apparently expressed the "conservative" attitude.

2. In this passage, the term *jun zi* seems to suggest a rule-following nobleman, and is used in its original meaning with a touch of the new meaning, introduced by Confucians, of a morally exemplary person. I use the transliteration *jun zi* rather than either "nobleman" or "(morally) exemplary person" to preserve the double meanings.

3. "Inhumane" is the negation of *ren* (仁).

Confucius did neither. Instead, he dug into human emotions and sentiments and offered a rational argument on the basis of them. If one lacks these sentiments, he or she is not humane. Thus, Confucius actually offered a new ground to evaluate all values, *li* included. At another place, Confucius was more explicit about this: "What can a man do with *li* if he is not humane?" (*Analects* 3.3), implying that *li* (and the conservation of it) is not fundamental whereas humaneness is, which is the ultimate foundation of *li*. Therefore, instead of conserving *li*, which served well as the social glue in feudal society, humaneness was introduced as the foundation for the new political order.

Compassion by Mencius

From the idea of humaneness, Mencius further developed the idea of compassion. Here is a rather important passage from the *Mencius* on this issue that I quote in full:

> Mencius said, "Every human being has a heart that cannot bear [to see the suffering of] others. The former kings had the heart that cannot bear [to see the suffering of] others, which was why they had governments that cannot bear [to see the suffering of] others. Running a government that cannot bear [to see the suffering of] others with the heart that cannot bear [to see that suffering of] others, one can run the world (tian xia) as rolling it on one's palm.
>
> The reason for me to say that every human being has the heart that cannot bear [to see the suffering of] others is this. If anyone suddenly sees a child about to fall into a well, he or she will have a feeling of alarm and distress, not to gain friendship with the child's parents, nor to seek the praise of their neighbors and friends, nor because they dislike the cry of the child. From this we see that whoever is devoid of the heart of compassion is not human;[4] whoever is devoid of the heart of shame is not human; whoever is devoid of the heart of courtesy and modesty is not human; whoever is devoid of the heart of right and wrong is not human. The heart of compassion is the germ of humanity (*ren*); the heart of shame is the germ of righteousness (*yi*); the heart of courtesy and modesty is the germ of the observance of rituals (*li*); the heart of right and wrong is the germ of wisdom. A human being has these four germs, as he or she has four limbs. Possessing these four germs but claiming one's incapability [of developing

---

4. The word for "compassion" was translated as "the feeling of alarm and distress" one line back; "the feeling of alarm and distress" is the original meaning of this term (*ce yin zhi xin* [惻隱之心]), which, perhaps thanks to Mencius, is later used to refer to compassion.

them into four virtues] is to cripple oneself; claiming one's ruler's incapa-
bility [of developing them into four virtues] is to cripple one's ruler. If a
human being who possesses these four germs knows to develop them, it
will be like a fire starting up or a spring coming out. If one can develop it,
one can tend to what is within the Four Seas [i.e., the world]; if one can't
develop it, one can't even serve one's parents. (2A6)

We should see that the "thought experiment" Mencius introduced in this
passage is very well designed. First, the object that is used to call up our compassion is a small child, whose suffering is perhaps one of the most difficult
kinds for human beings to bear. A child is usually considered innocent, and
his or her life is not yet fulfilled, while a suffering adult might have done things
that merit his or her suffering (or so we rationalize) and usually has a far more
fulfilled life than a child, which would weaken our compassion. Second, Mencius asked about our instinctual reactions ("if one *suddenly* sees"), reactions
we would have before any second thoughts—"who this child is," "whose child
it is," "what reactions would be considered proper from others' perspectives,"
and so on come to mind. Third, he only asked if we would have felt bad in this
situation, and not if we would do something about it. Intuitively, the former
seems to be universal, and the latter is not.

If we understand how well this thought experiment is designed, it is hard
to imagine that anyone wouldn't have the kind of reactions described by Mencius. But there can still be some challenges. First, what if this child (or his or
her parents) posed a threat to you? For example, what if, right before the fall,
the child was, unintentionally, about to pull the trigger of a gun that is pointed
at you? But we can answer on Mencius's behalf that it is about our instinctual,
and not deliberative, reactions, and even if we had an instinctual sense of relief,
we would still have a sense of compassion as well.

Second, from our common experiences, a child might not react to someone
else's suffering with a sense of alarm and distress, and his or her reactions
might be the opposite. But we can argue that it is not because the child doesn't
have compassion, but because he or she doesn't grasp the fact that what happens to the object is suffering. That is, what the child lacks is not the moral
sentiment of compassion but a certain cognitive capacity.

Third, what about a psychopath who enjoys seeing the suffering of others,
and whose enjoyment comes precisely from the recognition that others are
indeed suffering? Here, there are two possible answers. It could be that this
psychopath has a sense of compassion as well, but it is deeply buried beneath
other sentiments that may have been the result of childhood abuse and other
traumatic experiences. If this is the case, it isn't a challenge to Mencius's
thesis. But it could also be that this psychopath was born with no sense of

compassion whatsoever. If we still wish to defend Mencius's thesis, we would have to say that this psychopath is not a human being but a beast that looks like a human. As was mentioned in chapter 2, for Mencius, "human being" is not merely a biological concept but a relational and moral concept. The distinction between human beings and beasts is very slight (4B19), and it lies in the moral sentiment of compassion.[5] The exclusion of those who are human beings in a biological sense makes Mencius's account not a descriptive one but a normative one. But at the same time, the fact that it catches what most human beings share makes this normative account a realistic one.

Compassion as a Modern Virtue

Why Is Compassion-Based Humaneness a Virtue?

There is another problem with Mencius's account. Even if we agree that he offered a very convincing account of the (near) universality of the sentiment of compassion, how could he, in 2A6, then argue that the sentiments for the other three virtues are also universal? In the history of Chinese thought, there is a long-running debate on this issue.[6] Whether there is an illegitimate move in Mencius's argument or not, what is obvious and uncontroversial is that compassion-based humaneness is *the* fundamental virtue among fundamental Confucian virtues, the virtue of virtues. Now, the question is: Why should compassion-based humaneness be taken as a virtue, even the most fundamental virtue? After all, what Mencius demonstrated is the (near) universality of the sentiment of compassion, but this doesn't make it the seed of a virtue.

5. According to the primatologist Frans de Waal, some primates have "seeds" of sympathy as well (2006). We can argue that what Mencius offered here is a normative account that is insulated from empirical challenges. We can also argue that the term "beast" is different from "animal," as the former is used to refer to animals that are cruel and lack any sympathy. To develop Mencius's original account further, we can say that what is essential to the human sentiment of compassion, as suggested by the metaphor "seed," is that it can be consciously developed into a "nonnatural" virtue ("nonnatural" in the sense that we are not born with it), where animals' inborn elements of sympathy can't. Interestingly, de Waal thinks that his theory resonates with Mencius's, but this is perhaps a misunderstanding. See Bai (2012a) for more discussions.

6. Shaoming Chen (2012) offers both a historical account and a solution to this problem that resonate with my own thoughts on this issue. Zeng Zhenyu (曾振宇) offers a very good survey of the debates over this and other issues related to Mencius's idea of the original goodness of human beings, and discusses many relevant issues as well (see chap. 5, sec. 1, in Zeng 2013; 222–49).

To this question, it seems that Mencius would simply say that this senti-ment and the virtue built on it are what define human beings as human beings, and if one keeps asking him why this is the case, he would have nothing else to say but thump on the table, if not on the questioner's head. That is, Men-cius's account of compassion as (the seed of) a virtue has a metaphysical touch. Confucius's answer seems to take a more "naturalistic" and less dog-matic or metaphysical tone. Of course, Confucius's idea of humaneness is not necessarily the same as Mencius's concept of compassion, but both refer to one's care for other human beings. When asked why we should have this care, especially when the world is chaotic and other human beings don't seem to be very lovable, Confucius said,

> One cannot associate with birds and beasts. Am I not a member of the human race in this world? If not human beings, with whom should I associ-ate? (*Analects* 18.6)

But we can ask: Why can't we associate with birds and beasts, living like a Rousseauian noble savage? Even if we had to associate with other human be-ings, why should we value caring among human beings but not something else (such as our tendency to fight against others, as in a Hobbesian jungle)?

Nietzsche's Account of the Origin of Pity

To offer an explanation, I have conducted some comparative studies in the following, especially with Friedrich Nietzsche's account of the origin of pity as a virtue. Before I do so, an important conceptual clarification is due. Nietz-sche distinguished between pity (*Mitleid*) and compassion (*Mitgefuehl*). The target of his criticism, and thus the focus of my following discussion of Nietz-sche, is the former, whereas the latter is the term we have used in Mencius's case so far, and is also what Nietzsche endorsed. For Nietzsche, presumably, "compassion" has a meaning of "shared passion," which is perfectly fine among friends, especially those of the master race. But "pity" in Nietzsche's under-standing lacks a genuine sense of other-regarding, and his criticism was tar-geted at his great teacher and enemy, Arthur Schopenhauer.[7] In the follow-ing, I also mention the idea of compassion in Buddhism (慈悲). In contemporary literature on moral psychology, there are many discussions about the connections and distinctions between concepts such as sympathy and empathy. But in the discussions of this chapter and throughout the book,

---

7. Many of the above distinctions in Nietzsche's account were made by Hans Feger, and I am grateful to him for them.

the Confucian idea of compassion simply means a sense of care toward others, including strangers. Issues such as what is the moral psychological structure of this care, is it sympathy or empathy, is it among equals or unequals, is it pity or compassion, and so on, do not really matter. One could object by arguing, for example, that when I have a sense of care for the suffering of another, as in Mencius's hypothetical case of the falling child, I am superior to the target of my care. If so, this sounds like pity in Nietzsche's sense, and shouldn't be called compassion. But it is possible that I care about another's suffering while I am also suffering, even suffering the same misfortune. For example, I can feel a sense of care for someone who is tortured while I am tortured by the same perpetrator in the same way as the object of my care. The root of my uncomfortable feelings, as described in Mencius's case, can be a shared feeling, and can be something else. For Mencius, and for the Confucian sense of care discussed in this book, all these different situations exemplify one and the same sense of care for others, which Mencius considers (nearly) universal, and can be cultivated and turned into a virtue.

With the above clarification, let us take a look at Nietzsche's account of the origin of pity, and see if this can shed some light on our question of why compassion should be elevated as the basis of a virtue, maybe even the most important virtue, by early Confucians. According to Nietzsche, the "value of the 'unegoistic,' the instincts of pity, self-denial, [and] self-sacrifice" were "the *great* danger to mankind" (1994, 7). He thought that the morality of pity was "the most uncanny symptom of our European culture," and that it originated from "the disgraceful modern softness of feeling" (ibid.).[8] In antiquity, morality was defined by the aristocrats as egoistic and aggressive, and it was "only with a *decline* of aristocratic value judgments" that "the herd instinct" finally rose up (ibid., 12).

Nietzsche's claim that the morality of pity was a modern concept seems to be corroborated by the history of Western philosophy. For example, he mentioned that Plato never valued pity (1994, 7), and this seems to be the case. The four cardinal virtues mentioned in Plato's *Republic*, and likely also endorsed by ancient Greeks, are wisdom, courage, moderation, and justice— pity is nowhere to be found. In book 1 of the *Republic*, Socrates offered three reasons for someone to want to rule: money, honor, and avoiding the penalty of being ruled by a bad ruler (347a–d), and the reason that we moderns take, that is, the care for one's compatriots, was not mentioned at all. It can be argued that Socrates offered these self-interest-based motivations to rule as a response to Thrasymachus, who argued that to rule is to satisfy one's self-

---

8. The late Robert Rethy once suggested to me that "uncanny" is not a good translation, and the proper word is "sinister."

interest (by exploiting the ruled). But we must see that none of his companions found it strange for Socrates to list only these reasons, and throughout the *Republic* there is no place for pity, either. In book 7 of the *Republic*, where Thrasymachus became mostly a silent partner of the dialogue, to answer the question of why philosophers should accept the task of ruling in a good state, Socrates appealed to the idea of paying back the rearing by the state (520b–c), an idea based on a definition of justice (paying back what one takes) that was apparently refuted by Socrates himself.[9] However, philosophers don't have an obligation to become the ruler of a bad state. In any event, pity or compassion, an obvious motivation to us "moderns," is peculiarly neglected in these passages. Of course, whether all these actions and virtues are good is ultimately determined by their relations to the Good (504a–6b). But the Good is never defined in the *Republic*, and it's hard to imagine that it has anything to do with compassion.

In Aristotle's *Nicomachean Ethics*, pity is also not considered a virtue, although Nietzsche didn't mention him.[10] He did mention pity as a feeling or a passion (*pathos*) (1105b20–25), but made it clear that virtue is not a feeling (1105b29–1106a6).[11] He later mentioned virtues concerned with feelings, such as bravery, as the mean between the feelings of fear and of confidence (1107a35–b5), and pity was also not mentioned. There are means in feelings or concerned with feelings that, though not virtues, are given praise (1108a31–b1). Once more, pity is not mentioned. Only on involuntary feelings and actions are pardon and sometimes pity bestowed (1109b30–35). But clearly, pity here is not taken as a virtue. An interesting contrast that is also relevant to what I will discuss later is how important friendship—which, similar to compassion, has something to do with goodwill among people—is in Aristotle's ethical system. Two out of the ten books of the *Nicomachean Ethics* are devoted to the discussion of friendship, and Aristotle explicitly stated that friendship "is a virtue, or involves virtue, and besides is most necessary for our life" (1155a1–5; Irwin 1985, 207).

Therefore, the neglect of pity as a virtue in the case of ancient Western philosophers, especially in the case of Aristotle, who considered pity a

9. Of course, how much of this definition is actually defeated and how much of it can be saved is yet another difficult question to answer. I thank Liu Wei (刘玮) for pointing this out to me.

10. Some scholars like to compare Confucianism with Aristotelian virtue ethics. But it seems that no one has paid any attention to the fact that compassion, which is the core of Mencius's moral values, is not listed as a virtue by Aristotle.

11. I thank Liu Wei for pointing this out to me. The English translations I have consulted are Irwin (1985) and Ross (1925). Terence Irwin translates *pathos* as "feelings," while David Ross translates it as "passions."

common passion or feeling, highlights the aforementioned problem with Mencius's account of compassion. That is, even if pity or compassion is a universal or nearly universal sentiment, why should we elevate it to the level of virtue, even the most fundamental virtue?

According to Nietzsche, the decline of aristocratic values and the rise of values of the herd, which are symbolized by the elevation of pity as a virtue, were a result of a conspiracy by the Jews. He said that among the nobles, there are two subclasses, the priestly and the chivalric. The members of the former cannot get involved in the actions (aggressions, killings, rapes, etc.) of the latter because the former need to remain literally (and not symbolically) pure for their priestly activities, including being away from the flesh and blood of the lowly and the conquered (meaning no killings and rapes).[12] In the noble values, the chivalric activities are valued, and the priestly people have to try to rationalize their sorry status by claiming that their passive and peaceful way of life is superior. A different value system thus emerges (Nietzsche 1994, 16–18).

The priestly class, however, is too weak to rebel against the chivalric class, or the moral values the latter embraced. Here a priestly people arose—the Jews. They were enslaved by one group after another, and were not happy with their status (of being oppressed and looked down upon by the Romans), but they were too weak to change it. They were also too bitter to accept their fate. So they revolted through conspiracy. That is, they wanted to turn the moral values of the nobles upside down, making the weak (i.e., the Jews) morally superior and the strong (i.e., the Romans) morally inferior. They tried to spread this new set of moral values—the slave morality—in which, among other things, pity becomes a virtue, in contrast to the ancient Greek and Roman values. According to Nietzsche, they succeeded at doing so through Jewish "black art" and by reinventing Judaism in the form of Christianity. In particular, through Jesus, they changed the message of resentment into one of love, which is more appealing, and by killing Jesus, they presented the message as non-Jewish (ibid., 19–20).

With regard to this blatantly anti-Semitic account, some, especially those who wish to enjoy Nietzsche without a guilty conscience by "whitewashing" him, believe that Nietzsche only offered a general account of the moral decline among human beings, and it was merely a historical accident that this decline was triggered and promoted by the Jews. Indeed, the moral decline discussed in Rousseau's *Discourse on the Origin of Inequality* or the master-slave dialectic

12. What Nietzsche covered up through his powerful rhetoric is the fact that it is often the priests who have the right to touch flesh and blood in sacrificial rituals. I thank the late Robert Rethy for sharing this point with me.

in Hegel's *Phenomenology of Spirit*, for example, bear some similarities to Nietzsche's account, and they are meant to be universal, describing the general principles and inevitability of human spiritual and moral development. However, although Nietzsche criticized "priestly" morality and spokesmen for it (Socrates, Buddha, etc.) within many civilizations, for him, it seems that only by the Jews, a priestly people with unprecedented hatred and "black art," could this priestly morality infect a whole body, a whole civilization. That is, for Nietzsche, the existence of the Jews is essential to the moral decline in Europe.[13] If not for them, to Nietzsche, who started out as a classicist, the glorious Roman Empire he loved would still stand. Here, Nietzsche's unprecedented hatred is palpable.

Resentful or not, a more serious problem with Nietzsche's account is that it simply doesn't work in the case of Mencius, because, obviously, there were no Jews in pre-Qin China. Even if we argued that Nietzsche's account was meant to be universal and not purely anti-Semitic, it is hard to say that early Confucians were an oppressed people, or were the priestly class who is barred from actions (e.g., wars).

Thus, by looking at Nietzsche's account of the origin of pity, instead of solving our problem, now we are faced with one more problem. On the one hand, it is unclear why Mencius's elevation of compassion as a virtue is justified, if we don't buy his assertion that compassion makes us human; on the other, Nietzsche's explanation doesn't seem to work, either, especially in the early Confucian case.

Compassion as a Bond under the Modern Condition of the Society of Strangers

There is, in fact, a solution for both problems, and it is implied by my discussion of the political changes during Mencius's time, as well as Nietzsche's own description of pity as a modern virtue. That is, the introduction of compassion as a virtue addresses some pressing issues of modernity.

As I argued in chapter 1 and earlier in this chapter, a key feature of modernity is the emergence of large, populous, and well-connected societies, in which the social glue that was effective in the de facto small, close-knit communities of a handful of acquaintances no longer worked. A new social glue that could bond a world of strangers together was needed. Compassion as Mencius understood it fits this need, because it is a feeling that connects a person with a stranger. As analyzed earlier, in Mencius's thought experiment about the falling child, he made it clear that it is about how one feels when one

---

13. I thank Rethy for pointing this out to me.

suddenly sees this falling child. At that very moment, the child represents an innocent person almost on an abstract level. That is, he or she is not this or that particular child but just a stranger child. This is why the emergence of our compassion is "not to gain friendship with the child's parents, nor to seek the praise of their neighbors and friends" (*Mencius* 2A6). That is, any possibility of this child's being our acquaintance is blocked by the condition "suddenly," and the feeling that is conjured up is a feeling toward a total stranger. In another place, Mencius made it clear that an exemplary person is "humane toward the people, but isn't *qin* 親 toward them," and the latter feeling, *qin*— which is hard to translate but can be translated as "loving," "holding dear," and "being intimate"—is reserved for family members (7A45).[14] Thus, compassion and the humaneness that is built on it are for strangers. We can then further speculate that the introduction of compassion-based humaneness as a virtue is early Confucians' answer, intentionally or unintentionally, to the search for a bond for a society of strangers that emerged from the collapse of a feudalistic society.[15]

The idea that compassion is suitable to address a key issue under modern conditions has a strong explanatory power with regard to the history of Western thought as well. The ancient Greek world, compared to traditional China since the Qin dynasty or Europe since its modernity, consisted of city-states. The fact that these states were relatively small and the citizens of the same state were not strangers to one another is perhaps why in Plato's and Aristotle's works, compassion is not taken as a virtue. One important bond, if not *the* bond, for citizens of an ancient Greek state is friendship. This also explains the emphasis on friendship in the *Nicomachean Ethics*. But during the Hellenistic and Roman imperial times, when small and close-knit states evolved into states with a large and interconnected population, compassion was taken more and more seriously, which eventually lent a hand to the spread of Christianity. Here we can also see that the evolution from Judaism was essential for the ascent of Christianity. Judaism, a religion of a particular people in a relatively close-knit society, didn't emphasize compassion, whereas Christianity

14. Some uses of the concept of humaneness in the *Mencius* seem to differ from its use here. For example, Mencius claims, "the content of humaneness is to serve one's parents" (4A27) and "to be *qin* toward one's parents is humaneness" (7A15). But what he meant here is perhaps that the humaneness toward others comes or is nurtured from one's feeling toward parents. However we interpret these passages, what is clear is that compassion and humaneness have a dimension toward strangers.

15. To clarify, that compassion may have been an answer to the search for a bond in a society of strangers doesn't mean that it is the only possible answer. Other answers are examined in chapter 7.

did, which may be one of the reasons that it became a dominant religion in Roman imperial times. But following the establishment of a pyramid-like "feudal" structure that divided a large state into smaller communities and halted the development of societies of strangers, the spread of compassion as a virtue was contained. Nietzsche took note of this, because he claimed that "the Church rather slows down and blocks the passage of poison instead of accelerating it,"[16] which seems to be referring to the hierarchy and the Crusades, which partially preserved "aristocratic morality." Finally, this halt was broken during the European transition to modernity, where modern societies of strangers emerged and compassion was celebrated because of its function in such societies. This change was also noticed by Nietzsche, for he claimed that the freethinkers of his time, in "a truly modern state," "loath the Church, *not* its poison" (ibid). In fact, they "love the poison" (ibid). That is, the freethinkers of modernity loath the hierarchy of the Church and its religious wars but not its message of compassion.[17] Nietzsche keenly observed all these "symptoms" of antiquity and modernity, but he gave the wrong diagnoses. That is, that compassion became a key moral value is not due to a Jewish slave revolt of morality but a possible reaction from moral philosophy to the emergence of societies of strangers and a consequence of modernization.[18]

16. Nietzsche, section 9 of the First Essay in the *Genealogy* (1994), 21.

17. In section 5 of the preface in the *Genealogy*, Nietzsche included Kant in the earlier "premodern" philosophers who considered pity worthless. But he may have been misleading here. It is true that in the *Groundwork for the Metaphysics of Morals*, Kant maintained that to be beneficent because one's soul is sympathetically tuned and finds inner satisfaction in spreading joy has no true moral worth, although he considered it praiseworthy (4:398–99; Kant 1998, 11). In *The Metaphysics of Morals* (6:456–57; Kant 1991, 250–51), apparently he had low opinions of pity and compassion. But if we read both texts closely, we may realize that the reason for his low opinions is that pity, sympathy, or compassion means the kind of humanity that is located "merely in the *susceptibility*, given by nature itself, to feel joy and sadness in common with others" (ibid., 250). Sympathy so understood fails to achieve the necessity or the a priori status that Kant wishes for his moral philosophy. But one has an obligation to the kind of humanity that is located "in the *capacity* and the *will* to *share in others' feelings*" (ibid.; italics in the original). Thus, on the issue of sympathy, Kant, who is commonly recognized as a modern philosopher, was not really on the side of the ancients, whether ancient Greeks and Romans or those of the Middle Ages, but on that of the moderns.

18. This understanding of the role of compassion in society can also explain other phenomena in the development of philosophical ideas. For example, after reading an earlier version of a paper on which this section is based, the Buddhism scholar Yao Zhihua (姚治华) speculates that this understanding may be used to explain the fact that the Buddhist idea of compassion was introduced and developed in the Kushan empire, which was a large-sized, populous, and interconnected state, and not during its origin in a small kingdom.

Therefore, the introduction of compassion as a virtue by Mencius was an attempt to answer a key question during the Zhou-Qin transition to early modernity. It is true that Mencius never explicitly framed this transition in the way I have done in this book, and he wouldn't offer such a social or political explanation of the origin of compassion as a virtue. This kind of explanation is more in the spirit of another early Confucian philosopher, Xun Zi, who paid special attention to the social origin of morality,[19] and it was one of his pupils, Han Fei Zi the Legalist, a fierce critic of Confucians, who offered a more explicit account of the political changes of the times that resembles mine.[20] But we can still see clues of Mencius's awareness of the issue at stake. The passage 2A6 begins with his attempt to promote a government that practices policies that "cannot bear" the suffering of its people, which is built on a heart that cannot bear to see the suffering of others. The passage ends with his emphasis that the heart of compassion, if fully developed, can be sufficient to protect the whole world. Although it is not specified to which particular person Mencius presented his account, it is rather clear that it was the rulers of a state who were the intended audience. In many other places, it was very explicit that he was addressing a ruler. For example, in the *Mencius* 1A7, King Xuan of Qi implied that he wished to dominate "the world" (the world known to the Chinese) by force. Mencius refused to give any advice on this but suggested that one become a "true king," that is, the deserving leader of the world, by protecting the people. The king then asked if he could do it. Mencius mentioned a story of the king in which he revealed the seed of compassion, and argued that if he could expand it to his people and even the people of the whole world, he could become the "true king." From this dialogue, we can see that after the collapse of close-knit communities in feudal times, the lord of a state lost the motive to care for his people, most of whom were now total strangers, unlike the situation in the feudal age, when the lord would only interact with a handful of nobles who were his close relatives and friends. As a result, the lord retreated to his sheer self-interest and used it as the motivation to rule. Mencius, however, tried to use compassion as a new bond between the ruler and the people, and as a new motivation for a leader of state to rule his people.[21]

---

19. I thank John Berthrong for suggesting that my reading is Xunzian.

20. See Bai (2011) for a preliminary discussion of Han Fei Zi's appreciation of the nature of the Zhou-Qin transition.

21. I have argued that compassion is a possible bond among strangers, but in this paragraph, the focus is the bond between the rulers and the people. Empirically, although a definitive feature of "modernity" is the emergence of a society of strangers, yet for common people, much of their social environment is still relatively closed. In contrast, the kings in Mencius's time and rulers today have to face people who are mostly not their acquaintances. Normatively, early

Therefore, to address an issue of modernity—the search for a new social bond—may have been the hidden reason for Mencius to introduce compassion, or the reason for his teachings to gain traction later on in "modern" China. If this interpretation holds, then, the moral concept of compassion is primarily a political concept, and is an ethical one only in an instrumental sense. This means that it is not necessary for Mencius, Neo-Confucians, and twentieth-century overseas New Confucians to elevate the discourse on compassion to the level of moral metaphysics (although they can do so). That is, we don't have to argue that the heart of compassion is inborn and innate to human beings (the original goodness of human nature), as many of these Confucians have argued. All we need to argue is that it can become a moral value for human beings, and in a modern society of strangers, it can be used as a bond. Although Mencius and Xun Zi sharply differed from each other on whether the original nature of human beings is good or bad, they both agreed that human beings can and need to be good. Thus, my "Xunzian" explanation of the issue of why compassion should be a virtue resolves this divide between Mencius and Xun Zi by rendering it irrelevant in my political philosophical reading of Mencius and early Confucianism.

Post-Qin China as a Modern State of Strangers?

My reading is based on a key feature of the Zhou-Qin transition, that is, the emergence of a society of strangers. But the mainstream view of traditional China is that it is a society of acquaintances. The late sociologist Fei Xiaotong (费孝通) held this view (1998, 6–17), and it is also shared by many contemporary Chinese scholars. But it was against the social turmoil and wars after the fall of the last traditional dynasty that Fei observed the village society and concluded that it was a close-knit society of acquaintances in which people stayed in the same community generation after generation. The China after the communist revolution that gives people the same impression that Fei observed is a result of the above social turmoil and upheavals, developed to their extreme through Maoism over the first thirty years of the communist takeover.

Confucians distinguish between the common people and the rulers on the basis of whether one can expand care for strangers, and the rulers should be those who are capable of caring about strangers. That is, it is mostly the ideal rulers who shoulder the task of bonding strangers. Therefore, although the bond among all strangers is important, both empirically and normatively, the bond between rulers and subjects is a key aspect of the issue of bonding among strangers under modern conditions, and was also naturally a focus of Mencius's. For a more detailed discussion, see "Care-Based Neofeudal Hierarchy" in this chapter (below). I thank Reviewer #2 for pushing me to clarify this point.

During these upheavals, traditional institutions, political structures, and social networks were nearly completely destroyed. If we look into Chinese history, we see that when there was political stability and order, agricultural productivity increased and commerce developed. Only in political chaos and during constant warring were these lively communications interrupted. Thus, a society of acquaintances may not have been the normal state of traditional China; rather, it may have been the result of more than a hundred years of social and political turmoil. The claim that traditional Chinese societies were those of acquaintances may have been a mistaken projection of contemporary observations on the whole history of China.

Moreover, even if we accept the judgment that the economy of traditional China was agriculture-based, and its villages were societies of acquaintances that were mobile (moving from one area to another under pressure to find new farmable land or to find security during wartime) only at a rather slow pace, we should see that there were two major activities that promoted social mobility in traditional China: commercial and "industrial" activities (though the industrial ones may not have been as developed as they were in the European and American industrial revolution) and the mobility of government-appointed officials who were often not even allowed to take a post in their hometowns (in order to prevent cronyism and corruptions). We should see that, especially regarding the latter type of mobility, since the Qin dynasty, these officials had had to deal with a relatively large number of strangers, rather than the acquaintances one level lower in the feudalistic structure, as rulers and officials in the Western Zhou dynasty had. In fact, if this dual structure—in which there were communities of acquaintances on the level of common people and societies of strangers on the level of the political and commercial elite—existed in traditional China, not only does it not challenge my interpretation of the function of compassion in Mencius's thought, but it actually supports it. As I argued earlier in this section, the primary goal of Mencius's discussion of compassion was to offer a motive for rulers (kings in Mencius's time and emperors and Confucian scholar-officials in post-Qin traditional China) to take care of the affairs of countless strangers, an imminent issue when bonds in a feudalistic regime stopped being effective in the emerging society of strangers.

Of course, we must acknowledge the fact that the level of "strangeness" is not as high in traditional China as it is today. Even for businessmen and officials in traditional China living in cities, their economic base was still often in rural areas, and thus they couldn't sever the ties with the communities of acquaintances they grew up in. In contrast, the industrial revolution happened in or was a sign of late modernity, "modernity 2.0," as it was called in chapter 1. In an industrialized society, the mobility of people in the lower stratus increased tremendously compared to that in early modernity, and the "strange-ness" of late modernity was also more comprehensive than that in early mo-dernity, which was largely restricted to the commercial, social, and political elite. Nonetheless, the bond developed by Mencius for the society of strangers remains relevant.[22]

The Cultivation of Compassion: From What Is Near to the "Transcendent" and the "Eternal"

Therefore, the sentiment of care for strangers, or compassion, is (almost) uni-versal among all human beings, and it should be elevated to the status of a virtue, even the most important virtue, because it can serve as a bond in a society of strangers. Nevertheless, as analyzed at the beginning of this chapter, the force of Mencius's argument for the universality of this moral sentiment is partly due to his "trick" of asking us what our immediate emotional reactions are when we see someone in danger, for instance, but not whether we would act upon them. This sentiment, as any sentiment, may also lead us to act in ways that are morally suspicious. For example, we could show care toward those who don't deserve it, and our care for our family members may be so strong that we ignore the suffering of strangers. Thus, in order for compassion to be strong enough to lead us to truly moral actions, this universal "seed of humaneness" has to be "grown," as Mencius suggested in the latter half of 2A6. This growth includes both increasing compassion's strength and guiding it toward morally right actions. In the following section, I will discuss how to grow this seed.

Self and Family as the Training Ground of Humaneness

Although Confucius didn't offer an argument for the universality of compas-sion, what he said in a passage in the *Analects* can be taken as the principle of moral cultivation: "to take as analogy what is near at hand can be called the method of humaneness" (6.30). That is, we should start with what is nearest

22. This change can explain another puzzle. As we saw in chapter 2, early Confucians advo-cated the idea of education for all. As a result, the educational level in traditional China was rather high compared with other societies. But it was dwarfed by the educational level in indus-trialized societies, for in an industrialized society, the need to move to a new place and to work in a factory demands basic education for all, whereas in spite of the Confucian advocacy, in traditional China, where the majority of the people work in small villages, to be literate and to be able to speak a common language is not that necessary. This explanation is partially suggested by Fei Xiaotong (1998, 6–17).

to us as a stepping-stone for our moral cultivation and expansion. What is nearest to oneself is one's own self, and what belongs to one's self. Mencius offered good illustrations on how the self and its possessions are important to moral cultivation. As mentioned in chapter 2, according to Mencius, stable ownership of private properties is crucial for the common people to have a "stable heart" or "character," as today's virtue ethicists call it (1A7 and 3A3). Common people's moral capacities may be limited; their goodness may not be strong enough to resist the challenges encountered in a materially deprived life, which Mencius clearly indicates in 1A7 and 3A3. Another reason for this limitation, which he didn't specify here but is more related to Confucius's principle of moral expansion through analogy, may have been that owning property helps us understand others' need of the same, and thus may help us be truly generous toward others, whereas in a communist society, there is no true generosity because nothing belongs to anyone.[23] Mencius was explicit about this reasoning in another place (1B5). A king of a state confessed to Mencius that he had weaknesses (literally "illnesses"): he was fond of money and women. Mencius pointed out that some good kings in the past were also fond of money and women, but these were not a problem because they shared their fondness with the people, making sure that, in the case of the desire for companionship, there were "neither girls pining for a husband nor men without a wife." What is implied in this passage is that without the king's own fondness of women—a private interest—he would not be able to understand the interest of his people, or the public interest.[24]

But understanding one's own needs is merely a necessary condition in taking care of others' needs. Compassion leads us outward, expanding our self-love toward others. For this to work, we need to grow our inborn compassion. A unique place to cultivate it is in the family, for on the one hand, family is a universal institution. Even an orphan, if he or she grows up, has to have a family, a group of people raising him or her.[25] Family is what most people feel

23. Aristotle actually made this argument in his *Politics* (1262b1–6), but Confucians could happily accept it.

24. This account poses an interesting contrast to Immanuel Kant's. In one of the examples in which he discussed how an action can have moral worth, Kant said that if a man is overshadowed by his own grief, which extinguishes all his sympathy for the fate of others, or if by nature he is cold and indifferent to the suffering of others (and if it brings no material benefit to him), the philanthropic action that he commits then has "its genuine moral worth" because it must have come from his sense of moral duty (1998, 12–13; 4:398–99).

25. Thus, the family that Confucians value is not necessarily one's biological family but the family that raises the person in question. Indeed, as clearly suggested by a later Confucian, Dong Zhongshu (董仲舒) (179 BCE to 104 BCE), if a biological father abandons his duty to raise his son, the son owes filial piety to the adoptive father and not to the biological father, or to a very

akin to and have a loving feeling for, almost as natural as one's self-love. On the other hand, the care for family members is also the first step in going beyond one's mere self and self-love and going toward others. This is perhaps why Confucians pay so much attention to family relations. Many misunderstand this as an unreflective and thus unphilosophical expression of familialism, that is, putting family's interests above all others', as embodied in the godfather's motto "never go against the family," which is natural and still prevalent, especially in many rural and somewhat autonomous societies. But the Confucian reason for emphasizing familial love is that it is naturally the first step in our path toward moral expansion. This rationale is explicitly stated in the *Analects*:

> It is a rare thing for someone who is filial to his parents and respectful to his older brothers to defy superiors. And it is unheard of for those who do not defy superiors to be keen on initiating rebellion. Exemplary persons [jun zi] concentrate their efforts on the root, for the root having taken hold, the Way will grow therefrom. Being filial to one's parents and being respectful to one's older brothers is the root of humaneness! (1.2)

Answering someone's worry about having no brother, a good pupil of Confucius pointed out that to be an exemplary person means to have everyone in the world as his brother (12.5), presumably by expanding the filial and brotherly love to people in the whole world. In the discussion of *zheng ming* (正名), "making the name right," a crucial political teaching in the *Analects*, there is a clear analogy between the father-son relationship and the ruler-subject relationship (12.11). It has become rather clear through these passages that communal and political relations are analogous to and should be modeled after familial relations, and the state, even the whole world, is an enlarged family. The devotion to the enlarged family is developed from the devotion to the natural family.

Mencius was fully with Confucius on this point. As he put it,

> Treat the elderly of my own family [as they should be], and extend this treatment to the elderly of other families; treat the young of my own family [as they should be], and extend this to the young of other families ... Thus extending one's humaneness outward can protect everyone within the Four Seas [the alleged boundaries of the world], and not extending one's humaneness cannot even protect one's wife and children. (*Mencius* 1A7)[26]

---

limited extent at best. See the extant text of Dong's *Chun Qiu Jue Yu* (春秋決獄) (e.g., S. Cheng 1963, 164). See Loewe (2009) for an English translation.

26. There are some subtle but significant differences between the *Analects* and the *Mencius*.

Thus, the Confucian emphasis on the centrality of family should be distinguished from familialism because expansion is key to the former. But some (especially the twentieth-century Chinese antitraditionalists) argue that the Confucian emphasis on family is to produce obedient subjects by cultivating filial piety at home and then projecting it to blind loyalty to the ruler. This is clearly a misinterpretation because the familial care early Confucians emphasized is explicitly mutual, and the ruler-subject relationship is also one of reciprocity. If early Confucians had really intended to use familial care to produce loyal subjects, they would have presented both relationships (son-father and subject-ruler) as one-directional (from son to father and from subject to ruler).[27] But it cannot be denied that there are far more discussions of filial piety than parents' care for the children in early Confucian classics. A reasonable and charitable explanation is this: Parents' care for their children seems to be rather natural in the sense that maybe out of evolutionary or animalistic instinct, parents have a strong natural tendency to care for their young, whereas adult children's care for their parents is not that instinctual and natural. The Confucian emphasis on familial care is intended to push human beings to go beyond one's instinctual emotions, and it is then only natural to pay more attention to the not-so-natural care for the parents.

Transcendence through Family

If one keeps expanding it, eventually one's care will embrace everything in the universe. This ideal is beautifully illustrated by a later Confucian thinker, Zhang Zai (张载) (1020–77), in his famous "Western Inscription":

Heaven [*qian* 乾] is called my father and Earth [*kun* 坤] is called my mother. And I, this tiny thing, find an intimate place in their midst. . . .

Both texts seem to follow the method of starting from what is near and paying special attention to the family. But Mencius introduced the idea of the innate goodness of human beings, which is lacking in the *Analects*. Then, in the case of Mencius, it seems that family and the private sphere only offer a "near at hand" environment for the original goodness to grow, and he paid far more attention to the cultivation starting from the self. In contrast, in the case of the *Analects*, the focal point of moral cultivation seems to be the family, and it leaves open the question about whether this natural kinship is a fact of human life, or it has a metaphysical root or not. The *Analects* is thus less metaphysical than the *Mencius* on this issue.

27. For the former, see 13.18. For the latter, see 3.19. For both, see 12.11. In chapter 51 of the *Han Fei Zi* (a Legalist text that is highly critical of Confucians), which is titled "Loyalty and Filial Piety," the relations are indeed one-directional, and it may be justified to say that this chapter or the Legalists in general, but not the Confucians, are promoting a subject's blind obedience to the ruler through a son's blind obedience to the father.

Hence, what fills Heaven and Earth is my body, and what directs Heaven and Earth is my nature. All people are my siblings, and all things are my companions. The great ruler is the eldest son of my parents, and his ministers are his retainers. To respect those great in years is the way to treat the elderly as [the] elderly [should be treated]. To be loving to the orphaned and the weak is the way to treat the young as [the] young [should be treated]. . . . All in the world who are tired, infirm, crippled, or sick; brotherless, childless, widows or widowers—they are all my siblings who are helpless and have no one else to appeal to. . . .

Riches, honor, good fortune, and abundance shall enrich my life, while poverty, humble station, care, and sorrow shall discipline me to fulfillment. In life I follow and serve [Heaven and Earth], and in death I shall be at peace.[28]

We can see from this passage that the ideal of universal love is both ethically and politically significant. It is ethically significant because it brings great peace to the person who achieves it. It is politically significant because if one governs with this universal compassion, as Mencius stated in 2A6, "one can run the world (tian xia) as rolling it on one's palm." That is, finally, the bond for a society of strangers is found.

In addition to its crucial role in the "spatial" expansion of care, family also introduces a temporal dimension into moral cultivation. An individual's life is limited, and through his or her family, through his or her ancestors and descendants, he or she gains a kind of transcendence and eternity.[29] This transcendence is not external to the individual, as he or she is part of this transcendence. The eternity through family can answer the problem of death, a key philosophical problem ("philosophical" in the sense of eternal and universal), because one can overcome death (to some extent) through the eternity gained through family. The temporal and spatial dimensions of human care also

28. The translation is mine. For the Chinese version, see Z. Zhang (1978, 62–63). For other English translations, see W. Chan (1969, 497–98) and Bryan Van Norden's translation, which is available online at http://facultysites.vassar.edu/brvannor/Phil210/Translations/Western%20Inscription.pdf.

29. To be clear, the "Western Inscription" passage, Zhang Zai's philosophy, and Neo-Confucianism in general often imply, or are interpreted as, a form of moral metaphysics. But the transcendence and eternity discussed in this chapter are meant to be naturalistic. There is no assumption of metaphysical or mystical cosmic order. Transcendence and eternity are a natural result of expansion from family. Indeed, the following interpretation of Christianity and God is also conducted from a functional point of view. One *can* give a "thicker," metaphysical reading of all these, but I will stick with a thin, naturalistic, and functional reading of transcendence and eternity in this chapter. I thank Reviewer #2 for pushing me to clarify this point.

address a key demand in moral philosophy: to transcend the mere self and the rational calculation of self-interest. Moral philosophy, concerned with what human beings ought to do, often presupposes this transcending because "ought" in most moral philosophy is understood differently from "is," from what human beings are and are actually doing. In many schools of Western philosophy and Abrahamic religions, both the philosophical problem of death and the need of a moral philosophy to transcend the mere self are answered through Being, God, or Being-like or God-like figures. Thus, in these regards, we can say that in Confucianism, family is the counterpart to Being or God in these traditions.[30]

Since eternity is achieved through and internal to family, and history is a record of families and other human interactions, for Confucians (and for Confucianism-influenced traditional Chinese societies), history is associated with things eternal and transcendent. Moreover, for Confucians, wisdom and principles are shown through history, and thus history is also related to reason and the pursuit of truth. This poses an interesting contrast to the Western philosophical term "historicism," which emphasizes historical contingencies and is understood as the opposite to the eternal, the true, the transcendent, and the divine. This is perhaps related to the fact that for many Western philosophers, eternity is related to Being or God, and in comparison, history must be condemned to the changing world of becoming. In this understanding, the pursuit of truth cannot be done through the study of history but through logic, metaphysics, or other kinds of "first philosophy," whereas for Confucians, history offers the "empirical a priori" and helps us to grasp being through becoming.

The Restraints on Self-Interest through Family Values

On a less abstract level, if one can expand one's care through family, it means that even if one is merely rational, one's behaviors would change. If the unit of calculation is the individual, he or she would have a hard time resisting the

30. See Sun (2014a) and Sheng (2008 and 2010) for similar discussions. Sun Xiangchen (孙向晨) elaborates on the corresponding roles between God in Christianity and family in Confucianism. He also argues that after God was declared to be dead by Nietzsche, Heidegger tried to discover the meaning of life through the end point of an individual's life, which is death. In the sense that Heidegger's maneuver is a reaction to the "death" of God, his philosophy is still related to Christianity and is "theological." More importantly, the idea that the death of the individual marks the end of his or her life is challenged by the Confucian understanding of the individual. According to the latter, one's existence and meaning are enlarged spatially and temporally through the family, and thus the death of an individual is not the end of his or her life and meaning.

temptation to do whatever it takes for his or her immediate interests, or to resist the attitude of "Après moi, le deluge" (After me, the flood; a famous line allegedly said by Louis XV of France). In contrast, Chinese economist Sheng Hong (盛洪) has elaborated on the different economic behaviors and their merits if the unity of rational calculation is changed to family.[31] One very clear implication when one calculates on the basis of family is that one would do long-term planning rather than making merely short-term decisions, for one would consider the material consequences of one's actions to the ancestors and descendants (a consideration that would be very handy, for example, in the case of environmental issues), and one would also consider whether one's actions would bring honor or shame to one's ancestors and descendants, the consequences of which will not cease to exist after one's death. In sum, as it is well put in the *Analects* by a good pupil of Confucius, Master Zeng (曾子), "Treat the death [of one's parents] with care and keep remembering those who are long gone, and the morals of the people will be thickened" (1.9).

Moreover, the idea that history can be used as a check to the natural human tendency to be self-interested can and should be embodied through institutions. In traditional China, the extended family had a "communal" family shrine, where the ancestors were memorialized and the good members of the extended family were honored. Although extended families are disappearing now, we can still practice these kinds of activities in nuclear families. We need to update the practices by, for example, including women in them. There should be a book of family history that records both the paternal and maternal lineages, and memorial tablets for ancestors from both sides as well. If the parents have only one daughter, she will carry all these items with her when she is married, and they will be enshrined in the new family. These are examples of changes that should (and can) be made.[32] But the general idea that

31. Sheng (2008 and 2012). For a criticism of Sheng (2008), see Zhiwu Chen (2008). In addition to giving some theoretical analyses, Sheng Hong tries to argue that the family-based rational calculation was a characteristic of traditional Chinese societies. Chen's criticism is partially focused on the empirical side of Sheng's article. But a serious problem with Chen's challenge is to use experiences of contemporary Chinese societies to challenge Sheng's claims about traditional Chinese societies. This can be a mistaken comparison though, because China has gone through some radical breaks with traditional Chinese societies, and it may have been completely wrong-headed to project one's observations of today's Chinese societies onto the traditional ones, a mistake often committed by antitradition Chinese "liberals." More importantly, my concern is normative, and I would stay away from the complex reality of traditional Chinese societies. Therefore, even if Chen's empirical criticism stands, it wouldn't affect the normative force of Sheng's (and my) argument.

32. Confucianism is often criticized as being androcentric, if not misogynistic, and it can be

through family one can broaden one's vision remains the same and is relevant. Other political and institutional arrangements that encourage these kinds of family values should also be in place, for example, certain birth, marriage, and death rituals that are intended to strengthen the sense of family should be promoted. There are many historical examples and interpretations that we can draw from traditional China and Confucian classics, and naturally, they need to be updated as well.

On a national level, there are also practices that still remain relevant. For example, in certain traditional Chinese regimes, under the Confucian influence, there were court historians who would record the words and actions of the emperor, and a deceased emperor would be given posthumous names (*shi hao* [谥号] or *miao hao* [庙号]) that were meant to be a judgment of his administration.[33] In an ideal regime (such as the Confucian hybrid regime), then, these practices could still be preserved in spirit. There could be independent offices of historical records that would record the words and actions of elected and selected politicians, and each administration would be given a *shi hao*, a one-word description and judgment by some offices after the administration steps down for a certain "grace period."[34]

Although we have drawn our inspirations from traditional Chinese practices and Confucian reasoning, the underlying rationale is not particular to the Chinese or Confucianism, as long as we acknowledge the idea that the familial and historical dimensions can strengthen people's long-term perspectives, and they are good for good governance, which is considered an ultimate good in politics. They can be abstract or minimalistic, so that people with different comprehensive doctrines can endorse them by their own readings.

For example, the American political theorist Jeffrey Green has offered his own criticisms of present representative democracy, or what he calls the "vocal model" (2011). Many of his criticisms actually resonate with those of mine offered in chapter 3 of this book. As an alternative to the vocal model, he proposes an "ocular model," or "plebiscitary democracy." In this model, the critical ideal is candor, which means "the institutional requirement that lead-

challenged whether the above changes can be made. I will address this issue in chapter 6 (under "A Confucian Argument for Gender Equality"). For now, let us simply assume that a progressive reading of Confucianism can endorse the above attempts to make the family-based practices gender-equal.

33. I was inspired by the discussions in Sheng (2008 and 2010).

34. To adapt these traditional Chinese practices to more diverse political arenas in the contemporary world, there can be more than one office, and they can sometimes offer competing versions of the records and "posthumous" names.

ers not be in control of the conditions of their publicity" (ibid., 13). The offices of historical records and the practice of *shi hao* giving can be two institutions that satisfy the plebiscitary requirement of candor.

In short, the aforementioned updated practices are meant to be political in the sense that they are not limited to one people, one culture, or people of one particular comprehensive doctrine, and they are a part of the overlapping consensus of a pluralistic and liberal society that nevertheless takes good governance as a primary goal.[35]

The Hierarchy of Universal Care

Hierarchical Care

As I have argued, compassion is introduced as a bond in a society of strangers. The issue of a bond in a political entity is a crucial political issue. But one can criticize the Mencian idea of universal compassion by making an accusation that is the polar opposite to the one that confuses the Confucian emphasis on familiar care with familialism. That is, one can argue that this Mencian idea fails to distinguish those within a political entity and those without, and thus it cannot be used to justify any in-group identity (such as patriotism). This is a simple misunderstanding of the Mencian ideal, because the Mencian ideal of universal care should be distinguished from the universal love allegedly held by the Mohist school and by certain readings of Christianity, or the French Revolution, communism, or some egalitarian idea of fraternity. For Mencius, even if one could achieve the stage of universal care, an extreme rarity among human beings, the care should be graded and hierarchical (愛有差等). It is natural and justified for one to care about close relations more, such as trying to save his or her drowning mother before saving anyone (or anything) else. According to Mencius, the Mohists advocated the idea of universal and equal care, and he argued that this view "amounts to a denial of one's father" (*Mencius* 3B9). Rather, as quoted earlier in this chapter, Mencius claimed,

> an exemplary person is sparing with things [or not wasting things; 愛], but is not humane toward them; he is humane toward the people, but isn't holding them dear (*qin* 親). He is holding his parents dear but is [merely] humane toward the people; he is humane toward the people but is [merely] sparing with things. (7A45)

35. I will come back to the issue of the possibility and necessity of this kind of arrangement in a pluralistic and liberal society in the following chapters.

Wang Yangming (王阳明; 1472–1528), one of the most important later Confucians who was greatly influenced by Mencius, illustrated this universal but hierarchical and graded care nicely. According to the *Record of Instructions* (传习录),

> [s]omeone asked, "A great man and an object are one [which was, as we saw in the discussion in the section 'The Cultivation of Compassion' earlier in this chapter, the ideal of the expansion of care], but why does [the Confucian classic] *The Great Learning* also say that something is favored [literally, the Chinese term *hou* (厚) means 'thick'] and something is not [literally, the Chinese word *bo* (薄) means 'thin']?" The master [Wang Yangming] said, "In principle, there are naturally something favored and something not. For example, body is one, but [if there is a danger,] hands and feet are used to protect head and face. Does this mean that hands and feet are not favored? This is how it should be. We love both beasts and plants, but the heart can bear to use plants to feed beasts. We love both human beings and beasts, but the heart can bear to slaughter beasts to feed family, to make sacrifices, and to treat guests. We love both the closest kin and people in the street [i.e., strangers]. But if there is little food and soup, one can survive if one gets it and will die if one does not, and the food is not enough to save two, the heart can bear to save the closest kin and not the person in the street. This is how it should be. When it gets to my body and the closest kin, we cannot make distinctions anymore. For to treat people humanely and to treat things lovingly comes from this [love of one's own body and closest kin]. If one can bear [to do anything] here, one can bear [to do anything] anywhere." (1992, 108; my translation)

Care-Based Neofeudal Hierarchy

Another challenge to the Mencian idea of universal care is that it is too demanding, especially with regard to the common people. But as we saw in the discussion of his "elitist" side in chapter 2, for Mencius, there is a hierarchy among people with regard to the level of proper care that they can achieve. The majority of the people, the masses, simply can't expand their care too far out and apply it properly to others. Their care might be only adequate to maintain their families and maybe the close neighbors, and thus to maintain a good social order within their communities. If there are some who can expand their care to take care of a community, they should become community leaders. We can then continue to move to higher and higher levels, and a Mencian would thus reestablish a pyramid-like "neofeudal" order that is based on one's compassion and the intellectual and political capacities of taking care of others.

This is a "*neo*feudal order" because the ruling structure is not based on birth, as it was in the case of feudalism, but it is based on one's capacity to care. The determination of one's capacity for taking care of others would be done in the way that is suggested in chapters 2 and 3.[36] With the Mencian project so understood, we can say that early Confucians are indeed "reactionary" in that they are trying to reestablish a feudal order, but it is actually a bottom-up, merits-based reinvention of the "feudal order." Thus, the task of expanding one's care to the whole state and even to the whole world is only for the few and not for the masses. The hierarchical requirements are nicely expressed in the *Zhong Yong*, which was quoted earlier in chapter 2. Let me quote it again here:

> The Way of the exemplary person [jun zi] is everywhere yet hidden. Man and wife of simple intelligence can know it, and yet in its utmost reaches, there is something that even the sage does not know. Man and wife of no moral character can put it into practice, and yet in its utmost reaches there is something that even the sage is not able to put into practice. . . . The Way of [the] exemplary person has its simple beginnings in [proper relations between] man and woman, but in its utmost reaches, it is clearly seen in Heaven and Earth. (chap. 12, my translation; see W. Chan 1969, 100)

In this hierarchical, neofeudal structure, the ruling class, conforming to the Confucian ideal and developing their compassion to the extreme, bonds together countless communities of acquaintances that follow proper relations within families and small communities. This solves the problem of the social bond within a large state of strangers. Thus, both those who argue that Confucianism, due to its emphasis on morality, is applicable only to societies of acquaintances and those who argue that the Mencian requirement of universal care is too demanding are mistaken.

Effectiveness of Compassion

But even with regard to the exemplary people who can cultivate their compassion much better than the masses, one can still doubt the effectiveness of compassion. It can be argued that familial care is too weak, and is being constantly diluted in the process of being expanded, so much so that it can't serve as a bond among strangers (Fei 1998, 24–30; Zhao 2007a and 2007b). An idea implicit in this challenge is that the expansion of compassion is through an almost mechanical process from the self to outer circles step-by-step. Then, in the circles very far from the center of the Confucian concentric circles of

---

36. I thank Reviewer #2 for pushing me to clarify this point.

moral expansion, the residue compassion would be too weak to serve as a bond. But this mechanical picture of expanding circles of care is mistaken. For example, in the *Mencius* 1A7, it is recorded that King Xuan of Qi couldn't bear to see an ox being slaughtered for a sacrificial ceremony. In this story, in order to feel compassion toward the ox, it is not the case that the king tried to recall the care of his family and then expanded it to his neighbors, and so on, all the way to the animal—this would indeed be ridiculous! Rather, when he saw this ox, he said, "Spare it. I cannot bear to see it shrinking with fear, like an innocent man going to the place of execution." That is, seeing the innocence and helplessness of the ox directly conjured up the horrible image of an innocent man being killed and the distress that the king would feel in this situation. This is another meaning of Confucius's claim of "finding an analogy near at hand" (*Analects* 6.30): we should be able to connect what we strongly feel directly with the intended object of our emotion rather than mechanically going through all the "intermediate" steps. Indeed, what is crucial to a Confucian exemplary person is to pay attention to the object of compassion that is not easily in our vision, and then make a direct connection between what we easily feel compassion for and the object in question.

Another challenge related to the effectiveness of compassion concerns whether it is possible to bond strangers with compassion, especially in an industrialized and globalized society in which even common people have to face strangers often. In fact, during the SAWS, the Chinese philosopher Han Fei Zi argued that the compassion among people was too weak to bond a state together, and what was effective were institutions and laws that were based on reward and punishment, a "banner" that every human being could easily bow down to.[37] In my view, Confucians should and do accept the necessity of institutions and laws. In fact, Confucius explicitly said, "If punishments are not proper, the common people will not know how to put their hands and feet" (*Analects* 13.3). That is, common people are not regulated by compassion or virtue but by political and legal institutions. The reason for this has something to do with Confucians' low expectation of common people, as discussed in chapter 2. But directly before the line quoted above, Confucius also said, "If rites and music [which are commonly understood as the embodiment of humaneness and morality in general] do not flourish, punishments will not be proper" (ibid.). That is, legal institutions should embody morality, and it is the job of the "great people" to see to this. Meanwhile, laws and institutions cannot regulate every aspect of people's lives, especially in a complex society. On

37. This idea can be found throughout the *Han Fei Zi* (see, in particular, chap. 49). For an incomplete translation of this book (that nevertheless contains chap. 49 in its entirety), see Watson (1964).

the matters that are outside of legal regulations, for example, seeing an old lady carrying heavy bags, we need to have compassion to motivate us to help her. This is hardly a demanding requirement even for a "small person." In short, the Confucian virtue of compassion is still significant even in the contemporary form of a society of strangers, because it is compatible with—and can serve both as the foundation of and supplement to—laws and institutions.

6

Conflict in the Expansion of Care

THE PRIVATE VERSUS THE PUBLIC

The Issue of the Private versus the Public

As we saw in chapter 5, for Confucians, there is a continuity between what is "near at hand" and what is far away, and our care for the latter is rooted in our care for the former. Using a pair of concepts that are commonly used in moral philosophy, we can say that for Confucians, there is a continuity between the private and the public. But clearly, there are also conflicts between them. From the idea of hierarchical care, we can argue that the Confucian can solve the conflicts by rank-ordering different duties, making one yield to the other. The passage from Wang Yangming that was quoted near the end of chapter 5 offered an example of this. Still, we can imagine that there are more complex cases of the conflict of duties than Wang's example, and the Confucian picture of expanding hierarchical care presupposes the possibility of harmoniously rank-ordering the conflicting duties. Therefore, we need to look into more cases of the conflict between the private and the public to show the viability of what I call the "Confucian continuum and harmony model."

Moreover, how to deal with relations between the private and the public is also a universal issue in moral philosophy. As I argue in this chapter, early Confucians were aware of the conflict between the private and the public, but their solution was to identify and develop the constructive aspect of the private and use what was cultivated from the private to suppress the conflict. Contrary to Confucians, Plato's *Republic*, for example, offers to suppress the private almost completely for the sake of the public. Thinkers such as John Stuart Mill and most late modern and contemporary Western liberal thinkers have switched their focus and are primarily concerned with how to protect the private against intrusions from the public. In contrast, early Confucians and Plato (in the *Republic*) were primarily concerned with intrusions to the public good from the private. But both Plato and modern liberals insist on the sheer divide between the private and the public. To look further into how early Confucians addressed the issue of the conflict between the private and the public may shed light on the universal philosophical issue of the private versus the public. With a fuller understanding of the Confucian rationale on this issue, we can then apply the Confucian idea of expanding care to other political and moral issues.

Before beginning these discussions, some clarification on the concepts of the private and the public may be helpful.[1] It should be noted that these two concepts are relative.[2] The private is what is one's own, and the public is what is beyond one's own. But "one's own" has some indeterminacy. If we take the interest of one person as private, the interest of his or her family or extended family can be taken as a form of public interest. But with regard to the interest of a community that is not merely based on kinship, one's own family's interest should be regarded as a private interest. Again, the interest of one's own community can be considered private with regard to the interest of a collection of communities or the interest of the state. Thus, in the Confucian expanding picture of care, we can say that Confucians urge us to keep enlarging the private sphere and then transcending it, until we can embrace the whole, including everything in the world.

However, in spite of the relative nature of the private and the public, it seems that it takes little effort, perhaps no effort at all, for human beings to be self-interested ("self" here means the individual person), and for the majority of people, it takes a little more effort, but it is still quite natural ("natural" in the sense of "effortless," through either natural affinity to or the nurturing and supportive environment of one's own family or extended family) to develop a

1. I wish to thank Loy Hui-chieh for pushing me to clarify these two concepts, James Peterman for emphasizing Mill's different understanding of these two concepts, and Hao Changchi (郝长墀) and especially Zhou Xuanyi (周玄毅) for helping me to see the relative nature of these two concepts.

2. Guo and Chen (2009) offer a detailed discussion of the original meanings of these two concepts and the Confucian renderings of them in pre-Qin China. They also point out the relative nature of these two concepts in Chinese history, especially under the pyramid-like, multileveled feudal system of the Western and Eastern Zhou dynasties (roughly from 1150 BCE to 249 BCE). Originally, one denotation of the Chinese word for "the public," gong (公), is the "superior," while the corresponding denotation of the Chinese word for "the private," si (私), is the "inferior" (thus, who represents gong depends on which level of the pyramid we are concerned with). But, as I mentioned, this structure was disappearing during the Eastern Zhou period, and was replaced by more centralized governments. Gradually, gong was associated only with the state (and its sole ruler), while the private with individual subjects. See also Q. Chen (2008), and Q. Guo (2008b).

concern with the interest of the family. Thus, although what is private is relative, one's own self-interest and one's own family's interest are often taken as
private. That is, they are often the primary sources of private interests, in spite
of the relative nature of what is taken as private interest. But as I argued in
chapter 5, we should also see that the interest of family, including the interest
of other family members apart from one's self, is the first step for a person to
go beyond the narrow interest of the individual self and to be concerned with
others. The double features of one's family interest, often "naturally" considered one's own (private) on the one hand,[3] and being the first step to go
beyond the private in its narrowest and most "natural" (most effortless) sense
on the other, together with the fact that, as I argued in chapter 5, family is a
universal institution that is available to anyone, explain why Confucians emphasize family relations.

With these two key concepts clarified, I first take a look at how early Confucians (again, the primary texts the discussion is based on are the *Analects* and
the *Mencius*) dealt with the conflict between the private and the public, especially between the family and the state, and then take a look at how the *Republic* dealt with this issue. We will see that the *Republic* puts more emphasis on
the conflict between personal interest, broadly construed, and public interest,
while the *Analects* and the *Mencius* place greater emphasis on the continuity
between the two.

Early Confucians' Solutions

Conflict and Harmony between the Private and the Public

Confucius and early Confucians were (painfully) aware of the conflict between the private and the public, because it was mirrored precisely in the
chaos of their times. The unity and the common interest of the Zhou dynasty
(the public) were increasingly challenged by the growing powers of its vassal
states (the private); the unity and the common good of each vassal state (the
public) were increasingly challenged by the growing powers of its noble families (the private), whose heads often served as ministers of the feudal state;
and the unity and the common good of the noble families (the public) were
increasingly threatened by ambitious lesser lords (the private) who served
them, and so on. When he was a minister of the state of Lu, Confucius was
obsessed with reducing the powers of the three most powerful noble families—who had usurped the power of the ruler of the state—and restoring the

---

3. I put "naturally" in scare quotes because the term here shouldn't be understood as carrying any a priori, metaphysical necessity.

proper relations between the private and the public, a fact to which the later Confucian Mencius explicitly referred (Qian 2002, 30–38).

Recognizing the distinction and the conflict between the private and the public, and seeing the conflict between them gone wild on every level, however, Confucius (in the *Analects*) and Mencius (in the *Mencius*) also discovered a constructive aspect of the private (constructive to the public good), that is, the care that can be expanded outward, which was discussed in chapter 5. In other words, Confucius and Mencius also discovered the continuity between the private and the public. For example, in the *Analects*, when Confucius was asked why he was not employed in governing (holding a public office), which might have been a ridicule of his being a political busybody, he replied,

> [t]he *Book of Documents* says: "Oh filial conduct! Just being filial to your parents and befriending your brothers, and applying this to governing [politics]." This is also employed in governing [or involved in politics]. Why do I have to be employed in governing [in a narrow sense, in order to be involved in politics in a broader sense]? (2.21)

As quoted near the end of chapter 2 in this book, a passage in the early Confucian classic *Zhong Yong* (中庸) states, "the Way of [the] exemplary person has its simple beginnings in [the relations between] man and wife," and even common men and women can know and practice it (chap. 12).

To deal with the conflict between the private and the public with the above insight, instead of suppressing or even abolishing the private for the sake of the public, early Confucians argued that we could develop the constructive aspect of the private, so that we could eventually use this aspect to suppress the destructive and conflicting aspect of the private and embrace the public. But the issue is whether our care for the private and for the public can be reconciled in our attempt to expand our care. The Confucian proposal to address the conflict between the private and public through expanding care presupposes the possibility of reconciliation.

The Mutual Concealment Case in the Analects 13.18

Early Confucians understood the issue at stake, and answered it in their own ways. In the famous mutual concealment case in the *Analects* 13.18, a local magistrate boasted to Confucius that the upright person in his village was someone who bore witness against his father, who had stolen a sheep. Confucius replied by saying that the upright people in his (ideal?) village would behave differently in that a father would cover for his son, and a son would cover for his father.

How to understand this passage and other related passages has been hotly debated among scholars in contemporary China.[4] Some argue that these passages show that Confucianism is a conspirator of authoritarianism, if not despotism, and it is the root cause of the lack of the rule of law and the rampant corruption in traditional and contemporary China. This has been a typical line of understanding since the antitradition New Culture and May Fourth movements. But it is a rather crude, superficial, and wrong understanding of these texts. In this sense these criticisms don't deserve the attention that they have received. But sadly, they have represented the popular understanding of Confucianism among many contemporary Chinese who are brainwashed in the antitraditional political, social, and educational environments, and they also resonate with the bias against Chinese culture held by many Westerners. Therefore, I must respond to these interpretations throughout this chapter.

The first thing that a careful reader of passage 13.18 should notice is that Confucius was talking about *mutual* concealment, that is, the father covering for his son and the son covering for his father. This is a clear debunking of the typical antitraditionalist reading that Confucianism, by advocating a one-directional piety of the son to the father, helped to promote the absolute power of the emperor over his subjects. But the care Confucius was advocating in 13.18 is clearly bidirectional.

Second, as I illustrated in chapter 1, a crucial characteristic of early Confucian texts, especially the *Analects*, is their contextual nature. By failing to understand this and not paying close attention to the text, some believe that Confucius was saying that family (private) interest *always* trumps public interest.[5] But we shouldn't ignore the simple fact that Confucius and the magistrate were discussing a case of stealing a sheep, not a heinous crime like murder.[6] How Confucius or early Confucians would deal with the latter kind of case remains to be seen.

However petty the crime, there is still a clear conflict between familiar care and the duty to justice in the public interest. It seems that in the case of petty crimes such as stealing a sheep, Confucius put the mutual familial care above

4. Q. Guo (2004 and 2011) has collected many essays in this debate. For discussions in English, see the articles in the special issue of the journal *Dao: A Journal of Comparative Philosophy* 6, no. 1 (March 2007).

5. As I said, these readers don't really deserve serious scholarly responses, but because their claims are so outrageous, they have received much attention, which some of them use to show how important their works are. I won't perpetuate this cynical abuse of scholarship, and I try not to refer to their articles. But they can easily be found in the aforementioned anthologies and the special issue of the journal *Dao*.

6. H. Wang (2011) argues that sheep-stealing in the state in which the magistrate resided was a capital crime. I don't agree. I will come back to this point later in this chapter.

the public interest. But clearly, what Confucius supported was *yin* (隐), which is usually taken to mean "covering up."[7] Thus, he didn't suggest that the son or the father facilitated the crime in any way but, in the context of the conversation with the magistrate—who wanted his village people to testify against their close kin—he may have simply suggested that they refuse to testify. Even in today's American legal system, a spouse can legally refuse to testify against his or her spouse in many situations, and what Confucius and early Confucians defended was merely to extend the privilege to father-and-son relations.

The defense in the last paragraph means that the violation of the duty to the public is not as serious as it first appears. Still, is there anything that, according to Confucius, one should do to fulfill one's duties to public justice, as well as helping the offender to become a better person? Confucius didn't say in 13.18. But if we follow the philosophical hermeneutics or take a continuous reading, we should try to make explicit what is implicit and hidden in a classical text by imagining what the author or the main character of this text would have said in response to our inquiries. Following this method, we can argue that, for Confucius, to conceal one's close relative's misconduct does not mean to let this person go free. One could, for example, tell this relative that he did a wrong, and he should correct it—in the case of 13.18, by returning the sheep to its rightful owner. It is not controversial to say that a father could admonish his son this way. But even if the father is the perpetrator, he could be admonished by the son, within some limits. In the *Analects* 4.18, for example, Confucius said,

> In serving his parents, a son may gently remonstrate with them. When he sees that his will is not followed, he is still respectful and does not disobey them. Though worried, he does not complain.

In spite of the limit of admonishment, the son could have done something further. For example, he could have returned the sheep on his own, taking the responsibility himself. This could shame his father into behaving himself in the future.

But why don't we just obey the law, or some abstract kind of justice, and turn the father in? Let's assume that the son does this. What would happen to the father? To the father, the person he trusted the most (the son) betrayed

---

7. In the attempt to explain away this conflict, some scholars try to use obscure meanings of this term, which would render the advice in this passage apparently innocuous. See, for example, Liao (2013). As I argued in chapter 1, being a philosophical reader, I resist this kind of attempt and instead follow the common meanings of the terms in question and try to offer a philosophically coherent reading of the relevant text.

him; is it possible that he would thus become a law-abiding person in the future? Yes, he may choose not to violate the law anymore, but it is not because he thinks it is wrong but because he is afraid of the punishment. But if there is a chance that he can violate the law without getting caught, he may still do it. This time, though, he wouldn't even let his son in on the dirty secret. Confucius put it well:

> Guide them by edicts, keep them in line with punishments, and the masses will be saved [from getting into trouble] but will have no sense of shame. Guide them by virtue, keep them in line with rites, and they will have a sense of shame and will obey willingly. (*Analects* 2.3)

Is a society full of apparently law-abiding but shameless people with no trust in anyone desirable? The rationale for Confucius's advocacy for mutual concealment is not that to obey laws is not important, but that without caring and trusting relations among members of society, the demand to obey laws will become oppressive and eventually ineffective, and the society will disintegrate. The short-lived, Legalistic Qin dynasty (that allegedly emphasized the use of strict rewards and punishments and ignored and even suppressed family relations) is a favorite example for the Confucians to illustrate this point.[8] Rather, by concealing this person's misconduct, thus preserving the loving relationship and trust, one can then more effectively help this person to right the wrongs.

A More Serious Conflict in the Mencius 7A35

Through the discussion of the *Analects* 13.18, we can see how Confucius could resolve the conflict between the private and the public. But what if the conflict is more serious than what is involved in 13.18? For example, what if the father committed a heinous crime such as murder? Confucius didn't deal with this kind of case in the *Analects*, but Mencius did in the *Mencius*. In 7A35, a pupil asked Mencius's advice in a hypothetical case. That is, if Gu Sou (瞽瞍), the father of the sage king Shun who, according to historical records, was said to be a terrible father and perhaps a terrible person, had murdered someone, what actions should have been taken? Clearly, there is a conflict of duties for Shun the sage ruler: a filial duty to his father and a public duty to the state. More importantly, the conflict is far more serious than the one in the *Analects* 13.18. For the crime in question here is murder, which is far more serious than the crime of theft in 13.18. Moreover, Shun's public duty in this case is also

---

8. To be clear, although the Confucians like to argue that Legalism was responsible for the quick demise of the Qin dynasty, this is a case that requires careful studies.

stronger than the father's or son's duty in 13.18. In the latter, the father or the son is merely a private person, but in the former, Shun is the ruler who is responsible, or, more precisely, more responsible than a private person, for maintaining order, which includes making a criminal pay for his or her crimes.

To the hypothetical case, the first response Mencius gave was to let Gao Yao (皋陶), the attorney general and police chief of Shun's court, arrest Gu Sou. The pupil, who was perhaps shocked by the lack of filial piety in Mencius's answer, asked, "But would Shun not forbid it?" Mencius's response was, "How could Shun forbid it?! Gao Yao had authority to do it." Pressed again about Shun's duty to his father, Mencius finally said,

> Shun would consider giving up [his reign over] the world [tian xia] like throwing away a worn shoe. He could have secretly carried [his father] on his back and fled to the seashore, living there happily ever after and forgetting [his reign over] the world.

The first and rather obvious thing I wish to make clear here is that this is clearly not a case of corruption, for corruption means the abuse of power of an office by its holder for the sake of private gain. In this hypothetical case, Mencius rejected the suggestion that Shun forbid his police chief to arrest his father. Indeed, it is likely that in Shun's time, it could have been in Shun's legal power to pardon his father. Thus, in the hypothetical case, even a *lawful* use of power that is in favor of one's close kin, but is in conflict with the public interest, was rejected by Mencius, and this makes the accusation that Confucianism is the root cause of corruption, especially with a clear reference to the *Mencius* 7A35, simply ridiculous.

Ridiculous as it is, the accusation has been made.[9] As I mentioned, although this kind of accusation is not worth responding to, it is, unfortunately, the mainstream belief about Confucianism in contemporary China, thanks to the past 150 years of the antitradition "tradition." On the accusation that Confucianism is the or a root cause of corruption, there are a few general issues the accusers fail to address, or fail to address adequately, making their accusations simply frivolous. First, is the corruption in traditional or contemporary China worse than that of countries of different cultures? Second, how can the corruption be traced back to a particular philosophy? As we know, philosophy enjoys certain freedom to become embodied in practice. One could read Nietzsche and become a Nazi or a postmodern feminist. There are also many traditions in China, and careful studies—philosophical, historical, and/or sociological—need to be conducted before one can pin something in practice

---

9. Again, for references, see Q. Guo (2004 and 2011), and the special issue of *Dao: A Journal of Comparative Philosophy* 6, no. 1 (March 2007).

on a particular philosophical school. I am not saying that philosophy can always be exonerated from this kind of accusation, but that we should be careful because it is a rather risky business to make such accusations. Third, a philosophical teaching can have practical implications through traditions and culture. But given the devastating and comprehensive effects of the antitradition movements in the past 150 years in China, it is dubious to attribute anything in contemporary China to the Chinese traditions, Confucianism included.

Most importantly, as we have seen in the *Mencius* 7A35, there is no advocacy for corruption, and Mencius paid attention first and foremost to public duty. Only when pressured did he suggest how Shun could fulfill the duty to his father: to give up the throne (and all the material interests and glories that come with it) with no modicum of regret, to become a fugitive instead, and to live in a godforsaken land without any complaint.[10]

In this fulfillment of private duty, public justice is also served. The father couldn't enjoy the "perks" of being the king's father anymore, and Shun himself was punished for helping his father to escape as well. Mencius's phrase "happily ever after" was meant to emphasize Shun's filialness through his willingness to suffer from the consequences of escaping with his father. Nevertheless, we can still ask, what about his people who, without a sage ruler like Shun, may suffer? And what about the victim's family? Mencius didn't consider these scenarios, and we could defend him by saying that if he had been pressured more, he would have said something. For example, he could have argued that with a competent and humane official such as Gao Yao in position, people would still be served well, and he could also have suggested that, although he lived "happily ever after," Shun did feel sorry for the victim's family and sent money to them.

However, it is easier to excuse Confucius from not making these further statements, because the *Analects* is known for its aphoristic and brief style, than to excuse Mencius, who seems to like to give elaborate accounts in the *Mencius*. Moreover, in these accounts, it seems that Mencius quite consistently ignored some remaining conflict between different duties, and offered a "rosy" picture of harmonized duties instead.[11] Indeed, many later Confucian think-

10. To a contemporary reader, "seashore" may sound like a nice place. But in the agrarian society in which Shun and Mencius lived, it is a symbol of barren land that is outside of the civilized world and the jurisdiction of any political entity, which is why Mencius would have Shun choose it as an ideal hiding place.

11. There are other cases in the *Mencius* that are worth exploring, for example, the discussion in 5A3, about how Shun treated his ill-willed half brother Xiang who plotted repeatedly to murder him. Again, we can see that Mencius tried to find a reconciliation among various concerns: Shun's family duty to his half brother (instead of punishing Xiang, Shun enfeoffed him), and his duty to the public (not allowing Xiang to run the affairs of his fiefdom because, given the fact

ers have discussed the conflicts among various duties (see C. Huang 2008, 90–97). In particular, alleged followers of Mencius, such as members of the Cheng-Zhu school (程朱学派), were also concerned with the relation between the oneness of the principle (理) and the diversity of its embodiments (see *The Surviving Works of the Cheng Brothers* [程氏遗书] vol. 18), and the metaphor about the moon and its myriad reflections is what the Neo-Confucian Zhu Xi (朱熹) used to discuss this issue.[12] But it seems to me that these later followers of Mencius also tended to believe that these conflicts could always be resolved perfectly. In contrast, although Confucius in the *Analects* did not always offer an adequate resolution of this conflict and other conflicts, it seems that he had a greater appreciation of the difficulty of harmonizing difficult moral concerns.[13]

In Mencius's defense, we should see that he lived in an era of far less hope of restoring the order of the "good old days" than Confucius did. In hopeless times, to "accentuate the positive" might serve as a good rhetorical tool to inspire people. There were also more dangerous but popular ideas in these hopeless times, and Mencius may have had to scream and to talk forthrightly

---

that Xiang was not a humane person, he would make his people suffer if he had actually been given the authority to rule). Thus, contemporary critics are simply wrong to claim that Mencius failed to appreciate the conflict of duties, or that he embraced one duty at the price of completely ignoring all others. But it is debatable whether Mencius's treatment of all duties involved is adequate or not. In the case of 5A3, although he used Shun's enfeoffing Xiang as a sign of Shun's forgiveness and filial love, and he did some "damage control" by now allowing Xiang to run his fiefdom, he did not address the issue that by rewarding, though to a very limited extent, this utterly immoral person, people would be given a wrong sense of a moral exemplar. After all, a ruler, according to the Confucian tradition, should be a role model for his subjects, and Xiang clearly was not. Nevertheless, from a "solution" of the inadequacy in Mencius's treatment a critic offered, which simply holds to one duty (different from what he accused Mencius of holding on to) while ignoring all others—that is, not offering any real solution, evading the conflict completely, and doing exactly what Mencius was accused of doing—we can doubt that this (and maybe other) critics understood the problem in the first place. For a more detailed discussion, see Bai (2008b).

12. He may have borrowed this analogy from the Chan Buddhist master Yongjia Xuanjue (禅宗永嘉玄觉禅师); see *Classified Conversations of Zhu Xi* (朱子语类), vol. 18 and vol. 94, and, for an English translation of this analogy, see W. Chan (1969, 638).

13. For example, Confucius was critical of the realpolitik that Guanzhong (管仲) and Duke Huan of Qi (齐桓公) played but praised them for using it to save the civilized world from barbarians' threats (*Analects* 3.22, 14.9, 14.15, 14.16, and 14.17). In contrast, Mencius's position on these two figures was far less ambivalent and subtle (*Mencius* 2A1 and 2B2). In general, I think Sharon Sanderovitch (2007) was right to claim that there is a "bug" (residue conflict) in Mencius's philosophy, although I would argue that it is Mencius and his followers, not Confucius, who believe that an adequate "debugging" is always possible.

in order for people to hear him. This might have been a reason for the differences between Confucius and Mencius; or, perhaps more accurately speaking, this might have been the reason why in Mencius's time, it was Mencius rather than a Confucius reincarnate who stood out. But it cannot be denied that Mencius is more exoteric, and less subtle and sophisticated, than Confucius.

Becoming Human through Resolving Conflicts in Context

We can debate on the adequacy of various Confucian treatments of the conflict between the private and the public, and on how much they actually differ from each other, but we should appreciate the rationale of their treatments. The early Confucians understood how natural affection for family members could be a source of social ills. But they were also aware that this affection was also a starting point for individuals to learn to care about others and to learn public-spiritedness. Then, instead of suppressing familial care for public interests, which is what the Chinese Legalist and many Western thinkers advocate, they proposed that we should take advantage of the constructive aspect of this care and extend it to the public sphere. The demand of expanding one's care outward, and the understanding that there can be a continuum and complementarity between the private and the public, is what is distinctively Confucian. Early Confucians considered familial love a natural starting point of extension, not the end point. In the act of extending one's natural filial love outward, there are always inevitable challenges and tensions, and one can only become a truly humane person (仁者) by overcoming them. Through the act of overcoming, one's commitment to humanity is tested, and his or her understanding of the meaning of humanity and of the ordering of different concerns is deepened. In this sense, the inevitable tension and conflict is also necessary for the development of a full Confucian person. One may well claim that he or she loves everyone equally, but without the act of overcoming, this person's claim is nothing but an untested and empty one and cannot be taken seriously, especially given the fact that human life is full of conflicts and tests.

Challenges and tensions are context-dependent, and one has to deal with them in one's own life. In Confucianism, there is a guiding principle for handling the tensions, that is, extending one's love to everything in the world while keeping the hierarchy or gradation of love. However, there are no ready-made, universally applicable formulae or "field manuals" to deal with all the practical challenges. Various accounts and stories in the *Mencius* and the *Analects* serve only as context-dependent examples that offer hints and inspiration for us to handle our own problems. This combination of the universal (the guiding principle) with the particular (the context) is another distinctively (early) Confucian feature (perhaps more Confucian in the sense of Confucius's than Mencian).

We can argue, as I do in the following, that sometimes the conflict can be irreconcilable, or the early Confucian treatments are not always adequate. But at least they recognized the conflict and didn't wish it away or simply hold on to one duty while ignoring all others. For example, if one's mother (or anyone whom one feels close to) and a stranger are both drowning, Confucians would argue that, naturally and justifiably, one should save one's mother first. We can debate about how much one should do, or how much remorse one should feel in this case of choosing one's mother over a stranger. But it sounds so much more reasonable than someone who chooses to save either the mother or the stranger on the basis of some a priori or absolute principle, without experiencing any conflict whatsoever.[14]

Han Fei Zi's Challenges

As mentioned in chapter 1, there was an early Chinese thinker, Han Fei Zi, who lived toward the end of the SAWS. He was allegedly a former pupil of the influential Confucian Xun Zi but then became a leading voice of the Legalist school, which was harshly critical of Confucianism. On the Confucian proposal of overcoming conflict between the private and the public by expanding on family care, he waged some serious attacks.[15] Apparently, he didn't reject Mencius's idea that compassion is a universal sentiment, but he argued that the innate kindness toward others was too fragile to do any real job. In his typical powerful rhetoric, he said, "in the fall of a year of plenty, it is considered necessary to feed even a stranger," seemingly acknowledging Mencius's idea of universal care, but right before this line, he maintained, "in the spring of a

14. Michael Ing (2017) offers a fascinating contrast to the harmony picture I have offered so far. He points out that those who argue for the overcoming and harmonization of moral conflicts tend to focus on the *Analects*, the *Mencius*, and the *Xun Zi*. But if we look into other early Confucian texts, we will find that, according to them, the conflicts cannot always be resolved (ibid., 3). As I have mentioned previously, my book is mostly focused on two early Confucian texts, which, as Ing argues, tend to be read as offering a "harmony picture." I am also clear about the fact that what I have offered in this book is only one possible and coherent reading of the two texts. But I am highly sympathetic to Ing's emphasis on tragedy and vulnerability when dealing with moral conflicts, even by Confucian sages, which, I believe, is present in the *Analects*, if not in the *Mencius*. As I argue in the following sections, the harmony picture has its limits, and it will break down on certain points. I thank Reviewer #2 for bringing Ing's work to my attention.

15. The following is merely a simple summary of Han Fei Zi's attacks. For a more detailed account, see Bai (2012b).

year of famine, even one's little brother is not fed" (*Han Fei Zi*, chap. 49).[16] For him, the SAWS were precisely the trying times for human beings that would completely suppress our inborn yet fragile sense of care (ibid.), and what can never be suppressed, "the fact of human beings," is that we are driven by (getting) rewards and (avoiding) punishments (ibid., chap. 48).

To be fair, Mencius understood the fragility of our inborn care, which was why he and other Confucians, including Han Fei Zi's alleged teacher Xun Zi, argued for moral cultivation through family. But Han Fei Zi further argued that, with regard to producing good subjects, the love among family members is not as reliable as strict laws that are based on rewards and punishments. Again in his powerful rhetoric, he said, "In a strict household there are no unruly slaves, but the children of a caring mother turn out bad sometimes" (*Han Fei Zi*, chap. 50).

But as we discussed regarding the morals of the *Analects* (13.18), resorting only to laws would produce shameless people, and a society that consists of apparently law-abiding yet shameless people is on the verge of chaos and disaster. To counter this, Han Fei Zi argued that to weigh different duties, as we discussed earlier, is too demanding for the masses. In contrast, the use of laws and other governing techniques is the only effective way to govern a state, especially when the state is already too large and too complicated, and there is a competition for limited resources, which is, for Han Fei Zi, a reality of the SAWS (and of the ages to come) (*Han Fei Zi*, chaps. 49 and 50).

To respond to this challenge, Confucians could argue, in line with their elitist tendencies, which we have witnessed clearly in this book, that for the common people, laws are what regulate their actions, but we need to produce a handful of elites who are moral and sophisticated enough to weigh different duties. This brings us to Han Fei Zi's core challenge to the Confucian solution to the conflict between the private and the public: the private and the public are in such a profound conflict that it can't be reconciled. To illustrate this, he offered his own twist on the sheep-stealing case, which he may have been familiar with through his Confucian training, and he also offered a story that implicated Confucius directly, an ingenious (as in "evil genius") joke on the Confucians (*Han Fei Zi*, chap. 49).

In his version of the sheep-stealing case, the upright son from the state of Chu reports his father to the minister, and the minister orders him (the son) to be killed because his conduct, though showing loyalty to the ruler, is unfilial to his father. According to Han Fei Zi, the moral of this story is that "the up-

---

16. The Chinese version of the *Han Fei Zi* I am using is Han (1991). Throughout this book, the translations of passages in the *Han Fei Zi* are mine. For another English translation, see Watson (1964).

right subject of the ruler is the brutal son of the father." In the other story, which was very likely made up by him, a subject of the state of Lu, Confucius's home state, runs away from the battle three times because he is concerned with the well-being of his father, should he die from the battles. In this case, Confucius finds this man as filial and recommends him for a promotion in the government. According to Han Fei Zi, the moral of this story is "the filial son of the father is the traitorous subject of the ruler." As a result of the Chu minister's and Confucius's actions, no evil deeds are reported to the authority anymore in the state of Chu (because reporting evil deeds may not get one reward but punishment instead), and the soldiers of the state of Lu are quick to surrender (because dying for one's country may not get any reward, but surrendering and escaping may). All these stories, according to Han Fei Zi, show that the conflict between the private and the public is fundamental.

A characteristic of such a sharp thinker and powerful rhetorician as Han Fei Zi is that he can deceive us with his eloquence. As I argued earlier in this chapter, the Confucians also acknowledge the conflict between the private and the public, and the key difference between them and Han Fei Zi is whether the conflict is "fundamental," that is, irreconcilable. In the case of the deserter from the state of Lu, Confucians might suggest that the state establish laws that would exempt at least one son from being enlisted, support soldiers' families, and provide for them if the soldiers are injured or killed in action. These arrangements would at least lessen the worries that a soldier may have. Moreover, soldiers who die for their country should be glorified, which would make their parents proud. For Confucians, to serve one's parents is not merely to serve them physically; to make parents proud is also a great sign of filial piety.[17] In the case of how to treat the sheep-stealing father, although Confucians didn't encourage the son to testify against or "rat out" his father, they wouldn't support the draconian punishment of executing the son who did this. To make his case, Han Fei Zi exaggerated the Confucian idea so much as to make it look ridiculous.

Although he exaggerated, Han Fei Zi did offer us a powerful image of the conflict between the private and the public. Although Confucians wouldn't necessarily support the execution of the son, they wouldn't encourage him to report petty crimes by their close ones to the authority. This could jeopardize the stability of the government. Confucians would argue that by encouraging familial care, people would become virtuous, which would benefit governance

17. Later, we will consider the treatment of the conflict between the private and the public in the *Republic*. It is suggested there that brave soldiers be given high honors (467e–69b), but the focus in the *Republic* is the soldiers themselves, while the focus of the Confucian proposal includes concern for the families.

in the long run. But Han Fei Zi would argue that virtues are not reliable, and if the state is in clear and present danger, the promise of the long run wouldn't help. To illustrate the latter point, he used a powerful analogy:

> One who cannot even get his fill of the coarse grain does not pursue meat and fine millet; one who cannot even have shabby clothes covering him does not wait for embroidered robes. (chap. 49)

Moreover, the case in the *Analects* 13.18 is about the petty crime of stealing sheep, and Mencius's treatment of a murder case, as we saw, is not fully satisfactory, although we could help him make a stronger case by following general Confucian concerns. But what if the conflict is even more difficult to reconcile? Nowhere in Confucian classics can I find a case like this. But in the *Shi Ji* (史记) (*Records of the Grand Historian*) by Sima Qian (司马迁), there is such a case (1981, 339).[18] Shi She (石奢), a minister of Chu (楚) in charge of catching criminals, chased a murderer down, only to find that the murderer was his father. Letting his father go, he turned himself in and asked the king to punish him with death. The king forgave him. But he argued that it was unfilial not to let his father go, and it was disloyal not to follow the king's law. Although it was up to the king's discretion and leniency to forgive him, it was his duty to pay for his crime. He committed suicide. The conflict here is even more serious than the one in the *Mencius* 7A35 because Shi She was directly responsible for arresting the criminal, whereas Shun was not. Shi She's "solution" of this conflict is not so much a solution as an acknowledgment of the lack of a solution or the lack of a reconciliation in this kind of conflict. I doubt that a Confucian can really find a reconciliation or a better "solution" here. In this situation, the continuation and the compatibility between the private and the public breaks down, and the conflict cannot be completely overcome through a reconciliation.

In addition to the problem of the unreliability of virtues, and the problem of irreconcilable conflict between the private and the public, there is also a problem of abuse. As I have shown, a characteristic of the Confucian attempt to reconcile different duties is its lack of a "field manual" and its contextual nature. But how could we prevent people from using this to bend the rules for their own gains? As Han Fei Zi put it, it is difficult even for the wisest to understand the subtle words of the wise, and thus these words cannot be what regulate the common people, and they will lead to irresolvable plurality or faction among the wise.[19]

---

18. Sima Qian's attitude toward Confucianism is ambiguous, but in the following case, he seems to be sympathetic to it.

19. See both chapter 49 and the first few paragraphs of chapter 50 of the *Han Fei Zi*.

In another history book, the political views of which are not dominantly Confucian but rather eclectic, there is an example of such abuse (*Y. Gao* 1986, vol. 11, chap. 3, 110–11). This is another version of the sheep-stealing case. The "upright" man first turns his sheep-stealing father in, and his father is to be executed as a result.[20] He then offers to take the penalty for his father. But before he is executed, he tells the officer that his action of turning his father in shows trustworthiness or loyalty to the state, and his action of taking the penalty for his father is a sign of filial piety. Should a trustworthy and filial man be executed in a state, everyone in the state would deserve execution. The king of his state, hearing this argument, stops the execution. Confucius is said to deplore this display of manipulation.

From Confucius's disapproval, this story shows that what that man does is not Confucian. But this story also reveals how the Confucian teaching can be easily abused. The exoneration of the man in this story can also lead us to reflect on another problem with the Confucian teaching: it is difficult to incorporate a moral understanding of the law without diluting the moral burden of the individual and the sanctity of the law. That is, in the concealment case, if to conceal for one's father is protected by the law, then this action loses much of its moral value, for this value depends precisely on the risk of being punished by the law, and the value of moral cultivation that this action offers is based on overcoming the conflict and thus discovering the continuation between the private and the public on a deeper level. However, if the concealment is not protected by the law, the state will then morally wrongfully punish a good person ("good" both in a private and a public sense). Of course, the state can overturn this ruling by some special pardons (such as presidential pardons in the American setting). But if we keep doing this, the law will become a joke and lose its authority among people.[21]

20. All these different versions of the sheep-stealing case were clearly meant to illustrate some morals, and it is likely that some details were dramatized to make the storyteller's points. They shouldn't be taken as being historically accurate, in spite of the fact that the book in question here resembled some traditional official historical records. Therefore, we shouldn't use this story to show that stealing sheep is a serious (capital) crime, as H. Wang (王怀聿) did (2011).

21. A similar set of concerns can be applied to one kind of torture case in the contemporary debate. That is, should we allow a CIA agent to torture a terrorist suspect when the latter is believed to hold a piece of crucial information that could be used to prevent an immanent terrorist attack that would kill many innocent citizens (with the assumption that torture could be effective in this case)? If torture becomes legal, then there will be an escalation of its use and, as a result, there will be many injustices committed to the suspects, and torture will also become ineffective or even counterproductive in that it may produce many false testimonies. But if not, and if the CIA agent takes the risk of being punished by the law in order to save his or her compatriots, to punish him or her may be unfair. The best solution, then, seems to be to keep torture

An Alternative Model in the *Republic*

In this section, I explore an alternative model offered in Plato's *Republic*. One reason to use this instead of a model from Han Fei Zi is that, as we will see, the model offered in the *Republic* poses a very neat contrast with that in the *Analects* and in the *Mencius*, even more so than that offered in the *Han Fei Zi*.[22] Moreover, by introducing a model from Western philosophy and by offering comparisons and contrasts in this and the following sections, which are drawn from both Chinese and Western philosophy, we will see that the issue of the private and the public is universal, and many views from different traditions resonate with one another, while views from the allegedly same culture can be in profound disagreement. This may help us to become disillusioned with the "China versus the West" dichotomy.

Although there are profound political and social differences between the failing feudal system of Confucius's and Mencius's time, and the failing Athenian democracy in Plato's time, there is one issue in common among them. During and in the aftermath of the Peloponnesian War, Plato witnessed an Athens plagued by factions. Each faction was often based on extended families or clans.[23] If we take the common good of the city as the public, the interest of the family and the clan (as well as the interest of an individual person) should then be considered the private. So, the problem of factions is a problem of the conflict between the private and the public. This may help us to understand that, in the *Republic*, (much of) the private and the public are taken to be in conflict with each other, the private (that is considered in conflict with the public) is denounced, and unity is apparently taken as the highest goal of the city (polis).

In the *Republic*, the aspects of private interests and family matters that are commonly regarded as not harmful and even beneficial to the public, and are considered key starting points and even crucial for cultivating public-spiritedness by the Confucians, are largely ignored. A telling example is that when discussing which laws to establish in the ideal city, Socrates lists a few

---

illegal but give some authoritative figure, such as the president, the power to pardon. However, if pardoning is used regularly, the sanctity of law will again be in danger. I thank Qian Jiang for making this point with me.

22. The views discussed in this chapter are what the *Republic* offers on the surface, with some necessary, minimum hermeneutical treatments. But whether Plato took these views literally, or he actually had a secret teaching, is not a concern of this chapter.

23. In the *Republic* 494a–95a, Socrates describes a phenomenon that may have been based on Plato's understanding of political reality in Athens. That is, a young, rich, noble, good-looking, and tall man in a big city is often allured early on by his kinsmen and fellow citizens with flatteries and honors so that he will become an ally who promotes their interests.

things as small and secondary conventions,[24] for which no laws need to be established. Among these are appropriate conduct for treating elders and the care of parents, and they are listed next to what are considered proper hairdos (425a–c).

In contrast, Socrates pays far more attention to the clear distinction and conflict between the private and the public. For example, at one place, he states that a private man cannot lie to the rulers, although it is appropriate for the rulers to lie for the benefit of the city (389b–c). In his footnote to this occurrence of the term "private" (*idion*), Allan Bloom—a contemporary translator and a commentator of the *Republic*—points out that the "opposition between the private and public is an important theme in the *Republic* and, in some respects, it is the core of the problem of justice" (1991, 445–46n41). Indeed, much of the *Republic* is focused on how the private can be a threat to the public, and thus the aspects of the private that are in conflict with the public have to be suppressed. In particular, almost anything private is forbidden in the two ruling classes (guardians and guardians' auxiliaries). For example, in his discussion of the material conditions of their lives (415d–17b), guardians are not allowed to have private property, including land, house, and money. There is not even a private space, such as a house or a storeroom, for the guardians (416d). The reason for abolishing these things is that private possessions will turn the guardians into "masters and enemies instead of allies of the other citizens" (417a–b). This transformation will lead to factional conflicts and eventually the destruction of the city. Instead, the city has to provide the guardians with sufficient—with no surplus and no lack—sustenance and other necessities of living. The guardians live and eat together, and this communal life is clearly intended to nourish the camaraderie among them.

Nevertheless, although their self-interest ("self-interest" in a narrow sense of this word, in which "self" refers to one's individual self) is largely suppressed, the guardians may still form factions based on their family ties because, as we have seen in the discussion on the concepts of the private and the public at the beginning of this chapter, family interest is the other primary source of private interest. This is why Socrates later proposes that families be abolished altogether (457c–71b). Through some complicated and almost impossible arrangements, only the best men—"the young who are good in war or elsewhere" (460b)—and the best women are allowed to reproduce. The newborns are immediately taken away from their mothers, with any possible identification of them with their birth mothers eliminated. These babies will

24. In this chapter, by "Socrates," I mean the character in the *Republic*, a play created by Plato. Whether this Socrates is based on an accurate portrait of the historical one is not a concern here.

be raised by the city. As a result, the male and female guardians have to treat all citizens of the city as blood relations, and cannot favor some over the others on the basis of family ties. Again, Bloom spells out the rationale of these arrangements: "To become either a member of a city—or a philosopher—one must break with one's primary loyalty" (1991, 385).

These arrangements also help to solve another crucial problem in politics: how to make rulers care for the city and the citizens. As discussed in the previous chapter, at two separate places Socrates offers two good reasons for good men or philosophers to rule. The first reason Socrates offers (347a–d) is self-interest-based (to avoid the penalty of being ruled by a bad ruler). Even if we read his argument charitably, an undeniable fact is that this reason doesn't offer much motivation for good men to rule. But in an ideal regime, it is desirable that the very best take up the task of ruling willingly. Moreover, self-interested rulers may do a good job because of their knowledge of ruling, but they will do an even better job if they are devoted to the public interest. The other reason that is offered at a separate place (520a–b) is based on a sense of justice: since the (ideal) city begets and rears philosophers, philosophers need to pay back (what is owed) and to rule. But the problem is that this reason is based on a problematic understanding of justice, which seems to be refuted in book 1 of the *Republic* already. This problem aside, some may argue that to follow this kind of business transaction–like cold justice doesn't sufficiently motivate philosophers (although some others may believe that philosophers would be motivated by a sense of justice as a virtue).

Perhaps aware of these problems, Socrates introduces means to strengthen the motivation of potential rulers. At another place in this dialogue, in his construction of the ideal city, "a city coming into being in speech" (369a), Socrates argues that the guardians have to be selected on the basis that not only do they have the knowledge of how to guard the city, but they also believe that what is advantageous to the city (public) is also advantageous to themselves (private). Only those who can hold to this belief against all sorts of tests will be chosen as guardians (412b–14b). It seems, however, that Socrates does not think that mere education is sufficient to instill public-spiritedness in the guardians; rather, a "noble lie" has to be told to all (male) citizens (414b–15d). They are told that they were born from the earth or the land of their city. As a result, the land is their mother, and they are all brothers to one another. With this belief, the rulers will love the land of the city literally as their mother and the citizens as their brothers. The aforementioned proposal of the abolishment of family, which is actually introduced in the dialogue after the introduction of the noble lie, can be taken as a further reinforcement of the noble lie. That is, through abolishing family altogether and adopting a community of women and children, any citizen the guardian meets is "a brother, or a sister,

or a father, or a mother, or a son, or a daughter or their descendants or ancestors" (463c).[25]

To be clear, not all private interests are suppressed.[26] As pointed out, the
city offers sustenance to the ruling class, thus satisfying some of its private
interests. But this satisfaction is so basic that these guardians and their auxiliaries of the city may not be happy, because they are like poorly paid mercenar-
ies (419a–20a). Of course, a particular private interest, their sense of honor, is
indeed adequately satisfied (413e–14a and 468b–69b). Moreover, it can be
argued that the producer class (the masses that are ruled) also has some private interests satisfied. It is possible that the masses can have private properties
and families, and their way of life is protected by the ruling class. But the *Republic* never makes this explicit, and we can infer from some passages that the
satisfaction of their private interests should be limited by the concern with the
good of the city and can even be violated. For, after all, as Socrates argues (in
his answer to the complaint that guardians are not happy), the happiness of
the city as a whole should be our only concern, and this suggests that if the
private interests of the masses have to be suppressed for the greater good, or
for the Good (which, in the *Republic*, is not defined as the sum of the private
interests of all citizens', as we moderns often understand it), we can suppress
them. Indeed, an important task of the guardians is to distribute wealth in
such a way that there is no poverty and too much wealth in the city (421c–
22a), and the city as a whole is described as not rich (422a–23c).

Therefore, as pointed out earlier, the private interests that are not harmful
to the common good or that are too difficult to discard, such as certain physical needs that can only be cast aside by the impossible act of taking away one's
body—which, interestingly, is actually considered in the *Phaedo* (61b–65b; see
also *Theaetetus* 172c–77c)—are not suppressed and are (often meagerly) satisfied, but the *Republic* pays little attention to them. In contrast, the focus is how
the private interests that are in conflict with the public good are suppressed.
With these interests completely suppressed, the public interest is not threatened anymore. Unity, the *allegedly* greatest good of the city,[27] is achieved,

25. It is debatable how effective Socrates actually thinks all these arrangements are to make
the good men devoted to the public interest. For example, in book 7, the philosophers (the best
men), after seeing the Good, have to be *compelled* to serve the common people (514a–21b).

26. I wish to thank Liu Wei (刘玮) for pushing me to make this clarification, and I have
benefited from the discussions with him in some of the points that will be made in the
following.

27. The reason to claim that unity is *allegedly* the greatest good is that Socrates later claims
that the Good is the highest good (504d–5b), and it is questionable whether unity is always
part of the Good. A reasonable guess is that unity, like justice, is only good by its relation to
the Good.

with the help of maintaining a proper size of the city (423b–c and 461e–66c). All its citizens, especially those of the ruling class, will have a shared sense of pain and pleasure among themselves, "like a single man" (462c). There are no factions among the citizens, and the conflict between the private and the public is solved by the total annihilation of the private interests that are in conflict with the public interest. However, it should be pointed out that Socrates thinks that the aforementioned arrangements—especially the abolishment of family—are unlikely to actually be carried out in a real state, unless the philosophers become kings or kings happen to be philosophers, a very rare, if ever possible, event (471c–74c).

Some may argue that the political proposal on the surface of the *Republic* is too "crazy" to be taken literally, realistically, and seriously. I do not deny that there may have been hidden teachings in the *Republic* that are "saner" and subtler than the model discussed in this section. Indeed, to deny the possibility of hidden teachings is a sign of hubris that we have toward Plato, one of the most profound thinkers in human history. However, isn't it also a sign of hubris not to examine the surface teachings of the *Republic* carefully with the excuse that they are too crazy and too simple? If one cannot even understand the surface, how can he or she be expected to understand the depth, the hidden, or the esoteric?

Moreover, it also cannot be denied that the surface proposal offered in the *Republic* has been taken literally and seriously—though often not correctly—throughout history, and it is also a paradigm that nicely underlies many political proposals in history. For example, the conflict model discussed in this section is a (significantly) revised version of the real-world regime of the Spartans and has inspired various forms of utopianism and totalitarianism throughout history. It was also criticized by philosophers such as Karl Popper as a blueprint for totalitarianism (1971). Of course, Popper's understanding of the *Republic* is deeply flawed, but even Aristotle—the great and yet not necessarily faithful pupil of Plato's—also offered in his *Politics* a comprehensive criticism of the political proposal in the *Republic* (1260b25–65a25 [chaps. 1–5 and part of chap. 6 of book 2]). A focus of Aristotle's criticism is precisely the suppression of the private for the sake of the public, which is the same focus as we have discussed and will discuss in this chapter. If this model were considered too crazy to be taken seriously, it would be difficult to explain why Aristotle took so much pain in attacking it.

There is another, more technical challenge to this reading of the proposal in the *Republic*. That is, this reading presupposes that the political proposal is independent, separable from other parts of the *Republic*. But on the surface, the discussion of political issues is to answer the question of justice in an individual soul (367e–69a). This seems to suggest that the political discussion in the *Republic* cannot be understood by itself.[28] In my own defense, first, let's see how Socrates introduced the political discussion. He and his companions started out with the question of justice, including the question of whether the most just man is happy or not. Encountering tremendous difficulties, Socrates acknowledges the fact that justice of an individual soul is hard to define, and the solution might lie in our examination of justice in a larger object, that is, the city.[29] This is, according to Socrates, like the situation where we can recognize little letters by looking at the bigger ones in a bigger place. But there is a problem with this analogy, because that "magnifying" process (such as walking closer to the letters that appear little from a distance) doesn't change the letters. However, given the fact that we still don't know what justice in an individual soul is, how can we know that justice in a city is really the justice in an individual soul enlarged? How can we know that the former resembles the latter? Answering these questions eventually depends on our understanding of the Good, but Socrates later admits that he can only suggest what the Good is by way of analogy and cannot offer a direct and clear description of it (506b–11e). Therefore, in the *Republic*, the connection between the ethical question of justice in an individual soul and the political question of justice in the city is not fully established. This gives further support to our treating the political discussions in the *Republic* separately.

Comparisons between the Two Models

With the introduction of the model offered in the *Republic*, we should already see some clear contrasts between it and the model offered by early Confucians. These comparisons and contrasts can further reveal hidden features, merits, and problems with each model, and help us to understand them more. This is the beauty of doing comparative studies between two allegedly different traditions, and even within allegedly the same tradition (e.g., the comparative works between Plato and Aristotle).

Two Models Compared

Against this comparative background, we can call the picture offered by early Confucians as one of continuum and harmony. They did acknowledge and try

28. I thank Hui-chieh Loy for pointing this out to me.

29. The idea that the city (state) is an enlarged individual soul poses interesting contrasts to different analogies in political philosophy. For many modern Western thinkers, the state is an enlarged individual body. For early Confucians, the state is an enlarged family. The underlying reasons for these different analogies and their implications are an interesting topic in their own right.

to deal with the conflict between the private and the public, but their solution resided in strengthening the constructive aspect of the private (constructive to the public good) to overcome the damaging aspect of the private (damaging to and in conflict with the public good). Moreover, although there is a conceptual distinction between the private and the public, the line in reality is not fixed. What is private in one setting (e.g., communal interest versus the interest of the state) can be public in another (e.g., communal interest versus family interest). Due to this relativity, family values, for example, cannot be said to belong to the private only. Since family values don't belong to the private only, a good family person has the potential to become a public person. That is, there is no clear separation between the masses (who are concerned with their narrow self-interests and family interests) and the Confucian ruling elite (the public-spirited).

In contrast, the picture offered in the *Republic* is one of discreteness and conflict. As we saw in the previous section, the private interests that are not harmful or are even constructive to the public are largely ignored, and the focus is the conflicting aspect, which is to be suppressed. There is also a clear cut-off line between the private and the public: the individual's self-interest and family interest are considered private and, in the case of guardians, need to be largely suppressed. As a result, there is also a clear cut-off line between those who are left in the private (the masses) and those who are in the public (the guardians).

The contrasting pictures of continuum and harmony on the one hand, and of discreteness and conflict on the other, can help us to understand other key differences between the *Analects* (and other early Confucian texts) and the *Republic*. In the *Analects*, the superior person performs a significant role of civilizing the masses because, according to the early Confucian picture of continuum and harmony, the masses, though largely limited to their private spheres, contribute to the public good by being good family and community members, and may move further up in the continuous line from a more private role to a more public one. In contrast, in the *Republic*, due to the picture of discreteness and conflict, the masses are assigned a very passive role of obedience, and the issue of how the rulers can civilize them is largely ignored.

The contrast between these two pictures can also help us to understand how the public good is defined in each model. In the Confucian model, the public interest is an extension of the private interest. It means that the public interest is nothing but the sum of the interest of the people that form the state. It sounds similar to how the public interest is understood today, but it should be noted that for the Confucians, the sum of interest is not the same as the sum of mere material interest, and is also not a simple accumulation of individuals' interests. There can be interests that only emerge in a group, such as those based on family or communal relations, so to promote the right kind of family relations, for example, is within the realm of the public. In contrast, due to the break between the private and the public, it becomes possible, in the picture offered in the *Republic*, that there can be elements of the public good or the interest of the state that are totally disconnected with any individual of the state. As mentioned in the previous section, the city in speech constructed in the *Republic* is suspected to be such a state that, paradoxically, although the city as a whole is happy, no group in it seems to be happy (419a–21c).[30]

Criticisms of the Model in the *Republic* from the Confucian Perspective

One reason for me to introduce the model in the *Republic* is that there seem to be problems with the Confucian continuum and harmony model. But how does the alternative model fare? Through the noble lie and the community of women and children, Socrates tries to turn all citizens into brothers, sisters, or other close family members, presumably using family ties to create unity in the city. Confucius and other early Confucians, following their understanding of the role of family in the cultivation of public-spiritedness, would challenge this attempt by saying that if family is completely abolished, where do citizens get a sense of family ties? A key problem here is that on the surface, in the *Republic*, much of the private is abolished for the sake of the public, but by making the city a big family, Socrates secretly wishes to take advantage of the beneficiary aspects of the private. Unfortunately, the guardian is deprived of any connection with the family, and nowhere in the *Republic* is the education of filial love and compassion closely examined. This makes empty the demand that the guardian must love his or her country and its citizens, because the country is his or her home or motherland, and all the citizens are his or her brothers and sisters, for without family, "home," "mother," and "brothers and sisters" carry no significance, and they can only gain significance when the feeling for family members is cultivated in a family environment. One may argue that guardians can gain a sense of camaraderie through community.[31] But a Confucian can argue that the close ties that are necessary for camaraderie would secretly reintroduce de facto family relations into society and thus lead to the conflict between the private and the public about which Socrates

---

30. Another reason or symptom of this disconnect may have something to do with how the Good is understood. In the *Republic*, the Good seems to transcend human affairs and to dwell in the realm of pure *theoria*. But in the *Analects*, wisdom is equated with serving the good of the people (the humanity, *ren* [仁]), and humanity is defined as loving people (12.22).

31. I wish to thank Tao Lin (陶林) for pointing this out to me.

is worried, or the ties are not so close, making the alleged camaraderie too diluted to be meaningful.[32]

In contrast, according to the *Analects*, the natural love among family members, present in a family environment, can achieve what the artificial noble lie and the practically impossible arrangements of community of women and children in the *Republic* try to achieve. An anecdotal support for the viability of the Confucian model is that although Socrates dreams of a world in which people call strangers with names usually reserved for family members, this practice of, for example, calling a stranger of a similar age "brother" or "sister" is an actual practice in China, probably thanks to the Confucian heritage.[33]

In defense of the model of the *Republic*, we can say that the family relations among citizens of the ideal state in the *Republic* are more or less literal, rather than the "as if" kind of family relations that result from ever-expanding familial care in the Confucian model. The community of women and children and the founding myth of the state (all citizens are born from mother earth beneath the city) in the *Republic* literally make the city a big family, thus the (secret) use of the private in the public in the *Republic* is more direct than in the Confucian model.[34] But the challenge from the previous paragraph that these family relations are meaningless in a place where there are no families, and the challenge that the founding myth (the noble lie) may not be effective—something even Glaucon acknowledges to a certain extent (*Republic* 415c–d)—still stand.

Therefore, it seems that the Confucian has a valid argument against the model in the *Republic*. Simply put, the unity the latter model tries to achieve is rootless. It may work to some extent through brainwashing and through quite radical arrangements such as the community of women and children, but without some proper root, devotion to the public and to a set of laws and codes of conduct will eventually wither. It may function when the conflict is not serious, as a dead tree can still resist breezes, but it will break down when faced with extreme cases, as the dead tree will fall in a thunderstorm. But as we have seen in the challenges to the Confucian model, it, too, will break down in some extreme cases. Perhaps no profound political teaching can offer

32. There is a curious passage in the *Republic* that tries to argue that the fights among guardians wouldn't lead to factions (464b–65b). The artificialness of some of the arguments there may reflect the difficulties that are discussed in this paragraph.

33. Interestingly, when we call a stranger "sister" in English, it usually means that this stranger is a nun. In other words, the idea that all human beings belong to an extended family in the West may come from Christianity. But there are significant differences between the idea of universal love in Christianity and the Confucian idea that "all human beings are my kin and all things are my friends." This is an important topic that I cannot go into in this book.

34. I thank Su Dechao (苏德超) for pointing this out to me.

a perfect solution to the ultimate conflict between the private and the public because any model may break down somewhere. After all, as it is claimed in the *Lao Zi*, "Heaven and Earth are not humane; they treat human beings as straw dogs [i.e., some kind of instruments that can be discarded after they are used up]" (chap. 5). We cannot always get things our way. Or, put in a simple and yet vulgar way, life sucks. There are fundamental dilemmas in human life that just can't be solved or resolved perfectly. Nonetheless, we can and should investigate the "breaking point" for each model, and find a model that works in most ordinary cases. The early Confucian model begins with something very accessible to ordinary human beings (the cultivation of family relations), while the model in the *Republic* is radical from the beginning. In this sense, the early Confucian model is more viable than that in the *Republic*.

Not Chinese versus Western but Only Two Representative Models

There are two clarifications I would like to make. First, the model in the *Republic* poses a very sharp contrast to that in early Confucian texts, which helps to illustrate features of both models. But we shouldn't rush into a simplistic understanding that Western thinking emphasizes the discreteness and conflict between the private and the public, while Chinese thinking emphasizes the continuity and harmony between the two. As we have seen, it was Han Fei Zi, a traditional Chinese political thinker, who challenged the Confucian harmony view on the relation between the private and the public, and the general Legalist approach to politics is said to be adopted by the Chinese rulers to a certain extent. The Confucian criticism that a rootless care for the whole community couldn't sustain itself was actually leveled against the Mohist school, a dominant school of thought in pre-Qin China.[35]

On the other side, Aristotle, a Western political thinker, offered in his *Politics* a profound critique of the political proposal of the *Republic*. Some of his criticisms and his own ideas of politics are actually very close to the Confucian understanding of the role of the family in public affairs, in spite of the differences between the Confucians and Aristotle on many other subjects of political philosophy.[36] In his *Politics*, the relationship between husband and wife in a family is described in political terms (it is a "partnership" instead of "the

35. But again, this kind of criticism can be translated into a criticism of, for example, the kind of utilitarian idea that would advocate treating everyone's utility equally and thus demand a coherent utilitarian to share his or her wealth with every poor person in the world, however remote he or she is (see, e.g., Singer 1972). On this issue, then, we can see that there is more kinship between the Chinese Mohist and some utilitarians than between the Chinese Mohist and the Chinese Confucian.

36. I wish to thank Robert Rethy for some very helpful discussions.

naturally ruling and the ruled"), although he also emphasized the fact that there are differences between "a large household and a small city" as well (1252a1–b35). Also, in his criticism of the *Republic*, he implied that the private and the family are an important locus for the education of public virtues. For example, Aristotle argued that without private property, one would not be able to learn generosity and affection for "friends, guests, or club mates" by overcoming one's self-love and using one's own possessions to help out (1262b1–6).[37] Without the family setting, one cannot learn proper respect for family members and, eventually, an appropriate attitude toward strangers (1262a25–33). Generally, Aristotle is known for emphasizing the education of virtue through habituation, and family and the "private sphere" are a natural setting for it (1263b40). Additionally, like the early Confucians, he also believed that by treating all citizens as family members and distributing affection to all of them, as proposed in the *Republic*, "affection necessarily becomes diluted through this sort of partnership," and without what is one's own and what is dear, human beings would not be able to cherish and feel affection for one another (1256b6–35).

The second clarification is that the models in the early Confucian texts and in the *Republic* are "samplers" on the treatment of the issue of the private and the public in the history of philosophy. Even within the Confucian tradition, contemporary scholar Huang Chun-Chieh (黃俊杰) argues that there is a change from the view of continuity between the private and the public in the pre-Qin era to the affirmation of the priority of the public over the private among Song Confucians (2008, 90–97).[38] Some philosophers in the Qing dynasty challenged the belief of the Song-Ming Neo-Confucians, arguing that, for example, the self in the Confucian moral tenet of "expanding the self to covering the realm of others" (推己及人) is not the same as the private denounced by the Song-Ming Neo-Confucians. In addition to the criticisms, the Ming-Qing Confucian scholars, such as Gu Yanwu (顾炎武) and Wang Chuanshan (王船山), had many other interesting things to say on this subject.[39]

37. I used this argument in chapter 5 (under "The Cultivation of Compassion") to illustrate a Confucian idea.

38. But Song Confucians put some human sentiments on the side of "heavenly principle" (天理) or the public. These sentiments seem to be very similar to the part of the private that is constructive to the public in our discussion. Thus, the change Song Confucians made on the issue of the private and the public may not have been as radical as it appears to be.

39. In Gu Yanwu's (顾炎武) treatise on the *jun xian* system (郡县论九篇) (1983, 12–17), for example, he offered insightful analyses of the merits and problems, with regard to the issue of the private and the public, of the feudal system that Confucians were commonly believed to defend, and the centralized *jun xian* system to which the Confucians were commonly said to object.

Although they are samplers, the two general models discussed in this chapter are very useful paradigms for us to think about issues in both the history of political thought and real-world politics, both in the past and in the present. As I have argued, both models break down somewhere, but the breakdown point of the Confucian model is "remote" enough for it to be useful in most ordinary cases. I won't deny that there can be some hybrid models that can address some of the problems the Confucian model encounters. Indeed, as I have repeatedly argued, the Confucian model can embrace the use of laws and institutions, unlike how Han Fei Zi and other critics have portrayed it. But I doubt that there will be any model that can completely resolve all these human dilemmas with regard to the issue of the private and the public.

A Confucian Criticism of the Contemporary Evasion of Virtue

After illustrating and defending the Confucian continuum and harmony model on the issue of the private and the public, in the following two sections, I illustrate some of its implications for contemporary liberal democratic politics, in addition to what has been alluded to so far.

From the Threat to the Public to the Oppression of the Private

It should be noted that in spite of the aforementioned contrasts, the *Republic*, the *Analects*, and the *Mencius* all seem to be concerned with the threat from the private to the public. But from Western later modernity to the contemporary world, the focus has been shifted to the possible threat from the public to the private and to how to guard against the infringement of the private by the public. Mill's *On Liberty* is a very good example of this. In spite of this shift, a shared assumption between the *Republic* and *On Liberty* is the possibility of a strict separation between the public sphere and the private sphere. In general, most virtues promoted by—and many vices condemned by—the "ancients" are now put in the private sphere by the "moderns," both protected from public infringements and prevented from entering into the public sphere and infringing on other private individuals' lives. There are good reasons for the concerns of the moderns (of the West). For one thing, pluralism of values is inevitable in contemporary states, if these states don't resort to oppressive means. But at the same time, later modern and contemporary states have developed far more powerful state machines (than the ones in Western antiquity) that enable governments to have a coercive effect on their citizens, an effect that tyrants of antiquity could only dream of.[40] This development makes

40. By "late modernity," I mean the industrialized and postindustrialized world.

totalitarian government possible. If this is the case, both later modern and contemporary thinkers on the one hand and Plato and early Confucians on the other have good reasons for their apparently opposite concerns, and we shouldn't blame either side for ignoring the issue that concerns the other side. In particular, we shouldn't use contemporary criteria to criticize early Confucians for ignoring the possibility of totalitarianism. Indeed, totalitarianism as we understand it is a misnomer when describing traditional regimes.[41] That is, there was oppression in traditional regimes, but the oppression was far from totalitarian.

With regard to traditional Chinese regimes, there is another reason that "totalitarianism" can be misleading, because totalitarianism means a comprehensive and complete control of common people's lives, including both the material and the moral, imposing something alien to their interests on the people. What is imposed upon the people can be the private interest of a narrow group (mostly the ruling minority)—we can call these types of regimes "selfish totalitarianism"—or a "common good" that is separate from people's interests, which we can call "idealistic totalitarianism." Thus, to appeal to the interests of the people doesn't really challenge the legitimacy of these regimes internally, that is, within the paradigm on which these regimes are based, and to make this challenge means a paradigm shift. In contrast, in traditional China, thanks to the Confucian influence, the governments have to use the banner "for the people" to justify governmental actions, wars included. A nice contrast is Alexander the Great, who is said to have conquered the world for the pursuit of glory (rather than for the interest of his people). He is often considered a hero in the West, and this is simply impossible in traditional China. Of course, the banner "for the people" may have been just that, a banner, and it doesn't mean that there were no oppressive regimes in Chinese history. Nonetheless, it still makes these regimes vulnerable to challenges internal to the political paradigm they allegedly adopt, such as whether the rulers have actually done a good job to serve the people's interests. If the above description is correct, then it may have been misleading to apply the term "totalitarianism" (as it is understood in Western political philosophy and history) to regimes in Chinese history.

The communist regime under Mao is a tricky issue. There is no doubt that it was a totalitarian regime, but perhaps partly thanks to the Confucian heritage, even under this regime, "to serve the people" (为人民服务) was still often considered the highest good. But there may have been a twist to this

---

41. As I understand it, there is a trace of totalitarianism in, for example, some Legalist doctrines. But it becomes a full-blown political mechanism only in late modernity, thanks to the industrial and later information revolutions.

banner that is alien to the Chinese traditions. That is, here "the people" is not inclusive but excludes the classes of "capitalists," "landowners," and so on. Although, as we have seen, early Confucians have a broader reading of people's interests, they are not detached from the ordinary, and, more importantly, they trust people for making judgments on whether their interests are served or not. But there was an abstract, even mystical dimension to the people's interest or the "common good" under Mao's communist regime, so much so that it could lead to the aforementioned strange phenomenon that the city was happy, but no one in the city was (*Republic* 419a–21c); or the "people's" interest was served, but no person or very few in this regime were happy with their lives. Thus, on the normative issue of what makes a regime totalitarian, it is not enough that the regime endorses the appeal to the people; rather, people's interests have to be accessible to most of the people themselves, and their judgment is the ground of legitimacy to the regime, which is a key Confucian requirement, as I argued in chapter 2.

After Mao, the Chinese regime has gradually gone back more and more to the Confucian understanding of the legitimacy of governance. There may still be Maoist residue, and the regime still has totalitarian elements, but the difference between it and the oppressive regimes in the Arabic world (which are oppression by some minority groups over the majority of the people) is clear: the former has a clear dimension of taking the satisfaction of people's ordinary needs as its goal and the foundation of its legitimacy, while the latter doesn't. The failure to appreciate this difference may have been why many Western observers mistakenly believe that following the downfall of some oppressive states in the Arab world, the present Chinese government must collapse soon.

Challenges to Liberal Value Neutrality

Although the Confucian idea "for the people" sounds democratic, as already mentioned, the needs that the government should satisfy include basic relationships and moral needs, not merely material needs, while according to the mainstream understanding of democratic accountability, a government only needs to satisfy people's material needs. This emphasis on moral values can make the liberal-minded people in the contemporary world feel uneasy because, as discussed earlier in this section, they are worried that this emphasis will lead to the infringement of the public and the government on the private. As has been shown, to avoid this infringement, liberal-minded people advocate a state neutrality on the issue of the Good, considering it a matter of free choice of private citizens. To be clear, this value neutrality only regards what is considered to be in the private sphere and about the Good. Liberal value neutrality still presupposes values such as justice as fairness, equality, autonomy, and so on, which are considered as belonging in the realm of the public.

But the problem is whether a functioning and flourishing human society can remain value-neutral in regard to the "private" virtues. Advocates of various doctrines may say "no" to this question, but we ignore them on the basis that their vision of a good society violates some of the important principles and ideas of a liberal society, and is thus considered unreasonable and even crazy. For example, constant wars among different political entities and the killing of innocent people are clearly considered bad from a liberal point of view. But for thinkers like Nietzsche, all the wars and killing would be justified for the realization of the best regime, however fleeting it is. Indeed, the wars may be an indispensable component of the emergence and preservation of this regime. In contrast, peace and stability that are achieved by evading the attempts to realize the best regime are nothing but banality and staleness, and are not desirable.

In order not to digress from the main issue, let us assume that these non-liberal thinkers are indeed unreasonable and even crazy, which is actually a debatable issue. Let us see instead whether there can be some reasonable concerns with state neutrality.

As we have seen, a main reason for state value neutrality is to prevent the government from stifling the plurality of private lives. Before the collapse of the Soviet Union, a highly visible source of this intrusion was the kind of communist governments that imposed values on all aspects of a citizen's life. But this danger seems to have disappeared with the collapse of the Soviet Union and the loss of attractiveness of communism in much of the world. Now the danger seems to come from liberal neutrality itself, for in reality, radical individualism and a free market economy have dominated many, if not most, contemporary liberal democratic societies. The former, in celebrating radical equality and individualism, may have destroyed all authorities except for, intentionally or probably unintentionally, the tyrannical power of the crude and unchecked narrow self-interest of each human being. This is worrisome. For example, if we are not too naive, we know that to sacrifice one's life for the common good is a sad and yet sometimes inevitable task for citizens from any regime. So if individualism means the primacy of one's self-interest, and this version of individualism is taken as the sole moral basis of a liberal democratic state with a large population, how can citizens of this state be persuaded to die for his or her country (the following argument can be applied to smaller sacrifices as well)? Why do they wish to join the military, risking their own or their loved ones' interests in order to protect the interests of millions of strangers? Why can't they choose to be free riders, that is, why can't they trick others to fight for the country while they enjoy security and prosperity without taking the risk? Even if they join the army, can such an army defeat an army from a state that celebrates the love of one's country and the common good?[42] As I argued in chapter 5, if what we were dealing with here was a small community centered around a family or a clan, or a small and close-knit polis, we could use familial love or friendship as a motivational force to sacrifice for others. This would be both easily accessible and nonoppressive. But the sixth fact of modern democracy poses a dilemma: we don't have easy access to some universally recognized virtues anymore, but we are definitely in more desperate need of them.

Moreover, when everything sacred is destroyed by a radical form of individualism, the remaining real and invisible authority, the new God after the death of the old God(s) is unrestrained pursuit of short-term material interests in the free market. Equality becomes equality in the free market, as every human being is a potential buyer of the product that the seller has created for the buyer's (also created?) needs. In a so-called liberal democratic society in the real world, then, the equality that the citizens really enjoy is the equality before the market, and the liberty in such a society is a freedom that liberates people from any other concern than the concern with their short-term material interests. The new God of self-interest and the free market, which has been running wild, may have suffocated a lively plurality of visions of private citizens, and the supply and demand of values. Put another way, the economic free market may have destroyed the free marketplace of ideas. This de facto tyranny of one set of values is protected by liberal value neutrality because the latter doesn't allow the state to challenge the formidable force of the free market by promoting certain values of the Good.

Indeed, this kind of criticism has been raised by many thinkers, such as the so-called communitarians and left-wing and egalitarian thinkers. Common to all these criticisms is the conviction that a desirable liberal society cannot be maintained through liberal neutrality. The Confucianism-inspired political theorist Joseph Chan offers a well-argued and comprehensive criticism of liberal neutrality and a defense of a moderate form of perfectionism, in which perfectionism is defined as "the view that the state should promote valuable conceptions of the good life" (2000, 5). I should add that these values are more than what liberals would typically want the state to protect and promote, such as a framework of justice that would allow people, with their autonomy, to choose values from the free marketplace of ideas. Chan's conclusion is that, on the one hand, the liberal arguments against perfectionism "would either exclude the state from pursuing social justice and other traditional goals or fail

---

42. In Plato's *Republic* (421c–23d), there is an interesting discussion on this issue and the issue of the proper size of the state.

to exclude perfectionist goals at all" (ibid., 41–42). That is, a liberalism excluding perfectionism would pay the price of giving up goals that even liberals would cherish. On the other hand, with regard to perfectionism, Chan states,

> (1) The pursuit of the good life requires the support of an appropriate social environment. (2) The maintenance of the social environment depends on the assistance of the state. (3) Different parts of the political community are interconnected and have a great impact on people's lives. (4) The state should be accountable for this impact and cannot evade the responsibility of evaluating it. (5) A moderate perfectionist state is much more sensible and acceptable than liberal neutralists thought it to be, even if judged by the common standards in liberal-democratic societies. (6) Moderate perfectionism does not violate, and can in fact be justified by, a liberal contractualist account of political legitimacy. (ibid., 42)

In his paper, Chan explicitly claims that Confucianism is a form of perfectionism (ibid., 5n1). In a recently published book, the Confucian scholar Stephen Angle also offers a preliminary proposal based on a moderate perfectionist understanding of Confucianism (2012, especially 139–42).

In fact, we can offer a criticism of liberal neutrality from the Confucian understanding of the relations between the private and public that has been illustrated in this chapter. A premise for the state to stay neutral on the issue of a good life and to allow citizens to make their own choices is the sharp separation between the private and the public. But if what I have argued in this chapter stands, this separation is precisely what early Confucians denied. For them, one's virtues at one's own home (which is outside of the "public sphere") often have implications regarding one's actions in the public sphere, and family environment is a constitutive part of the public sphere. Even if we are only concerned with the public sphere, certain things in the private sphere, including certain "private" virtues, should be of our concern as well.

But the liberal challenge to the Confucian emphasis on the cultivation of virtues is how a regime can apply this without becoming oppressive and endangering pluralism. Compared with the model in the *Republic*, which is focused almost exclusively on the conflict between the private and the public and thus advocates sheer oppression of (much of) the private, the early Confucian model appreciates the constructive aspect of the private to the public, and thus may be less oppressive.

Nevertheless, we still need to show that the Confucian insistence on promoting virtues through social, political, and even legal regulations is not in conflict with pluralism and doesn't lead to oppression. I will come back to this issue in chapter 9. But it should be clear by now that the Confucian model of continuum between the private and the public poses a serious challenge to a fundamental assumption for liberal neutrality, the clear line between the private and the public. If this challenge stands, the liberal defense of state neutrality becomes deeply problematic, and the liberals owe us a further justification for their value neutrality and evasion of virtues in the public sphere.

A Confucian Argument for Gender Equality

The Confucian continuum model that denies a sheer separation between the private and the public may also contribute to the issue of equality between men and women in politics. To be clear, early Confucians were not feminists, and they didn't speak highly of women; nor did most thinkers until rather recently. But as I pointed out in chapter 1, my approach is a continuous and philosophical one. On the issue of gender equality, my concern is what Confucians *would* say about women and about the (newly emerged) issue of equality between men and women, and the really important question is whether the low opinion of women is rooted in the Confucian philosophical system itself or is merely a reflection of the common views of its time that can be discarded in an updated version of Confucianism. Moreover, even if the Confucian objection to gender equality is rooted in some fundamental Confucian principle, we can still put aside the issue of the compatibility between Confucianism and gender equality, and ask if the Confucian idea of the continuum understanding of private-public relations can be useful to support gender equality. The last question is the focus of this section, and I will not comment on the more general question about how Confucianism, as a system of thought, can address issues of gender equality and even feminism.[43]

To see how the continuum understanding can contribute to gender equality, it is helpful to look at an account offered in the *Republic*, which, on the surface, may be considered the first "feminist" account in human history. As we have already seen in this chapter, in the construction of the ideal city, Socrates proposes to give equal opportunities of education and political participation to women. But a careful reading of the text reveals that Socrates doesn't embrace gender equality fully, for he believes that women as a whole are weaker than men in all practices, and thus, even in his radical proposal of educating women and selecting the best women to become rulers and soldiers, he argues that, in general, women should be given lighter parts of the

43. On the general issue of Confucianism and feminism, see, for example, S. Y. Chan (2003), C. Li (2000), and R. Wang (2003).

tasks than men of the same rank (451d–e, 455a–56a, and 457a). It is just that although the best women on average may be only as good as the second-best men, we should still include women in education and in the selection of the ruling class if the second-best men are included in these.

But there is an even more serious challenge to the proposal based on (partial) gender equality in politics. That is, if the best women have to stay away from education (including military training) and political activities for child-rearing duties (for producing the best offspring; Socrates considers it necessary that these women are encouraged to produce as many children as possible with the best men [459a–60a]), it seems that they will be put at an even worse disadvantage than their male counterparts. This is perhaps an unstated reason for Socrates to propose abolishing traditional families and delegating the child-rearing duties to the city, so that women guardians will have "an easygoing kind of childbearing" (460d). If we put all these reasons together, we should see that the apparently feminist proposal in the *Republic* actually offers a serious challenge to the claim of gender equality: if women are still the main caretakers of giving birth to children, feeding them, and rearing them, it seems that they simply couldn't do as good a job of ruling as their male counterparts (unless, of course, the best women choose not to have children, which, for Socrates, would have negative effects on the quality of the next generation of citizens). This is also a spoken or unspoken worry that many employers or voters have when they consider hiring or voting for female candidates in the contemporary world. The message from the *Republic* seems to be a rather depressing one to those who advocate gender equality: unless traditional families are abolished, or at least the state takes over the child-rearing when it is the most burdensome, gender equality cannot really be achieved. The arguably first proposal for gender equality in human history actually poses a hidden and seemingly fatal challenge to it!

A key assumption in this challenge is that to rear children means being away from politics and public life, and retreating to the private, which is a waste of precious training time in public affairs. This is, in turn, premised on the sharp separation between the private (rearing children) and the public (serving in an office), which, as we have seen, is rooted in the *Republic*, and in many contemporary liberal models, on the issue of the private versus the public. Early Confucians, in contrast, denied this separation and emphasized the continuity between the private and the public. From the Confucian understanding of private-public relations, then, one can argue that although women may have to leave office to rear children for a few years, this doesn't necessarily make them less experienced in public affairs. To serve well in the private sphere is related to serving well in the public.

Clearly, early Confucians didn't offer this defense for gender equality in politics, but this argument is in line with their general idea of the role of private life in public service. As I discussed at the beginning of chapter 5, Confucius (as well as Confucians after him) defended the practice of the three-year mourning ritual. Obviously, to stay away from political office for three years after one's parent dies, which is one of the things that the three-year mourning ritual required, was not considered a hindrance to this person resuming his office later. Indeed, if we follow Confucius's reasoning, this retreat may help the mourner to strengthen and even rediscover his sense of care through remembering the care from his parent, and the strengthened and rediscovered filial love could also help him to rediscover life's purpose. We can say that the three-year mourning ritual is a Confucian way of dealing with a midlife crisis, far better than buying a Porsche and having a few mistresses. After all, one is likely to be in midlife when one's parents pass away, and a reason for a midlife crisis is precisely the loss of life's purpose when one has gained a comfortable life, which may have been the goal until now. In the case of a political figure, spending three years away to remember his or her deceased parents and their care, and to think about the meaning of his or her life in the enlarged temporal scale (one lives not just for oneself but for bringing honor to his or her family as well) rather than the mere here and now, a political leader may emerge as a more motivated and caring leader after the absence from politics. Similarly, we can argue that the rearing of children may even help women become better politicians than they would have been without rearing children, because this activity can strengthen their compassion and give them a sense of long-term deliberation, which are both key characteristics in a good public figure.

From the above arguments, we can also see that it still makes sense today to reinstitute some form of the three-year mourning practice. Obviously, even among Confucian "originalists" or fundamentalists, few can follow this practice today. Still, can we institute policies that require the employer to give a one-month paid leave to those whose parents have passed away? There can be certain ritual practices over the three years that wouldn't interfere with the person's work (other than perhaps taking certain days off over the three-year period).[44] The underlying idea may be "thin" enough for people with different comprehensive doctrines (religions) to accept, and

44. In fact, for Jews who still observe their tradition, many activities are suspended during the first thirty days of the death of a first-degree relative, and in the case of mourning a parent, the ritual can last twelve months, although after the first thirty days, many activities are resumed. The fact that Jews observe a similar mourning ritual also supports my following claim that the

this state-sponsored policy that promotes virtues is hardly oppressive and threatening to pluralism.[45]

To be clear, on the gender equality issue, I have only shown that Confucians have resources to support gender equality in the case of public service by women. But, for example, if a woman mathematician has to take a few years off in order to raise her baby, will this necessarily put her at a disadvantage compared with male mathematicians with similar talent and drive? If it does, how should we address the concern of the hiring committee that to hire a female mathematician is not as beneficial to a university's research profile as it is to hire a male mathematician? The Confucian continuum model, as I imagine it, doesn't really help to make a case for gender equality in situations like this one. But I hope that readers can appreciate the possibility for Confucianism, not known for advocating gender equality, to be able to offer some support for it.

---

mourning ritual can be endorsed by people with different religious and comprehensive beliefs.

45. A more general and detailed discussion of the compatibility between some Confucian promotion of virtues and pluralism is offered in chapter 9.

7

Tian Xia: A Confucian Model of National Identity and International Relations

Patriotism Justified and Restrained

Confucian Justification of Patriotism

In chapter 5 I introduced the Confucian concept of compassion, which has three key features. First, it is universal in the sense that everyone has (a seed of) it. Second, it is care that we have for strangers, and if developed fully (which only the few can achieve), it can help us to embrace the whole world. Third, it is hierarchical. Usually we have a stronger sense of care for the ones closer to us than the ones further away, and *justifiably* so. The second feature means that we should care about everyone, and the third one means that we prioritize duties to some over others. This is not necessarily a contradiction, but it demands a skillful balance. In chapter 6, I discussed how to achieve this in a few difficult cases, showing how prioritizing the private and taking care of the public can be in harmony. These cases were about conflicts between one's familial duties and one's duties to the state. If we expand our care one step further, we encounter the issue of one's duties to one's own state and people versus the duties to other states and peoples. The same reasoning discussed in chapter 6 can still be applied to this new situation. Indeed, the Confucian idea of compassion, along with a few other conceptual tools, can be used to address the two remaining key political issues against a "modern" background: how to bond together people of a large, populous, and well-connected state that doesn't have a feudal structure with intermediate and autonomous units, and how to deal with state–state (international) relations when there is no overlord above the states anymore.[1]

1. I have developed this "Confucian" idea based mostly on the *Analects* and the *Mencius*. In this chapter, I mostly use these two texts, although there are references to other Confucian texts that are used to supplement Confucius's and Mencius's ideas on these issues.

Therefore, following the Confucian reasoning, which should be clear by now, and applying it to the issue of one's duties to one's own state versus to other states, one can argue that, given the hierarchical structure of expanding care, one should prioritize duties to one's own state over those to foreign states, thus justifying some form of patriotism. But given the all-embracing characteristic of expanding care, one should still try to take care of the interests of foreigners, thus rejecting a strong form of patriotism as embodied in nationalism, which takes one's homeland's interests as supreme and absolute.

Why should we prioritize the interests of our own state over those of other states? To achieve all-embracing care, one has to expand one's care step-by-step. In the case of the family versus the state, care for the family is the root of care for the state, and the root should naturally be stronger. Similarly, if the state is also a necessary stage of the cultivation of human care, care for the state is the root of caring for the rest of the world, and the former should naturally be greater than the latter. Otherwise, our alleged care for all the people in the world would become rootless and empty. As a later Confucian scholar-official, Sima Guang (司马光) (1019 CE to 1086 CE), put it, "I have heard that the exemplary person holds his kin dear, and extends this feeling to the kin of others; he loves his own country, and extends this love to the countries of others" (zi zhi tong jian [资治通鉴 · 秦纪一 · 始皇帝上]).

A crucial question that needs to be answered here is about the necessity of the state. As long as we don't live in the kind of ideal state proposed in the *Republic*, in which families are completely abolished, we can't imagine human beings doing without the institution of the family. But why do we have to have the political entity of the state? In a passage in 3A4 of the *Mencius* (which is quoted in chapter 2 under "Confucian View of Political Legitimacy" in this book), Mencius argued for the necessity of government. Thus, he would reject an anarchist proposal for eliminating the government. But the government can be a world government. Indeed, a criticism of Confucianism by thinkers such as Liang Qichao (梁启超) (1873 CE to 1929 CE), who witnessed the humiliating defeat of China by Western and Japanese powers, is precisely that Confucian teaching was responsible for Chinese to have a sense of family, community, and then care for the world, but no sense of the state and thus no sense of patriotism (Bell 2011, 113). I make further responses to this criticism throughout this chapter. For now, let me just say that although early Confucians didn't offer any strong defense for the necessity of the state, they didn't offer any rejection of it either. The existence of various states is a natural phenomenon in human history, and early Confucians such as Mencius had strong objections to a state annexing another for the former's own self-interest. As we will see in my discussion of Mencius's idea of just war in chapter 8, only in extreme cases, in which a state is purely tyrannical, can it be eliminated with force by a truly humane state. Given this rather high criterion of legitimate state elimination and annexation, a grand unification that eliminates all states can never be justifiable for Mencius because it would presume that all the other states that are eliminated would be so tyrannical as to be able to be eliminated justifiably by a humane and powerful state, a sheer improbability in the real world. Thus, the existence of individual states, instead of a unified world government, is what Mencius would envision as realistic and justifiable. With this as a basic assumption, our home state and our compatriots are then naturally closer to us, because they are those with whom we have more dealings than foreigners. If we cannot even treat those close to us well, according to the Confucian reasoning, the claim of treating those further away well will just be an empty claim, or a claim that cannot resist serious tests.

In addition to a Confucian rejection of the elimination of states, there can be more direct justifications for the necessity of the state that are drawn from resources other than Confucian texts. If we follow the Nietzschean argument, that a world with no competing units is a world of the last man, while competitions can make human beings' drive for greatness by keeping their will to power alive, which will in turn make human lives worth living and flourishing, then we can say that a unified world without competing units is not desirable. To render this Nietzschean argument innocuous, however, we should stipulate that competition should remain "healthy," that is, for example, violent struggles among these units should be forbidden. But one can object to this line of justification by saying that the units don't have to be states. They could be quasi-autonomous communities under a world government. But these units would need to be large enough to maintain their competitiveness. A small community with even a few thousand people may not be able to maintain even the most basic technologies and institutions to sustain itself as a significant competing unit. Almost all states today are large enough to be competing units. So if there is no justifiable reason to recreate units of competition, why shouldn't these states be kept for the sake of preserving competitions that are essential for human flourishing? Moreover, competing states can perform the function of checks and balances against each other, and against a world government that could become oppressive. The above justifications are not strictly from a Confucian text. But as we have seen, early Confucians were against some radical form of equality and supported meritocratic competitions. In their discussions of the relative merits of feudal (partially autonomous) and *jun xian* (highly centralized) political systems, some later Confucian thinkers also worried about the possibility that the oppression of a highly centralized government could not be challenged anymore when local autonomy was completely eliminated.[2] Therefore, the above justifications of the

2. See, for example, Gu Yanwu's (顾炎武) treatise on the *jun xian* system (郡县论九篇) (1983, 12–17).

necessity of states are in line with some Confucian ideas, and Confucians can endorse these justifications.

But Confucian Patriotism Is Not Unconditional

We have seen so far that although Confucian compassion is all-embracing and thus can bond strangers of the entire world together, its hierarchical nature and the necessity of the states can justify a stronger bonding of people within a state and thus can justify patriotism. This is part of the Confucian answer to the issue of state identity in modern times. But this stronger care for one's compatriots doesn't mean a total disregard of foreigners. Rather, it serves as the basis for our (weaker) care for foreigners. If we have no care for them at all, then, according to Mencius, we lose the one thing that distinguishes us from beasts (*Mencius* 4B19). That is, if we completely disregard other peoples' interests when protecting ours, we cease to be human and become beasts. For early Confucians, to love one's country was justified, but this country had to be one of humans and not beasts. An example here may help. If a few states suffer from flooding at the same time, it is justified to help one's own state and compatriots first. But if in order to prevent one's own state from being flooded one leads the flood to a neighboring country, this act is not justified. Moreover, after the flooding of one's own state is under control, one should then try to help people from other states. What Confucians justify is priority and not supremacy.

Therefore, Confucians do not support the kind of patriotism that promotes one's national interests at all costs, and people don't even have to stay loyal to one's home state at all costs. As discussed in chapter 5 (under "The Cultivation of Compassion"), the father-son and ruler-subject relations are those of reciprocity. It should be noted, however, that although for early Confucians, there is a family-state analogy, it seems that a father enjoys a stronger demand on a son's love than a ruler does on his or her subjects. Although the Han Confucian Dong Zhongshu (董仲舒) seems to suggest that a biological father who abandoned his son shouldn't enjoy the status of a father in some cases,[3] Mencius praised Shun for his steadfast care for his murderous family members, including his father, who even conspired to murder him a few times.[4] To be clear, Shun was a sage, and Mencius's praise of his devotion to the family is not meant to be a universal requirement. But according to early Confucians, the state clearly doesn't enjoy this kind of devotion. As we saw in chapter 2,

---

3. See the extant text of Dong's *Chun Qiu Jue Yu* (春秋決獄) (e.g., S. Cheng 1963, 164). See Loewe (2009) for an English translation.

4. See, for example, the *Mencius* 4A28, 5A1, and 5A2.

early Confucians had reservations with voting with one's hands (i.e., one person, one vote), but they fully embraced the idea of "voting" with one's feet.
This applies to the Confucian exemplary persons (jun zi [君子]) and scholar-
officials (shi [士]) in the sense that they can move from one state to another,
away from a tyrannical ruler, and search for a humane ruler to realize their
political ambitions. Confucius and Mencius were examples of this, and they
supported the free movement of the political elites (see, e.g., the *Mencius*
4B4). Voting with one's feet also applies to the people. For example, when
talking about the right way to make a state strong, Confucius's suggestion is
to make itself so attractive through its humane governance that people from
other states would love to move to said state, thus making it stronger by having
more happy producers, and putting pressure on the not-so-humane states to
shape up (*Analects* 16.1 and 13.16; see also *Mencius* 4A9).

Moreover, for early Confucians such as Mencius, both the common people
and elites can choose not to defend their failed or tyrannical states and thus
choose to welcome and even assist the invading liberators.[5] This is analogous
to the hypothetical case in chapter 6 (under "Early Confucians' Solutions"),
in which Mencius argued that Shun should not stop Gao Yao from arresting
and prosecuting his murderer father, although the devotion to one's father is
considered by Mencius to be stronger than that to the ruler and the state, because he also suggested that Shun should give up his throne and become a
fugitive with his father (7A35). Indeed, in very rare occasions, a rebellion
against a tyrannical ruler and his regime can be justified,[6] although no early
Confucian texts ever justified the killing of a bad father.

In sum, the Confucian concept of compassion can be used to justify patriotism, but this patriotism is not unconditional. The pursuit of national interest,
one's loyalty to the state, and the sovereignty of the state are all limited by the
same Confucian concept of compassion and humaneness. This conditionality
is interpreted by some critics as a lack of state identity and patriotism in Confucianism, but this is a clear misunderstanding. It cannot be denied, however,
that Confucian patriotism is weaker than an extreme nationalist version, but
as I argue later in this chapter, this may be a merit of Confucian patriotism. Of
course, though conditional, one still shouldn't abandon his or her country
whenever it becomes inconvenient to stay loyal to it. The Confucian elites
should especially try to save their troubled country rather than abandoning
their patriotic and humane duty and moving to another country, as long as

5. See, for example, 3B5. I will come back to this in the discussion of a Mencian theory of
just war in chapter 8.

6. But as shown in chapter 2, people don't have the right to start and lead the rebellion, and
only elites with certain political status do.

their country is not going down a tyrannical path and there is nothing that can be done to change it.[7] For the common people, when one's own country's trouble is not so serious as to meet Mencius's rather stringent criteria of liberation, to defend one's country is also (partially or completely) just.[8]

The Civilized and Barbaric Distinction
and a Confucian World Order
Early Confucian Tian Xia Model

When we expand our care beyond state borders, it seems that we will embrace all of humanity. But for early Confucians, there was another stopping point in the expanding circles of care. To understand this, let me introduce another crucial Confucian distinction between the civilized (xia [夏]) and the barbaric (yi [夷]). This distinction is sometimes understood as a racially based distinction between ethnically Chinese people and non-Chinese people. But this is clearly not the case for Confucius and Mencius. In the *Mencius* 3A4, Mencius criticized Chen Xiang, a former pupil of Chen Liang (who is no relation to Chen Xiang):

> I've heard that xia convert yi, but not that xia is being converted by yi. Chen Liang was a native of the state of Chu. Being delighted with the way of Duke Zhou and Confucius, he came north to study in the Middle Kingdoms, and no one from the north could excel him.

In the traditional Western Zhou feudal world, the states and peoples who followed the Zhou feudal order were considered xia, and those who didn't were considered yi or barbaric. Even in this understanding, the distinction was not racial but political. In this passage, Mencius pushed the nonracial feature of this distinction even further. In the traditional feudal sense, the state of Chu, which didn't follow the feudal order under the Western Zhou regime (let alone under the Eastern Zhou regime, when the feudal order was collapsing), was considered a yi state by the northern Chinese states that followed the Zhou feudal order and considered themselves xia. In Mencius's opinion, however, in spite of his "barbaric" origin, Chen Liang became a member of the xia people because he learned the way of Duke Zhou and Confucius, which symbolizes xia. In contrast, although it is likely that Chen Xiang was from a xia state, he failed to follow xia and thus degraded himself to the level of barbar-

---

7. For a more detailed discussion about an exemplary person's duty to a nonideal state, see Bai (2010b).

8. I discuss this in detail in chapter 8.

ians and should be considered a barbarian, not a member of the xia people, which was implicitly indicated by Mencius.[9]

It should be clear, then, that whether someone is a member of the xia people or the yi people depends on whether he or she adopts the xia way of politics and life and not on one's race or country of origin. Thus, we can safely interpret xia in Mencius's use as "civilized."[10] "Xia" or "Hua Xia" is often used to refer to the Chinese. But in this sense, "Chinese" means the civilized, and not the so-called ethnically Chinese people of today. This understanding of the distinction between xia and yi can be found in other early Confucian classics such as *Spring and Autumn Annals* (春秋) and its classical commentaries.[11]

During the SAWS (roughly from 770 BCE to 221 BCE), there were more than one xia states, and the Chineseness in the broad sense of this term, the identity of the civilized way of life, became a bond among all civilized states. The question, then, is what distinguishes one civilized state from another? One Confucian answer is the hierarchical nature of compassion that was already illustrated in the previous section. Another answer, which was not explicitly made by early Confucians, but was a common practice during the SAWS and in later traditional China, is culture. During the SAWS, each Chinese state had its own spoken and written language (although the differences among the written languages of different Chinese states may not be very significant), they had different history and customs, and their people were known to have different general characteristics. These cultural distinctions could be taken as the identity of a state that further bonds its people together.

With all these clarifications, we can finally give a complete picture of the Confucian world order—I call it the "Confucian tian xia model,"[12] which was succinctly expressed in the *Gongyang Commentary*: a people should "give preferential treatment to their own state over other *xia* [civilized or Chinese] states [which, presumably, implies that this state is a civilized state], and give

9. What Mencius didn't point out is that in terms of legendary origin, the state of Chu came from the same ancestor as the xia peoples, and it was considered barbaric because it didn't adopt the xia way of politics and life.

10. To make an artificial distinction, in this book, the term "civilized" and its variants refer to the common features of different civilized peoples, while "culture" refers to what distinguishes one people from another.

11. X. Guo (2012) has a more detailed discussion on this issue. This article also addresses more textually based claims that the Chinese-barbaric distinction is racially based, and defends the thesis that this distinction is between the civilized and the barbaric.

12. The term *tian xia* literally means "all under Heaven." But for early Confucians, the heavenly way has a moral content, and thus their tian xia model is not a world order in reality but an idealized and moral one. In the following, I use the term "tian xia system" to refer to the system in the traditional Chinese world that is inspired by the Confucian tian xia model.

preferential treatment to all *xia* states over *yi* [barbaric] ones" (春秋公羊传 · 成公十五年). The preferential treatment concept, or the hierarchy of care, has its roots in the Confucian concept of compassion, as well as in cultural and civilizational identities. Of course, identity with the civilized way of life is also an implication of identity with the Confucian concept of compassion and humaneness.

World Order in Post-Qin China

But then, all the so-called civilized states in the known world were unified by the state of Qin, with the means and theories that early Confucians wouldn't endorse. In the following unified dynasties, Confucianism was reintroduced into the mainstream. But as different Chinese states disappeared, so did the cultural identities that would be used to differentiate one Chinese state from another. What served as the identity of all the "Chinese" (civilized) people, that is, its civilizedness, became identical with the identity of all the Chinese in the unified Chinese state, that is, its culture. The Chineseness in the sense of being civilized became one and the same as the cultural identity of the unified Chinese state. That is, the Chineseness now took up the dual identities of civilizedness and culture. Even during disunity, the strong dual identities still persisted, partly because there were no clear political, cultural, and civilizational alternatives available.[13]

In this unified world, another version of the world order that was partly inspired by the Confucian tian xia model—I will call it the tian xia system—emerged. In this tian xia system, China was the center of civilization of the whole world, and other states either accepted the influence of China and became an unequal member of the world system (Korea, Vietnam, and so on during certain historical periods) or kept their barbaric ways, waiting to be civilized by China or taking the initiative to follow the China model. During the periods when China was a unified empire, all the civilized world (that was known to and recognized by the Chinese) was subsumed under this tian xia system. In this system, Chinese civilization and political institutions were considered identical and represented the universal principle of all civilized peoples. It should also be noted that both the cultural and civilizational identities in this system do not have a racial dimension.

---

13. This is a rather simplified picture of traditional Chinese history; there are many exceptions to this picture in the real history. One significant exception is the relations between the Song dynasties and Liao and later Jin dynasties, as well as the Xi Xia dynasty. These "dynasties" were more or less equal members of a world system rather than members on different levels of a tian xia–style hierarchy, and how they dealt with one another resembled relations among sovereign states. Tian Ye (田野) offers a very interesting discussion of this in his conference presentation (2015).

With this understanding, we can offer a further response to Liang Qichao's criticism, mentioned in the previous section, that Chinese had clan and tian xia identities but no national identity and thus no patriotism. The reason for the lack of state identity in post-Qin traditional China (206 BCE to 1911 CE) is that the China in which Liang lived was in fact a unified "world" system, in which there could be changes of (world) government (dynasties) but no changes of states. If today's world became unified under a one-world government, the people's sense of national identity would likely also be weakened.

Although I keep emphasizing the idea that there is not a racial aspect in this system, in certain periods of traditional Chinese history, as Tang Wenming (唐文明) points out, the Chinese-barbaric distinction did have a racial dimension due to the oppression from invading peoples, but this was not the usual case. Normally, Tang argues, Chineseness "is created and developed by the Chinese people" and "is the civilizational ideal that takes the Chinese people as its main subject," and the identity of the Chinese people "is also gradually formed in the development of this ideal." According to Tang, this is cultural nationalism. But in this chapter, I use "culture" to refer to what belongs to a specific people, and "civilization" or "civilizedness" to refer to what distinguishes it from the barbaric. Since the unification after the SAWS, the cultural and civilizational distinction collapsed, and thus we should call this kind of "nationalism" civilizedness-based and culture-based nationalism. Tang further argues,

> In fact, only under one kind of circumstances did the racial implication of the Chinese-barbaric distinction become prominent; that is, when an alien race conquered the Chinese state and governed it in a way in violation of the Chinese civilizational ideal. Under these circumstances, the civilizational distinction overlaps with the racial distinction. Borrowing the distinction between cultural nationalism and political nationalism, which has been introduced since modern times, we can say that the Chinese-barbaric distinction both expresses itself as a cultural nationalism and as a political nationalism. In particular, when the alien race imposes a clearly racial policy [on the Chinese], discriminating against the Chinese, the racial implication of the Chinese-barbaric distinction presents itself in an even more extreme manner. Clearly, the political nationalism is a reactive nationalism, and deep down, it is based on anti-racism. The political nationalism with a strong racial sense finishes its historical task as soon as the external institutional pressure of racial control is removed. (2010, 10)[14]

14. For a somewhat different but far more detailed analysis of the emergence of Han Chinese identity, see Elliot (2012).

But China was eventually defeated by the West. It was defeated by other peoples and powers before then, but the perception had always been that these peoples didn't represent competing political, cultural, or civilizational models. If anything, they (often the nomads) just had better horses, which, during the cold weaponry times, would have given significant advantage to those who had them. Only a foreign influence such as Buddhism seemed to offer something culturally competitive, but the Buddhists didn't have an invading army, and Buddhism was also absorbed into the Chinese culture. The defeat by the West, however, seems to suggest to the Chinese that not only did the Westerners have superior military forces, but they had superior political, cultural, and civilizational models. This is indeed a challenge that the Chinese haven't witnessed for thousands of years. Thinkers of late Qing and early Republican periods, such as Zhang Taiyan (章太炎), reacting to Western nationalism, downgraded the Chinese civilization to what constitutes the particular language, customs, and history of the Chinese as a particular nation (Tang 2011, 104). That is, now the dual meanings of "Chinese" (civilizedness and culture) are reduced to the meaning of culture alone.[15]

Confucian New Tian Xia Model

Reduction or not, we have to acknowledge today that outside of the traditional Chinese tian xia system, there are other civilized states that are independent of the Chinese system. So the Chineseness in the Confucian tian xia model has to assume two identities in the contemporary world. First, in a narrow sense, Chineseness is "what constitutes the particular language, customs, and history of the Chinese as a particular nation." Here we adopt a "thick" understanding of Chineseness, which refers to the collection of what constitutes the Chinese culture that serves as the bond of the Chinese nationals, including Chinese history, important figures, classics, and institutions. This is a possible foundation upon which to distinguish contemporary Chinese people from non-Chinese people. Second, in a broad sense, according to the understanding of early Confucians, Chineseness is referred to as "the universal values of all civilized peoples." Using classics that are an important bearer of civilization, in today's world, not only Chinese classics, but also classics from other traditions that meet the criteria of civilizedness (such as Plato's *Republic*) should be included in the repertoire of civilized people. The mean-

15. If this account is correct, those cultural conservatives who are against (Western) universal values, and insist that Confucianism is a culture specific to the Chinese, are actually following the understanding of Chineseness as offered by the antitraditionalists, violating the universalist understanding of early Confucians, which is a little ironic.

ing of "being civilized" still needs to be further elucidated, but it should include the following Confucian values: the legitimacy of the state lies in service to the people, humane governance is the ideal of the government, and Confucian compassion is a key virtue.

Therefore, in the contemporary world, according to Confucian theory, cultural elements such as geography, history, language, and customs constitute state identity. The state so formed becomes a step in the effort to extend care outward. Through the Confucian universal but unequal love concept, the love of one's state is justified. Although Confucians don't consider sovereignty sacred, state borders should still be respected and cannot be changed arbitrarily. Even if two states are both civilized states and share the same culture, it is not justified to unify these two states by force as long as they already exist as independent states and are not inhumane states. If one of the two states tries to annex the other state by force, this action disqualifies the former as being civilized, and the defense of the latter is justified. Above states, all civilized states should be bonded together by their shared commitment to the civilized way of life. As an entity, they should defend the civilized way of life and guard against and exert positive influence on the barbaric states. As mentioned above, the meaning of "civilized" needs to be further elucidated, but the following can be said of a barbaric state: it is one that either tyrannizes its people or, out of incompetence or indifference, fails to offer basic services to its people, leaving them in great suffering; moreover, it threatens the well-being of other people or completely disregards its duty to other people, such as the duty to protect a shared environment. Simply put, "civilized" is a term deeply associated with the Confucian idea of humaneness. Using a real-world example, we can say that the sovereignty of such a country as North Korea should not be respected at all, and should not be given a seat, let alone an equal membership, in the world community. A telling sign of a civilized state is the recognition of the above and its willingness to contribute to bringing down such a regime, if it doesn't lead to great suffering of the North Korean people and other people who are threatened by this country.

According to this new tian xia model, which is based on the early Confucian tian xia model and is updated to the new reality of the contemporary world, the people of one civilized state should "give preferential treatment to their own state over other civilized states," and people of all civilized states should "give preferential treatment to all civilized states over barbaric ones." To love one's own state and to love all civilized states are justified, and to put one's own state's interests above other states' interests and to put all civilized states' interests above the barbaric ones are also justified. In the meantime, however, giving preferential treatment doesn't mean having a total disregard of the interests of "the other." Rather, people have a moral duty (based on the

Confucian idea of compassion and humaneness) to the other. Civilized states can justifiably intervene with the business of the barbaric (failed, tyrannical, and ultranationalist) states. Of course, we should first try to be a moral exemplar, "the beacon on the hill," as a way of moral intervention, and only under some extreme circumstances can military interventions be justified. In the latter case, the sovereignty of a tyrannical state should not be protected, and the defense of this state can be unjust. This is comparable to the domestic case within a constitutional and liberal state in which those who commit extremely heinous crimes are punished with state-sanctioned violence—and in both cases, a state's sovereignty and a person's liberty are conditional upon some basic humane duties. Among civilized states, although a civilized state can prioritize its own state's interests over another civilized state's, and the former can even be in fierce competitions with the latter, the competitions can never be conducted through violence because otherwise, these states wouldn't be considered humane, which is a key feature of being civilized. This is a thesis of "civilized peace" rather than democratic peace. The situation is comparable to the domestic case within a constitutional and liberal state in which, as described by Rawlsian political liberalism, the quarrels among reasonable citizens should never be conducted violently. Overall, as already mentioned toward the end of the second part of chapter 4 in this book, the Confucian hierarchical international system mirrors the hierarchy within a state, and answers the objection to Rawls that there is an asymmetry between his international order and his domestic order.

Although there can be additional definitions of civilizedness, we can already see that it must include the following ideas: First, the legitimacy of the state lies in service to the people (to its own people first and to other people second), and humaneness should be the overarching principle within a state and among states. To be clear, the service to its own people should be considered primary, but a state's duty to all humanity should also be considered. For example, if by serving its own people, a state causes an environmental crisis abroad, it loses its legitimacy to some extent because of this. Second, the reflection of the supremacy of humaneness in international relations is that a civilized state should never use force to solve a conflict with another civilized state, while violence is an acceptable (but last) resort to interfere with and to civilize a barbaric state. Third, not on the basis of an originally Confucian position but on a position that Confucians can endorse,[16] another element of civilizedness is the protection of some basic rights and liberties. Fourth, we need to preserve the classics and other heritage that constitute the civilized way of life.

16. See chapter 9 for more discussion on this issue.

A clarification is due here. The promotion of a new tian xia system that is inspired by the Confucian new tian xia model may sound threatening to the people on a lower ladder of the traditional Chinese tian xia hierarchy, such as the Koreans. But it should be clear that the system I am proposing is a normative one that is drawn from early Confucian resources and is meant to have universal applications. In reality, not only was traditional China a member of the tian xia system, but it was its core, creator, and guarantor. But in the enlarged and updated new tian xia system, whether contemporary China or its leader can even be a member of the civilized world is not a given but something that China has to earn and other countries can earn as well. Indeed, contemporary China may not be a fully "Chinese" state yet, if "Chinese" is understood in the broad sense of civilizedness.

Is Nation-State the Only Path to Modernity?

China's Nationalist Path to "Modernity"

From what I have argued in this chapter, it should be clear that although the encounter with the modernized West has made China realize that the world was not unified in a tian xia system in which China is the center, and China is but one state among many, the normative Confucian version of the tian xia system, if adapted to the contemporary world (as presented in the previous section), can still be used to address problems in a world of competing states—a reality since the advent of Western modernity.

Unfortunately, the mainstream view seems to be the opposite. A received narrative in the past 150 or more years, which is intended to explain the repeated and humiliating defeat of China by Western powers and a rising Japan, is that the West entered modernity while China was premodern. To escape from the fate of defeat, then, China needs to modernize itself. A key feature of a political entity being modern is that it is a nation-state: to be modern is to become a nation-state.

In this narrative, it is important, then, for us to understand what a nation-state is. In the process of European modernization, the concept of a sovereign state was developed from the Westphalian treaties, according to which other states could not legitimately interfere with the internal affairs of a sovereign state. This concept was then combined with the idea of nation-state that was developed in the eighteenth century, which led to the sovereignty-based nation-state model.[17] In the complicated process of the evolution of the

17. I wish to thank Qian Jiang for drawing my attention to the distinction between sovereign states and nation-states, and the fact that nation-states were only fully established after World War I. But as I will argue, the concepts of sovereign state and nation-state were introduced to

nation-state model, different versions of it have emerged. But when this model becomes dominant through the ascendency of the West over the rest, a particular version of the nation-state model is often perceived as *the* nation-state model. In this version—let me call it the nationalist version—"nation" is understood as a race, and it offers unity to a nation-state; sovereignty makes the nation-state an individual entity; in the world of nations, each nation-state is justified to pursue its national interests at all costs, and the basis of the relations among these "monads" or individual nation-states is power or realpolitik.

Traditional China was obviously not a nation-state in this sense, and is often compared with pre-nation-state political entities such as empires. Among those who know a little about traditional China, what the American right-wing sinologist Lucian Pye said about China may be a rather popular account:

> China is not just another nation-state in the family of nations. China is a civilization pretending to be a state.[18] The story of modern China could be described as the effort by both Chinese and foreigners to squeeze a civilization into the arbitrary, constraining framework of the modern state, an institutional invention that came out of the fragmentation of the West's own civilization. Viewed from another perspective, the miracle of China has been its astonishing unity. In Western terms the China of today is as if the Europe of the Roman Empire and of Charlemagne had lasted until this day and were now trying to function as a single nation-state. (1990, 62)[19]

However one understands the nature of traditional China as a state, the mainstream narrative is that traditional China was premodern and not a modern nation-state. The traditional Chinese model of state identity and international relations ceases to be relevant to the modern world, and cannot offer guidance in a constructive manner anymore.

Moreover, as I presented in the previous section, a historical version of the tian xia system is one in which China was the center of the civilized world, dominating all other states and accepting homage from the latter. It is then argued that not only was China premodern, but the vision that China has been

---

address issues caused by the collapse of feudalism. In this sense, these two concepts are closely related to each other. To be sure, the history from the establishment of the concept of sovereign state, the transition from sovereign state to nation-state, and to the development of the concept of "nation" is long and complicated. What I offer in this chapter is merely a rather simplified account.

18. In another article, the same sentence is almost exactly repeated with one important revision: the last occurrence of "state" is replaced with "nation-state" (Pye 1993, 130).

19. It is not that difficult to find accounts, especially among sinologists (e.g., Joseph Levinson), that are similar to Pye's. See Z. Yang (manuscript) for more examples.

accustomed to will make a rising China a threat to the existing world order, for the latter is built on a vision of states being equal members of the world community, while in the historical version of the tian xia system, China is not an equal member in this community. A rising China, if it returns to its old path, will destabilize the world, to say the least.

Therefore, from the consideration of both modernization and world peace, it seems that China must follow the West, establishing a nation-state and becoming an equal member in the world of nation-states. The establishment of the Republic of China and the People's Republic of China may be interpreted as efforts toward this end. With the modernization of China so understood, some argue that the destruction of Chinese traditions, both on the material and on the spiritual levels, and the atrocities committed in the past 150 years by Chinese revolutionaries can be defended as a necessary evil or a necessary sacrifice—the good end justifies all the ugly means. This defense is also used as an excuse for some Chinese to become apologists and underlings for the present Chinese government, and to become nationalists.

Ironically, when some Chinese intellectuals and politicians hope that by waving the nation-state flag, China can finally join the club of modern states, "stand up," and look "normal," many Western countries start having different thoughts about nation-states. They realize that the kind of nation-states that pursue nothing other than their narrowly defined national interests (short-term material interests) and follow only power politics are also a source of instability and war in the world. The later-developed and newly rising powers, such as Nazi Germany and Jingoist Japan, brought great damage to the world order, which is why the rise of China is worrisome to many in the world as well. To correct the wrongs of the nation-state model, now many Western countries have tried to transcend it by flying the banner of "human rights override sovereignty" and continue to be suspicious of the rise of China. Many Chinese are perplexed and even angered by this suspicion, and keep emphasizing the peaceful rise of China. But as long as the Chinese government keeps using typical nation-state language, such as "our national interests and sovereignty are sacred and cannot be threatened," the rest of the world will continue to worry and justifiably so, because almost no nation-state rises peacefully. A rising nation-state will demand a larger share of the benefits of the world order, if it pursues its national interest by power only, and will thus be doomed to disturbing the existing world order and peace.

Nation-State Is Only One Possible Path to Modernity

It is both ironic and tragic that being criticized by the West and Westernizing forces, China has tried to become a Western-style nation-state, and this becomes a new source of criticism by the West. Ironic as it is, however, if the nation-state model is the only path to modernity, and if modernity is desirable, China will have to emulate the West while looking suspicious and even ridiculous. But as I argued in chapter 1, what happened during the SAWS or the Zhou-Qin transition is comparable to European modernization in many aspects. We could debate on the meaning of modernity, and whether the Zhou-Qin transition is an early modernization. But I think that the following statement is not really very controversial.[20] In both medieval Europe and Western Zhou China, the ruler of a political entity, for example, a feudal state, didn't directly control all the people and land in his state, and he had delegates (lesser nobles) who ruled over smaller and somewhat autonomous units within his state. That is, this ruler didn't have absolute sovereignty even within his own state. In Western Zhou China, the king served as an overlord of all feudal states. He could intervene with these states' affairs to a limited extent, and this conditional intervention was another limit to the sovereignty of the lord of a feudal state. In medieval Europe, there was no overlord who enjoyed a status as stable as the Zhou king did, but there were often trans-state authorities, such as the pope, who had the right to intervene with state affairs. Moreover, although the whole feudal system may appear to be large, through the multilevel delegatory structure, on each level, only the ruler and his delegates (on the lowest level, the ruler and his people) form a closely knit and small community of acquaintances, and an apparently large state is thus divided into many communities of this kind. Each community is bonded by a shared sense of the Good, by rituals, and by (explicit and implicit) laws or noble codes of conduct.

During the Zhou-Qin transition and early European modernization, however, the above political structure collapsed. In the ensuing jungle politics, in which political entities were faced with the Hamlet question, "to be or not to be," or to conquer or be conquered, eventually a new type of large states emerged. Within these states, the delegatory system by the nobles disappeared and was replaced by a centralized government. In the meantime, no legitimate arbiters existed above the states anymore. In other words, absolute or near absolute sovereignty emerged. Although there were no Westphalian treaties in China to recognize the naturally developed sovereign status of states in a legal form, giving it a touch of sanctity, states in the Warring States period all gained de facto independence and sovereignty similar to those in modern Europe. International relations as we understand them today also emerged. With no overlord to play the role of arbiter, and with noble codes of conduct no longer functioning, international relations would have to be built upon the naked and oftentimes brutal pursuit of national interests, if we don't find alternative trans-state authorities and rulers. Within each state, without the del-

20. I have already discussed these comparisons in chapter 1, but let me repeat a few key points that are relevant to the discussion in this chapter.

egates, the rulers would have to face thousands and even millions of strangers. The internal bonds in feudalism (kinship, rituals, codes of conduct, a shared sense of the Good, etc.) that are applicable to small political communities are not effective in large, populous, well-connected, and centralized states. To discover new bonds between rulers and their subjects and among all the people under such conditions becomes an urgent issue.

With China's Zhou-Qin transition and European modernization understood in this manner, we can see that the kind of understanding well expressed in Pye's quote is rooted in a false analogy. What is comparable to today's world is the Warring States period of Chinese history; the contemporary world is an enlarged version of the Warring States. After the Warring States period, the "world" was unified, until the Chinese came to the painful realization that China was merely a part of a much larger world with many more states. Where the contemporary world is going remains to be seen. In theory, political philosophers will have to address the problems in this enlarged Warring States version.

In this light, we should see that the nation-state model is one way to address two of the emerging issues of modernity: how to bond a society of strangers together as a state and how to deal with state–state relations. But even in the West, this is not the only answer offered. For example, in Karl Marx's *The Civil War in France*, he introduced the concept of class to replace nation as the social glue for strangers in modern societies (Sun 2014b). Before the Middle Ages, the Roman Empire used military force and laws to regulate the whole empire, applying different laws to the Romans and other peoples, and the contemporary Western ideas of constitutional patriotism and cosmopolitanism can be considered a modern development of the Roman practices. Facing similar problems, pre-Qin Chinese thinkers offered their own answers, including the Confucian model, an updated version of which was just offered in this chapter. So, it is simply wrong to claim that to become a nation-state is the only path to modernity. Among all the different paths, a question that a normative theorist needs to answer is which model addresses the aforementioned issues of modernity best, and I argue that the Confucian new tian xia model is one of the best answers. To do so, I compare the Confucian model with the nation-state and cosmopolitan models, and show the viability of and even the superiority of the Confucian model.

Confucian Model versus Nation-State Model

The Nationalist Version of the Nation-State Model

There are many different forms or versions of the nation-state model that have emerged in modern Europe. A fair and comprehensive evaluation of all these different versions is an important project but is beyond the scope of this chapter. In the following, I have chosen one version of it, the so-called nation-alist version, which was introduced in the previous section. According to this version of the nation-state, although a nation can have cultural, linguistic, and geographic elements, the defining element of a nation is blood relations or race. If the majority of the people of a state belong to the same nation in this sense, and the majority of the people who belong to this nation live in this state, this state is a nation-state. The merit of this version of the nation-state is that the identity is clear, and the bond can thus be very strong. The line be-tween the "self" and the "other" is also clear. Within the borders is a big family of kin, and outside are strangers who are no relation. Under this clear division between the self and the other, national interests can be well established, and they are the sole and supreme concern in the nation-state's dealings with other states. In this framework, if there is no conflict of interests among states, they can peacefully exist with one another. But if there are conflicts (which are inevitable in a globalized world), the state can resort to bribery, coercion, and even war in order to satisfy its own interests. There could be international laws, but the nation-state uses them only when they are convenient to advance its national interests. When international laws are not convenient, they will be manipulated or outright ignored, if the nation-state is skillful, powerful, or shameful enough. If there are other races within a nation-state and they have a conflict of interests with the majority race (which is also inevitable), similar to the case of international relations, this nation-state will resort to all kinds of means, including genocide. If outside of a nation-state there are settlements by people of the same race as the majority of this nation-state, the nation-state will try to unite with these settlements.

It is fair to say that the version of the nation-state that I offer here is an ex-treme nationalist one. But historically, this is a model that many states have followed, and it has been emulated by many non-Western countries, including China. Even in the West, there is a recent rise of right-wing nationalism that embodies this version of the nation-state. Thus, to evaluate the merits and problems of this version and compare it with the Confucian model is still an important task.

Before we evaluate this version of a nation-state, a clarification needs to be made. This version of a nation-state is built on the purity of the nation or race, but this can be purely imaginary and artificial. Indeed, contrary to the nation-state story according to which a nation makes a state, what actually happens is that the state makes a nation. That is, a large unified state emerges first, and in order to bond itself together, a nation is invented. In this sense, although it is commonly understood as a doctrine that is intended to transcend nations, a cosmopolitan ideal may have played a constructive role in nation-state build-ing, because its emphasis on transcending communal identities can help to form a nation.[21] Nation-state, then, is rooted in a contradiction: it adopts cosmopolitanism within the state but rejects it without. This contradiction can be better contained when the identity of the "within" and boundaries between the "within" and the "without" are more sharply drawn.

Comparisons and Contrasts

Imagined or not, the idea of blood relations is intuitive and strong, more so than, for example, the kind of state identity offered by the Confucian idea of hierarchical care. Since it treats all people in it as a big family, a nation-state can have a strong motivation to protect its people, and even promote individuals' rights within the state. This kind of protection and promotion can facilitate the creativity of the individual and the community.[22] But in the benefits of this model also lie its drawbacks. The bond is strong in this kind of nation-state because it is using blood relations, and blood relations are exclusive. A person of a different race (nation) can never become a citizen of this nation, and other states and other people are forever the other. As a result, the conflict of interests can be resolved with whatever means possible, including wars. Within a state, ethnic cleansing can be accepted, and internationally, this version of a nation-state model is also a root cause of wars among nations, including the two world wars, which were caused by European nation-states and Japan, which closely followed the Western nation-state model. This kind of nation-state can appear to be self-contradictory in another way (than the aforementioned contradiction between cosmopolitanism within and nationalism without): it can be humane to its own and tyrannical to the aliens. A good example of this is King Leopold II of Belgium, who was a promoter of rights and liberties in Belgium and of brutal colonization and mass killings in Africa. As Jack Donnelly puts it, the nation-state is both the "principal violator and essential protector" of human rights (2003, 35). But if we understand the logic of this version of the nation-state, there is nothing contradictory between these two sides of a nation-state.

In contrast, as I argued earlier in this chapter, the Confucian model acknowledges the (conditional) sovereignty and sanctity of individual states and is not meant to be a complete rejection of the nation-state,[23] but instead of using race, which is exclusive, in the Confucian model, the bond is hierarchical care and culture. The drawback with this kind of bond is that it is not as strong as blood relations, but here lies its merit: precisely because it is not very

21. I thank Theodore Hopf for making the latter point with me.
22. I thank Chong Ming (崇明) for making this point with me.
23. I thank Mathias Risse for pushing me to be clear on this.

strong, it can be inclusive. As we saw in the passage from 3A4 of the *Mencius*, which I mentioned earlier in this chapter, one could become a xia person by adopting the xia culture and way of life. Historically, an important reason that the Chinese civilization could continue and expand is that it adopted (partly) the Confucian model of state identity and not the race-based nation-state model. If traditional China had adopted the latter, it would have been impossible for the Chinese to assimilate so many different races (by mixed marriages, by aliens' voluntary conversions to the Chinese way of life and thus becoming Chinese, and sometimes by wars, of which the Confucian model wouldn't approve), and the collapse of any Chinese state, which happened a few times in Chinese history, could be the end of the Chinese civilization in the sense that the "Chinese" wouldn't be the bearers of the Chinese culture and way of life anymore, as was the case for ancient Egyptians, ancient Greeks, ancient Romans, and ancient Indians.[24] In contrast, the Confucian model helped the continuation of the Chinese civilization and the *relative* peacefulness of its expansion.[25]

Therefore, the Confucian new tian xia model is not intended to eliminate nation-states but to offer a more inclusive foundation for them. One can argue that there are versions of the nation-state model that don't use race but instead use something "soft" and inclusive, similar to the cultural identity in the Confucian order. Moreover, the nation-states are also required to respect international laws that are based on "natural laws," that is, laws that are considered to have moral content and are a priori. On this point, there may be two differences between this kind of nation-state model and the Confucian model. First, the ultimate principle on which the Confucian model is based, the Confucian idea of humaneness and compassion, can be ametaphysical and naturalistic. Second, the kind of international order the Confucian model would embrace is clearly different from today's UN model if we take it as a community of equal member states, because the Confucian order is hierarchical, and it is also different from the UN model if we understand it as a hierarchy with the five permanent members of the security council on top, because the Confucian hierarchy is determined by the humaneness of the states and not by some historical contingencies that are not relevant anymore. But we can imagine a version of the nation-state model that can also embrace some ametaphysical

24. To clarify, the Confucian understanding of Chinese identity may have been merely a contributing factor to—but is neither a sufficient nor necessary condition of—Chinese cultural continuity. I also don't mean to suggest that the reason that the other three cultures failed to preserve their cultural identity was its adoption of the nation-state model, which is simply historically false. I thank Wang Caihong for pushing me to clarify this point.

25. I deal with the objection that the historical expansion in China was not as peaceful as some may wish to believe later in this section.

principle of international order, and the de facto world police system that is built on the above principle. If so, I am happy to accept the possibility that the Confucian model is not the best model but one of the best.[26]

Reply to a Realistic Objection: Icing on the Cake Matters

As mentioned in the previous section, many Western countries have realized the great danger caused by the strong exclusiveness of the nationalist version of the nation-state and its unconditional pursuit of national interests. As a result, they are deeply worried about the rise of China, which seems to follow this kind of nation-state model. On the one hand, the hypocrisy beneath their worries and accusations—"we have got our lion's share through our nationalist policies in the past, but you cannot do the same"—is ironic, if not shameless. On the other hand, as my above criticisms of the nationalist model shows, their worries have a legitimate foundation. As Tang Wenming points out,

> If we have a clear understanding of the logic of capitalistic development and the political economy of modern imperialist states, from a rational perspective, it is hard to believe in the rhetoric of a "peaceful rise" once adopted by the Chinese government: who can believe that a China that emulates America in every step will adopt a pacifist ideology after its rise? (2011, 105)

Tang's conclusion presupposes the following understanding: the United States is a hegemon that is driven purely by national interests. This is a well-held belief among those, in China or elsewhere, who have a cynical view of American and Western involvement in international affairs. Such an accusation can be generalized as a nationalist and realist criticism of the Confucian model. That is, what each state will actually follow is its national interests, and the talk of humaneness or, in the case of the United States and Western powers, the talk of human rights is just that: empty talk. The realist has a point: it may well be true that any state in the real world (including traditional China, which was under a strong Confucian influence) couldn't help but take national interests as the primary concern. But as Mencius put it, what distinguishes us from beasts is rather slight (4B19). To a large extent, we are rational animals, and either as individuals or as a group in the form of a state, our own material interests usually take priority. But if we or our state are human in Mencius's sense, we/it must show a slight distinction from rational animals.

---

26. To address this issue adequately, I need to compare the Confucian model with, for example, the liberal nationalist models proposed by David Miller (2000) and Yael Tamir (1993). But this is beyond what this chapter can handle, and I will leave this issue for future research.

Failing to understand this, and evaluating the moral dimension of a state's policies by asking if its citizens are driven by national interests, we will deny the morality of any state and embrace the relativist view that every state is equally immoral. A really meaningful and *realistic* perspective, in contrast, is to look at whether a country takes anything else other than national interests into account, especially when the sacrifice of national interests is not great.

Taking this perspective, we can defend the contemporary American and traditional Chinese regimes by arguing that among all the hegemons in history, although state interests are a priority, traditional China and contemporary America do have a moral dimension that distinguishes them from the *purely* interests-driven hegemons. Confucius made this kind of distinction among the hegemons in his time. He gave conditional praise to Duke Huan of Qi, whereas he was far more critical of Duke Wen of Jin (see, e.g., *Analects* 14.15 and 14.16), although both dukes were considered hegemons in those times. Although Duke Huan pursued his state's interests and personal gains, just as other hegemons did during the Spring and Autumn period, he did try, to the extent that immediate harm would not come to these interests, to help the weaker states and restore and maintain the "world" order, oftentimes through peaceful means, in contrast to a far more ruthless self-interested hegemon such as Duke Wen.

Of course, the way China was unified at the end of the Warring States period was almost opposite to the Confucian ideal. Even among regimes in post-Qin China that allegedly followed the Confucian way, there were discrepancies between historical reality and the ideal types, as is always the case between the normative and the empirical. But as I argued above, the really meaningful question is whether the traditional Chinese regimes, under the Confucian banner, did better than those states that completely lacked Confucian-style ideals. Arguably, the strongest Confucian elements can be found in the Han and Song dynasties. But even in the Ming and Qing dynasties that wouldn't be considered as Confucian as the Han and Song dynasties, according to David Kang, between the late fourteenth century and the middle of the nineteenth century, there were only six major wars in East Asia that were allegedly under Confucian influence, and among them, only two were fought between Confucian states, with the remaining four between Confucian states and nomadic and Western powers (2010, 83). He suggests that a strong China was good for the peace and stability of East Asia, while a weak one was not. Giovanni Arrighi's estimate of the number of wars during this period is higher than Kang's, but there were still fewer wars in East Asia than in Europe over the same period.[27] Moreover, even the wars of expansion in Ming and Qing

27. Of course, if my comparison between Chinese history and European history stands, Western Europe in this period went through a "Warring States" period, whereas in East Asia,

China were deeply defensive, and instead of exploiting resources from the newly gained territories, as was the case for European colonialists and later the Japanese, the Chinese government actually used the resources from the "old" territories to support the new ones (Arrighi 2007, 314–29).[28]

In the American case, as the master of geopolitics Henry Kissinger once observed, "[I]t is above all to the drumbeat of Wilsonian idealism that American foreign policy has marched since his watershed presidency, and continues to march to this day" (1994, 30).[29] If true, this also supports the idea that the United States is not a purely national interest–driven hegemon, and the nationalism that contemporary China emulates is much worse than the one adopted by the United States, unlike how Tang argued above.

Coming back to the normative issue, in a more realistic Confucian order, then, we can acknowledge the fact that it is not possible for a state to transcend its interests, and it is extremely difficult and rare for a state not to put its interests first. As I argued earlier in this chapter, civilized states don't go to war with each other, but a realist can object to this by arguing that this is the case only because not going to war with another state for national interests is one of the definitive features of a civilized state. A more realistic Confucian, then, can even accept the realist idea that the peace between two states, even between two states with a sense of moral obligations, in reality, can only be maintained for good if these two states have a balance of power. There can even be competing unions of civilized states,[30] which, as the Nietzschean argument for the necessity of the existence of states goes, can be good for the flourishing of human civilizations. But the realistic Confucian differs from a typical realist in that the former argues that the "slight" difference between a state purely driven by national interests and a state with a sense of moral obligations matters. It may be just the icing on the cake, but sometimes icing can make a difference with regard to the taste of the cake! Put less metaphorically, all the realistic Confucian expects is for a state with a Confucian-style ideal to have restraints on its interests with humaneness.[31]

China was the absolute dominant power over some periphery states. Nonetheless, this doesn't affect the argument that a world system that is dominated by a power with some kind of moral obligation is more stable and less prone to war.

28. The above account about Ming and Qing China is based on Cai Menghan's (蔡孟翰) summary of Kang's and Arrighi's discussion in Cai (2017, 60–61).

29. An irony about the fact that the United States doesn't always do things out of geopolitical calculations might have something to do with its peculiar geographical location, being isolated from other important geopolitical powers and thus protected from their threats.

30. Again, the fact that they are civilized means that their competitions are peaceful and are not in any way violating some basic humane principles.

31. In the building of modern India, to avoid the problems of aggressive nationalism, the

Confucian Model versus Cosmopolitan Model

The "Thin-Identity" Model and Its Problems

Recognizing the danger of the nationalist version of the nation-state model, some liberal thinkers, such as some cosmopolitanists, wish to dissolve nations and nation-states by resorting to some universal values, thus eliminating national identity and anticipating a post-nation, post-state era—let us call it the "no-identity model." Some more moderate liberal thinkers try to make the identity as thin as possible, grounding it, for example, in constitutional identity—let us call it the "thin-identity model." The beauty of the thin-identity model is that people of different (imagined or real) blood relations, cultures, and geographic areas can become members of the same state. There is a similarity between this way of bonding a state and the way the Romans bonded their empire. The Roman Empire controlled its vast land through political, military, and legal methods, tolerating cultures of the dominated peoples and even leaving intact some of their political institutions. The pre-Qin Legalists such as Han Fei Zi (韩非子) also advocated similar means of control and bonding. As discussed in chapter 6 (under "Han Fei Zi's Challenges"), he thought that elements such as Confucian compassion, culture, and civilizedness were too weak to bond a large and populous state together, and the unity of the state would only be achieved by institutions that applied the "two handles"—rewards and punishments—to the people who were invariably profit-driven. Han Fei Zi was obsessed with the unity and strength of the state, and tolerance didn't even occur to him. But he also didn't appeal to banners such as nationalism. Some may argue that the identity of Americans is also based on the US Constitution, and to be an American means nothing more than pledging allegiance to the Constitution, in spite of race, culture, and state origin.

Using the thin-identity model could also help a state to expand quickly, absorbing different nations (in the racial sense of this term) with little difficulty. A serious problem for China today is that the last traditional Chinese dynasty included Tibet and Xinjiang (新疆), but the Qing dynasty didn't promote cultural assimilation of the Tibetans in Tibet and the Uighurs in Xinjiang. If "Chineseness" in the narrow sense of the term becomes the basis of state identity for the Chinese, how the Tibetans and Uighurs can be Chinese and their lands remain part of China could be a problem. This doesn't seem to be an issue for a state whose unity is based on a constitution.

---

solution offered is pacifism, or a disarmed nation-state. I will leave it to the readers to decide whether this solution is desirable and possible. I thank Rahul Sagar for pointing out the Indian solution to me.

The problem with the thin-identity model is that its bond may be too thin. For example, due to the lack of bonds other than institutions (on the highest level), laws, and military oppression, when the center of the Roman Empire fell, the whole empire fell with it rather quickly. The quick demise of the Legalist Qin dynasty also revealed this problem. As for the United States and other states whose identity seems to be based on a constitution, contemporary Chinese liberal thinker Zhou Lian (周濂) argues, in agreement with the liberal nationalist David Miller, that constitutional identity cannot replace national identity as an effective bond of the state (2011, 101). That is, in the case of the United States, if it relies on constitutional identity alone, its unity won't be stable; or, there are other kinds of bonding that are neglected by those who think that the United States is based on constitutional identity alone. To resort to constitutional patriotism and civic consciousness only and to completely reject historical traditions, according to Zhou, is "to undervalue the significance and the value of 'national character'" (ibid.).[32]

To be clear, different from the Legalist Qin dynasty and the Roman Empire, liberalism that uses the thin-identity model can use equality, universal rights, universal and equal love, and respect for and endorsement of diversity to bond human beings together—which is premised on the tenet that diversity produces unity.[33] But obviously, this kind of bonding cannot help distinguish between two equally liberal and pluralistic states. One can answer this by saying that maybe there is no need to make this distinction. In this case, then, the thin-identity model is turned into the no-identity model, at least among liberal states. If we think that the existence of states is still necessary, as I argued at the beginning of this chapter, then this thin-identity model becomes problematic. But if an advocate of the thin-identity model still wishes to preserve states, the identity based on liberties and pluralism seems to be too weak to hold a people together. Moreover, the liberal commitment to pluralism can sometimes evolve into an active promotion of different kinds of identities (racial, sexual, etc.). This kind of promotion leads to thicker and thicker substate identities, while the state identity remains thin and becomes even thinner and thinner by the liberal suspicion of any form of national identity, because some liberals and left-wing intellectuals consider the affirmation of national identity not only unnecessary but oppressive, nationalistic, and even racist. This kind of liberal or left-wing identity politics

32. The bond doesn't have to be "national character" only. In the Cold War era, the fear of the "other," the oppressive communist regimes, may have been an effective bond for liberal states to hold themselves together. With this external threat largely gone, liberal states are now facing how to distinguish one another.

33. I thank Theodore Hopf for sharing this point with me.

(promoting substate identities while ignoring or even suppressing state identity), which was once popular in many Western countries, now leads to right-wing, nationalistic backlashes throughout the West, partly due to its failure to pay sufficient attention to state identity.[34]

To solve this problem, Zhou proposes that first we still need to take the constitution and the most abstract principle of justice as the foundation of a state. Second,

> [i]n order to strengthen the legitimacy and solidarity of a political society, political liberalism need not and should not maintain "absolute" neutrality, and should be mixed with [a] thicker value system that belongs to a particular tradition. Otherwise, the centripetal force of a nation-state cannot be maintained, and all the centrifugal forces will eventually have an "avalanche" effect. (2011, 102)

Zhou's liberal account of national identity (as well as other similar liberal accounts) is an important correction of the somewhat naive account of constitutional identity. Liberalism cannot reject all "thick" doctrines, and actually needs to be supplemented by some of the latter. Zhou seems to believe that liberalism can be "thickened." Meanwhile, the rule of law and the protection of rights in a liberal regime are effective tools to guard against the dangers of a strong version of nationalism. Zhou finally concludes, "I'd rather give up a weak version of Confucian nationalism and choose a thin version of liberal nationalism" (2011, 102).

But why is there a preference for liberal nationalism over Confucian nationalism? Zhou offers two reasons. First, he thinks that Confucian nationalism, unlike liberal nationalism, doesn't have constitutionalism, rule of law, and rights regimes to rein in the danger of nationalism. A crucial line is removed from the published version of Zhou's article: "what is urgent now is for China to become first a normal state with the rule of law, not a nation-state with special characteristics."[35] After this line, he points out, on the basis of this, for a liberal, the issue of national identity can then be raised (2011, 102). But as I argue in chapter 9, Confucians can endorse the rule of law and rights. Although the rule of law and rights cannot have as sacred a status in Confucianism as in some thick versions of liberalism, Confucians can still wholeheartedly endorse and support them by offering their own (thin) readings of the rule of law and rights. Therefore, Confucian "nationalism" can be as strong as liberal nationalism in protecting the rights of the people.

34. See Lilla (2016) for a criticism of "identity liberalism."
35. From the manuscript Zhou sent to me.

The second reason for Zhou's defense of the superiority of the liberal nationalist model is his belief that Confucianism lacks resources to support state identity. He writes:

> If we use the "tian xia" idea [Zhou uses this term in the sense that all civilized people should treat each other humanely, without any special attention to a state's boundaries; my note] to replace the existent "nation-state," the "Confucian nationalism" will then be self-defeating: it will essentially deny a sense of state borders and the foundation of the nation of a nation-state, thus becoming a form of "cosmopolitanism" with Chinese characteristics and making "Confucian nationalism" a self-contradictory concept. (2011, 100)

But if my account of the Confucian model is correct, then Zhou's account of the Confucian idea of tian xia is deeply mistaken. It is true that in the Confucian tian xia model, state borders and even sovereignty are not regarded as sacred; nor does it hold to the idea that a state should pursue its narrowly defined national interests by all means. But isn't this transcendence of the nation-state model a common merit of Confucianism and the liberal thin-identity and no-identity models compared with the nationalist nation-state model that was discussed in the previous section? More importantly, the kind of cosmopolitanism to which Zhou alludes seems to be the no-identity model, which denies national identity, sovereignty, and the necessity of becoming a nation-state. But as I argued at the beginning of this chapter, in the Confucian model, the necessity of the state is recognized. Another crucial difference between the cosmopolitan model and the Confucian model is that Confucian care is hierarchical, while the kind of cosmopolitanism in Zhou's use seems to endorse an equal treatment for all, without any preferential treatment of one to another. With the recognition of the necessity of the state, the Confucian model can endorse a thin version of patriotism, while the cosmopolitan version in Zhou's article can't.

In addition to hierarchical care, the Confucian model that I have offered in this chapter has another resource to strengthen state identity, which is culture. As we saw in the previous section, compared to race, culture is more inclusive. But it can still be used to distinguish "us" from others, in a softer way than race. Its effectiveness is corroborated by Chinese history. The historical expansion of China was built on the dual identities of culture and civilizedness, including politics, customs, written language, and so on. This made the expansion of post-Qin China slow but kept a relatively thick and stable bond among its people. Though the country had been invaded and conquered, the many people who had a strong sense of Chinese identity could not be eliminated, which is why the Chinese culture and its people continued, in spite of the collapse of individual political regimes and dynasties. This poses an interesting contrast to the Roman Empire, which, once quickly expanding and seemingly invincible, collapsed suddenly and almost completely when the center of the empire was destroyed.[36]

In fact, there is another theoretical tool from Confucianism that can be developed to address the issue of liberal or left-wing identity politics and its nationalist backlash. An important idea, and even ideal, for Confucius is "harmony without uniformity" (*Analects* 13.23). In Confucius's time, "harmony" (*he* [和]) was often referred to as the harmony of different flavors or of different musical tones. Thus, it presupposes diversity and rejects uniformity. But the diverse elements need to constitute a harmonious whole. Using this conceptual tool, we can say that the problem with the nationalist version of the nation-state model is that it has uniformity but no diversity, and the problem with liberal or left-wing identity politics is that it emphasizes diversity but fails to find a harmonious whole. To clarify, what I just offered is merely heuristic, and more serious theoretical analyses need to be done: for example, the scope of Confucius's idea of harmony (whether it can be applied to the issue of state identity) and its meanings. Otherwise, we could say, for example, that liberal tolerance is actually the same as Confucian harmony. We also need to show how this idea is connected with the key ideas that I have used in this book up to this point.

Zhou is wrong to claim that the Confucian tian xia model lacks tools for state identity, and it is nothing but cosmopolitanism with Chinese characteristics, making Confucian "nationalism" self-defeating or self-contradictory. Of course, Zhou also rejects his version of cosmopolitanism and tries to offer a liberal nationalism that embraces some "thicker" traditions in order for it not to be self-defeating. But the question is: What is the theoretical basis for liberalism to do so? In order to thicken cosmopolitanism, we may end up with the aforementioned liberal nationalism, proposed by thinkers such as David Miller (2000) and Yael Tamir (1993), and presented in the previous section as a thinned-down version of nationalism. Liberal nationalism can be considered a liberal attempt to find a middle ground between the nationalist version of the nation-state model and thin-identity cosmopolitanism, which is why in the section criticizing nationalism and the section criticizing cosmopolitanism, we end up with the same alternative. An adequate analysis of this alterna-

---

36. The Chinese historian Qian Mu offered a similar account about the differences between traditional China and the Roman Empire (1996, 13–14). Of course, there was no higher political culture in the world known to the traditional Chinese, which was an important reason for the cultural continuity of China.

tive and a comparison between it and the Confucian model, as I mentioned, is important but beyond the scope of this chapter. Again, if it turns out that there is little difference between the two models, I am happy to accept the idea that the Confucian new tian xia model is one of the best models available, if not the best model.

The No-Identity and Communist Models

Finally, let me make a few comments on the no-identity version of cosmopolitanism. If we accept the arguments for the necessity of the state, we should reject this kind of cosmopolitanism already. There is another Confucian objection to it. A possible theoretical foundation for this kind of cosmopolitanism is the demand to treat everyone with equal care, but Confucian universal care is hierarchical. The reason, as we saw in chapter 6 of this book, is that our care for those further away is built on or rooted in our care for those closer to us. To care for everyone equally sounds wonderful, but it is rootless and thus too demanding for human beings to sustain over a long period of time. Human beings could achieve this status with quasi-religious zeal, as the Chinese did in the Cultural Revolution, which is not so much different from the "high" a drug user feels when doing drugs. But just as the euphoric stage of doing drugs eventually dissipates, this universal and equal love can't sustain itself for too long and will inevitably fail. When it does, again, similar to a drug user when the effect of the drug wears off, one will go from one extreme to the other, from complete selflessness to extreme selfishness, which was what happened to many Chinese people after the Cultural Revolution. Moreover, because the ideal of equal care is too demanding, and a state often cannot achieve it even to a very limited degree, other countries will quickly grow suspicious of the state that waves such a banner as "human rights override sovereignty." This cynicism will lead us from high morality to moral relativism and nihilism, if not something worse. The cynicism and suspicion of international interventions after the failure of the second Iraq war, and the nationalist backlash against the European Union and the German refugee policies are contemporary examples.

In fact, the above criticisms of equal care can be found in the *Mencius*. Mencius criticized two dominant schools of his time, Yang Zhu (杨朱) and Mo Di (墨翟), as well as their followers. According to Mencius, Yang Zhu advocated an extremely selfish moral philosophy, whereas Mo Di advocated an extremely altruistic one. But they are two sides of the same coin, and both lead to chaos in the world (*Mencius* 7A26 and 3B9). On the international level, we can say that the nationalist version of the nation-state model is built on extreme (national) selfishness, while the equal-care-based cosmopolitan model is built on extreme altruism. The Confucian model (and maybe some version of liberal nationalism), then, strikes a middle ground, more idealistic than the nationalist version of the nation-state model and more realistic than the cosmopolitan model of equal care. Again, using Rawls's terminology, the Confucian new tian xia model of state identity and international order is a realistic utopia.

As I mentioned earlier in this chapter (under "Is Nation-State the Only Path to Modernity?"), another model to address the issues of identity and international relations in the modern setting of large and populous states of strangers is communism. The above criticisms of cosmopolitanism can be applied to communism as well. A simple fact is that in a time of extreme conflict, such as in the past two hundred years, instead of "all workers unite," we see time and again that workers identify themselves with their home states and not with workers of other states. Right now, we see that blue-collar workers of Western countries are strong supporters of left-wing antiglobalization, anti–free trade policies, and even right-wing nationalist policies, which are detrimental to the well-being of the workers in the developing world. If reality tells us anything, it is "all workers divide"!

To be fair, there can be different versions of cosmopolitanism. According to one version, cosmopolitanism doesn't demand that people care about each other equally, and can make its policy proposals within the framework of states.[37] It is cosmopolitan in the sense that when we create international regulations and policies, we should take advantage of the Rawlsian veil of ignorance, screening off our own nationalities and the condition that our states are in, and thus treating everyone equally. In my Confucian model, what is rejected is equal care, and it can embrace this form of cosmopolitanism and the international order created through the veil of ignorance as a fair procedure of establishing laws and legal norms on the international level. But Confucians would emphasize that even behind the veil of ignorance, we can screen off knowledge of our particular states, but it is fine if we are asked to consider whether one should give preferential treatment to one's own state and compatriots (whatever and whoever they are), for example, during natural disasters. If a cosmopolitanist can accept this, there is a consensus between Confucians and cosmopolitanists (of this sort).

Let me illustrate the discussions in this section with a current example: immigration and the refugee issue. As the flooding example that I offered at the beginning of this chapter suggests, the general Confucian principle is that refugees and immigrants can only be allowed into the state when the lives of

---

37. I thank Thomas Pogge and Thomas Christiano for suggesting this version to me on different occasions.

the citizens are not seriously disrupted. Of course, a clear mechanism to evaluate the influence on the lives of the citizens, and to define what "seriously disrupted" means, needs to be worked out, but it is clear that based on its basic theoretical principles, the Confucian model would reject open borders to refugees. This Confucian principle may sound cold-blooded compared to a more cosmopolitan, open-border policy. But the latter policy may actually be bad for bringing justice and prosperity to the citizens, for such an open-border policy or loose immigration policy would only benefit the immigrants, who could afford to and/or dare to move to a more prosperous state, leaving their poorer and less-motivated compatriots behind and in a more hopeless situation (because the wealthier and more ambitious people have left the country).[38] Even with regard to the ones who are able and willing to take the immigration path, they often suffer from various forms of exploitation, enslavement, and even death. As the antirefugee, anti-immigrant backlashes in the West have shown, to strive for an ideal by putting an unreasonable demand on the citizens will likely be counterproductive as well. As the cultural identity in the Confucian model—expressed by the Confucian tenet "harmony with diversity"—requires, the refugees and immigrants need to be absorbed into the culture of the country that receives them. This means at least two things. First, the admission of the refugees and immigrants, if it is not a temporary solution due to some crisis, has to be gradual; otherwise, the influx of a large group of people with alien cultures is hard to absorb into the state with a different cultural identity. Second, while tolerant of their diverse cultures, the adopting state should actively use soft means, promoting the use of the national language(s), learning national history, and so on, to encourage cultural assimilation. This is a Confucian response to the left-wing identity politics in the West.

In fact, the peaceful assimilation of Jews and other peoples through the ke ju exams in traditional China offer a good, real-world example of this. In traditional China, the most important path to becoming a member of the political elite was through the ke ju exams, which were state-administered exams intended to select officials of different levels. To excel in these exams put soft pressure on new immigrants and encouraged them to study the common texts that were used for the exams. The institution of ke ju exams thus helped the immigrants of different substate identity groups to find a common language and culture. Partly because of this soft pressure, a very rare case of peacefully assimilating Jewish immigrants into a nation is found in traditional China.[39]

38. I thank Thomas Pogge for sharing this argument with me.

39. See Shapiro (1984), Pollak (1998), and Xu (2003). Also see http://en.wikipedia.org/wiki/Kaifeng_Jews.

A serious challenge to the Confucian solution here is: What if due to some humanitarian crisis, a very large number of refugees need to find a safe place? To accept them in one or several states may be too much for these states, but to reject them means to let them die. I don't have a good answer to this challenge and can only suggest that maybe something like a charter city could be a solution. That is, some international organization or alliance of states could use an unclaimed island or create a safe zone in a refugee-producing state to receive the sudden influx of refugees due to some grave natural and/or political disaster. This chartered place could be administered by the alliance, and aid could be offered by the states in the alliance. Factories could be set up to make this place economically sustainable to some extent.[40]

Finally, a few clarifications are in order. First, a point that has been repeated a few times in this chapter is that I am only arguing for the superiority of the Confucian new tian xia model for certain forms of the nation-state and cosmopolitan models. But it can be argued that this Confucian model and some forms of the nation-state or cosmopolitan models are not really fundamentally different. I have no problem if this is the case. What I wish to argue is that early Confucians already developed a model of national identity and international relations, and its updated version should be put on the same footing as models about these issues that have been developed in the West. Moreover, the Confucian model is still viable and one of the best models on offer. Indeed, the claim that there are equally good models from different traditions shows the universality of the Confucian model, which is also what I am arguing for. Of course, a valuable theory has to have its own special ideas. We will have to look into a particular theory in comparison to say more on this.[41]

Second, one can argue that liberalism is already deeply rooted in people's hearts, and Confucianism has been a wandering soul without a body for a hundred or more years. Thus, to construct a Confucian theory is but a game for armchair philosophers.[42] I think a hidden assumption beneath this challenge is the understanding of Confucianism as a particular culture and even as an ideology for the Chinese. An ideology cannot be isolated from a concrete political and social structure. But if we take Confucianism as a political philosophy, what a scholar sympathetic with it should do is attempt to make it as adequate as possible. Then, statesmen and social activists would be needed to put the theory into practice. If our theory is truly better than the mainstream models in the real world, even deeply rooted (but defective) ideas

40. See Sagar (2016) for a very good and far more comprehensive analysis of the idea of charter cities.

41. I thank Liu Qing (刘擎) for encouraging me to clarify these points.

42. I thank Liu Qing and Chong Ming for these challenges to an earlier version of this chapter.

can be changed, or at least we should try our best to change them. With the faith that "by character the exemplary person is like wind, and the small person is like grass. When the wind sweeps over it, the grass is sure to bend" (*Analects* 12.19), it is part of the Confucian tradition "to do what is known to be hopeless [to achieve because it is the right thing]" (*Analects* 14.38).

Treatments of Some Practical Problems in China

Finally, let me use the Confucian model to explore some difficult issues in contemporary China. The Confucian model is meant to be universally applicable, and showing how it can handle some political issues in China is just an example. As we will see, some of the issues in China have global resonance. In addition to this, to apply this model to China is significant because China, due to its fast rise, is an increasingly important player in the world order. Many of its policies haven't caught up with its fast-growing influence and its domestic political landscape, and the call for change of these policies from a traditional Chinese source may be a very useful tool.

One serious issue in contemporary China is the ethnic problems, the most extreme of which are the Tibetan and Uighur independence movements. As mentioned in the previous section, a historical reason for these independent movements is that contemporary China inherited land from the Qing dynasty. The control of the Tibetan, Uighur, and Mongolian territories by the Qing government was achieved by quick military expansion, which was similar to the way that the Roman Empire expanded its territory, and not to the traditional Chinese way. Moreover, the Qing dynasty was run by a minority group, the Manchurians, who considered themselves (and were considered by others) to be different from the majority of the Chinese, and although they adopted the Chinese identity to some extent in order to maintain control of the traditional Chinese territories, they intentionally separated the governance of the above areas from that of the traditional Chinese areas, not promoting Chinese identity or a common identity in the former areas. As a result, much of the population in these areas made little progress in adopting the Chinese identity under Manchurian rule. To solve this problem, a Confucian would suggest that we try to promote Chinese identity in these areas. But after the demise of the Qing dynasty, both the Republic and the People's Republic of China, under the conviction that the nation-state was the inevitable path to modernity, adopted the nation-state model, which worsened the existing ethnic problems.[43] In fact, the People's Republic of China has done much worse

---

43. With the independence of Outer Mongolia, the Mongolian independence movement is not a serious threat to the unity of China anymore.

than the Republic of China by creating fifty-six ethnic groups in China. Perhaps for Mao Zedong, being a nation-state was just a means, or an intermediate step, and these ethnical groups would be replaced by class distinctions, which would in turn be transcended by communism.[44] In other words, the bond he would eventually adopt for China was the bond gained through classes. In Marx's theory, as Sun Xiangchen points out (2014), nations and classes are all intermediaries, and the ultimate end is communism. That is, this theory doesn't take seriously the issue of national identity. But class as a bond and communism doesn't seem to be working well. After the collapse of communism or Maoism in China, the contemporary Chinese government still holds on to the nation-state model and the related policies introduced at the founding of the People's Republic, without Mao's ultimate solution of the ethnical problems (to be clear, this solution is neither desirable nor possible). This is the root of ethnic conflicts and separatist movements in China.

To address this issue, we should understand that the nationalist version of the nation-state is merely one way to handle national identity and international relations, and is a rather problematic way at that. It becomes even more problematic when it is applied to China, which, historically, addressed similar issues with a rather different model. Therefore, from a Confucian perspective, we should firmly reject the policy of dividing Chinese into fifty-six ethnic groups and the related ethnic policies by the People's Republic, which were actually imports from the Soviet Union.[45] The identification of different ethnic groups is arbitrary. Among these ethnic groups, many of them already considered themselves Chinese when the ethnic policies turned them into ethnic groups distinct from the "Han Chinese." Some people who consider themselves as belonging to the same group are divided into different ethnicities based on their different settlements (e.g., those up in the mountains and those down in the valleys). Some people who don't really identify with each other as belonging to the same ethnic group are put in the same group. These phenomena testify to an aforementioned point: it is not the nations that make states, but states that make nations. In the case of the People's Republic of China, it is the unified Chinese state that has created most, if not all, of these nations (ethnicities). Among the so-called fifty-six ethnic groups, most had never had their own states in any period of history, and thus most didn't really have strong national or ethnical identities. Their identities have been largely manufactured by the People's Republic of China. Some, such as the Tibetans, did have a large state in the past, which helped to create a large group with a national identity. But even with regard to them, the People's Republic of China

44. This is a point Tang Wenming made with me in a private conversation.
45. For the Soviet origin of the ethnic policies of the People's Republic of China, see Ma (2010, 8).

put people who didn't identify with the Tibetans under the Tibetan identity, thus significantly enlarging the Tibetan base. This is similar to the experiences of the Soviet Union in that many ethnic groups in the Soviet Union were also manufactured through state mechanisms.

As a result, many of these created ethnic groups don't have rich traditions as a real ethnic group, but, encouraged by nationalism, are restless. This makes them very dangerous because they lack historical constraints and maturity, such as experiences with dealing with other peoples. From the experiences of the Soviet Union, after the disillusionment of communism and the loss of control by the central government, these created ethnic groups either became the foundation for nation-states that dissolved the Soviet Union or became seeds of ethnic conflict in Russia.[46] With such clear historical precedent, unfortunately, the existing state policies in China not only don't help to overcome the ethnic barriers but actually reinforce them by, for example, making an affirmative-action kind of policy for ethnic groups in college admission (which should have been based on economic status rather than on race), giving financial subsidies to ethnic regions and allowing ethnic people to have more than one child where the majority of Chinese were not allowed to do so. These policies artificially maintain and strengthen ethnic identities. To make matters even worse, while strengthening ethnic divisions politically, the Chinese government lacks proper understanding of and respect for the religions and customs of these groups, and because of ethnic conflicts, the government sometimes even actively oppresses the practice of their religions and customs.[47] This oppression only leads to even more fierce confrontations, and the policies that strengthen ethnic identities keep sending more new blood to these conflicts. But as has been shown in the discussions in this chapter, what the Chinese government should do is precisely the opposite: instead of strengthening ethnic identities politically and oppressing them culturally, it should weaken ethnic identities (by abolishing policies that encourage ethnic identities, such as the ethnicity-based affirmative action, which should be replaced by an economic status–based policy) and tolerate ethnic identities culturally.

In addition to criticizing policies that follow a certain version of the nation-state model, Confucians can also offer constructive proposals, such as the encouragement of discovering common cultural identity among different ethnic groups in China. In order to achieve this, the Han Chinese, who should

46. Ma (2010) also offers a comparison with the Soviet policies and is concerned with a possible breakup of China if the Chinese government doesn't change its Soviet-style ethnic policies.

47. This makes the present government even worse than the Qing rulers, who could be very flexible with regard to ethnic customs and practices.

have been the main bearer of Chinese traditions, should try to restore the traditional Chinese culture. Through more than a hundred years of antitraditionalist destruction, especially during the Cultural Revolution, the Han Chinese have become a people with no culture and are close to becoming barbarians in the traditional Chinese sense of this term. Naturally, Chinese ethnic groups whose traditions have not been damaged as severely as the Chinese traditions should challenge the idea that the Han Chinese, an almost cultureless people, should lead the cultural assimilations of those whose cultures are better preserved.[48] Therefore, the Han Chinese should first try to restore their own culture. While doing so, those concerned with Chinese identity need to answer another important question. As I mentioned, one root cause for the Tibetan and Uighur problems is that traditional Chinese culture is too narrow to include Uighurs and Tibetans. Therefore, among all different groups in China, a thinner, commonly shared culture should be actively constructed. This identity could then be promoted by policies and used to unify different ethnic groups in China. As I mentioned in the previous section, the ke ju exams were an effective institution for promoting this identity. A contemporary educational system could play a similar role. In fact, it could be used to address both the issue of unity and that of diversity, achieving a Confucian harmony, for the common texts on which a centralized educational and examination system is based could help form a national cultural identity. At the same time, there could be optional courses tailored to different minorities, and instead of giving extra credits to minority students in the national college entrance exams, as it is practiced now in China, there could be a special exam tailored to test the knowledge related to the religions and cultures of minorities, for example, a test about Tibetan history and culture that is conducted in Tibetan. Anyone, not just the so-called Tibetans, could take this exam, and the extra credit could be based on the test scores.[49] In contemporary Chinese government, the State Ethnic Affairs Commission should not be an institution that maintains and promotes ethnic identities, as it currently does, but an institution that promotes integration and a common identity of all ethnic groups in China.[50]

48. The Chinese Communist Party, being an ultra-left-wing party, considered ethnic groups in China oppressed by the majority, that is, Han Chinese. It tried to play the role of the savior of the allegedly oppressed, so ironically, this radically antitraditional party became the protector, promoter, and even inventor of ethnic traditions, while destroying the mainstream Chinese culture, Confucianism in particular, at the same time.

49. I thank Daniel Bell for suggesting this line of thought to me.

50. See X. Guo (2012). In general, many of the policy proposals I have made in this section resonate with the so-called second-generation ethnic policies (第二代民族政策; SGEP) pro-

Although I am discussing the issue in China here with an allusion to the Soviet Union, the problem is not limited to (former) communist countries. Liberal and left-wing identity politics also suffers from some similar problems. Perhaps from the same left-wing root, both the communist and the left-wing policies toward minorities politically encourage their ethnic identities. In a liberal democracy, the cultural practices of the minorities are not as oppressed as in despotic or authoritarian regimes, but from the same radical Enlightenment ideology of forcing one to be free, some form of oppression also exists, such as the burka ban in France. On this issue, a similar Confucian-style set of corrections can be offered, including downplaying ethnic identities politically and tolerating cultural practices of the minorities. At the same time, the myth that to promote national identity has to be "nationalistic" in a bad sense, xenophobic, or even fascist has to be challenged,[51] and a state should actively promote a culture-based identity through soft powers (such as unified educational and examination systems) that don't violate basic principles of liberty.[52]

---

posed by some sociologists, political scientists, and policy analysts in China. One good representative is Ma Rong (马戎). He has numerous articles on this issue. For example, see Ma (2004, 2007, and 2010). Hu and Hu (2011) is also a representative article in this endeavor. Elliot (2015) offers an extremely clear and insightful review of these policy proposals. According to Elliot, although critical of the first-generation ethnic policies (the policies I have described in this section) and proposing instead a more assimilation-oriented, state-identity-building policy, there are still important differences among those who propose SGEP. For example, while Ma emphasizes more on tolerance and pluralism in the gradual assimilation process, Hu and Hu (2011) focus on a rapid assimilation of ethnic groups and the centralization of power with little attention paid to basic liberal values (Elliot 2015, 193–94). The proposal I have made in this section is closer to Ma than to Hu and Hu.

51. For example, because of the shadow of Nazism, any mention of the German spirit or the like becomes almost taboo in contemporary Germany. Germans' attempts to redeem themselves should be applauded and even admired, especially in contrast to the lack of sincerity in the efforts made by the Japanese, but they should find the balance between the complete rejection of Nazism and a healthy embrace of culture-based national identity.

52. There may be more issues in common between ethnic issues in China and those in the West. In the aforementioned article by Mark Elliot, he argues that the best analogy in the West with the Chinese issue of ethnicity is that of native peoples (2015, 206). He also acknowledges that not all Chinese ethnic groups fall into this category (ibid., 207n71). But I would argue first that there are far more groups in China that don't fall into this category, and second that even among those who do, the issue is not as clear-cut as that in Australia, the United States, or Canada. For the interactions between the ethnic group in question and other people groups (including those who would later be labeled as the Han Chinese) in China have a far longer and more intertwined history than those between white settlers and the native peoples. In this sense, at least for some minority groups in China, maybe a better analogy is the relations among Irish,

To the independence movement, a radical expression of ethnic conflicts, there is another Confucian response. That is, Confucians don't support the idea of national self-determination. One reason for this is the Confucian reservation with one person, one vote. Another is the Confucian rejection of using ethnicity as a bond of a state. Moreover, Confucians also reject a sheer divide between the self and the other, as we saw in the discussions in chapters 5 and 6, and thus the fate of a people is not merely considered their own business.

We can apply all the above reasoning to another issue for contemporary China, that of Taiwan's status. For example, Confucians would reject the self-determination argument for Taiwan's independence. In order to promote independence, Taiwan, under the rule of the Democratic Progressive Party, has adopted policies of "de-Chinese-fication" (去中国化). The underlying assumption is that if there are shared cultural elements between the peoples of the two sides of the Taiwan Strait, there cannot be two countries. But as was mentioned, early Confucians had no problem with the existence of different xia states that had shared cultural elements with one another. For Confucians, people with the same language and even the same ancestry don't have to be in the same country, and whether they should form one or more than one state needs to be evaluated on the basis of historical and other contextual factors. The ultimate principle in this deliberation is humaneness, the care for the well-being of the people involved. For example, let us assume that Taiwan's independence has little to do with the well-being of the people in Taiwan, but because of the push by some demagogues, the people of Taiwan falsely believe that independence is good for them. In reality, however, an independent Taiwan would become a pawn of Japan and the United States, and its people's interests would be sacrificed for the interests of Japan and the United States; the people from mainland China would also be hurt in this process. Under these circumstances, Confucians would object to Taiwan's independence, and some form of pressure—what measures are acceptable will be based on the principle of humaneness—can be applied to keep Taiwan from becoming independent.

Scots, Welsh, and English in Northern Ireland, or among European peoples in a region with a long history of group interactions and even conflicts. Moreover, an important issue is what the proper reparation to the American Indians or First Nations should be. Intuitive ways of reparation, such as giving back the land that was taken from them, cannot be easily justified, and a truly fair solution can only be found after we take all stakeholders and circumstances into account. See, for example, Waldron (1992) for some in-depth philosophical analysis of the issue of reparation.

In the international arena, the Chinese government should realize that one of the biggest obstacles to its peaceful rise is the nationalist discourse that it has adopted. China should abandon the nationalist version of the nation-state model of international relations and adopt the Confucian one instead. If China can further embrace the Confucian hybrid regime, or at least make its government truly accountable to the well-being of the people, and if China can respect the rule of law and protect people's liberties—that is, if China can become a "Chinese" (i.e., civilized) state—it can become a member of the union of the civilized states. Indeed, to make the Confucian model a reality, people need to see the problems with the present models. But then, we need those who adopt the Confucian-style model ("Confucian-style" because it can be drawn from other sources, such as a coherent version of liberal nationalism) of state identity and international relations to form a union, a "coalition of the willing and the civilized." Realistically, it will depend on a few great powers in the world to reform themselves, and then form such a union, or a few civilized unions that peacefully compete in a pluralistic setting with each other and together try to defend a civilized way of life against barbarism. Therefore, a China that reforms itself and then takes up its responsibility may contribute to the formation of this union of the world police, which will in turn bring civilizedness and international stability and order for the right reasons to the world. Then, China will truly rise peacefully, saving both it and the rest of the world from apparently inevitable conflicts and devastating destruction.

8

Humane Responsibility Overrides Sovereignty

A CONFUCIAN THEORY OF JUST WAR

A City upon a Hill: "Isolationism" as
International Intervention

In chapter 7, I offered an outline of a Confucian new tian xia model of state identity and international relations. An important issue in international relations is international conflicts and interventions. As I have mentioned, the SAWS in China was full of interstate conflicts, and early Confucians had a lot to say about them. In this chapter, then, I discuss how they approached these issues. These discussions are illustrations of, elaborations on, and developments of the general model introduced in chapter 7. To maintain coherence, I will again mostly use the *Analects* and the *Mencius*.[1]

But before I get into early Confucian discussions on these issues, including what I call "theories of just war," I need to answer the question of whether "justice" and "just war" are applicable to the discussions in the *Analects* and the *Mencius*, because these terms were originally from Western philosophy and political theories.[2] There are different understandings of these terms even within Western philosophy. In spite of the differences, however, there is

1. In chapter 2 of *Beyond Liberal Democracy*, Daniel Bell has discussed the ideas of a just war in the *Analects* and in the *Mencius*, and compares and contrasts them with Western theories on this matter (2006). I share many of Bell's ideas. What I hope are the distinctive features of this chapter are, first, it is based on a more general theory of world order, which was offered in chapter 7, and on my general thesis of China's early modernity; second, the focus of this chapter is a close textual analysis of the *Analects* and the *Mencius*; and third, there are a few different ideas in the details between Bell's treatment and mine.

2. Early Confucians used the term *yi zhan* (义战) (see, e.g., *Mencius* 7B2), where the term *yi* is also used in the translation of the Western term "justice." But it is debatable whether this term means the same as justice.

a common use of these terms: When a war is called "just," it means that it is
good, right, and proper, and follows at least some moral rules. The differences
among philosophers are about how they understand the Good, the right, or
the moral. In the broad sense of the term "just war," clearly, both Confucius
and Mencius considered some wars just and some not. It is legitimate, then,
to discuss just war theories in early Confucian thought.

In a conversation (*Analects* 16.1), two of Confucius's pupils who served
Lord Ji, a powerful lord in the state of Lu, were plotting with Lord Ji to attack
another lord, the lord of Zhuanyu. Confucius pointed out that the lord of
Zhuanyu and his fief had been a bulwark of the state, and the lord did not do
anything wrong. But one of his pupils pointed out that this fief was close to
one of his lord's fiefs (the fief of Bei [費]), and it was strongly fortified, which
was why he and his lord wished to destroy it. Confucius then pointed out that
the stability of the state or a fief depends on treating its own people well.
When this is done, "if people from afar [i.e., from different states or fiefs] are
still unsubmissive, we should improve our civilizedness and moral character
to attract them to come; once they come, we should make them content."[3]
Finally, Confucius pointedly observed that the threat to Lord Ji's fief did not
really come from outside but from inside, that is, from Lord Ji's lack of humaneness and from the practice of realpolitik.

The background of this conversation is the serious conflicts between the
private and the public on different levels, which I mentioned in chapter 6.
Lord Ji was one of the three powerful ministers who, out of their private interests, usurped almost all the real power of the rightful ruler of the state of Lu.
What Confucius implied in the end is that this kind of self-interestedness was
contagious, and if Lord Ji could do things purely out of self-interest, the lesser
lords who served him would follow his immoral example, which would be a
threat coming from inside and a (real) threat to the stability of his fiefdom.
Perhaps as a validation of Confucius's prediction, in the next chapter of the
Analects, it is mentioned that the lord of the fief of Bei, which was said to be
threatened by the other lord's fief in 16.1, used his fief's strong fortification to
rebel against his master, Lord Ji (17.5).[4]

Therefore, self-interest-motivated wars were not approved of by Confucius.
We could eliminate external threats through these kinds of wars, including

3. A similar idea is expressed in the *Analects* 13.16. A local magistrate asked about governance, and Confucius's answer was "[m]ake sure those who are near are pleased, and those from
afar are attracted to come."

4. Of course, whether these allegedly historical events actually happened, and if they did
and had these connections, is a question for historians. I am merely making a speculation from
the arrangement of these two passages.

preemptive strikes, but this would only be a temporary fix that would be counterproductive in the long run, because it would encourage amoral and interest-driven realpolitik, which perpetuates the conflicts among states. Then how should external threats be dealt with? As was said in 16.1, we should make our own state prosperous and civilized, and attract foreigners, including those from the state that poses a threat to our state, to live in our state. If people leave their home state, the foreign state that poses a threat to the home state loses the manpower to wage war. If the foreign state doesn't want to lose its people, it will be pressured to change its inhumane ways and emulate the humane state. In fact, we can further argue that in a situation in which a few states are engaged in war with each other for morally dubious reasons (such as rational calculations based on self-interests)—World War I among European states could be such an example—instead of helping one or the other side, maybe the most humane and effective policy is for foreign states to stay out of these wars and to make one's own state (in the WWI case, e.g., the United States) a "city upon a hill," exemplifying to these warring states and their people a humane alternative, by pressuring, shaming, or persuading them into changing their ways. That is, an apparent "isolationist" policy—"isolationist" in the sense of not directly getting involved in the conflicts—can be the most humane to foreigners who are suffering in these conflicts. In traditional Chinese history, perhaps under the influence of this Confucian idea, rulers of traditional Chinese states who were keen on waging war—even if with the intention or excuse of doing good to the people—were rarely praised and often criticized.

Crucial here is the Confucian idea of "voting with one's feet," which has already been discussed to some extent at the beginning of chapter 7. Let me make a few more comments on it here. First, as we saw in chapter 2, early Confucians had reservations about common people's capacity for making sound policy decisions, but from their support of voting with their feet, they seemed to believe that common people had the capacity of choosing what they considered to be the best place to have a flourishing life. This understanding of common people's capacity seems to have both an egalitarian side and an elitist side, and it is worth exploring in future research. Second, the idea of voting with one's feet can be used to measure a Confucian "happiness index." For any state, we can, under the condition of adequate exposure to the lives of different states, measure the percentage of those who wish to emigrate in this state (over their compatriots, who wish to stay), and we can also measure the percentage of people from other states who wish to immigrate to this state (over those foreigners from these states who don't). These measurements can be further used to evaluate the legitimacy of a government and offer the basis to replace a failing or tyrannical government from within or without. To be sure, the defender of any type of regime will claim that their regime is legitimate, and even offer a priori reasons to support his or her claim. To use people's feet to decide on which regime is better may offer a way out when those with two different a priori reasons cannot agree with each other. Of course, this has to presuppose that the idea of voting with one's feet can be accepted by both sides. But it seems to be a measurement standard with greater "objectivity," or, more accurately, greater potential to be an overlapping consensus among people with different metaphysical and religious beliefs than, for example, voting with one's hands or asking people how happy they are. Moreover, we don't have to defend voting with one's feet as the metaphysical foundation of legitimacy, and only need to argue that this idea is a revelation of some higher good that is recognized by the holder of the metaphysical doctrine of the legitimacy in question. Therefore, resorting to voting with one's feet has the potential of resolving conflicts among many metaphysical and religious doctrines of legitimacy.

Going back to the issue of international interventions, although it can make sense in some situations to stay out of some brutal conflicts among self-interest-motivated states, in some situations, it may not. Moreover, what if the people of a particular state are suffering from their government's tyranny or extreme incompetence? Confucius didn't say much on these issues. For example, he praised Duke Huan of Qi and his adviser Guan Zhong for their many successes at maintaining order among different feudal states without resorting to war, when the Zhou King couldn't play such a role of overlord anymore (14.16). Apparently discussing domestic governance with a pupil, Confucius stated that there are four bad actions in governance, two of which are: "to execute without education [moral cultivation] first" and "to demand results without warning" (20.2). We can apply this idea to international intervention by arguing that before we resort to war, there should be some measures taken first, such as helping the troubled state to appreciate its problems, giving its people proper assistance, and offering a clear statement about the conditions under which military intervention will take place. But I have to admit that on interventions, what Confucius offered in the Analects is rather sketchy. One reason for this omission may have been that Confucius lived in a time when the old feudal order was collapsing but was still maintained by the so-called hegemons, the feudal lords who temporarily played the role of the king to maintain order among the states under the Zhou feudal regime. In the Mencius, there are far more detailed discussions of international interventions.

The Strength of the State and the Justice of War

In the Mencius 6B9, Mencius argued that if one assists a ruler who "is neither attracted to Dao [the Confucian way, or humane governance] nor disposed to humaneness," making his state economically and militarily stronger, one is "to enrich Jie (桀) and to assist Jie [Jie is an infamous tyrant in Chinese history]," and this person should be looked down upon as a thief and a robber to the people. What is implied in this passage is rather obvious: it is not just that an inhumane ruler's state is rich and powerful, or that his state is victorious in wars against others. Indeed, a war waged by an inhuman ruler—his inhumanity means that he is motivated by self-interest ("self-interest" in a narrow, materialistic sense) in the case of war—must be unjust. Moreover, for Mencius, not only is humaneness critical to the strength of a state *for the right reasons* and the justice of war, but it is critical to the long-term stability of the regime. He said, "if one follows today's way [the inhumane way], but does not change its mores, he could not hold on to it for one day, even if he were given the tian xia [i.e., the whole world, under his rule]" (ibid).

In another dialogue, Mencius gave a more straightforward discussion of the above issues. King Hui of the state of Wei, which was one of the seven strong states during the Warring States period, bemoaned the fact that his state, though once the strongest among all, was defeated repeatedly by other strong states. He thus asked Mencius about how to make his state strong. Mencius answered,

A territory that is only a hundred *li* by a hundred *li* [i.e., a tiny state even in Mencius's time—*li* is a length unit, which might have been around half a kilometer during Mencius's time] can be sufficient for its ruler to become a king [not just a king of one state, but the overlord of all states, like the Zhou king during the Western Zhou period]. If Your Majesty will practice humane governance to the people—sparing in the use of punishments and fines, and making the taxes and levies light, so that the fields shall be ploughed deep and the weeds shall be removed in time, and that the strong-bodied, during their days of leisure, shall cultivate their filial piety, fraternal respectfulness, loyalty, and trustworthiness, serving thereby, at home, their fathers and elder brothers, and, outside home, their elders and superiors—then you can make these people who are armed with nothing but staves inflict defeat on the armies of Qin and Chu [two powerful states during the Warring States period] who are armed with the strong armor and sharp weapon.

[For] the rulers of those states rob their people of their time [during the farming season], so that they cannot plough and weed their fields to support their parents. Their parents suffer from coldness [due to the lack of clothes, which would rely on agricultural products in Mencius's time] and hunger, and their brothers, wives, and children are separated and scattered. Those rulers push their people into pits and into water. If Your Majesty should go to punish them, who will be there to oppose you? Hence it is said, "The humane person has no match." I beg of you not to have any doubts anymore. (1A5)

One problem with this passage is why did Mencius assert that Qin and Chu are so driven by the ruthless pursuit of military strength that their people are suffering miserably? He offered no historical or empirical support for this assertion. A possible interpretation is that Mencius was not really describing the reality of Qin and Chu; rather, he implicitly offered a normative account. That is, a war between two states is just only when one state is practicing humane governance and the other state is tyrannical—a possible meaning of "tyrannical" being specified in the above description of how the states of Qin and Chu treated their people. This normative account also indicates the timing of the war endorsed by Mencius—that is, when the tyranny is so bad that the people of the state lose any initiative to resist external forces anymore.[5]

Another problematic claim in this passage of the *Mencius* is his assertion that even a small state with far inferior arms ("staves") can defeat a strong state with superior weapons, as long as the former practices humane governance. Anyone with any sense of political reality, especially of the world of the Warring States, would find this assertion incredibly naive. This apparent naïveté seems to be in line with some people's image of Mencius, even Confucians in general: they are overly moralistic, pedant, and unrealistic. But it should be noted that the interlocutor of Mencius is King Hui, who was ruling over one of the seven strongest states at that time (in spite of the repeated defeats under his rule). His state was hundreds of times the size of the small state Mencius talked about in the conversation. But the humiliating defeats may have led the king to be anxious for revenge and impatient with or unconfident in humane governance. Therefore, Mencius's claim that a small but humane state can rule over the whole world may have been meant as an encouragement, or even to trick the king into believing the power of humaneness. The last line of this conversation, an outright plea to the king that he not doubt the power of humaneness, corroborates my interpretation.

Moreover, what Mencius said was that the ruler of a small-sized state *can* become the leader of the whole world. The discussion in another passage can be understood as a more realistic and detailed road map for such a state to become the world leader (1A7). In his dialogue with the king of another large state (King Xuan of Qi), the king reluctantly and indirectly admitted that his dream was to become the lord over all the "middle kingdoms." But Mencius pointed out that the state of Qi, in spite of being a powerful state, occupied

5. I thank Cheng Chung-ying for pointing out the relevance of the idea of timing in this passage.

only a ninth of the known world. If the king wanted to achieve dominance by conquest, he was actually fighting against an enemy (the rest of the world) eight times its size (and strength), which was clearly an impossible mission. But if the king practiced humane governance, his state would attract—recall the Confucian idea of voting with one's feet—scholars, peasants, merchants, travelers, and those who resented their own rulers, which would make this state invincible in the world (1A7). We should keep in mind that in Mencius's time, when agriculture was the driving force of economy and there was plenty of land waiting to be developed, population growth was almost the same as economic growth, and it would also provide more potential soldiers for the state. In other words, Mencius argued that a state is not strong simply because it practices human governance; rather, it becomes so through economic growth and the growth of the population that loves the state, which is brought about by humane governance. This is perhaps his real understanding of the connection between humane governance and the strength of the state. Using Rawlsian terminology, we can say that for Mencius, strength achieved through humane governance is strength for the right reasons.

From these passages, we can conclude that for Mencius, in a war between two states, if one practices humane governance and the other is tyrannical, the humane state is conducting a just war. Moreover, if a state can practice humane governance long enough, its population (the source for economic and military strength) will grow, and it will become so strong that it will be invincible in any war.

The Self-Preservation of a Humane but Small State

However, we can still question the chance for a humane but small state to become the leader of the world, especially when surrounded by powerful (and self-interest-driven) states. This state may have been annihilated long before it could, through years of humane governance, become invincible. In the *Mencius* 3B5, an interlocutor asked what could be done if the state of Song practiced the "kingly" way,[6] but was resented by the powerful states of Qin and Chu. When answering, Mencius still insisted that not practicing the humane way would lead to the defeat and elimination of a state, and if practicing humane governance, "what is there to be afraid of even though the states of Qi and Chu are large in size?" But this could still be an encouragement. Although the state of Song was not one of the seven strong states during the Warring

6. The kingly way is the way for the ruler of a state to become the leader of the world, which, according to Mencius, had to be achieved through humane governance. So the kingly way and the humane way are interchangeable in this context.

States period, it was still a medium-sized state, far larger than the state that Mencius described in 1A5. In particular, according to the *Shi Ji* (vol. 38; Sima 1981, 197), under King Junyan (君偃), Song once defeated Qi, Chu, and Wei (Liang), three of the seven strong states. It happened when Mencius was in his fifties. But then, Junyan fell prey to his lust for drinking and womanizing, killing those who dared to admonish him, and was labeled as a tyrant. Eventually, his state was annihilated by other states. The annihilation happened after Mencius's death. If the historical record in the *Shi Ji* is trustworthy, we can see that when the aforementioned dialogue took place, the state of Song was actually a medium-sized state that could have been on its way to becoming one of the strongest. Therefore, in addition to large states, as discussed in the previous section, even a medium-sized state could preserve itself through humane governance, and then develop its economy and become invincible.

In the *Mencius*, actually, we can find conversations between Mencius and the ruler of a truly small state, Duke Wen of Teng, who, though not ideal, came close to being a humane ruler.[7] When asked by the duke about how to preserve Teng against the menacing states of Qi and Chu that surrounded Teng, the apparent naïveté in 1A5 is nowhere to be found, and his answers sound rather realistic, which supports my reading in the previous section that Mencius's "naive" claim was meant to be encouraging.

In his responses, Mencius basically offered two options to the duke. The first option was that the duke should fortify his defenses by digging deeper moats and building higher walls. Then there was a chance that the state would be saved if the people would rather die than desert the state (1B13). He didn't mention anything about the happy and victorious people of a humane state with wooden staves; rather, military technology was quite central. But even with military technology and people willing to die for the country, Mencius only said, "then there is a chance," with no guarantee of victory and self-preservation, let alone becoming the king, the humane ruler of the whole world.

The second option can be summarized from two passages (1B14 and 1B15). The state of a legendary ruler in the past was threatened by some barbarians. The ruler offered all kinds of goods to buy them off, but the barbarians were still keen on an invasion. The ruler said,

7. In 3A4, it is claimed that this ruler practiced humane governance, although he may have fallen short of the highest standard of a humane ruler. Indeed, the simple fact that he still styled himself as a "duke," a title under the Zhou feudal rule and thus implying his respect for the old regime—as some early Confucians urged rulers to do rather than "king," which was assumed by most of the rulers in the Warring States period who had no respect for the old order anymore—is a sign that he was indeed close to being humane in a Confucian sense.

What the Di tribes [the invading barbarians] want is our land. I have heard that a jun zi [in this context this term can be understood as both a ruler of noble descent and a Confucian moral exemplar] does not use what is to support the people [i.e., the land] to harm them [i.e., by asking them to die for the land]. Why should you guys be worried about having no ruler? I am leaving. (1B15)

But when he left, his people thought, "This is a humane man, and we can't lose him. . . . They follow him as if going to the market" (ibid.).

The story doesn't end there. If the ruler and his people could find a safe place, and subsequent rulers of the state could keep governing humanely for generations, eventually a ruler would become the king. According to the available historical records, a later ruler of this state indeed became the founding father of the Western Zhou dynasty, and the leader of "all under Heaven." This seems to support Mencius's idealistic claim that a small but humane state could (eventually) lead the whole world. But this world leader was not the present ruler of the humane state. More importantly, immediately after the uplifting claim, even with the promise of the coming of a future king, Mencius said that this was up to "Heaven" (1B14). Some classical commentators also noticed this not-so-idealistic claim, and their interpretation of this claim is in line with a Confucian stance that, on the one hand, one should not resign oneself to fate but do one's best; and on the other, "Heaven's will," fortune, fate, or whatever you like to call it, also plays an important role in what happens in the world.[8] In short, Mencius did not really think that a state of humane governance could achieve security and prosperity, come what may.

In his own summary of these two options, Mencius pointed out that not every ruler could choose to run away (with his people) because some may think that "this has always been our land for generations, and to abandon it is not my decision to make. I would rather die for it than run away" (1B15). This claim was made in the tone of the ruler, which suggests that if defending the state to death was the choice, the ruler should be part of it as well. The last line of this group of conversations is Mencius's suggestion that Duke Wen of Teng should choose between the two (ibid.).

To sum up, in Mencius's view, a small but humane state, when faced with powerful enemies, could either defend itself with the risk of perishing or run away. In the second choice, it is possible that after finding a safe place, and after a few generations of humane governance, a future ruler could become the king of the world. But there is no guarantee. Therefore, for Mencius, humane gov-

8. See, for example, Zhu (1985, 16) and Jiao (1986, 97).

ernance did not necessarily guarantee the stability and even the survival of the state, in spite of his sometimes rosy claims. The self-preservation of the state relied on its strength (size, population, economy, the military). Whether it could become a powerful state depends on fortune, among other things. The guaranteed reward of practicing humanity is that even if all the people of a humane state (including the ruler) die with it in a defensive war, they would die as human (humane) beings, and the state as a human (humane) state. This is perhaps what Mencius meant by claiming "there is a chance" (1B13). That is, the chance was not necessarily the survival of the state and its people, but that they would die as human beings, with human dignity.[9]

In these passages, not only did Mencius offer a more realistic and subtler account of the connection between humane governance and the power of the state, but he shared some telling signs of a just defensive war. As we will see later in this chapter, for Mencius, a defensive war was not necessarily just. But if the defensive side was a state that practiced humane governance, its defense was necessarily and fully just.

But almost every state under attack likes to play the card of an innocent victim. What is offered in the aforementioned passages, then, can be considered decisive signs for us to determine whether a state under attack is truly and fully humane, and thus the defense is truly and fully just, while the invasion is truly and fully unjust. One of the signs is that both the ruler(s) and the people of a state under attack are willing to die for it. The other is that if the state is abandoned to the enemy, the people would follow their leaders to "the world's end." Although, especially in the second sign, it seems that Mencius was describing a historical case, but if we take him as a philosopher, we should consider the apparently descriptive account to be normative and universally applicable. In short, the mere claim, especially by a ruler, that his or her state is humane and is thus unjustly attacked is not enough, and there have to be some clear verifications, such as the voluntary following of the ruler by the people (to die for the state or to move to a safer place).

The Duty to Protect by a Humane and Powerful State

Now, what if a state is both humane and powerful and the problem of self-preservation is not an issue? Is it ever justified for it to wage war against others? From the previous discussions, we can infer that the general principle for Mencius is that in a war of invasion, if the invaded side is a tyrannical state,

9. Han Fei Zi also discussed how a small state could preserve itself in *Han Fei Zi* (chap. 49); so did Socrates in Plato's *Republic* (422a–23c). There are similarities and differences among these three accounts, which would be an interesting topic to investigate.

while the invading side is led by a humane state with the aim of saving the suffering people of the tyrannical state, and all other means have been tried and have failed, then this war of invasion is just. But these discussions can come dangerously close to empty talks, and can be easily abused. Perhaps aware of this danger, Mencius again offered decisive signs on how to gauge if a war of invasion was just.

Before we discuss these signs, I should first emphasize that for Mencius, war is the last resort. In the *Mencius* 3B5, the lord of a neighboring state, Lord Ge, refused to make certain sacrifices, and when Lord Tang of Shang asked him why he failed to do so (which is presumably a lord's duty), Lord Ge used the excuse of lacking the stock and other agricultural products. But when Lord Tang offered him these things, Lord Ge consumed them himself. When Lord Shang sent his own people to help farm the land in Lord Ge's state, and to bring food to Lord Ge's subjects, Lord Ge robbed them, even killing a child who was bringing food over. This finally triggered Lord Shang to start a (just) war against Lord Ge. From this example that Mencius offered, we can see that the war of invasion should only be resorted to after all other means have failed and a truly tragic event (the killing of a child) occurred.[10]

In the *Mencius* 2B8, a person who was likely a minister of the state of Qi asked Mencius in private whether the state of Yan could be invaded,[11] and Mencius said yes, with the justification that the former king of Yan gave his throne to his prime minister while it was not his to give. What would be a justifiable reason to give one's throne to another, according to Mencius (as discussed in chapter 2 of this book), is Heaven's will, which is expressed by the people.

The state of Qi took up the task of invading Yan for its former king's wrongdoing, and people suspected that Mencius supported Qi's actions. In response to this suspicion, Mencius argued that he only said that the state of Yan could be marched against, but those who could justly take up this duty had to be "heavenly appointed ministers" (*tian li* [天吏]). What is implied here is that Qi was not such a minister. But who was?

In two other passages, Mencius offered more detailed descriptions of the telling signs of a justifiable invasion in the context that Qi marched against Yan. Qi conquered Yan within fifty days, which King Xuan of Qi claimed to be beyond human power and to be the will of Heaven. So if one didn't annex Yan, Heaven would punish him. He asked Mencius whether he indeed should do so. Mencius answered,

---

10. There are some problems with this example and the example of the state of Yan being invaded. I will come back to them later in this chapter.

11. See Jiao (1986, 168 and 170) for more discussions of the position of the interlocutor.

If the people of Yen will be pleased with the annexation, then do so ... If the people of Yen will not be pleased with the annexation, then do not do so ... When, with the strength of your state of ten thousand chariots,[12] you attacked another state of ten thousand chariots, and the people brought baskets of rice and bottles of drink to meet Your Majesty's army,[13] was there any other reason for this but that they hoped to escape from fire and flood? Should the flood become deeper and the fire hotter, they would have no alternative but to turn elsewhere [for help].[14] (1B10)

It becomes clear in this passage that for Mencius, whether a war of invasion is just depends on whether the people of the invaded state are pleased or not. But considering the fact that some invaders like to put up an image of the invaded being pleased, we need to find some clear evidence. For Mencius, if "the people brought baskets of rice and bottles of drink, to meet Your Majesty's army," this acceptance must be real. In the *Mencius* 3B5, he further added that members of the ruling class of the invaded state (presumably minus the tyrannical ruler) should also welcome their counterpart of the invading armies. That is, the welcome of the invaded is sincere and widespread.

Moreover, in the passage quoted above (1B10), Mencius also argued that if those who are liberated find the rule of the invader to be worse than before, they could turn elsewhere for help. This means that the welcome by the people has to stand the test of time. In 1B11, Mencius offered a more detailed account about why people would change their attitude toward the invaders. After Qi's conquest, other kings planned to attack Qi. Consulted by the king over this situation, Mencius said,

If [the invaders] kill the people's fathers and older brothers, bind their sons and younger brothers, destroy their ancestral temples, appropriate their valuable vessels, how can this be right? The [rest of the] world has already been fearful of the power of Qi. Now your land is doubled, and you don't practice humane governance. This provokes the armies of the [rest of the] world.

12. How many chariots that a state had for war was a symbol of the strength of the state especially during the Spring and Autumn period, and "a state that has ten thousand chariots" was a figurative expression, commonly used during the SAWS, referring to a strong and powerful state.

13. This welcoming scene by the people was mentioned two more times in the *Mencius*, when he talked about just wars of liberation (1B11 and 3B5).

14. "Turn elsewhere" is based on one interpretation of the original Chinese text (see B. Yang 1960, 45; and Zhu 1985, 15). Another interpretation is that the coming of the new ruler turns out to be merely a change from one bad ruler (the former one) to another (the present one), and there is no improvement of governance (B. Yang 1960, 45).

His solution for the problem is,

> [i]f you hasten to order the release of the old and the young, stop appropri-ating the valuable vessels, and leave after setting up a ruler by consulting with the people of Yan, there is still time to stop [the armies of other states from attacking you].

In contrast to the opposition by the people of Yan and other states that King Xuan of Qi experienced, the military expeditions by Lord Tang (and later King Tang) of Shang have the sincere and long-standing support of all the people, and a reason is that during the invasions,

> [t]hose who went to the market didn't stop, and those who farmed didn't change [what they were doing]. He [King Tang] executed the rulers and comforted the people, like the fall of timely rain. (ibid.)

That is, people's lives were not interrupted, and only the tyrants who made people suffer paid the price.

From these passages, we can already see that there is another telling sign of a war of invasion being just, that is, the support of the trust of the people all over the world. In 1B11, Mencius explicitly said that the military expeditions of King Tang gained the trust and confidence of all under Heaven. A telling sign is that

> [w]hen King Tang marched on the east, the western barbarians com-plained; he marched on the south, the northern barbarians complained. They said, "Why does he not come to us first?"[15]

These people were anxious to be invaded (liberated) because "we are waiting for our king [i.e., the humane ruler Tang]; when he comes, we are going to be revitalized" (1B11). There is almost an identical passage somewhere else in the *Mencius* (3B5). Unfortunately, King Xuan of Qi didn't listen to Mencius, and eventually lost the state of Yan when its people rebelled, feeling ashamed in front of Mencius (2B9).

A Mencian Theory of Just War

From the analyses of the aforementioned passages of the *Mencius*, we can now construct Mencius's just war theory. Its fundamental principle is that in inter-national relations, especially in wars among states, humane responsibility overrides sovereignty. As was argued earlier in this chapter (under "The Self-Preservation of a Humane but Small State"), a defensive war is fully just only

---

15. A similar passage can be found in 7B4.

if the state practices humane governance. From the discussion following this section (under "The Duty to Protect by a Humane and Powerful State"), we can infer that if a state doesn't practice humane governance but actively puts its people under unbearable misery, and if the "invaders" are meant to save these people from their misery, then to defend the invaded state is fully unjust, while to welcome the invaders (liberators) is fully just. Therefore, to Mencius, sovereignty is not sacred. The justification of sovereignty comes from the sovereign state's having satisfied its people's basic material and moral needs, as discussed in chapter 2. No humane duty, no sovereignty!

But this doesn't mean that a suffering people should welcome just any invaders. Some Chinese democratic activists once claimed that it would be good if the British colonized China for three hundred years. But to Mencius, this is a rather problematic claim, for his theory requires that an invasion be conducted for the sake of saving and liberating those who are suffering, while the majority of British colonists clearly had no intention of liberating the suffering Chinese. Moreover, Mencius's theory also presupposes that the people have to suffer to such a degree that they are ready to welcome the invaders with open arms, and many states colonized by the British didn't meet this requirement.

In general, under the principle that humane responsibility overrides sovereignty, a just war of invasion has to have the following signs or meet the following conditions:

1. The invading side has to have sufficient power to carry out the liberation, and the use of force has to be the last resort.
2. The invaded side has to have proof of a clear violation of humane governance that leads to the suffering of its people, which cannot be corrected by nonmilitary means.
3. The suffering of its people has to be to such a degree that they are ready to welcome the invaders with clear and unmistakable gestures.
4. The invasion has to be done out of the intention of saving the invaded people from suffering, and this intention has to be put to a long-term test by the invaded people, so that it is certain that the appeal to humaneness is not merely an excuse.
5. The action of liberation has to be endorsed by the international community; the hope of those who suffer from similar inhumane governance to be liberated by the same armies is a telling sign of the endorsement.
6. Whether the invaders should stay in the invaded state should also be subjected to the will of the invaded people and international consensus.

One question about the above criteria is whether a Mencian just war of invasion must meet all of these conditions. Other than the consensus of the international community, these conditions seem to be closely connected with one another in the text, and it makes sense against the overall picture given in the *Mencius*. So the issue is really whether the consensus of the international community has to be included here. This item is mentioned in different cases Mencius dealt with. More importantly, for Mencius, the justification of war comes from the satisfaction or dissatisfaction of the people, whether the states are directly involved or not. Therefore, to exclude other people, especially other suffering people's perceptions from the legitimacy issue, is not in line with Mencius's general understanding of this issue.

The reason for Mencius insisting on the telling signs of the legitimacy of a war of invasion is the concern that the legitimacy may have been engineered by the invaders. One could argue that the welcoming scene required by the Mencian theory can be staged by the invaders as well. I can answer this challenge by making the following claims: First, the judgment of whether the invaded people's feelings are freely expressed has to presuppose the freedom and the adequate flow of information. Second, Mencius's demand that the invaders' behaviors have to stand the test of time also reduces the risk that the invaded people are misinformed. Third, his demand for the consensus of the international community offers another guarantee that a reliable evaluation of the legitimacy of the war is made.

Now, let us consider a concrete example from Mencius's just war theory presented in this chapter. With regard to the legitimacy of the second Iraq war, a key issue common to those who were for and against it was whether there were weapons of mass destruction that would pose a "clear and present danger" to the United States. That is, both sides presupposed the same principle: only under such a danger is a war against another state justified. Now, let us assume a case in which state A practices inhumane governance to such an unbearable degree that state B, out of compassion for the suffering of the people of state A, attacks it. In this case, state B poses a clear and present danger to state A. But according to Mencius's theory of just war, the defense of state A to dissolve clear and present danger is unjust, while the invasion by state B has nothing to do with any clear and present danger but is triggered by the miserable situations of the people in state A; thus, it is a just action for state B to invade state A. That is, in Mencius's theory, "clear and present danger" is neither a necessary nor a sufficient condition for a war to be just. In the case of the Iraq war, if the suffering of the Iraqis had been so great that they were ready for a regime change, to invade Iraq with the sole intention of liberation would be just, even if it posed no clear and present danger to the invading state(s). In fact, some American politicians (especially some of the neocons) indeed used this argument to support the war on Iraq, claiming that Iraqis would come to the streets, welcoming Americans with flowers. The Bush administration also emphasized repeatedly that Americans were liberators, not invaders or occupiers. Many antiwar people were against the principle behind these claims, but Mencius would support it. From Mencius's point of view, the mistake in the Iraq war was not that Americans used this principle to wage war against Iraq (if this were the real and only reason for Americans to invade Iraq, which is extremely controversial) but that those who claimed to follow this principle made a wrong evaluation of the reality on the ground. Some Iraqis indeed came to the streets, but they carried bombs, not flowers.

So is there a good example of a just war in Mencius's sense in human history? Perhaps the best example is the Americans' involvement in World War II. Under the fascists' rule, many Asians and Europeans suffered greatly. When Americans, (partly) motivated by saving people from mass annihilation, invaded Europe and Asia, these people indeed welcomed the Americans with good food, drinks, flowers, and so on. Their only complaints were "Why did you invade our country so late?" and "Why didn't you invade our country first?" The welcoming of the Americans, in most cases, was sufficiently long-standing.

Obviously, the principle offered here is the normative ideal of a just war, and it is unlikely that any war in reality can be considered fully just or fully unjust according to this ideal.[16] But a just war theory is meant to offer a normative ideal, against which we can measure the degree of justice in any real-world wars. At the same time, an adequate just war theory should offer treatments for real-world cases that are often, if not always, "impure." Unfortunately, there is almost no discussion of the nonideal cases. But, for example, as was mentioned at the beginning of this chapter, in his discussions of Guan Zhong (管仲), a shrewd politician of his times, in the *Analects* Confucius did show that on the one hand, he could be critical of Guan Zhong's actions for falling short of the Confucian moral standard, and on the other hand, he acknowledged that some of these actions may have saved the Chinese and the civilized world from being completely wiped out (*Analects* 3.22, 14.9, 14.16, and 14.17). From these discussions, we can imagine that we could develop Mencius's just war theory to deal with the nonideal cases more adequately. Nevertheless, we shouldn't deny the value of Mencius's theory for offering a set of criteria against which we can measure the level of justice in real-world wars, and for offering an ideal for human beings to strive for.

16. Some then argue that the reason that Mencius set the criteria so high was to deny legitimacy to any war in reality, and he was actually a pacifist. See Hagen (2016). Clearly, I don't agree.

Compared with "Human Rights Override Sovereignty" and the "Responsibility to Protect"

Compared with the Rights-Based Theory

Now that we have explored the Mencian theory of just war, how does it compare with contemporary, mainstream just war theories? The issue of just war has a long history in Western thought, and there are many refined and complicated discussions about it today. Clearly, in this chapter, I can't compare Mencius's theory with contemporary mainstream theories in any comprehensive and profound manner, but I will compare it with some "textbook" versions of humanitarian intervention and the Responsibility to Protect doctrine (with an eye toward preparation for future studies).

First, a key idea in liberal and cosmopolitan theories of humanitarian intervention is the principle that "human rights override sovereignty." There is overlapping between human rights and humaneness, but they are different with regard to their theoretical foundations and practical implications.[17] On the issue of just war, first, what Mencius emphasized was the duty of the liberator, as well as the loss of sovereignty due to the failure to fulfill the responsibility of protecting its people by the invaded state's government, whereas a rights-based intervention theory is focused on the violation of rights. As I will argue in chapter 9, the responsibility-based approach puts the burden of action on the party that is able to take action, the potential liberators.

Second, according to the humaneness principle of Mencius's theory, determining whether people need external assistance depends on if, under the condition that they are adequately informed, they themselves feel that they are suffering from poor governance in their state and not on whether some abstract rights are violated. If the intervention is based on rights, one issue is whether the people who are the potential target of assistance recognize these rights. If they don't, but the external helpers do, the latter can still intervene. This can be used as an excuse and justification for colonialism. Even if the external helpers are sincere, they are guilty of condescension and hubris. What they are doing is "protecting" a people's rights by violating their rights to determine which rights to embrace, and to determine whether their suffering is grave enough to justify external intervention. In contrast, although it can be controversial, whether people are suffering from inhumane governance or not is *far less* controversial than whether their rights are being violated. Another issue with the rights-based intervention is that it has a greater risk of being overly aggressive than the humaneness-based one, for external helpers can

17. See chapter 9 for more detailed discussions.

always introduce new rights and give new interpretations of rights, whereas a people's suffering is less subject to this kind of invention.

Third, according to Mencius's theory, even if people are suffering (or their rights are being violated), but they are not ready for a regime change, an invasion is not just, even if other means have been exhausted. But according to the rights-based theory, a war of invasion in this situation can be just. Some may see the Confucian mechanism of caution as cold-hearted because it seems to ignore people's suffering if it hasn't reached an unbearable level. But this strategy may come from a profound observation of political reality. When the people of the invaded country are not prepared to welcome invaders yet, a goodwilled invasion may push them to the side of their inhumane ruler, in the name of patriotism, and the consequent resistance could lead to death and destruction, which would further fuel the resistance. This would prolong the life of an inhumane regime and give it some legitimacy that it wouldn't have had if not for the premature invasion. A similar reasoning can be found in a famous allegory that Mencius offered about a stupid farmer: he was so anxious for his seedlings to grow that he pulled them up, and he killed all of them as a result (2A2). For Mencius and many Confucians, timing is important, in addition to being on the right side of history. Of course, when military interventions are not justified, a Mencian can still offer assistance to the suffering people through other means, such as helping those who are fed up with the ill-governance in their state to escape.

One can defend the rights-based theory of intervention by arguing that we can develop a rights-based theory that puts the burden on those who can act, is limited to some basic and noncontroversial rights, has a mechanism to take the liberated people's feelings and judgments into account, and has a mechanism of caution in the use of military interventions. But all these are already present, innate, and natural to Mencius's theory.

Compared with the Responsibility to Protect Doctrine

Partly due to the problems with the humanitarian intervention theory, which is based on the principle that human rights override sovereignty, the Responsibility to Protect (R2P) doctrine was developed.[18] Facing the Rwandan genocide and the Srebrenica massacre, the Canadian government established the International Commission on Intervention and State Sovereignty (ICISS)

18. I wish to thank Ping Cheung Lo for referring me to the significance of R2P to my discussions. For the history and the basic ideas of R2P, https://www.un.org/en/genocideprevention/about-responsibility-to-protect.shtml.

in 2000, and ICISS issued a report in 2001.[19] The idea of R2P was unanimously adopted by the 2005 World Summit, where the largest number of the heads of state and government attended, and it was written into the outcome of the summit.[20] In 2009, the secretary general's report, "Implementing Responsibility to Protect," was issued.[21]

In the report, it is stated that R2P rests on the following three pillars:

(a) Pillar one is the enduring responsibility of the State to protect its populations, whether nationals or not, from genocide, war crimes, ethnic cleansing and crimes against humanity, and from their incitement.... That responsibility ... lies first and foremost with the State.... (b) Pillar two is the commitment of the international community to assist States in meeting those obligations.... (c) Pillar three is the responsibility of Member States to respond collectively in a timely and decisive manner when a State is manifestly failing to provide such protection.[22]

From these documents, especially the three pillars listed above, the R2P theory greatly overlaps with Mencius's just war theory. First, the R2P theory stipulates that the cases in which intervention is applicable are genocide, war crimes, ethnic cleansing, and crimes against humanity. Similar to a merit of Mencius's humaneness discourse that I have shown earlier, to consider the above cases unacceptable and to use them as a cause for intervention is far less controversial than the rights-based discourse. One can argue that the cases in R2P are different from the corresponding condition in Mencius's theory, that the people of the invaded state have to welcome the liberators with good food and drink, but these cases may be precisely those in which the people would have the kind of reactions described by Mencius.

Second, R2P replaces the rights discourse with the responsibility discourse. This change can have two beneficial effects. By accepting the idea that each state is the primary responsibility-holder for protecting its own people, R2P acknowledges sovereignty. At the same time, by linking sovereignty with this responsibility, it also limits the former. With this understanding, we can see

19. The Responsibility to Protect, Report of the International Commission on Intervention and State Sovereignty, December 2001, http://responsibilitytoprotect.org/ICISS%20 Report.pdf.

20. Technical Meeting for the Development of a Framework for Universal Access to HIV/ AIDS Prevention, Treatment and Care in the Health Sector, WHO, Geneva, October 18–20, 2005, http://www.who.int/hiv/universalaccess2010/worldsummit.pdf.

21. Implementing the Responsibility to Protect: Report of the Secretary-General, General Assembly, January 12, 2009, http://responsibilitytoprotect.org/implementing%20the%20rtop .pdf.

22. Ibid., 8–9.

that international intervention doesn't violate the sovereignty of a state; rather, the incompetence and tyranny of the state intervened causes the loss of sovereignty. This can lead to additional moral, political, and legal clarity. R2P's emphasis on other states' duty to assist the people of a failed or tyrannical state can also be more effective for calling other states into action. One reason that a desired international intervention may not be carried out is that although other states have a right to intervene, they can refuse to use this right, which only *allows* them to do certain things but doesn't *demand* them to do so. In contrast, the discourse of responsibility can put more pressure on (i.e., through the "shaming factor") and be more attractive to (through the "glory factor") those who would be able to help out.

Third, the R2P theory specifies which responsibilities the international community has: a responsibility to prevent, a responsibility to react, and a responsibility to rebuild.[23] In the discussion of these responsibilities, we can clearly see that war is the last resort. In my presentation of Mencius's theory, the focus is the discussion of just war, and I haven't paid much attention to other aspects of his theory of humane responsibility. But from the beginning of this chapter, we can see how Confucius offered one way to deal with inhumane states. In the aforementioned case of Lord Tang marching against Lord Ge in the *Mencius* (3B5), we can see that Lord Tang only resorted to war after all other means of assistance had failed. In his discussion of how to deal with other states' opposition during Qi's occupation of Yan (1B11), Mencius's suggestion about restoration resonates with the responsibility to rebuild in the R2P theory.

Therefore, Mencius's just war and intervention theory overlaps to a very large extent with the R2P theory. One important difference between the two is that in the R2P theory, the idea that sovereignty is limited by how much service a state offers to its people is implicit, whereas in Mencius's theory discussed in this chapter and in the Confucian new tian xia model illustrated in chapter 7, this idea is explicit. Indeed, if the idea was explicit in R2P, it would be a miracle if it was unanimously adopted by the states that attended the 2005 World Summit. Related to this issue, in the UN document, R2P is undertaken by the United Nations, which is the collection of all sovereign states. But in the Confucian world order, the world should be hierarchically structured on the basis of humaneness. The coalition of humane states has a collective responsibility to protect people from inhumane states (where there is no need to protect people from the coalition because being a member of the coalition requires that each member state protect its own people to a satisfactory degree). The humane responsibility or R2P should be resolved among the

23. Ibid., 7.

member states of the coalition, rather than by consensus of all states or the permanent members of the UN Security Council. That is, the undertaker in a Mencian theory may be different from the present R2P model.

Problems with Mencius's Theory

In the last section of this chapter, I discuss some problems with Mencius's just war theory. First, there are usually three components of a just war theory: *jus ad bellum, jus in bello*, and *jus post bellum*. Mencius's theory deals with the first component, just cause to go to war, in detail, and touches on the third component, justice after war, in the discussion of postwar restorations. But it says little about just conduct during war. In contrast, another important early Confucian, Xun Zi, deals extensively with this issue, as well as the other two.[24] A possible reason for this, as Tang Qingwei (唐清威) points out, may have been the different interpretations of human nature between Mencius and Xun Zi (2014). For Mencius, human beings have the innate potential to become good, and tyranny is the result of a particularly bad tyrant, an extremely abnormal case. Therefore, in order to liberate suffering people, all we need to do is to remove this beast-like tyrant, and the people will naturally support us, seeing the goodwill from their own good potential.

The Opaqueness of People's Will

This also leads to another problem with Mencius's theory.[25] Even if Mencius's conception that a single tyrant is the sole cause of people's suffering was true in his time, in all the tyrannical states in today's world, it is not the case that a single tyrant oppresses all his or her people, and the oppression is almost always carried out by a group of people, often a minority group, that is "bought" by the tyrant. For example, in Saddam's Iraq, the Sunnis, especially those from his hometown, were the co-perpetrators in the oppression of the Shiite majority. This fact has something to do with the chaos after the forceful removal of Saddam, and something similar has also happened in the Arab Spring upris-

---

24. Xun Zi may also have had more adequate treatments of the use of the popular will to justify a war of invasion, an issue, as we will see, that poses challenges to Mencius's theory of just war. But for the sake of offering a coherent Confucian theory throughout this book, I have decided to mainly use the *Analects* and the *Mencius*, so I won't go into Xun Zi's theory in this book (which is particularly regrettable here because he had a richer theory to offer on the issue of just war). See Tang (2014) for a detailed discussion of Xun Zi.

25. I thank Qian Jiang for pointing out to me this problem, as well as the problem with the stability of the popular will, which will be discussed later in this section.

ings. Even in the best-case scenario, the example of World War II, the majority of Japanese and Germans may not have welcomed the Americans with open arms. In today's world, the scene in which all but the tyrant welcomes the liberators almost never comes true, if it ever did. To resort to the welcome of a simple majority can be inadequate, because in some cases of ethnic cleansing, it is the majority group that kills off the minorities.[26]

There is another issue with using the people's will as the basis for the legitimacy of liberation. Before the war of liberation, if the people of a state suffer from tyranny, it is likely that their will cannot be freely expressed. Even if we could somehow measure their will through the kind of surveys suggested at the beginning of this chapter (the ratio of migration), the people in a tyrannical state may be so brainwashed that they think their way of life is not that bad after all, in spite of the fact that from a Confucian or any reasonable point of view, their countries should be liberated. The Chinese during the height of the Cultural Revolution and today's North Koreans are two good examples of this possibility. We could try to spread the right kind of information to the people, but it is very challenging to do so when they are under a regime that oppresses the freedom of information. Even if we found a way to do it, as I argued in chapter 2, it takes time for people to get adequately informed before they can express their satisfaction or dissatisfaction with a regime, which makes the practical challenge to the Mencian criteria of the legitimacy of liberation even greater.

To these two challenges, Mencius could have two formal answers. First, those who conspire with the tyrant and choose to ignore the suffering of the common people are inhumane and even inhuman in Mencius's sense, and their will should not be part of the will of the people. Second, as mentioned a few times in this chapter and earlier chapters, the people's will can be used to offer legitimacy to a regime change only if people are adequately informed. But due to the aforementioned practical difficulties, both responses will make the judgment of the will of the people opaque, in contrast to clear signs of welcoming (such as offering good food and drink to their liberators). As a result, we can imagine that the invaders can ignore the will of some people, even the majority of the people, in the invaded country by saying that their voices don't count because they are the oppressors,[27] or are not adequately informed. If the invaders are sincere, this can lead to false judgments, and rash and even counterproductive actions. If the invaders are not sincere, this can be a good excuse for them to justify their ill-willed invasion.

26. I thank Liu Xiaofei (刘晓飞) for pointing this out to me.
27. Similar to the issue of whose voices count within the state to be invaded, there is also the issue of which states' voices count in the international community.

As I argued in the previous section, the R2P theory clearly specifies the cases in which military intervention can be applied, and these cases may have been precisely the ones that can meet the Mencian criteria of the just war of liberation. Moreover, they are relatively easier to identify than the Mencian conditions of liberation. Instead of using the people's will and the consensus of the international community, a Mencian can argue that in reality, we should use these cases as the ones that justify liberation. Moreover, on the issue of international consensus, whether what happens in a state should be considered to be one of these cases or not should be determined by the alliance(s) of the civilized states and not by all states. This may help to avoid the aforementioned challenges.

Thick Meanings of Humaneness

Another issue of Mencius's theory is the multiple meanings of humaneness, some of which are so thick they are very controversial. The examples I used in this chapter are mostly about the suffering of the invaded people. But in the case of Yan being invaded (2B8), what was explicitly mentioned was that the king gave his throne to a minister, which violated the customary rule of succession, and it was not mentioned whether the people of Yan suffered from this illegitimate succession or not.[28] We could argue that the violation of this customary rule would lead to the harm of the people of Yan—the quick collapse of Yan under Qi's invasion did seem to suggest that Yan's people were not keen on defending their state because of the suffering that they probably endured. This violation could even be harmful to people of other states because, for example, it could encourage the violations of the rule of succession and the ruthless competitions among ambitious ministers in other states. Even so, it should be clearly stated that the justification of a war of liberation has to lie in the fact that the suffering people are ready for a regime change.

Another, far more problematic case is Lord Tang's military march against Lord Ge (3B5). The initial reason for Lord Tang's intervention was Lord Ge's refusal to make sacrifices. This is a matter of ritualistic choices. But to use whether a state conforms to rituals or not can be easily used by another state for its self-interest-motived military expansion, and in the contemporary world, if the mere difference between religions and customs becomes the reason for conflicts and wars, it will violate liberal pluralism and even destabilize

---

28. Cf. Confucius's urge to march against the state of Qi because a minister committed regicide (*Analects* 14.21). But this is apparently a more serious issue than the case Mencius discussed here, and a war during Confucius's times, when the feudal order hadn't totally collapsed yet, could be rather limited.

the world order.[29] For example, the late Qing and early Republican thinker Zhang Taiyan (章太炎) (1869–1936), who witnessed the invasions of China by the "civilized" West and Japan with their hubristic reasons, offered a cynical interpretation of this example from the *Mencius* (1986, 40).[30] According to him, Lord Tang's military expedition against Lord Ge's state was really a setup. First, he used the excuse of religious differences to criticize Lord Ge. Whether the lord of one state observed his state's own rituals was probably not for his neighboring state to inquire or to criticize, and the sacrificial goods should only be offered by the lord himself and not the lord from another state, especially when the former hadn't asked for any assistance.[31] When Lord Ge was annoyed by the criticisms and inferences, Lord Tang sent his people to Lord Ge's state, making the latter deeply worried. Finally, presumably out of suspicion and animosity, which could be a rational reaction in these circumstances, a child from Shang was killed in the state of Ge, an incident almost doomed to happen, and Lord Shang quickly used it to justify his military march against Lord Ge's state. Zhang further pointed out that it has happened many times in human history that a state attacks another state with the excuse that the latter is barbaric while the former is civilized.

To prevent these kinds of problems, we need to go back to the "thinnest" and most commonly shared criteria, that is, those based on the well-being of the people, rejecting the thicker ones that are based on the rule of succession, observance of rituals, and so on. On Lord Tang's case in the *Mencius*, it is said that his military march against Lord Ge's state got "international" support in that his liberation was anxiously anticipated by other suffering people, even barbarians. Presumably, these barbarians may have had different views on rituals, and their support implied that the justification of Tang's war was based on some overlapping consensus. This can answer Zhang's challenge, and can support my thin reading of the Mencian theory.

To be clear, although it cannot be so thick as to include the violation of the ritualistic or religious system of one particular state, a Confucian wouldn't

29. I wish to thank Takahiro Nakajima (中島隆博) and Fang Xudong (方旭东) for pushing me to clarify this point. But on ritualistic and religious plurality, Chan Kang (詹康) offers an interesting response. One can examine whether a state violates its own religious faith. But this response risks moral relativism. For example, if the Nazis decide to violate their own values by treating the Jews nicely, should we intervene? Generally, intervention, especially military intervention, should use the higher criteria of the violation of humaneness. Otherwise, it could easily be abused.

30. I thank Takahiro Nakajima for pointing out the relevance of this interpretation to me.

31. Chan Kang pointed out to me that the assistance by Lord Tang is similar to our aid to Africa today. But the problem is that the assistance by Tang was imposed on the state of Ge, in spite of the latter's protests.

accept the satisfaction of the short-term material interest of the people as the whole content of the well-being of the people. Rather, people's long-term interests, including the interests of descendants, and basic moral needs, such as the cultivation of basic human relations, should also be part of the well-being of the people. For example, a country's total disregard of the harm to the environment can be harmful to foreigners and future generations (long-term interests), and this can be grounds for intervention, although, clearly, it wouldn't be grounds for a military intervention.

Stability through Oneness

Finally, let me clarify Mencius's view of the unification of the world. Daniel Bell argued that the ideal world for Confucians is "a unified world," "a harmonious political order without state boundaries and governed by a sage by means of virtue, without any coercive power at all" (2006, 36 and 24). In this ideal world, naturally, there wouldn't be any wars. Mencius seems to express this idea. In 1A6, he claimed that the world can achieve stability by "being settled on oneness," and only someone who doesn't like killing people can achieve this. But in what sense did Mencius talk about this "being settled on oneness"? It could be the centralized government, as the unification by the state of Qin achieved. It could be the feudal order in which the king of Zhou was the overlord, while the feudal lords still enjoyed much autonomy. It could also be a loose union in the case of the European Union, even of the United Nations. From Mencius's suggestion of restoring the conquered state of Yan (1B11), we can see that physical unification is not an important goal for him. Indeed, according to his just war theory, even under a true king, that is, a humane person who could become the overlord of the whole world, who only appears every five hundred years (2B13), if another state doesn't practice inhumane governance, or even if it does but does not go to such an extreme that its people are ready for a regime change, this true king cannot attack and annex another state. So the precondition for a physical unification of the whole world by the true king is that all the other states are so tyrannical as to be ready for a regime change (ready in the sense that their people are ready to welcome the liberators, and that their states are easy to liberate), and obviously, this is even rarer than the emergence of the true king. Thus, even in the time when a true king is present, it is extremely likely that state boundaries would still exist. For this king to be a true king, what is necessary is not that the true king actually unites the whole world, but that the true king leads other states toward humane governance by being "the city on a hill," by attracting the suffering people to migrate to his state, and, only in some extreme cases, by stopping an unjust war of conquest or by conquering another deeply tyrannical state. The world thus becomes one, not because it is physically united, but because it is now under the leadership of the true king in the aforementioned manner, or under the leadership of what the king represents—humaneness. As I have argued, it is likely that the "true king" is not a particular state but a coalition of humane states. If it comes into being, it will offer not only peace and stability but peace and stability for the *right reasons* to the world.

But can we have a humane ruler who happens to be powerful enough to be the overlord of the world? Mencius seems to be optimistic about the power of humanness, but, as I argued in this chapter, he didn't really believe that a humane state could always preserve itself, let alone lead the whole world, which shows the realistic side of Mencius. Still, we can question whether even a charitable reading of the realistic side of Mencius can resist the challenge of reality. For example, Mencius claimed that "it happens that a state is acquired through inhumanity, but it never happens that the whole world is acquired through inhumanity" (7B13). But it was precisely the state of Qin, which would be considered inhumane by Mencius, that conquered the whole known world and unified China. A Mencian could comfort himself or herself by pointing to the quick demise of the Qin empire. After all, as was quoted earlier, Mencius argued that an inhumane ruler could not maintain control over the whole world for too long (6B9). We can also argue that Mencius, like John Rawls, was concerned with stability for the right reasons. The dominance of the whole world by an inhumane ruler may be possible, but that doesn't make it right. Besides, as I argued in the last paragraph, Mencius was not that hopeful of a world order under a humane ruler. Still, it cannot be denied that Mencius didn't discuss how an inhumane state could dominate the whole world, how its power could be preserved (for however short a period), and what we could do about it, the discussion of which is important for an adequate theory of humane governance and international order.[32]

32. Again, this inadequacy may have something to do with Mencius's optimism with regard to human natural tendencies, and Xun Zi may have more realistic teachings to offer.

9

A Confucian Theory of Rights

Four Camps on the Compatibility between Confucianism and Liberal Democracy

Since the introduction of the Confucian idea of compassion in chapter 5, I have shown how it can be expanded from family to state and from state to all humanity. I have also shown the implications of the expansion of care for some key issues in political philosophy. The next natural step of expansion is to apply this care to animals, which I will do to develop a Confucian theory of animal rights. But before I do this, I must revisit a recurring issue in the previous chapters: the compatibility between Confucianism and rights. Again, the main Confucian texts I am using are the *Analects* and the *Mencius*.

As mentioned at the beginning of chapter 1, liberal democracy is considered to be the end of history in terms of political models, the ideal for all states to follow. Although liberal democracy has encountered more and more problems, it is still widely believed that the first thing for any defender of the contemporary relevance of Confucianism (or other schools of "nonliberal" ideas) to do is to argue for the compatibility between it and liberal democracy.

In order to show compatibility, we need to define what liberal democracy is. A dominant understanding among Western politicians and Chinese prodemocracy intellectuals is that the fundamental ideas of Western democracy are individualism (the primacy of the self-interest of each individual) and equality. Human rights regimes and the rule of law are considered as related to, or even based on, these two ideas. If we add the idea of autonomy to the above "minimalist" version of individualism, that is, each individual should be the master of his or her own fate, or if we further argue that the individual is the best judge of his or her self-interests (for argument's sake, I will call the "fundamental ideas" and the added ideas "democratic ideas"), at an institutional level, these ideas imply that political matters are to be decided only and ultimately by the individuals involved through the one person, one vote model. As argued at the beginning of chapter 3, some might also believe that a market economy—one dollar, one vote—is what represents these fundamental ideas on the economic level. This is why, for many people, the establishment of one person, one vote and a market economy is essential for a state to be considered democratic.

Against this background, those who are concerned with the compatibility issue between liberal democracy and Confucianism, as well as the so-called East Asian values in general, can be divided into four camps. The first camp is the prodemocracy incompatibility camp. Taking the democratic ideas as essential to liberal democracy, people in this group argue that Confucianism is not compatible with liberal democracy, for it is commonly believed by this group and many laypeople that Confucianism advocates ideas that are exactly opposed to the aforementioned liberal democratic tenets. In particular, Confucianism gives priority to the state and the community over the individual, thus opposing individualism; Confucianism advocates a kind of elitism or meritocracy, even authoritarianism, which presupposes inequality among human beings and opposes equality and one person, one vote; the Confucian idea of the rule by the virtuous (which is also described as "rule by [virtuous] men") is apparently at odds with the idea of the rule of law; and the alleged Confucian belittlement of commerce, and the emphasis on the moral role of the government, seem to be in conflict with market economy and autonomy.

Based on this incompatibility view, people of the first camp can be further divided into two subcamps. The first subcamp contends that we need to get rid of Confucianism in order for Confucianism-influenced countries to embrace liberal democracy. This was a tenet of the radicals of the New Culture and May Fourth movements. It is still very popular among Chinese prodemocracy intellectuals, and promoted by international figures such as Ronald Dworkin. In contrast to the first subcamp, the second subcamp includes more realistic thinkers, such as Samuel Huntington and Amy Chua, who think the Confucian values have deep roots in East Asia and cannot be uprooted, the implication being that these deep-rooted but incompatible values will lead to clashes of civilizations between the East and the West.[1]

The second camp is the prodemocracy compatibility camp, to which many so-called overseas New Confucians, especially Mou Zongsan (牟宗三) and his followers, belong. Their main strategy for the compatibility thesis is to show that democratic ideas can be derived from Confucianism. However, there are a few problems with this line of defense. First, on the issue of the compatibility between Confucianism and rights, for example, some of them have argued that a Kantian form of individual autonomy is inherent in Confucianism, and thus Confucianism is compatible with rights. But the crucial

1. For references and more detailed discussions, see Bell (2006, 1–6).

move in this strategy has been very controversial, and it doesn't do justice to either Kant or Confucianism.[2] Second, even if this derivation could be done, why should we bother to derive democratic ideas from Confucianism if they are already fully developed in some Western political philosophies? Simply put, why do we bother to read Confucius? We should just read Kant, who can offer a Kantian message without any massaging. This derivation, then, can at best have the pragmatic function of helping countries with a Confucian heritage or contemporary Confucians to adopt democracy. Generally, although the New Confucian approach appears to be very assertive, arguing that modern and Western liberal democratic values can be derived from Confucianism, it is actually waving the white flag to liberal democracy. That is, people of this camp actually share the conviction of the first camp that "West [i.e., Western democracy and science] is best" and only differ from the latter in the former's (oftentimes very forced) claim that Western values can be derived from Confucian ones. What they actually do is to show that Confucianism can be a cheerleader for liberal democracy, and the only constructive aspect of Confucianism comes from its moral metaphysics. But the thick moral values that they take as cures for some excesses of real-world democracies are in conflict with pluralism and are at best useful to the believers, who will only be a small sect among the people with diverse moral views. Indeed, more moderate Chinese prodemocracy thinkers would welcome, in an almost condescending manner, such a "neutered" Confucianism as a constituent of the plurality of values in a liberal regime. Third, common to both camps is the belief that democratic ideas are essential to Western democracy, and thus Confucianism can only be made compatible with democracy if we can derive these democratic ideas from Confucianism. On the issue of rights, the aforementioned New Confucian move presupposes that rights can only be justified by a strong (Kantian) version of autonomy. I will come back to these issues in the following two sections.

The third camp is the pro-Confucianism incompatibility camp, or the fundamentalist camp. People of this camp, like those in the first camp, also believe in the incompatibility thesis but assert the superiority of traditional Chinese values over Western ideas. The writings of the early twentieth-century eccentric thinker Gu Hongming (辜鴻銘) are an example of this, although they are not commonly considered scholarly. Contemporary scholar Jiang Qing (蔣庆) argues that liberal democracy is inseparable from Christianity, which is the root of Western culture. Hence, since China is a Confucian country, it can't adopt liberal democracy, which is culturally specific to Christendom, and it has to develop and adopt a Confucian constitutional regime, which is also

2. See, for example, Shi (manuscript).

superior to the Western liberal democratic regime. (I have criticized his proposal elsewhere and won't repeat it here.)[3]

The fourth camp is the revisionist camp. Members of this camp acknowledge the differences between mainstream liberal democratic ideas and Confucianism, and they want to offer some revisionist accounts. The revisions and how they are applied divide this camp into two subcamps. One subcamp is a more prodemocracy revisionist camp. People in this camp want to revise Confucianism so as to make it compatible with liberal democracy, thus, a liberal democratic state with some democratized Confucian values. Sungmoon Kim's recent works can be put into this category (2014). There are a few thinkers in China who currently appear to be taking on such projects. But most of them are not clearly formulated in a scholarly way yet. Moreover, the distinction between this group and the second camp can become murky. In the case of Kim, the real distinction between his works and the works of the overseas New Confucians may be that he is openly revisionist, while the latter are "closeted" revisionists. Therefore, I have criticisms of this subcamp (including Kim's works) similar to some of those raised regarding the second camp. In particular, other than promoting democratization by being sensitive to an allegedly particular cultural (Confucian) milieu, it is hard to see how this kind of endeavor could enrich reflections of the best regimes in a universal sense.

The second subcamp is the pro-Confucianism revisionist camp. To be sure, those who are in this camp acknowledge the merits of liberal democracy and want to preserve them, sometimes by updating, revising, or even abandoning some of the Confucian ideas. But different from the second camp and the first subcamp of the fourth camp, they also argue that in some of the differences, Confucianism may have merits, especially in regard to political institutions (and not only with regard to virtues in a pluralistic civil society), that can be used to improve on the political institutions of liberal democracy and even develop different political models. Daniel Bell, Joseph Chan, Stephen Angle, and I, just to name a few, belong to this subcamp.[4]

The above divisions are meant to be signposts—with both their significance and shortcomings—to guide the readers through the literature on Confucianism and liberal democracy. The categorizations can be crude, failing to do justice to the many nuances, even among the scholars who have been mentioned. For example, a defender of Mou Zongsan, Angle's work has features

3. For a more detailed introduction of Jiang's theory and some criticisms of it in English, including my own criticism of it, see Jiang (2012).

4. For Bell's works on this subject, see Bell (2006 and 2015). In a recent book, Joseph Chan has assembled many of his works in the past decade or more (2013b). For Angle's work on this subject, see Angle (2012).

resembling the second camp and the first subcamp of the fourth camp. The contemporary Chinese scholar Gan Chunsong (干春松) seems to offer a Confucian world order in one of his new books (2012) that resembles the works of the fourth camp, but it can be argued that this order comes fairly close to the liberal cosmopolitan order, which makes his work closer to those of the second camp, that is, sugarcoating liberal democracy with Confucianism.

In terms of mapping the intellectual field of reflecting on Confucianism in the contemporary world, there is another set of tools that may be useful for readers and intellectual historians: the distinction between the universalist and particularist readings—"universalist" or "particularist" depends on whether Confucianism is taken as a universal (philosophical) teaching or as a doctrine particular to a certain time (ideology) or people ("Chinese culture" or "East Asian values"). As I have made clear in chapter 1, I adopt the universalist reading of Confucianism.

With the above categorization of different camps on the issue of the compatibility between liberal democracy and Confucianism, and the clarification of my own stance in these categories, I can give an outline of how I deal with this issue. As I have shown so far, Confucianism can accept one person, one vote as one mechanism of selecting the good (rather than eliminating the bad, as is commonly understood as a function of democracy) and of revealing the popular will. But its ideal regime has a meritocratic component. Confucianism can also offer different models of state identity and international relations. All these models have their merits, and may even be superior to certain Western or liberal models. At the same time, these models have some compatibility with liberal models, and I will offer further arguments for the compatibility thesis. But as I have repeatedly stated, there are clear merits of liberties, human rights, and the rule of law, especially in dealing with the politics of large and diverse states. Thus, my project of arguing for the contemporary relevance of Confucianism can be summarized as: limiting democracy (understood as one person, one vote) and nationalism while embracing liberalism (understood as the protection of rights and liberties, and the rule of law). The remaining task for me now is to show how the second half of my project could work. That is, I need to show the compatibility between Confucianism and rights as well as the rule of law. Moreover, in order to illustrate that the first half of my task is only a revision and not a complete rejection of democracy, I also need to show the compatibility between a Confucian reading of the one person, one vote system and a democratic system. I argued for this compatibility in chapter 4, but in the following discussions, further arguments for compatibility between my critical and constructive proposals from chapter 2 to chapter 8 and liberal democracy are offered.

One thing that I would like to note here is that my position is different from a dominant understanding of liberal democracy. As mentioned earlier in this section, many believe that one person, one vote is the core of liberal democracy. As Bell points out, even conservative Chinese leaders and critics of democratization only focus on the timing of democratization (2015, 15). That is, their apparent reservation is only about whether the people are ready for democracy or not (at present), and they never doubt or dare to doubt the desirability of democracy, understood as competitive elections in the form of one person, one vote. An interesting (and depressing) phenomenon in China today (from 2012 on) is that the terms "constitutionalism" and "judicial independence" have become targets of censorship, while the open use of the term "democracy" has not. For prodemocracy people in China and in the West, the most important task is often promoting popular elections. That is, ironically, conservative (anti-Western) Chinese leaders and prodemocracy people in China and in the West are in agreement on this issue (that the key to democracy is one person, one vote). But according to my position, it should be the other way around. Liberalism (in the form of the rule of law and the protections of liberties and rights) is far less questionable and far more desirable than democracy (in the form of one person, one vote), and should be promoted first. As I mentioned in chapter 1, liberal democracy has been in trouble recently, and this leads many to reject it. Though critical of many aspects of liberal democracy, I argue that it is the democratic (and certain nation-state and cosmopolitan) parts that cause the problems and should be revised, while the liberal part should be defended. That is, my critical proposal is in fact a support of (a revised version of) liberal democracy.

Problems with Democratic Ideas as the Metaphysical Foundation of Liberal Democracy

Let me now return to the compatibility issue. To repeat, a dominant belief is that liberal democracy is built on democratic ideas, or the ideas of individualism, equality, autonomy, and so on. These ideas are often given a metaphysical status. But how can we justify them? That is, how can we argue that they are absolute and a priori? One way to justify these ideas is to appeal to human nature. That is, it can be claimed that human beings by nature are *only* capable of being self-interested or equal. Here, the restrictive word "only" is crucial, because many "nonliberal" doctrines don't deny the self-interest of human beings (as they are often mistakenly accused of) but only the claim that human beings are *only capable of* being self-interested. Oftentimes, this claim is corroborated with nothing more than a rather imaginary, vague, and ahistorical account of the state of nature, or a biological, psychological, or

behavioral account of human nature that is scientifically dubious. Scientifically and historically, it is not clear that human beings are only self-interested,
or that human beings enjoy equality and autonomy.[5]

More importantly, even if human beings by nature *are* only self-interested
or equal, does it follow that we *ought to* remain this way? An error in some
common rhetoric about the validity of democratic ideas is an illegitimate
move from what we are to what we ought to be, and to the celebration of what
we are. We are born ignorant, but usually we don't think that we ought to stay
this way. Various accounts of human nature (what we are) have a decisive
normative function only if human beings cannot be or are not capable of being
or becoming otherwise. For example, a political philosophy that is based on
the assumption that human beings ought not to eat is meaningless because
we cannot yet afford not to eat. But it is quite obvious that human beings can
be public-interested, unequal, or social. Of course, it is important to know
the natural tendencies of human beings, so that we can tinker with them according to certain norms, certain "oughts."[6] Therefore, the questions now
become whether human beings ought to be self-interested, equal, or indi-
vidualistic, and why we have to accept these "oughts." I will not go into the
many arguments for or against these claims but only want to point out that it
is even more difficult and controversial to defend the "ought" claims than the
"is" ones.

Having shown the problem associated with these ideas themselves, I now
turn to the issue of the relations between these ideas and liberal democracy.
Let me first examine whether these ideas are sufficient conditions for liberal
democracy, that is, whether the acceptance of these ideas necessarily leads to
the acceptance of liberal democracy. The answer seems to be negative. Let's
assume for argument's sake that human beings are and/or ought to be self-
interested. It is not clear why one does not want to establish his or her tyranny
over others if possible. One can argue that it is not possible for one or a few
people to rule over the majority, because we have relatively equal abilities (in
a war of all against all). But from Thrasymachus and Glaucon in Plato's *Republic* to Nietzsche, many have argued otherwise, and, historically, tyrannies and
oligarchies are not rare. Maybe these regimes are not stable, but why should
stability be a concern? A concern for whom? Nietzsche would say that stability is a concern for those with a herd instinct and ought not to be taken seriously by the superior race. Maybe the actions of the tyrants will have bad

5. In fact, the primatologist Frans de Waal has argued that, empirically, human beings were
originally hierarchical and social, and had seeds of compassion for others (2006).

6. The concept "natural tendencies" doesn't carry with it a sense of necessity, and only means
what, statistically, human beings tend to do without cultivation.

consequences, but as long as they don't happen—or these tyrants don't think that they will happen—during their lifetime, they can always take comfort in Louis XV's line, "After me, the flood" (quoted earlier in chapter 5). Indeed, even if they expected to pay for their wantonness, they could still comfort themselves with a revised line, "After the fun, the flood."

For argument's sake, let's put aside this "quibble" and accept the assumption that human beings are self-interested and relatively equal ("relatively equal" in the sense that it is not possible for one or the few to establish tyranny over the many). This assumption doesn't necessarily lead to the acceptance of democracy. One only needs to think of the textbook version of Hobbes's *Leviathan*, according to which any regime can be accepted as long as it is a result of the covenant of the people.[7] For example, monarchy can be accepted if the majority decides to have this regime. Now, what about the idea of equality, independent of the idea of self-interest? On this issue, one only needs to be reminded of the fact that a nondemocratic regime such as communism also takes equality as its basic principle and final goal. As for the idea that the right of an individual should be first and foremost respected, the relation between it and liberal democracy becomes complicated when there are conflicts among individuals, and solving these conflicts might lead to a regime other than liberal democracy. To be clear, what I am arguing here is not that these ideas necessarily lead to a regime other than liberal democracy but that accepting these ideas does not necessarily lead to adopting liberal democracy. In other words, accepting these "democratic" ideas is not a sufficient condition for adopting liberal democracy.

However, is the acceptance of democratic ideas a necessary condition for adopting liberal democracy? That is, is it the case that one will not accept liberal democracy if one does not accept these ideas? If this is the case, the nearly universal consensus of the legitimacy and supremacy of liberal democracy today will pose serious challenges to those who reject them. But clearly, many in the world don't accept some or all of the democratic ideas. Human beings differ, perhaps even more so on these fundamental ideas of human existence. This being so, how do we deal with those who don't believe in, for example, "Give me liberty or give me death" and can't be persuaded by us? Should we say to them, "If you don't want to be given liberty, we will give you death"? To follow "Give me liberty or give me death" is idealistic, but to impose it on others is tyrannical.

In general, a common misconception that we human beings tend to have is the belief that those who don't agree with us are either ignorant or crazy. If,

7. Of course, Hobbes's view may have been far more complicated than this textbook version of his teaching.

however, we think about the implication of the fact that there are so many different and conflicting philosophical schools in history, even among those who have intellectual connections with each other, for example, Aristotle versus Plato, Hegel versus Kant, Heidegger versus Husserl, Han Fei Zi versus Xun Zi, and so on, we should see the falsehood of this misconception. It is not the case that the best thinkers from all these schools establish and follow their own schools rather than others' because they lack appreciation of reality, they do not think clearly, or they are too narrow-minded to understand other schools of thought. These schools differ greatly on what human beings naturally are and what they ought to be, and these differences have rarely, if ever, been resolved after generations of communications (peaceful or otherwise). Moreover, even if two groups of people or two smart thinkers hold the same a priori tenet, they may still come up with totally different systems. There may have been more struggles and wars among various sects within Christianity, and between it and its "sister" religions (Judaism and Islam), than between them and other civilizations. In the realm of Chinese philosophy, both the Cheng-Zhu school and the Lu-Wang school believe in the original goodness of human nature, but their doctrines are often different from each other. On the irresolvable differences among (intelligent) human beings, commenting on his debates with Albert Einstein, physicist Niels Bohr quoted a beautiful old saying about two kinds of truth: "To the one kind belong statements so simple and clear that the opposite assertion obviously could not be defended. The other kind, the so-called 'deep-truths,' are statements in which the opposite also contains deep truth" (1958, 66).

Therefore, we should see that even among well-educated, sensible, intelligent, and well-informed people, there can still be profound differences, and these differences cannot always be resolved by persuasion.[8] The differences can be those concerning the validity of democratic ideas, and this means that the people who don't accept these ideas are not and never will be a negligible minority, if only persuasion is used. If accepting democratic ideas is a necessary condition of accepting liberal democracy, this group of people may feel uneasy about, and perhaps hostile to, liberal democracy, while those who are in favor of liberal democracy may not trust this group of people and may see them as enemies of liberal democracy.

To this group of people, propaganda or brainwashing can be applied in order to change their positions on democratic ideas. But this method is in

8. For a thorough theoretical discussion of this profound pluralism among human beings, see Rawls (1999b, 475–78; sec. 2, "The Burdens of Reason," in the 1989 article "The Domain of the Political and Overlapping Consensus") as well as Rawls (1996, 54–58; here we can find a later and slightly revised account on this issue—one of the revisions is that he changes the term "the burdens of reason" to "the burdens of judgment").

conflict with the democratic idea of autonomy (one is forced to embrace free-dom), and it probably would not produce a determinate effect on this group of people. So in order to establish and maintain liberal democracy, further oppressive forces that more blatantly violate basic principles of liberal democ-racy have to be exerted on this group of people who constitute a nonnegligible minority, are commonly viewed as sensible and law-abiding in other aspects, and yet reject "democratic" ideas and, by implication, democracy. If these forces are not exerted, they may reject liberal democracy, make it unstable, and even overturn it when the time is right. Given the fact that they do not consti-tute an insignificant minority, this scenario is not unlikely. The conclusion here seems be this: nonliberal democratic (oppressive) forces have to be used to establish and maintain liberal democracy. For those under the regime of liberal democracy who wish to maintain it and those under a nonliberal demo-cratic regime who wish to establish liberal democracy, this conclusion seems to be rather depressing.

A Revised Rawlsian Answer

A Rawlsian Answer to the Compatibility Issue

Therefore, if democracy and human rights have to be based on a metaphysical doctrine, then the universal applicability of democracy and human rights, the stability of a democracy, and democratization in the world will become prob-lematic. The political philosopher John Rawls in his later works sees this prob-lem, especially with regard to stability within a democracy, and offers a solu-tion.[9] In *Political Liberalism* (*PL*), he writes, "the political culture of a democratic society is characterized . . . by three general facts": first, "the diver-sity of reasonable comprehensive religious, philosophical, and moral doc-trines found in modern democratic societies is not a mere historical condition that may soon pass away; it is a permanent feature of the public culture of

9. There are other thinkers who also argue for a pluralistic understanding of liberal democ-racy and can thus be used to address the questions that have been raised. However, I chose Rawls for the following reasons: first, I think that the later Rawls offers a powerful theoreti-cal—rather than merely practical—challenge to any universalistic understanding of liberal democracy; second, as I have shown in chapters 3 and 4, there is a resonance between Rawls and a Mencian in their concerns with today's democracy and their understanding of the condi-tions necessary for a good democracy; third, Rawls has been a leading liberal thinker. So to show his challenge to the universalistic understanding of liberal democracy, and the resonance be-tween him and a Mencian, may have the practical benefit of persuading liberal thinkers, both Western and Chinese. In a series of articles, Chinese political philosopher Zhou Lian (周濂) offers a list of works by various Western political philosophers on this issue, as well as his own discussion of the issue of pluralism (2007, 2008a, and 2008b).

democracy";[10] second, "a continuing shared understanding on one comprehensive religious, philosophical, or moral doctrine can be maintained only by
the oppressive use of state power," which he calls "the fact of oppression," and
he lists the comprehensive liberal doctrines of Kant and Mill (that are based
on individualism and autonomy) as examples of such doctrines that can only
be universally shared, paradoxically, through oppression; and third, "an enduring and secure democratic regime . . . must be willingly and freely supported
by at least a substantial majority of its politically active citizens" (1996, 36–38;
see also 78). These facts lead to the central problem of PL: "the problem of
political liberalism is: how is it possible that there may exist over time a stable
and just society of free and equal citizens profoundly divided by reasonable
religious, philosophical, and moral doctrines?" (ibid., xxvii).

For Rawls, then, the aforementioned "democratic" ideas, if taken to be (a
part of) a comprehensive doctrine, cannot serve as the sole foundation of
liberal democracy. Rawls's solution, simply put, is to take the whole theory of
liberal democracy as a freestanding political conception, divorced from any
known metaphysical "doctrine." This maneuver makes it possible for different
reasonable, liberal, or nonliberal doctrines to accept a common core, a political conception of liberal democracy that does not preclude the fundamental
ideas of these doctrines. The content of liberal democracy is not predetermined by or derived from any a priori ideas but is an overlapping consensus
worked out and endorsed by every reasonable and comprehensive doctrine.
It is not even necessary for every reasonable doctrine to endorse the same
concept but only the same family of concepts of liberal democracy; the way in
which each doctrine endorses this family of concepts can also be different.

Following Rawls's insights, we can argue that the apparent conflict between
Confucianism and the aforementioned "democratic" ideas doesn't necessarily
mean that in order for democracy to be possible, we must either denounce
Confucianism or somehow derive these ideas from it, as some overseas New
Confucians have done, often through greatly massaging and distorting Confucianism. Rather, Confucianism doesn't have to embrace democratic ideas,
understood as "thick" (metaphysical) ideas, in order to endorse liberal democracy. Two facts make this task easier. First, endorsement is a weaker requirement than derivation. Second, Confucianism may be in conflict with some of
the democratic ideas, but we can argue that they are not part of the "thinner,"

10. Rawls in PL quite consistently uses "conception" or "concept" to refer to the political,
free from metaphysics, and uses "doctrine" or "comprehensive doctrines" to refer to the metaphysical. For example, almost all known liberal philosophical theories, including those of Locke,
Rousseau, Kant, and Mill, are such "doctrines." Rawls uses "idea" as a neutral term. Moreover,
the term "reasonable" is another crucial concept in PL that may have a special meaning different
from how it is ordinarily understood.

noncomprehensive conception of political liberalism depicted in *PL*, for an insight of the later Rawls, simply put, is that in order for the majority to endorse democracy, there cannot be just one reading of it. Therefore, Confucians do not have to accept the assumption that in order to accept democracy and human rights, one must accept certain metaphysical versions of individualism, and they do not have to reject democracy and human rights due to their rejection of these kinds of individualism. Confucians can offer interpretations of democracy and rights that don't betray their basic tenets. These interpretations can be different from dominant readings of liberal democracy, and Confucians only need to offer interpretations that bear a "family resemblance" to other readings.

Relativism?

Some clarifications are due before I apply the Rawlsian strategy to show the compatibility between Confucianism and liberal democracy. First, this thin version of liberal democracy, indeed, liberalism in general, might be criticized as being relativistic or even nihilistic by people such as the moral conservatives. Although trying to "thin down" the core of liberal democracy in order for it to be inclusive, Rawls was quite clear that his thin version of liberal democracy is not value neutral. As discussed in chapter 3 (under "Nonmeritocractic Solutions and Their Fundamental Limit"), Rawls's concept of "reasonable" and other related concepts are moral requirements, and the implied call for people to be considerate with other people's needs and interests is also a cure for the excesses of radical individualism. But these moral values are compatible with pluralism, and are thinner than the ones presupposed by a metaphysical moral doctrine. Indeed, for Rawls, the endorsement of liberal democracy should not be merely a convenience, a tactical move that is based on rational calculations. Rather, it should be a sincere moral commitment.

Moreover, people in this kind of liberal democracy are not what Nietzsche called the "last men," the men who do not have any profound beliefs and values and/or lack the courage or the strength to defend their beliefs and values. On the contrary, a major development of Rawls's political thought from *A Theory of Justice* to *PL* is precisely the recognition that in a liberal democracy, people have profound yet different beliefs and values. The concepts of "overlapping consensus" and "public reason," as well as the possibility of a stable liberal society in *PL*, presuppose that citizens in such a society actively express and defend their views, as long as the expression and the spread of their views meet the basic requirements of liberal democracy. In other words, the thin version of liberal democracy discussed in this chapter is neither completely value-free nor a modus vivendi that is used as a truce before one is able to eliminate those who differ with any means available. It does not force citizens to give up their profound beliefs; rather, it presupposes and even encourages them to fight for their beliefs and values *reasonably*.

Therefore, Rawls's liberalism is not a form of relativism or nihilism. The latter denies the existence of any ultimate truth and values. In Rawls's liberalism, there are thin but ultimate values, and people with different comprehensive doctrines have their own thick values as well. It is just that in defending their values or even attacking other people's values, there has to be a limit. Without such a limit, the attackers will pay the price eventually. Using as an example the consequences of the alliance between church and state, Rawls points out, as Tocqueville argued, linking a religion to earthly governments sacrifices the future for present short-term benefits, and this religion would go down when the rulers did; thus, the separation of church and state actually protects religion (1999a, 166–68). On the basis of this understanding, a moral conservative can have an interpretation of liberalism that doesn't violate his or her belief in the existence of the ultimate moral truth. To him, liberal democracy as a political concept doesn't deserve to have a metaphysical foundation. Rather, it is merely a compromise due to the imperfection of human reason, a protection of the kind of moral conservatism he or she believes in, and a procedural framework under which he or she can spread his or her beliefs. If, one day, all human beings become completely virtuous, that is, if they become God or the kind of sage even the Confucian exemplars Yao and Shun fall short of, then this compromise (liberal democracy) could be discarded. Until then, conservatives can accept liberal democracy as a second-best society and refine it within its framework.

A related point is that Rawlsian liberal democracy leaves room for private citizens to organize their lives in the way they prefer, as long as they endorse the political concept of liberal democracy in the public arena. That is, Rawlsian liberalism is different from the kind of moral metaphysics that is meant to apply to every aspect of human life. For example, even if we endorse a thin version of liberal democracy, we can still do things in other aspects of our social life, such as a private club, not in accordance with the principle of liberalism or democracy. Although in chapter 6 of this book, I expressed some reservations of Rawls's and other liberals' separation of the private from the public, I do think that a moderate separation can be made in certain aspects of human life.

Rawlsian Approach Revised

Second, there are some differences between Rawls and my own work. For one, Rawls is concerned with how to find stability for the right reasons in a liberal democracy that is inevitably pluralistic. While sharing this concern with him,

I am also concerned with helping people in a nonliberal democracy (as well as in a liberal democracy) to accept liberal democracy by showing that they can both endorse liberal democracy and cherish their ideas that are different from and even in conflict with "democratic" ideas. One's dislike of a certain ideology of liberal democracy does not necessarily mean that one does not want to have a liberal democracy.

For example, in China today, there are heated and sometimes extremely hostile debates between the leftists and the "liberals" over many political issues.[11] In spite of the differences on "thick" metaphysical ideas about the Good and about detailed policy implementations, it would be good if both the Chinese liberals and the leftists (including the New Leftists) in the Chinese context could agree on one point: there should be a fair process in various political, social, and economic matters. If so, then both groups could endorse a common and thin version of liberal democracy. The leftists want the government to have control over certain matters, and the thin version of liberal democracy is not against this. It only asks for a fair process. Similarly, even some socialists can and should endorse and even welcome this thin version of liberal democracy. The leftists should only be against a "thick" version of liberal democracy by some "liberals" or libertarians. The "liberals" should see that maybe some leftists are only against a certain version of liberal democracy and not liberal democracy per se. Discovering this common ground (the endorsement of a thin version of liberal democracy), and realizing that much needs to be done for China to become liberal democratic in this sense, Chinese "liberals," leftists (including the New Leftist), and "old conservatives" (e.g., Confucians) should first try to work together to fight against the common enemy (those who reject the thin version of liberal democracy, especially constitutionalism, rule of law, and rights), in order to lay down the common foundation for reasonable but diverse views to debate with each other. Unfortunately, in recent years (from 2010 on), partly confused by what the real problems and differences are, some Chinese "liberals" have become increasingly hostile to even moderate Confucian conservatives and New Leftists, and even

---

11. To clarify, Chinese scholars and the Americans use these terms in almost opposite ways. In the American context, liberals are understood as those in favor of maintaining social and economic equality through some normative principles, enforced by the government. So if the so-called New Leftists in the Chinese context are referring to those who want to protect the interests of common people from a crude market economy, they are liberals in the American sense. If the so-called liberals in the Chinese context are understood as those who want to support economic freedom or free market economy, free from governmental interference, they will be taken as hard-core Reaganite Republicans, or even libertarians, but definitely not liberal democrats in the American sense.

more New (and old) Leftists have become the "Maoist Leftists" and statists, cynical of any liberal arrangements and the rule of law and determined to eliminate, spiritually and even physically, their opponents. The latter group of people should then be considered "unreasonable" in a Rawlsian sense, and they won't even acknowledge a common basis, a fair process, or a "constitutional order," on the basis of which we can conduct our debates over issues on which we disagree.

Another difference between my approach and Rawls's is that, for Rawls, the basic principles of liberal democracy are based on equality, justice as fairness, or reciprocity, and cannot be "thinned down." In other words, what the later Rawls is doing is to search for a wider base for the ideas developed in his earlier work, *A Theory of Justice.* What his political liberalism is meant to achieve is not a compromise among existing doctrines (1996, xlvii and 39–40). For example, Rawls carefully distinguishes between overlapping consensus and modus vivendi (ibid., xxxix–xliii and 146–50; 1999a, 149–50 and 168–69). That is, people with different comprehensive doctrines should happily accept this fact of pluralism and treat people with different doctrines in accordance with the basic principles of liberal democracy. In other words, they should not take pluralism in liberal democracy as a political compromise, a truce that a certain happenstance plus some political maneuver can and should break. Although I maintain that certain political maneuvers should be excluded, I have not attempted nor will attempt to closely follow these requirements by Rawls and every particular liberal principle or idea that Rawls considers essential. Rather, I take inspiration from Rawls's notion that the political conception of liberal democracy needs to be freed from any particular doctrine and only needs to be endorsed by different reasonable teachings in their own way. But my version of the common core of liberal democracy may be explicitly "thinner" than Rawls's in certain aspects, and only on the common core do I try to show that Confucianism is compatible with liberal democracy. In particular, as I mentioned earlier in this chapter (under "Four Camps on the Compatibility between Confucianism and Liberal Democracy"), my focus is to show how Confucianism can be compatible with the liberal part of liberal democracy, although I have shown, and will continue to show, that there is some overlapping consensus between Confucianism and the democratic part (such as one person, one vote) of liberal democracy as well. Nonetheless, there are still remaining conflicts between Confucianism and liberal democracy, especially the democratic part. One crucial difference is about popular sovereignty, discussed in chapters 2–4, and there may arguably be some differences between the Confucian model and the liberal models of state identity and international relations, as discussed in chapters 7–8. But on these differences, if they are real differences, I have tried to argue that maybe the Confucian models have their merits; liberal democracy should revise and thin down their core of overlapping consensus and embrace these Confucian models instead.

Besides, on certain issues of fundamental differences, for example, abortion, I don't see how a Christian who truly believes that a fetus is a human being can offer an argument based on public reason or be reasonably persuaded otherwise. For him or her, the political reality that allows abortion is a modus vivendi that, as a democratic citizen, he or she has to accept. The best we can hope for in this kind of situation is perhaps for people of fundamental differences that cannot be resolved by public reason to accept the modus vivendi, without attempting to break it with force but only with democratic procedures. Otherwise put, to operate with Rawlsian public reason is the ideal, but some form of modus vivendi should be accepted as the second best, which Rawls excludes from his account of liberal pluralism, but should be accepted and examined within the range of liberal democracy.

Role of Democratic and Confucian Ideas in Democratization

Third, it should be noted that my argument for compatibility between Confucianism and liberal democracy is about possibility and not about necessity, and my criticism of democratic ideas is about necessity (that is, that they are sufficient or necessary conditions for liberal democracy) and not about possibility. Otherwise put, on the one hand, democratic ideas can be connected with liberal democracy as a political concept, but this connection is not necessary; on the other hand, nondemocratic ideas and liberal democracy as a political concept can be opposed to each other, but this opposition is not necessary. Philosophical ideas, as something "upstairs," often have different ways of coming "downstairs," that is, embodied in real regimes or other aspects of reality.

Of course, in a particular historical context, some ideas may have a closer connection with what is going on in reality than other ideas do. Indeed, ideas are often introduced in a particular historical context, and the connection between these ideas and what is going on in reality is often considered necessary. But this kind of "necessity" is context-dependent and not "pure," not in the same way that some metaphysicians usually understand the concept of "a priori" or "necessity."

Therefore, democratic ideas can be instrumental in promoting democracy, more so than nondemocratic ideas, in certain historical contexts. For example, when state power and public interest are distorted or misused for the interests of a small group of people, or for the imposition of some crazy ideas of a small group of people in the majority, the emphasis on individual liberty and even the justification and celebration of each citizen's private interest can become an important *practical* maneuver, but it is not the case that some radical version of individualism is always helpful and even essential to democracy.

To use a concrete example, constitutionalism, which is instrumental to the development of liberal democracy, was first developed in countries such as England, and many factors quite peculiar and accidental to the English regime and political situations at that time contributed to it. Some can argue, then, that people from other countries should reject constitutionalism because it was an English phenomenon. An argument for the Confucian fundamentalist Jiang Qing to reject Western constitutional democracy is precisely this kind of argument: the fact that Western countries were all Christian countries means that Christianity was the necessary condition for constitutional democracy. China is not a Christian country, and thus the Chinese should reject Western-style constitutionalism. Some others may argue that in order to develop a constitutional regime, we need to emulate all the factors that were instrumental for the English development of constitutionalism. This is one implicit argument among the Chinese May Fourth radicals and many other Chinese antitraditionalist prodemocracy people. But as previously discussed, the endorsement of liberal democracy does not hinge on a particular democratizing process or a particular way of endorsing liberal democracy, and such a particular process and a particular understanding of democracy do not exclusively determine how others should understand and accept liberal democracy.

Failing to appreciate the distinction between the historical and the normative, one could object to any attempt to defend the compatibility between Confucianism and liberal democracy by arguing that if they were compatible, why didn't China first develop liberal democracy? But whether a Confucian country (if China ever was such a country, which is highly debatable) developed liberal democracy or not is a separate issue from whether Confucianism can be compatible with liberal democracy or not. In fact, even on the issue of promoting democracy, Chinese prodemocracy dissident Wang Juntao (王军涛), for example, shows that many prodemocracy activists throughout modern Chinese history are Confucians, and that their work is actually partly inspired by their Confucian ideas (2003, 68–89), including such ideas as the duty of the educated elite to participate in governing the state.[12]

An implication of the distinction between democracy and democratization is that the democratization process doesn't have to be conducted in accordance with democratic principles. In fact, in history, many democratization processes are not democratic, and undemocratic conduct is tolerated and even supported by the prodemocracy camp. Some consider this tolerance and sup-

12. For more references, see Winston (2011, 229–30).

port a sign of hypocrisy and even conspiracy. But this criticism is a result of the confusion between democracy and democratization. Those who favor democracy can tolerate and support undemocratic elements in a democratization process, as long as these elements are meant to facilitate the democratization process, although this tolerance and support should end after this process is completed or after it turns out otherwise.

Confucian Rights

The Confucian/Rawlsian Strategies of Endorsing Rights

As I stated toward the end of the first section of this chapter, my overall strategy is to revise the democratic part of liberal democracy with Confucianism-inspired ideas and institutions, while defending the compatibility between Confucianism and the liberal part of liberal democracy, especially the rule of law and rights. Now, let me show how we can tackle the compatibility issue with the revised Rawlsian approach illustrated in the previous section. First, let me reformulate it by referring to Joseph Chan's paper on the compatibility between Confucianism and rights (rather than liberal democracy in general) (1999).[13]

In his article, Chan first makes it clear that with regard to the compatibility issue, Confucianism is not understood as a state ideology or as a set of practices that are "more a kind of product of time and historical circumstances," but as a philosophical thought that transcends time (1999, 213) and, I add, space or locales, a position I also take (see the discussion in chapter 1 in this book). Confucius and Mencius clearly did not think of the issue of human rights as we understand it today, but this does not mean that we cannot respond to contemporary and comparative issues while following the spirit of their thoughts. In other words, the central question about the compatibility between early Confucianism and rights is not really "*Is* Confucianism compatible with rights (in history)?" but "*Can* Confucianism be compatible with rights?" (ibid.).

Even with the compatibility issue so defined, however, there are still challenges to it. In Chan's article, he deals with four alleged Confucian reasons for rejecting the idea of human rights. First, it is argued "any assertion of human rights must presuppose that human beings are *asocial* beings and have rights independent of culture and society," while Confucians have a social,

---

13. There have been numerous discussions on the issue of whether Confucianism is compatible with rights. In this and the next sections, I rely mostly on two articles, Chan (1999) and Tiwald (2013). They offer comprehensive and critical reviews of various positions in these discussions, as well as their own well-argued proposals on this issue.

contextual, and role-based understanding of human beings (1999, 216). Second, "any assertion of human rights would be premised on the view that human beings are egoistic," in contrast to the Confucian ideal of familial and communal relationships (ibid., 219). The third alleged Confucian reason for the incompatibility view is that "the Confucian conception of personal relationships advocates hierarchy and submission" (ibid., 222), and the fourth reason is that "the appeal to rights would turn social relationships from harmonious to conflictual or litigious" (ibid., 226).

Chan acknowledges that these conflicts, though exaggerated, do exist. But he argues that if we do not suppose that there can be only one understanding of human rights, it is possible for Confucianism to endorse human rights from a different perspective and with a different reading. That is, what is needed to show the compatibility between human rights and Confucianism is not universal agreement but "overlapping consensus" (1999, 212).

Chan doesn't mention Rawls when he uses the concept of overlapping consensus, but as we have seen throughout the book, it is a key concept in Rawls's later philosophy. The focus of Rawls's discussion is how to establish a universal conception of justice, given the fact of pluralism in any democracy. But his arguments can be used to challenge the universalist understanding of human rights as well. That is, it is impossible for the people of a pluralistic liberal democracy to adopt one essentialist and metaphysical understanding of human rights without oppressive forces—forces that deny human rights—being used. Rawls's solution, applied to the rights issue, is that for rights to become "universal" among reasonable people, these rights must not be given only one universalist understanding. Rather, the common understanding of rights in liberal societies has to be thinned down to an overlapping consensus that is based on family resemblance. In contrast to Chan's more moderate criticism of the universalist approach, which emphasizes the practical need to take the Confucian context into account when applying rights to East Asian countries, I argue that the universalist approach is inevitably in conflict with the fundamental fact of a liberal and pluralistic society where people hold different and competing comprehensive doctrines. This conflict makes the metaphysical or universalist approach untenable in all societies that are and wish to be liberal, including the East Asian ones. In the case of compatibility between Confucianism and rights, acknowledging the conflicts between some basic ideas of Confucianism and the four ideas that are considered essential to rights, as illustrated above by Chan, I argue that Confucianism doesn't have to embrace these ideas to endorse rights.

In particular, using Rawlsian terms to recast and revise one of Chan's answers to the first two challenges, that Confucianism is not asocial and not egoistic, we can argue that for human rights to be universally adopted, one simply cannot base them solely on one and only one particular metaphysical moral doctrine—in this case, one specific form of metaphysical individualism, which is implied by the first and second challenges in Chan's formulation. It is true that rights have to presuppose individuals as their bearers, but this conception of the individual doesn't have to be "thick," and cannot be thick if we want rights to be universal. We can easily argue that Confucianism can endorse a thin version of the conception of the individual, and can thus be made compatible with rights that have individuals as their bearers. Of course, the Confucian individual is always in a social context, and his or her rights will be subjected to the social relations he or she is in. That is, Confucian rights may be more contextual and less absolute than the rights derived from an asocial and autonomous conception of the individual. But perhaps it can be a good thing that rights are contextual in certain contexts, the examples of which will be given later in this and the next sections.

Even with a thin version of the individual, we have to admit that Confucians rarely talk about rights. But they do talk about duties, and duties and rights are oftentimes two sides of the same coin. One can say that a child has a right to be raised by his or her parents, but one can also say that a parent has a duty to raise his or her underage children.

Another "tactic" that is inspired by a pluralistic understanding of rights is what Chan calls the "fallback apparatus." He uses it to answer the second, third, and fourth points on his aforementioned list, that is, Confucianism is not egoistic, not egalitarian, and not litigious. In spite of all these challenges, Chan argues that Confucianism can still endorse human rights as a fallback apparatus. That is, although Confucians prefer familial and communal care, benevolent paternalism, and reliance on rituals and the power of virtues, human rights can be endorsed by the Confucian as the last line of defense of basic human interests when and only when the aforementioned preferred mechanisms are inadequate or abused (cf. Tiwald 2013, 41).[14] For example, ideally, we hope that a father will care for his underage children, but just in case he fails to fulfill his duty, we can use legal constraint to force him to do so, thus de facto protecting the "right" of the children.

There is one more tactic that can encourage Confucians to endorse rights. We can reinterpret rights in the Confucian framework and then subject them to some higher goods rooted in and recognized by Confucianism.[15] Indeed, even the idea of a fallback mechanism can be considered the result of weighing different kinds of goods recognized by Confucians. An example of this tactic is the right to free speech. It can be endorsed by Confucians for three reasons. First, this right can help reveal the will of the people, which, as I argued in

14. The original English version of Tiwald's paper has not been published, but the Chinese translation has been. The direct quotes from this paper are based on the English manuscript.

15. I thank Liang Hao (梁颢) for pushing me to clarify this point.

chapter 2, is the root of the legitimacy of a government for Confucians; second, it can serve as a deterrent on rulers engaged in wrongdoing; and third, it can facilitate good policy making and thus promote good governance.[16] All the concerns here are recognized by Confucians. To be clear, for the third reason, we have to accept an observation that free discussion of policies helps to lead to good policy making, an empirical claim that is naturally open to empirical challenges. Moreover, from a Confucian "elitist" point of view, primarily those with merits can engage in meaningful policy discussions. However, the line between those with merits and those without is not fixed and predetermined. Therefore, free access to information should be open to all in general. Moreover, although those without merits (the masses) cannot "handle the truth," there should still be free access to information, otherwise the masses will lose their trust in governmental authority and will be subjected to the sway of rumors, if the cover-up and deception of the latter is revealed, which is almost always inevitable in this day and age, when absolute control of information is unlikely, especially in a liberal society. In short, although Confucians have no trust in the masses' ability to handle the truth, they would nevertheless argue against preventing the masses from having access to it.[17]

In sum, the key for Confucianism to be compatible with rights is to allow rights to be read differently. Based on a thin conception of the individual, which has to be presupposed by any rights regime, Confucianism can offer three specific strategies to endorse rights: (1) replace rights talk with duties talk; (2) use the fallback apparatus; and (3) refer rights to some higher good in Confucianism. Moreover, the case for this can be strengthened if it can be shown that in most cases, the Confucian reading leads to little significant practical difference, while in the cases in which the Confucian reading offers something significantly different, it has its own merits.

Obligations versus Rights

With the first tactic, one may object that obligations and rights seem different. As Justin Tiwald puts it, "If it is my responsibility to contribute to my brother's education, I then have merely an obligation to him. But if it is my responsibil-

16. Indeed, if we don't believe that rights can be deduced from some metaphysical principles, but have to be the result of fair discussion among citizens, that is, if we accept the fact of pluralism and fairness, the right to free speech should be taken as the condition for other rights to be possible. That is, free speech is the mother of all other rights. In a similar vein, it is also the condition for good governance, as I argue here, which also includes identifying and protecting people's "rights," though read differently by Confucians.

17. Of course, even in a liberal country, there has to be some secrecy, and a Confucian can certainly recognize this need.

ity to help him and he is morally permitted to demand it, putting in motion enforcement or redress, he then has a right" (2013, 43). Tiwald's account shows a key feature of rights: they have to be demandable, and can thus be a foundation for legal enforcement. He is also right to say that appealing to obligation instead of right, one cannot say that the receiver of a benefit can demand the benefit as his, her, or its right. But surely the receiver can claim it as the giver's obligation and duty. One may argue that obligation is voluntary and thus cannot be demanded, but this argument is perhaps a late modern Western understanding of obligation. It is true that for the Confucian, ideally, it is the doer who willingly undertakes his or her obligation, and to exert too much force on him or her is counterproductive.[18] But this does not mean that obligations cannot be enforced through a fallback apparatus of moral and legal codes, and the possible violation of "negative liberty" that this enforcement implies doesn't necessarily lead to oppression—clearly, oppression cannot be accepted in a liberal democracy and should not be accepted in the Confucian regime that we are building.

For example, in the American legal system, there are laws called "Good Samaritan laws." These laws protect good Samaritans from being held legally responsible for unintended harm that may occur in their attempt to help someone who is injured or imperiled. In this scenario in China, those who are assisted (or their family members) sue those who help if harm is done, so this phenomenon becomes a reason for many not to help others. Thus, by passing these kinds of laws, we may help people fulfill their moral duties. Moreover, we can imagine a more aggressive version of the Good Samaritan laws when, for example, bystanders who fail to help the injured are fined. Another example from the American legal system is when a child's right to be fed is enforced by punishing the parents who fail to fulfill their obligations to nurture their child. In this example, the interchangeability between rights and obligations becomes even more apparent. Thus, if it is so enforced, an obligation can be claimed, not as a moral right of the receiver but as a moral and even legal obligation of the giver.

Demandable or enforceable obligations have few, if any, practical difference from the claimable rights in the areas they overlap. The resemblances in practice reveal the falsehood of a dogma held by some liberals. According to this dogma, modern liberalism is based on the protection of negative liberties, and any emphasis on positive liberties or obligations must lead to oppression. But the examples mentioned above, fining bystanders who fail to help and

18. See, for example, a famous allegory in the *Mencius* (which was referred to twice in this book already) in which Mencius pointed out that the people who try to help seedlings grow by pulling at them not only "fail to help them but they do the seedlings positive harm" (2A2).

punishing negligent parents can hardly be considered oppressive. Indeed, the latter is actually practiced in the United States, a liberal democratic state. Jane Mansbridge has recently argued that perhaps it is time to offer more (legitimate) state coercions that would be similar to what I propose here.[19] There are two reasons for this. First, coercion is a way to address the free riders' problem and to protect those who are dutiful. Second, the need to use coercion is stronger today, because the world is more interdependent and we are closer to using up natural resources (collective property of all humans), which makes the threat from free riders rather real.

Of course, conceptually, obligations and rights are still different, but as I have pointed out, for rights to be universally adoptable, they have to be understood and interpreted differently. In general, we can say that many rights can be endorsed by Confucians, but the latter read some of these rights not as the demandable rights of the receiver but the demandable and (morally and legally) enforceable obligations and duties of the giver.

In fact, the classical liberal thinker John Stuart Mill argued in chapter 5 of *Utilitarianism* that what makes something a duty is precisely the fact that it can be exacted from the duty-bearer, and this demand is not enforced by law only because of prudence (2001, 48–49), that is, the fear of "trusting the magistrate with so unlimited an amount of power over individuals" (ibid., 48). He also makes a (not always clear) distinction between duties of imperfect obligation and of perfect obligation. The practice of the former is not toward any particular person or at a prescribed time but is left to our own choice, while the practice of the latter is specified for a particular person at a particular time. Mill then argued that the former do not give birth to any right, but the latter do. It is true that some of his distinctions are not always aligned with the idea of demandable duties discussed here; some of what he would consider duties of imperfect obligation would be considered giving birth to rights in our discussion, and some legal enforcements he might consider imprudent are considered otherwise here. But we can see that it is not that far-fetched to consider (some) duties and rights to be two sides of the same coin.

The Confucian emphasis on obligation also puts the burden on the strong, who can actually act, instead of on the weak, who cannot act to enforce their rights and whose claims to rights may thus end up being purely formal. Indeed, in the case of animal rights (discussed in the next section), animals can't

---

19. Mansbridge hasn't had a paper on this issue yet. What I offer here is based on her PowerPoint presentation with the title "The Case for Coercion: How Our Need for Legitimate Coercion Is Increasing, Just as Its Supply Is Decreasing." Mansbridge (1990) contains some earlier discussion of this idea. I thank her for pointing out the relevance of her discussion to what I propose here, and for sharing the PowerPoint document with me.

just claim rights, but we humans do on behalf of them. Therefore, the Confucian strategy may protect the weak more effectively. Put otherwise, there is *doing* justice versus *having* justice. Rights are more associated with the latter and duties with the former. But clearly, if no one is doing justice, no one will have justice. The emphasis on duties is essential for us to have rights.

Is Confucian Endorsement of Rights Fragmented and Too Thin?

Another objection is that the fact that Confucianism has to endorse rights through different tactics, and maybe even on a case-by-case basis, and thus lacks a universal justification, makes the Confucian endorsement fragmented. But a universal justification on the basis of inalienable rights of an individual is usually, if not always, based on some kind of metaphysics. It can be theoretically elegant and systematic. But there may never be a consensus on what rights are self-evident and inalienable, as the fundamental fact of pluralism in human life implies, and if we impose one systematical understanding on all, this imposition is clearly despotic and will likely be perceived as arbitrary. Otherwise put, if we accept later Rawls's understanding of pluralism, rights that are endorsed by the majority of a liberal and reasonable people have to be endorsed in a "fragmented" manner.

Yet another objection is that this thin version of human rights, as well as the kind of Confucianism that merely endorses it, would not promote human rights as forcefully as the "thick" version of human rights does. This may well be true in many historical contexts. But, as argued above, it is simply not possible for a thick version of human rights that is based on a metaphysical understanding of human beings to be universally adopted without resorting to oppressive forces. Also, at least in some scenarios, it can be those who adopt this thick version of human rights—that is, those who think that human rights have to be based on some metaphysical understanding of the individual and give absolute priority to certain rights that they consider fundamental—who should tone down their thick version of rights and benefit from a thin version instead. For example, should we allow neo-Nazis to march in a Jewish Holocaust survivors' community or pornography to be available at any time to anyone, because the right to free speech is absolute? As already mentioned, the Confucian endorsement of the right to free speech is subjected to some higher good, and can thus be conditional.

Moreover, it is argued that many ills in contemporary societies are related to some extreme form of individualism, on which the thick version of rights is based. As a result, some complain that "rights" are sometimes used to defend an individual's reckless and selfish actions and thus indirectly encourage such actions; otherwise put, "rights" are used to defend "wrongs." This fact makes some people doubt the desirability of human rights.[20] In contrast, as I argued earlier in this section, the Confucian reading of rights is partly duty-based, and can thus avoid the above problem and attract those who are repelled by the radical individualism and the rights theory based on it. For example, in the duties talk, an irresponsible chain-smoker doesn't have a right to health care. While it is true that the government has a duty to assist those in need, the shift of language takes some entitlement away from the chain-smoker. Moreover, the duties talk also implies that the smoker has a duty to take care of himself as well.

Tiwald offers some further challenges to the aforementioned tactics to make Confucianism compatible with rights. He first points out that both the "compatibilists" and "incompatibilists" now accept the (weakened) compatibility of Confucianism with the fallback reading of human rights. He then argues, "fallback rights are inconsistent with the founding moral and political doctrines of Confucianism, or not rights at all" (2013, 41–42).[21]

One argument he offers is that fallback rights are not rights as such or rights proper (Tiwald 2013, 47–48), whereas, as Michael Meyer puts it, a dominant understanding of rights among Western liberals is that "the existence of the right is itself one constitutive component of what makes the action virtuous" (1997, 159; quoted in Tiwald 2013, 46). Tiwald's argument may well be true, but the understating of rights that Tiwald uses is a thick version of human rights. As I pointed out earlier, the Confucian can endorse only a thin version of human rights. Not to insist on the universality of the thick version is crucial for human rights to be universally adoptable and, as we have already seen, there are problems with the thick version of rights. Indeed, as Tiwald points out, even in Western scholarship, many modern rights thinkers "also regard appeal to rights as something of a necessary evil" (ibid., 41).

Rights That Cannot Be Endorsed by Confucians?

A more serious challenge by Tiwald, I think, is his argument that (some of) the fallback rights, if we closely follow the classical Confucians, such as Confucius and Mencius, turn out to be much weaker than what the charitable reader may have expected.[22] One powerful example that he offers concerns

20. For example, Mary Ann Glendon has offered a scathing account of the abuse of rights talk in the contemporary United States (1993).

21. In the published Chinese version, this line is actually revised. The quote is from his original English manuscript.

22. Tiwald seems to suggest that this is a common problem of all fallback rights, but he does not go through all of them, and he may have overstated the case. Thus, I limit the claim to some of the fallback rights.

a common reading that Mencius allows "that the people might use extra-legal means to protect them, including the violent overthrow of tyrannical rulers" (2013, 48). That is, according to this reading, for Mencius, people have the right to revolt (and to vote). Those who hold this reading often refer to the *Mencius* 1B6 and 1B8, where Mencius justifies the removal and even the killing of a tyrant, but as Tiwald points out (ibid., 48–49), although serving the people is the goal of wise and virtuous Confucians, the love and resentment of the people are only "a passive indicator of Heaven's mandate, not as claims of right" (ibid., 49), especially not the right to vote, as we understand it in contemporary democracies. If we read 1B6 and 1B8 closely, we find that people are not entrusted with the direct action of removing a tyrant. Indeed, Tiwald's reading is in line with my own reading presented in chapter 2. That is, the popular participation that could be allowed by Mencius has to be more qualified than what the thin Rawlsian version embraces. For early Confucians, people's will plays a significant role in political decision making, but the role is in fact only consultative rather than decisive, as is the case in liberal democracies. Therefore, to take a strong reading of (some) fallback rights, "requires a great deal of massaging the textual evidence," as Tiwald puts it (ibid., 48).[23] This is true in the case of the alleged Confucian right to revolt. But this doesn't pose a threat to my version of Confucianism because, according the latter, there shouldn't be the right to revolt in the first place.

In the case of free speech, however, Tiwald's challenge becomes more serious. The direct target of his criticism is Joseph Chan's account of the right to free speech. In the discussion of this right, Chan points out, "Both Confucius and Mencius hold that social and political discussion and criticism are necessary to prevent culture and politics from degenerating" (1999, 228). The passages he refers to are from the *Analects* 13.15, 14.7, and 16.1; and the *Mencius* 5B9 and 3B9 (ibid., 228–29). He then claims,

> This does not prove that Confucius and Mencius valued free speech as such, nor is this my intention. What it shows, rather, is that both of them saw the importance of speech in politics and culture. Now if, as an empirical claim, it is true that freedom of speech in the long run helps society to correct wrong ethical beliefs and to prevent rulers from indulging in wrongdoing, then a Confucian perspective would endorse freedom of political speech. (ibid., 229)

However, this claim ignores a statement by Confucius in the *Analects*: "Do not plan the policies of an office you do not hold" (8.14). In case one might

---

23. This exact line doesn't appear in the Chinese version, but is in the original English manuscript.

ignore this statement as a misstatement, the very same statement appears twice in the *Analects* (8.14 and 14.26). Chan does not mention this statement in his discussion. Rather, he merely makes a general claim:

> One might think that, in these passages [the aforementioned supporting passages and not *Analects* 8.14 and 14.26; my note], Confucius and Mencius ask only those holding public office (ministers) to perform the task of admonishing the ruler, and so freedom of expression should be confined to them alone, but this is not true. Neither Confucius nor Mencius were state officials, but they were active in speaking publicly to criticize current politics and schools of thought. (1999, 229)

I think, however, that a more moderate conclusion from the conflict between the message implied in the *Analects* 8.14 and 14.26 and Confucius's own practical activities is that it is puzzling for those who try to understand Confucius. This conflict does not justify ignoring the two passages of the *Analects* completely and arguing instead that given some empirical considerations, Confucius would endorse freedom of speech. Indeed, Chan's argument for a Confucian endorsement of free speech is in part similar to what I offered earlier, so the two passages from the *Analects* also pose a serious challenge to my argument as well.

Then, how to resolve this conflict? One interpretation of passages 8.14 and 14.26 is that in an ideal state, where everyone does his or her own job and does it well, there is no need for a non-officeholder to interfere with the business of this office. During Confucius's lifetime, however, the feudal states were in such bad shape that many ministers and rulers not only did not do their jobs but also tried to usurp the office of others. Indeed, the Chinese word that is translated as "plan" here (謀) does have meanings of conspiracy and scheming, which are related to usurpation. Thus, we can take the message in these passages as a protest against the prevalent usurpations in Confucius's time. Paradoxically, in issuing this warning, Confucius became precisely someone who is planning policies of an office he didn't hold.

Still, we have to admit that the justification of freedom of speech on the Confucian ground is conditional on some higher good, as I argued earlier in this section. In the aforementioned two problematic passages, the Confucian restrictions are revealed. As Roger Ames and Henry Rosemont point out in the footnote to their translation of the *Analects* 14.26, "words are cheap" (1998, 261n240). The people who do not hold the office may enjoy the luxury of being critics without the burden of being constructive, may lack the ability to handle the problem, may have no extensive exposure to every aspect of the problem, may have no full dedication to the problem, may have no resources to solve the problem, and may have no comprehensive grasp of all the practical difficulties. If one is truly concerned, he or she should try to hold the office first. Indeed, in the discussion of justice in Plato's *Republic*, similar concerns with the problems of one man not doing the job he is good at have been expressed by Socrates.[24]

Of course, all this said, as was mentioned previously, Confucius himself was running around, planning policies of the office he did not hold. Indeed, Confucians do believe that people have a say about how well an officeholder does his or her job, and he or she can be replaced with a non-officeholder if the latter can do a better job. If people do not have some understanding of the office and its responsibilities, and if the replacement is not allowed to consider and discuss the policies of this office, how could people make sound evaluations and how could the replacement be trusted with the business of this office? Clearly, there is still tension between the two requirements for non-officeholders by the Confucian, and the Confucian endorsement of freedom of speech is rather limited. In contrast to a liberal's endorsement, which may take the right to free speech as sacred, thus defending any speech even if it is in conflict with the political concern, the Confucian endorsement has good governance as the ultimate constraint on free speech. If we accept the idea that we do not believe that free speech is divinely ordained,[25] and we should take good governance, or, more generally, the well-being of the people into account, we can see that Confucians do have good reasons to curb unlimited use of freedom of speech, and we had better address their concerns.

In sum, first, we can render rights compatible with Confucianism by allowing rights to be read differently. Second, the Confucian understanding of some rights is perhaps even "thinner" than the thin understanding many scholars would like Confucians to hold on to. However, we can argue that the further retreat from an already weakened version of human rights required by the Confucian may have some merits.

Although the Confucian restrictions on rights can be greater in some cases than some mainstream understandings would allow, early Confucians can also acknowledge some so-called positive rights, such as the right of the people to have enough resources, food, and means of livelihood (subsistence); the right of the people to obtain an education regardless of economic status; the right

24. There are numerous places in the *Republic* where the issue of justice is discussed. See, for example, 369e–70c and 432b–34d.

25. Indeed, "natural rights" sounds appealing. But what is "natural" and what does Nature actually give us? In a liberal democracy, the answers are inevitably different. As a result, there are no natural rights for everyone but only natural rights asserted by different groups. These natural rights in reality may be nothing but man-made rights, and often drive people to impose "nature" (their nature) on others.

of the people to be cared for when they are sick or elderly (though in Confucianism this is a duty of both the family and the state); and so on. Indeed, as I mentioned in chapter 2 (note 2), Samuel Fleischacker argues that the idea of satisfying everyone's basic needs was only introduced to the West in the eighteenth century (2004, 2 and 53–79), whereas it was introduced by Confucians much earlier (Perry 2008, 39). Moreover, for early Confucians, these "rights," or duties to satisfy people's basic needs, are part of the highest good the government should pursue, rather than a derivative from the highest good, like the right to free speech. These rights are thus ranked highest in the lexical order of rights or duties, and are "basic rights," as Henry Shue would call them (1980). As I mentioned in chapter 3, Rawls acknowledges that he agrees with Hegel, Marx, and even some socialists that liberties without basic needs met would end up being purely formal and not real liberties (1996, lviii; 1999a, 49–50). Therefore, Confucian rights theorists may have good reasons to consider these rights basic rights and put them at the very top of the lexical order of rights.

An Example: Confucian Animal Rights

Now that we've explored general strategies of how to render Confucianism compatible with rights, I will illustrate these strategies by showing how the Confucian can accommodate animal rights, and I will answer more challenges to these strategies. I choose to discuss animal rights for two reasons. First, the compatibility between Confucianism and animal rights is rarely discussed in the literature. Second, and more importantly, it seems to be quite difficult for the Confucian, who takes human affairs as their central concern, to have a positive account of animal rights. Given the "fragmented" and case-by-case nature of the Confucian endorsement of rights, if I can show that the Confucian can have such an account, the claim that the Confucian can accommodate most other rights that are commonly recognized will become very promising. After discussing the issue of animal rights, I will show how the Confucian treatments of this issue can be applied to the issue of the right not to be tortured.

As was mentioned earlier, a simple fact is that early Confucians didn't talk about rights, let alone animal rights. But from the strategies discussed at the beginning of this chapter, we can see that in spite of the above fact, we can still argue that Confucians can endorse animal rights, if we can show that Confucians can endorse something, such as the humane treatment of animals, that could be used as a basis to construct an account of how to treat animals that bears resemblance to, and is practically indistinguishable from, what animal rights would dictate in many scenarios. From the discussion of the Confucian conception of expanding care, we can already see that this care can and should be expanded to animals, and it can be used as the basis for a Confucian account of treating animals humanely, and thus a support of "animal rights." We will see that this account is still different from how many Western animal rights thinkers endorse animal rights, but I will show that the former may have some merits in these regards.

Confucius's and Mencius's Ideas of the Care for Animals

With the task so defined, let us look into Confucius's and Mencius's ideas of how we should treat animals. Unfortunately, from certain passages in the *Analects*, it seems that Confucius has little regard for the well-being of animals. It is clear that, according to the *Analects*, Confucius was not a vegetarian (see, e.g., 7.7, 7.14, and 10.9). Moreover, it is recorded that when a stable burned down, Confucius asked if any human being was hurt, but he did not ask about the horses (10.17). Of course, Confucius was not actively involved in the death of the horses in this case. But in another passage, when a disciple of Confucius, Zi Gong (子贡), wanted to do away with the sacrificing of a lamb at a certain ceremony, Confucius said to him, "you love the lamb, but I love the rituals [*li* (礼)]" (3.17). In this case, Confucius actively defended the killing of animals, not out of material needs but out of ritual needs.

A closer reading of these passages, however, reveals some subtlety of Confucius's attitude toward animals. According to the commentaries on the passage 10.17 (S. Cheng 1990, 712–15), a different (and perhaps highly problematic) way to read 10.17 is that Confucius asked about human beings first and horses later. Moreover, even in the common reading of this passage that is offered in the previous paragraph, we should understand that the emphasis is that human life is more important than the life of a horse that serves as a symbol of property. Similarly, what passage 3.17 emphasizes is also that the ritual propriety that is crucial to the moral education of human beings is more important than the life of an animal and the value of the animal as a property (ibid., 195–96).

But the above interpretation only shows that Confucius was not as bad toward animals as he appeared to be in the aforementioned passages. It doesn't show that Confucius had any care for animals. Only at one place in the *Analects* can we find a sign of Confucius's care for animals.[26] In 7.27, it is said that when fishing, Confucius "used a fishing line but not a big rope [to which a number of fishing lines are attached]," and when hunting, he "did not shoot at the roosting birds." From here we can see that although he acknowledged the

26. I wish to thank Li Chenyang (李晨阳) for pointing this out to me.

human need to catch or hunt animals, he was against wasteful killing, and killing that we find objectionable because of our compassion. If we look into texts other than the *Analects*, we can see that, though poor, Confucius tried to save the used curtains and covers of his carriage, and instructed a pupil of his to bury his horse and dog properly after they died by covering their corpses with these used things (S. Wang 1990, chap. 43, 121; and the *Tan Gong Xia* [檀弓下] chapter of *The Classic of Rites* or *Li Ji* [礼记]).[27] Although he didn't offer explanations, it is clear that he did it out of his care and compassion for animals, especially those close to him.

Nonetheless, it should be acknowledged that there is no elaborate account of Confucius's attitude toward animals in the *Analects* and other classical texts. In the *Mencius*, however, there is a more elaborate account of why animals should be treated humanely from a Confucian point of view. In the *Mencius* 1A7, King Xuan of Qi saw that an ox would be killed for some ceremonial ritual, and said to the person who led the ox, "Spare it. I cannot bear to see it shrinking with fear, like an innocent man going to the place of execution." He also thought that abandoning the ceremony was out of the question, and ordered the sacrifice of a lamb instead. Lambs were cheaper than oxen, which is why they were not considered as great a sacrifice as oxen (Jiao 1986, 48–50). The king was thus suspected by the people of begrudging the expense, though he vehemently denied this suspicion. However, Mencius explained why the people had this suspicion:

> You must not be surprised that the people thought you miserly. You used a small animal in place of a big one. How were they to know? If you were pained by the animal going innocently to its death, what was there to choose between an ox and a lamb?

After the king denied one more time that he was motivated by monetary concerns, Mencius offered an explanation of the motive behind the king's action:

> This is the humane way. You saw the ox but not the lamb. The attitude of a jun zi toward animals is this: once having seen them alive, he cannot bear to see them die, and once having heard their cry, he cannot bear to eat their flesh. That is why the jun zi keeps his distance from the slaughterhouse and the kitchen.

The last line of this quote is from the Confucian classic *Li Ji* (vol. 6, chap. 13), a book about the proper conduct of gentlemen, and what Mencius did here was to offer a (Confucian) philosophical explanation of this noble code of

---

27. I thank P. J. Ivanhoe for pointing out the relevance of these passages.

conduct. In 1A7, before the story about the king, Mencius argued that one can become a great king through practicing virtues. In particular, "he who becomes a king by protecting the people cannot be stopped." But the king didn't know if he could protect the people, which led Mencius to tell the story about how the king couldn't bear to see the death of an ox. In other words, for Mencius, the compassion that the king showed to the ox was a sign that he possessed (the seeds of) virtue, and these seeds made it possible for him to protect the people and to become a great king.

A Human-Centric Account of "Animal Rights"

Therefore, the moral of this passage resonates with the Confucian concept of compassion that has been discussed in the previous chapters, and our care for animals is a result of the expansion of the universal sentiment of compassion. On the issue of treating animals humanely and its implication for animal rights, a few distinctive features of Mencius's understanding of animal rights, and of rights in general, may be implied and constructed from this section of the *Mencius*. The key is that 1A7 is not so much about the rights of animals as about the moral obligations, responsibilities, and duties of human beings. But from the discussion in the previous section, we can see that we can replace the rights talk with the duties talk. That is, the Confucian account of "animal rights" is really an account of human and humane obligations to animals.

The move of focus from animals to humans has its merits. The Confucian justification of "animal rights" is based on human sentiments and not on animals' innate qualities and rights. In contrast, the discussion of the innate qualities of animals is, in the debates over animal rights, a focal point for some Western animal rights defenders and their dissenters. The traditional justification of the preferential treatment of human beings that is based on innate qualities is that human beings are superior in this regard. However, this superiority has been challenged by many thinkers, and this challenge is precisely the basis for some scholars to challenge the preferential treatment of human beings and to defend animal rights. For example, toward the end of part 5 in the *Discourse on Method*, René Descartes argued that two distinctive features of human beings are language and reason.[28] But Jeremy Bentham questioned whether human beings are really distinctive in these two features, and further implied that these two features are not even relevant to the question of whether we should treat animals humanely. He stated, "the question is not, Can they reason? nor, Can they talk? but, Can they suffer?" (1948, 311). Peter Singer, an important figure in the contemporary animal rights debate,

28. For an English translation, see Descartes (1998, 31–33).

develops Bentham's attack more fully (see, e.g., 1986). For example, he shows that at least some human beings, such as the mentally challenged, do not fare better than pigs with respect to these allegedly distinctive human features, and he argues for giving consideration to all sentient beings. But to prove that certain creatures are sentient or can suffer pain is a difficult matter, and the discussion based on innate qualities is a slippery slope. For example, if part of the reason that pigs should be spared is that they are as intelligent as mentally challenged human beings, then what about mentally challenged pigs? Can we breed pigs that don't feel pain and slaughter them instead? Another possible line of defense of animal rights is that we should follow what is natural, but animals kill each other in nature, and what is distinctively human is that thanks to our natural qualities, we can slaughter other animals more effectively. That is, what is natural is rather murky and does not offer a clear defense of animal rights.

The Confucian justification, in contrast, can show a way out of dangerous waters. For the Confucian, human beings should be compassionate about animals, not because animals can reason or converse, or because they can suffer, or because they treat each other nicely, but rather because we human beings perceive their suffering, the kind of suffering that reminds us of the suffering of our own kind, and, as human beings, we "cannot bear" to see them suffer, as in the idea of "the heart that cannot bear" in the *Mencius* 2A6. Of course, if it is proven that an ox does suffer when being killed, the Confucian will claim it as a concern for human beings. But the Confucian would claim that we are justified in our concern with merely the appearance of suffering. This means that even if during the killing or some other kinds of torture, an ox or a robot that is made to look like a human does not really feel any pain but makes expressions of pain—such as "shrinking with fear"—that appear to be similar to human expressions of pain, we human beings still should, prima facie, try to stop the killing or torture or, at least, should not be undisturbed by such scenes. This may sound like an overinterpretation, but a statement by Confucius that is mentioned in the *Mencius* corroborates my reading: "Confucius said, 'The inventor of burial figures in human form deserves not to have any progeny,' "[29] and the reason, according to Mencius, was that these figures were used due to their resemblance to human beings (1A4). That is, although they were just man-made figures, we buried them with the deceased because we

29. As I argued in chapter 5, family is a Confucian way toward transcendence, and thus "to have no progeny" is perhaps one of the worst curses a Confucian, and thanks to the Confucian influence, a Chinese person could give to others. It is the Confucian equivalent to the Christianity-based curse "Go to hell!"

imagined them to be real human beings and thus ignored their suffering of being buried "alive" in a virtual manner.

The shift of focus to human compassion also means that the Confucian care for animals is subjected to a human-centric hierarchy, a Confucian lexical order. As we saw in chapter 5, even if we achieve the stage of all-embracing care, this care is hierarchical, which is beautifully illustrated by a long passage from a later Confucian thinker, Wang Yangming (quoted in chap. 5 under "The Hierarchy of Universal Care"). The general idea is that although the Confucian exemplary people should treat people as kin and things as friends, many human needs, both physical and spiritual, should override the well-being of animals. They never encourage people to become vegetarians, let alone vegans. They do not even wish to give up ritual ceremonies that involve the sacrifice of animals.

From the Confucian lexical order, we can also argue that the animals that are closer to our daily life, such as our pets, or animals that look more like us (kitties that remind us of human babies) should be given a preferential treatment over animals that are more removed from our daily life or look less like us. This position was clearly seen in the aforementioned account of Confucius's attitude toward his own dog and horse. A statement that is intended to show the hypocrisy or inconsistency of human actions toward animals is that if cockroaches looked like humans, we wouldn't wish to kill them. But based on the Confucian lexical order, there is nothing wrong with this hypothetical reaction by human beings.

Of course, if one aspires to become a Confucian exemplary person, he or she should try to expand the care to those further and further away from his or her familiar circles. For example, although he praised the king for having the seed of compassion in 1A7, Mencius didn't mean to ask the king to stop his care at the objects in front of him. Rather, an ideal Confucian ruler is someone who is able to have a sense of care for his or her people, most of whom he or she would never meet in real life. In this regard, a Confucian can agree with the criticism of utilitarian thinkers such as Singer, that it is wrong to ignore the suffering of those far away from our daily life (in this day and age, it means those who don't show up on our TV or the Internet). Nonetheless, the care, though inclusive, needs to be hierarchical.

One may question the validity of the Confucian lexical order, and to this challenge, my answer is that *any* moral theory of rights has to give some lexical order of rights (which rights are the most important, the second-most important, etc.), and this order has to be defended in this theory. As I have argued in chapters 5 and 6 of this book, the beauty of the Confucian lexical order is that it starts with something very natural to us and uses it to push for a more compassionate, inclusive, and even universal care for everything in the world. It is true that in the Confucian model, the picture is rarely black-and-white, and there is often tension between different needs and duties. But the reality of human life is rarely black-and-white, and instead of finding a simple way out by appealing to some universal principles, to struggle through this tension and to learn to manage the nonintrinsic lexical order in different contexts is necessary for the moral life of human beings. In short, Confucians may defend their position by claiming that it is more realistic than the "rights fundamentalists."

Limited as the Confucian version of animal rights appears to be, in practice it can endorse many actions promoted by animal rights advocates, and even actions ignored by the latter. For example, a Confucian would support the animal rights activists in their attempt to improve the conditions in which animals are raised and slaughtered. In the Chinese context, the Confucian would object to some practices in Chinese cuisines and restaurants, in which not only is there no attempt to reduce or hide the suffering of animals eaten, but there is an attempt to show it to the eaters (in order to prove that the meat is fresh, something Chinese eaters take seriously). If the animals are not treated humanely (in terms of how they are raised, slaughtered, and served), Confucians may refuse to consume meat. Even if they were treated humanely, Confucians may still advocate the practice that we take meats as rare delicacies, as we did before the modern age of mass-manufactured meats, because the slaughtering of animals reminds us of the killing of innocent people, and it should be done only when it is really necessary, and, in the infrequent consumption of meats, we should eat them with ritual propriety, for example, by expressing our gratitude to animals sacrificed.[30] The fact that the production of meat puts more burden on the environment—which is the basis of a decent

30. For example, interpreting Mencius's claim that "[we should] eat things according to the season, and consume things according to ritual propriety" (7A23), the Song Neo-Confucian Zhu Xi (朱熹) offered reasons why we should eat meat with a sense of compassion and respect, and avoid unnecessary waste (Zhu 2001, 420). Actually, Mencius's original claim was focused on rulers not exploiting people for satisfying their own desires, and Zhu Xi shifted the focus to the humane treatment of animals, which might be a response to the Buddhist challenge concerning the consumption of meat. Indeed, it may have been the Song-Ming Neo-Confucians who should be given the credit for developing a fuller account of the expansion of care to animals and even all things in the world, although it is implicit and even implied by Mencius's idea of compassion. For a more detailed account, see Fang (2011). For an even more comprehensive and subtle account of Song-Ming Neo-Confucians' discussions, especially Wang Yangming's, on the issue of the humane treatment of animals than Fang (2011), see Lisheng Chen (2008), especially chapters 1 and 2.

and flourishing human life—offers one more reason for Confucians' demand of the reduction of meat consumption.[31]

Moreover, the Confucian account of animal rights can be applied to what is beyond the animal realm. That is, Confucians would also object to purely taking pleasure in the "virtual" suffering of human look-alikes, such as the aforementioned burial practices, or violent electronic games and movies. Of course, it is a different story if a violent movie is watched with a feeling of compassion for the weak, or, in the case of punishing the evil, with a feeling of justice. Trickier is the possibility that people may play violent video games or watch "kinky" pornography to "let off steam," which may prevent them from doing these things in real life. A Confucian, especially one who follows the more moralistic Mencius, would say that, ideally, we should overcome this animalistic impulse through our moral cultivation. If we claim to play or watch violent or perverted games and movies to let off steam, the worry is that they will strengthen our impulse instead, in addition to being a sign of the lack of moral uprightness. Issues such as whether playing violent video games in-creases the likelihood for the players to do really bad things in real life are open to empirical studies, and I personally think that to put such a high moral de-mand on people, even morally superior people, is to ask too much. But to have such a demand seems to be coherent with Mencius's understanding. Out of our own common sense, we can argue that we shouldn't be so moralistic. But we should be clear, when we do this, that this would be a revision of Mencius's understanding.

Why Slaughter? Who Slaughters?

Naturally, there are other problems with the Confucian treatment of tension and lexical order, and I will discuss only two of them. First, a hidden assump-tion in the Confucian account is that the consumption of meat is inevitable. For Confucians, the concern is not only mere survival but also the conditions for us to live a flourishing and decent life as human beings. But if these human needs in a broad sense can be satisfied otherwise, the implication to Confu-cians seems to be that we should abandon the consumption of meat com-pletely. In fact, when Buddhism became popular in China, and Buddhist monks showed the possibility of living a good (?) life without consuming meat, Confucians had a hard time defending the habit of eating meat (Fang 2011). Today, with so many vegetarians and even vegans apparently doing fine, the challenge to a Confucian defense of the consumption of meat remains

31. For a Confucian "environmentalist" account, see the first part of the postscript.

extremely serious, maybe even more so than the time when Buddhism became popular in China.[32]

Second, even if animals needed to be slaughtered for the physical and spiritual needs of human beings, who should do the slaughtering? According to
Mencius, viewing the slaughtering of animals is disturbing, and Confucian
gentlemen should keep themselves away from it. But what about the butcher's
moral well-being? For he or she has to get used to the slaughtering scenes and
might thus lose compassion, which, according to the Confucian, is crucial to
his or her moral cultivation.[33] One solution is that the butchers are those who
fail to develop their moral potential. This solution is similar to Aristotle's argument in *The Politics*, that if slaves are those who are defective in soul by nature,
then slavery is justified (1254b15–55a3).[34] In traditional Japanese society,
butchers were considered morally inferior and belonged to the outcast Burakumin class (De Vos, 1971). However, Confucians such as Mencius recognize
the moral potential of each and every human being, and encourage upward
mobility, which helps to balance the Confucian insistence on hierarchy. That
is, Confucians cannot accept the idea that some people are doomed to be
butchers. Moreover, if some butchers develop themselves and find slaughtering morally unbearable, they should leave their trade. The society and the government also have a responsibility to help them. In contrast, exposing them
to slaughtering seems to be very bad for the development of their moral potential, de facto locking them into "(un)natural butchery."

Another, perhaps more promising, solution is to take the job of slaughtering as something comparable to the job of soldiering. Difficult as it sounds, a
Confucian soldier still needs to kill and to be good at killing, although he or
she is and should be pained by the killing. Similarly, a Confucian butcher has
to slaughter, although he or she is and should be pained by the slaughtering.
The slaughtered animals are perhaps more innocent than enemy soldiers, although killing a human being is more serious than killing an animal. In this
scenario, butchery becomes almost a quasi-religious activity itself, similar to
butchery in the Jewish tradition. After all, it is the jun zi who was supposed to

32. Perhaps this is only a serious challenge to someone who is persuaded by the Confucian
argument for the humane treatment of animals and is an incurable lover of meat, such as the
author of this book.

33. It is an interesting empirical question to investigate whether butchers do have a lower
sense of compassion as a result of their job. Clearly, Mencius assumed that this is the case, and
it seems to make sense. But reality doesn't always "make sense." To be clear, what I am question-
ing here is whether a basic premise of Mencius's theory is violated by experience or not, and
not the consistency of Mencius's own account.

34. For Aristotle's treatment of the problem of slavery, see book 1, chapters 4–7, 1253b23–
55b40 of *The Politics*. For an English translation, see Lord (1984, 39–44).

be in charge of ritualistic activities, including sacrifices. Nevertheless, this solution still looks rather artificial. Moreover, the suggestion that it has to be the
Confucian gentlemen or superior people who slaughter is in conflict with
Mencius's advice (and the *Li Ji*'s) that Confucian gentlemen should stay away
from slaughterhouses. Of course, we can argue that given the fact that the *Li
Ji* is a book on noblemen's ("gentlemen" in the original sense of the term)
conduct, that advice is outdated in a postfeudal society. Although he quoted
it, Mencius didn't have to take it literally. Nonetheless, it seems that we have
to pay a price for making Mencius's theory coherent, and for remaining Confucian meat-eaters.

On Other Rights

Now that I've discussed the Confucian view of animal rights, let me briefly
comment on the Confucian views of one particular human right that is somewhat related to Confucian views on animal rights. That is, if some morally bad
people have committed heinous crimes, should they be treated humanely?
Following our general strategies, we should see that both Confucius and Mencius may phrase this right as the obligation of the superior to the inferior (i.e.,
morally good people's obligation to be compassionate toward the morally bad
people), rather than the right of the latter. If we follow Confucius's idea that
human beings are fallible, which will be discussed in the next section, a Confucian may well support some protection of the accused and the convicted. The
protection is not interpreted as a right of the convicted but as a cautious means
to safeguard against false judgments about these people. Moreover, especially
for Mencius, even the worst criminals can change, and proper humane treatment may help. Therefore, both Confucius and Mencius would support some
just but humane treatment of criminals.[35] Thus, unlike the Confucian reasoning over animal rights, the right of the bad has something to do with the potentiality of the bad. But one idea that distinguishes Mencius from Confucius
is that for Mencius, the bad who have lost their good hearts are nothing but
beasts that happen to look human (3B9 and 4B19, among many other passages). This does not mean that we should thus treat them inhumanely, because, as is argued in this section, a humane person should show some compassion even to the beasts. So for Mencius, the right of the truly bad not to be
tortured is really an "animal" or "beast" right, or, more precisely, an obligation
of human beings to animals and even beasts (i.e., those human look-alikes who

---

35. The restrictive words "proper" and "just" are important, for Confucius never supported
repaying bad deeds with good deeds ("turn the other cheek") but emphasized repaying bad
deeds with uprightness (*Analects* 14.34).

behave like beasts). Again, due to the unique changeability of even the bad into real human beings, according to Mencius, the reason to treat a morally depraved criminal humanely is based upon both the obligation of the superior and the potential of the inferior, whereas the humane treatment of animals is based upon obligation and our perception of the suffering of animals.

Through the discussion of the general strategies, and the particular and apparently difficult example of the Confucian endorsement of animal rights, I hope to show that Confucians are able to accommodate rights in a Rawlsian pluralistic framework. The detailed discussions in this section are meant to be a paradigm for demonstrating how Confucians can endorse other rights. As was pointed out in the previous section, the ways in which Confucians endorse rights can be fragmented. But there are a few common strategies for the Confucian endorsement: to endorse rights by interpreting them as (legally and morally) enforceable and demandable obligations, as a fallback mechanism, or by subjecting them to some higher good in Confucianism. Clearly, there are differences between how rights are endorsed and interpreted by the Confucian and how they are interpreted in the mainstream (Western?) rights regimes, but it is precisely these differences that may enrich our understanding and practice of rights. Therefore, to understand Confucian rights is not only important to the practical problem of helping societies under the Confucian cultural influence to accept rights, but it is also important to the theoretical problem of understanding rights and spreading rights regimes.

Compatibility between a State's Promotion of Virtue and Liberalism

Much of the work in this chapter has been intended to show that some of the Confucian ideas, though apparently in conflict with some of the "democratic ideas" or ideas considered essential to rights, can be made compatible with rights. But clearly, Confucians have a more ambitious agenda. As we saw in chapter 6, they wish to promote the public interest over private interest, although the path to it is not to suppress the private but to cultivate the constructive part of the private and use it to overcome the destructive part ("constructive" and "destructive" with regard to public interest). Given the Confucian continuum and harmony model (introduced in chapter 6) between the private and the public, they also reject the mainstream liberal idea that the state should remain value-neutral, and stay out of the realm of the private. Instead, the state has a duty to promote virtues, including some of those that are considered to be in the realm of the private. As I mentioned in chapter 6, according to Joseph Chan, for a liberal democracy to function well, the promotion of some virtues is necessary. That is, the virtues a liberal state needs to and should promote have to be "thicker" than what the liberal value neutrality or even a later Rawlsian would endorse (reasonableness, reciprocity, etc.). The question then is: Can this thickened morality be thin enough to be compatible with liberalism? This is what I will try to address in the last section of this chapter. Although the main focus is on Confucianism, the following discussion may also be useful for other schools that share a similar view of the significance of promoting virtues and the public interests, such as some moral conservatives and even leftists.

One concern with the state's promotion of virtues from a liberal perspective is that it will become oppressive and intolerant. For example, Thomas Metzger labels an alleged Confucian belief in the possibility of an infallible elite ruling class and the practicality of a utopian state run by this class as "epistemological optimism," and contrasts it to the Western belief in the epistemological (and political) fallibility of human beings (2005).[36] The implication is that an infallible elite ruling class could then impose their moral understanding on the masses, inevitably making the regime oppressive and nonliberal.

The above understanding is widespread but deeply problematic. I suspect that it is a result of reading twentieth-century Chinese thinkers' and politicians' ideas and practices, such as Kang Youwei's (康有为) and Mao Zedong's writings, into traditional Chinese history of thought. If we put this general observation aside, we can see that Confucius had a clear sense of the fallibility of human beings. In the *Analects*, not only was he suspicious of the perfectibility of ordinary people, but he even claimed that he had never met anyone who was drawn to humaneness (*ren*) (4.6) or anyone who was drawn to humaneness as much as being drawn to the beauty of women (9.18 and 15.13). Indeed, he claims that even Yao and Shun, the ideal Confucian sage rulers, fell short in assisting the people to have a good life, apparently a basic requirement of any good ruler (6.30). It is true that the Confucian exemplary people are better than the common people, but the former are not perfect or all-knowing but are fallible.

The case for Mencius is a little different.[37] While it is true that Mencius seemed to believe in the perfectibility of every human being (6B2), it could be interpreted that he just meant to be encouraging. But even if we took Mencius's claim at face value, he also stated that sage rulers only emerged every five hundred years, and then complained that it had been seven hundred years

36. I thank Daniel Bell for pointing out to me the relevance of Metzger's work.

37. I came to see the distinctions between Confucius and Mencius on this issue in a spirited yet friendly debate with Stephen Angle, and I wish to thank him for pushing me to clarify my own thought.

without a true king since the dawn of the Zhou dynasty till the time of Mencius (2B13). So when sage rulers are not around, safeguarding mechanisms can be introduced against the imperfect rulers in the real world. Even in the rare occurrence when sage rulers do come into being, for Mencius, it doesn't mean that they should simply force people to follow them. The reason, paradoxically, lies in the very belief that every human being is perfectible. Thus, sage rulers should only facilitate the common people to actualize the latter's potential for becoming perfect, leaving some room for free choice (and liberties), rather than making the common people blindly follow (Confucian) moral codes. In a famous allegory about personal cultivation of morality, which has been mentioned a few times in this book, for example, Mencius pointed out that the people who try to help seedlings grow by pulling at them not only "fail to help them but they do the seedlings positive harm" (2A2). From this allegory it is natural to infer that Mencius would argue that the moral role of government should be realized through education, and it would be counterproductive if this moral development was forced. Such an interpretation of Mencius—emphasizing moral persuasion, not force—is also consistent with his idea of winning people over by winning their hearts and minds (4A4 and 4A9).

The intellectual historian Zhang Hao (also spelled as Chang Hao [张灏]) has published a very influential article in which he argues that in spite of some Confucians' apparently optimistic claims (such as those of Mencius), the appreciation of the "darkness" of human nature, the precariousness of moral cultivation, and the difficulty of harsh reality was widespread among traditional Confucian thinkers, including even Mencius (2010, 22–42).[38] Theoretically, we can easily develop a Confucian theory that preserves many key Confucian ideas that have been used in this book while simultaneously insisting on the fallibility of human beings.

One may argue that my reading of Confucianism is too thin, and such a thin version of Confucianism is not really different from moral relativism. It is true that a Confucianism that doesn't take the pursuit of virtue as essential may be too thin. But the Confucianism that acknowledges the fallibility of human beings is one that rejects the dogmatic pursuit of virtue, but not the

38. The irony is that many Chinese use certain terms from Zhang's paper but completely miss his point. They think that Zhang argues for a thesis similar to that of the aforementioned Metzger. To be clear, although Zhang rejects the epistemological optimism thesis, he does argue that the Confucian appreciation of the darkness of human nature and reality is not as adequate as the case in the West, which is a crucial reason that democracy was first developed in the West and not in China. For a rebuttal of this claim, see Bai (2016).

dogged pursuit of it. The difference between a Confucian with a cautious and even skeptical attitude, as I propose here, and a moral relativist is that the skeptical attitude of the former is toward what any real human being has achieved in the pursuit of virtue, but not toward the existence of virtue itself, the existence of right and wrong, or good and bad, while the latter is skeptical of both. The appreciation of the limit of human capabilities is a Confucian reason to embrace free speech, which is a necessary condition for imperfect human beings to perfect themselves and their policies. The acknowledgment of our imperfection means that we don't have a God's-eye view of the Good, but it doesn't mean giving up using our imperfect reason. Using a metaphor of Quine's (and Otto Neurath's), "we can rebuild (the same boat we stay in) only at sea while staying afloat in it" (1969, 127). That is, this version of Confucianism, in the pursuit of virtues, takes a naturalistic attitude. Human beings make mistakes, and this means that we should be careful, but not that we should stop judging. Human beings have to use the defective reason in the pursuit of the Good that is essentially beyond human reason and to judge whether the judgment based on the defective reason is defective, for we have no better tools than this, and we have to make judgments in life.

With this understanding of fallibility, we can see one more reason for Confucians to embrace competitive elections. Confucians want the virtuous and wise to rule, but the problem is how one can know for certain who the most competent and most virtuous people are. If one likes to gamble and wants to take the risk that there might be a thousand years of chaos before and after a sage king,[39] one might as well let a small group of presumably virtuous people or one person make all the important political decisions. In doing so, one has to ignore the question of how and by whom this group of people is selected. If there is a chain of selection going back generations, one has to reject the possibility that in each selection, the selecting group didn't have a God's-eye view and thus could make mistakes or make their selection out of their self-interests. A moderate Confucian, then, can take competitive elections as a more sustainable process of selecting rulers, a balance between choosing the best and avoiding the worst, that is, interpreting this process as a reasonably cautious process of selecting and checking the meritocrats while safeguarding against the bad results of wrong selections, rather than reading this process as

---

39. Han Fei Zi the Legalist made this criticism (chap. 40 of the *Han Fei Zi*), and argued for an institutional and verifiable procedure for selecting members of the ruling class. As I mentioned in chapter 1, the kind of Confucianism I am using is an updated version that can handle Han Fei Zi's incisive critique.

a means to punish the bad politicians, a common reading in contemporary liberal democracies.[40]

It should be clear by now that in spite of the pursuit of virtue, the idea of the rule of the virtuous, and the proposal that the state should promote virtues, Confucianism doesn't necessarily lead to oppression because of the appreciation of the imperfection of human beings, the need of a safeguarding mechanism, and the belief in assisting people's moral cultivation rather than imposing virtues on them. But what about those who, although given the best possible education, still fail to or refuse to perform the virtuous deeds expected from a citizen? A Confucian's answer is that on the basis of the seriousness of the offense, the people who *truly* fail to share their part of moral duties should be punished with a state-sanctioned oppressive political force, such as imprisonment, being condemned by public opinion, or being left alone, if the matter in question is of no or little public interest. Imprisonment and public condemnation may sound harsh to some, but even in a liberal democracy, these methods are justified on certain occasions. For example, it is justified to put someone who commits treason in prison or to condemn, in public opinion, a corporate executive who takes advantage of the public through legal loopholes. What makes these oppressive means sound problematic or even horrific is the following concern. Matters like virtues and public interest are often highly complicated, and thus people often make wrong judgments or are simply deceived by demagogues who manipulate the public in order to achieve their own ignoble or crazy goals. As a result, oftentimes, the wrong people are prosecuting others, and people are wrongfully prosecuted. But this only means that when they have to make a judgment, people should be very responsible and careful not to be deceived by themselves or demagogues, and they should give their own judgments a reasonable doubt. Moreover, the people who are judged should be given the benefit of doubt as well. If we are not confident in people's own conscience and intelligence, we have to accept that to rely on people's own conscience and intelligence is not enough for them to behave responsibly, carefully, and humbly when they pass judgments on others. So proper education and institutions are needed. For example, people should be taught to be thoughtful, humble, and tolerant; open discussion should always be possible; and the best possible procedure that can effectively correct mistakes and compensate those who are misjudged should be established. These considerations, as I already argued in the previous two sections, can be a basis for a Confucian to endorse the rule of law and "human rights."

---

40. Joseph Chan discusses in detail the merits of the Confucian reading of popular elections in comparison with the common democratic reading (2013a).

So far in this section, I have only argued that the Confucian idea of promoting virtues, especially through the state, doesn't have to be oppressive. But how can the promotion of some of the "private" virtues—rather than "public" virtues such as autonomy, equality, and justice, which even those who believe in virtue neutrality would endorse and promote—deal with the fact of pluralism, an essential feature of a liberal society? That is, which "private" virtues can be promoted by the state and which can be recognized as virtues by people with different comprehensive doctrines? In this section and in chapter 6 (under "Challenges to Liberal Value Neutrality"), I have made the claim that "public" virtues that are endorsed by liberal value neutrality, or even a thicker Rawlsian account of public virtues, are too thin for a liberal democracy to function well. But the challenge to the Confucian stance is whether the virtues Confucians want are too thick for the state to promote. To answer this question, we will have to look at these virtues individually. As an example, then, let me look into a virtue that has been mentioned in the previous chapters, the virtue regarding the family.

In the past, some traditional Confucians did offer a more metaphysics-like account of the significance of family and family virtues, and many of the overseas New Confucians explicitly offer a Confucian moral metaphysics. If family virtues are built on this kind of metaphysics, they will surely be too thick to accommodate the fact of pluralism, as is the case for any metaphysical doctrine. But throughout this book, the account I have offered is intentionally ametaphysical, which, as I argued in chapter 1, is one possible way of understanding Confucius and (to a lesser extent) Mencius. In the case of family, I have argued in chapter 5 that family is important because it is a crucial institution in which to cultivate a person's care for others, and it helps a person have a vision that is beyond his or her mere short-term material interests. If these are reasons for promoting family virtues, reasonable people of different comprehensive doctrines may endorse these virtues. These people would only need to endorse the idea that care among strangers and long-term and nonmaterial considerations are important for maintaining a flourishing liberal society, and to recognize that certain family relations are good for helping people develop the aforementioned care and considerations. As I suggested in chapters 5 and 6, the state can promote family values by, for example, giving people paid leave when their parents have passed away, establishing an office that takes records of top politicians' words and deeds and gives an official one-word summary of their performance, and so on. The state can also encourage people to have a family book that keeps records of the life of everyone in the family, which will then be carried on by their children. There can also be taxes and other policies that encourage adult children to live close to their parents, and to encourage couples to stay together, especially when they have children.

These institutions and policies don't seem to be in conflict with pluralism in a liberal society, and may contribute to its well-being. In short, we may discover virtues that are thin enough for a liberal people to endorse and for a liberal state to promote, but are thicker than the ones that are usually promoted in a liberal society. For this to happen, we need to give up the taboo that a liberal state cannot promote any virtues other than thin ones such as equality and autonomy.

Postscript

Environmental and Technological Challenges: A Synthetic Answer

If we keep expanding Confucian care, it will go beyond even animals, and eventually reach everything in the world. It was recorded that the Song Neo-Confucian Zhou Dunyi (周敦颐) (1017–73) refused to cut the grass in front of his windows, and when asked why he did not do this, he said, "[it is] as if [they] were my own family" (Cheng and Cheng 1992, vol. 3, 54).[1] Another Neo-Confucian, Cheng Yi (程颐) (1033–1107), a private tutor for the emperor, once saw the young emperor playfully break a twig off a weeping willow tree. He scolded the very young emperor by saying, "[the tree] was being reborn and growing in early spring, and [you] shouldn't break [a twig from it] and damage [it] for no reason" (ibid., appendix, 266). From this, we can develop a Confucian ground for care for the environment.[2]

There are three more reasons for a Confucian to advocate environmental protection: first, our need to live a (materially and spiritually) decent life; second, our care for our ancestors (not to lay waste the environment they have left us) and future generations (to leave enough for them); and third, our care for foreigners and their ancestors and descendants. Although the Confucian may not take as radical a position as certain environmentalists who may put

1. Zhou's reply in Chinese, "与自家意思一般," can be interpreted differently, and my translation is merely based on one possible reading of it. Of course, one can suspect that he was merely giving a beautiful excuse for being lazy.

2. The Confucian idea of the unity of Heaven and man is now often used to develop a Confucian environmentalist account. But this can be misleading, for this idea mainly serves political purposes (e.g., to draw political implications from natural phenomena and to use them to criticize the rulers for their ill rule) or ethical purposes (e.g., to use Heaven as the moral ideal for human beings to strive for). See Csikszentmihalyi (manuscript) for a very good review of these different interpretations. In my view, the Confucian idea of expanding care offers a far better ground for a Confucian environmentalist account.

the concern with the environment on a par with, or even higher than, human needs, Confucianism, being anthropocentric, still offers plenty of good reasons for protecting the environment.

As we should know by now, early Confucians didn't think that we could enlighten the masses with these ideas.[3] Institutional solutions need to be offered.[4] In terms of domestic governance, the Confucian hybrid regime may offer a better answer to environmental issues than both the democratic and the authoritarian regimes, for the Confucian regime's meritocratic branch may be better equipped with taking long-term, nonmaterial, future generations', minorities', and foreigners' interests into account than the democratic regime can, while its liberal element and the element of popular participation may be better checks and balances of the power of the ruling elite than what is available in an authoritarian regime.

Another challenge to the environmental issue, as I have argued in chapter 3 (under "Climate Change: A Perfect Storm"), is that those who damage the environment and those who suffer from the damages may live in different states. To solve this problem, international interventions are needed. In the Confucian new tian xia model, certain interventions are justified because the sovereignty of the state is conditioned on its humaneness. To protect the environment for its own people and for foreigners is required by humaneness. So states that perform their environmental duties have the legitimate authority to intervene with the states that fail to do so.

In today's world, there is another set of serious challenges to the life of human beings: technological challenges.[5] The threats from technologies are threefold. First, on a moral level, technological advancements may lead to an

3. Many people in the contemporary world, dissatisfied with what they consider the Western, industrialized, or modern way of life, wish to make a difference by choosing a different way of life, and by changing others' attitudes. Someone with the above elitist attitude would doubt the effectiveness of their approach.

4. The Lao Zi can also be used to develop an environmentalist account. But in my view, for it to be effective, a political solution also needs to be developed. But a solution based on the Lao Zi may be too dystopic. See Bai (2009b) for a detailed discussion.

5. It is sometimes loosely referred to as the challenges from science and technology. But we should distinguish between the two. See Kuhn (1959) for the distinction between modern science or basic science and applied science (including technologies). The challenges really come from technologies, and not from basic science. For example, it is true that without Einstein's equation of $E = MC^2$, and without the development introduced by quantum theorists, we wouldn't be able to make the atomic bomb. But the goal of these scientists is to understand the world. Their achievements, without the pressure of war, or other social and political factors, and without the creativity of engineers and technicians, cannot be turned into nuclear weapons or power plants.

"addiction" to them when addressing issues in human life, and they may lead people to ignore the importance of virtues and the pursuit of a good life worth living. This is an "eternal" issue that existed even before the advent of modern technologies.[6] But such concerns can be rejected as "elitist" and undemocratic, for they imply that certain people's lives are worthless. Second, on an existential level, technological advancements, such as the development of the atomic bomb, new viruses, and artificial intelligence, may threaten the very survival of the human species. This problem existed before modern technologies,[7] but modern technologies have brought the existential threat vividly to the public through the clear and present danger they pose. Third, on a political level, the development of modern technologies makes it likely that inequality will become permanent and ever increasing.

If we don't wish to go down the road of rejecting modern technologies,[8] we need to find a moderate solution. One is to educate the public and encourage public participation in policy making.[9] As I have argued, a Confucian is all for informing the public, but he or she would also doubt how informed the public can be. Again, the Confucian hybrid regime would serve as a model for balancing public participation with meritocratic involvement. For example, in Germany, various expert councils play an important role in the decision-making process regarding the ethics of technologies (G. Wang 2016).

The problem of growing inequality caused or exacerbated by the advancement of technologies and globalization still remains. One might hope that people can be freed from their daily work and be free to do what they please in a constructive manner, thanks to technological developments. But the fact that there is an opioid crisis among unemployed Americans and they don't seem to engage in any family duties, let alone civic duties, doesn't bode well for this expectation (Eberstadt 2017). Indeed, those who use their free time to learn new things and are involved in meaningful projects tend to be those who have intellectual curiosity and political drive, which makes it more likely for them to survive and even excel in the technological age. In contrast, those who surrender to the technological challenges tend to be those who lack such curiosity and drive. If they can't use their free time to think about political issues,

6. See 405a–8c of the *Republic* and 14.43 of the *Analects* for Plato's and Confucius's account of what life is (and is not) worth living.

7. See Diamond (2011, 79–119) for such an example (the irreversible deforestation of Easter Island).

8. The price for achieving this may be too high for us to pay. See, again, Bai (2009b) for how high the price can be.

9. For a radically democratic proposal, see Feyerabend (1993, 2). For a more moderate proposal of public participation, see X. Huang (2016).

the result is that they will, through their votes (if they bother to vote at all), support those who don't necessarily have the right answers to their problems. Therefore, to give more voice to those with the right kind of moral and intellectual capacities becomes even more pressing today than ever before.

But even if the Confucian meritocrats were able to make better decisions, what would they be? They would have to battle with inequality within a state and would also have to develop international regimes to curb the bad effects of globalization. More concrete proposals, I have to confess, are still wanting.

Realizing the Confucian Alternatives?

In spite of the aforementioned inadequacy, I hope I have shown in this book that the updated models that are based on early Confucian ideas may address many political issues better than the mainstream liberal democratic models do. If my arguments stand, the next issue is how they can become reality. The first thing we need to do is to acknowledge that history has not ended with liberal democratic orders, and we need to search for better political models. Political philosophers and theorists can do whatever "conceptual engineering" they like to do, but they can only get more sympathetic ears if there is pressure from the real world. That is, the conceptual engineering of new models can only be taken seriously if present mainstream political models, such as liberal democratic ones, keep getting into trouble.

As I have alluded to throughout the book, these models encounter many problems both theoretically and practically. But in spite of questionable performances, liberal democratic regimes still enjoy what I like to call a "liberal democratic legitimacy premium," which helps them to resist performance-based challenges. One can argue that in the domestic case, this is because although the performances of some liberal democratic governments have been poor for a while, people feel that they can express their dissatisfaction with the governments through democratic procedures. This allows an apparently contradictory phenomenon: the dissatisfaction with the performance of consecutive democratic governments strengthens the sincere support of the democratic regime, because the dissatisfaction can be expressed, and voters feel that they have the power to make a change, even if new government after new government keeps doing poorly.[10] But if expressing their dissatisfaction through voting doesn't improve the performance of the current government,

10. In Min-Hua Huang's and Benjamin Nyblade's contributions to an anthology on legitimacy, they offer this kind of explanation about strong democratic legitimacy in Taiwan and Japan, in spite of their governments' poor performance (Chan, Shin, and Williams 2017, 166–89 and 218–37).

the power that average voters think they have may merely be an illusion. One can't help but wonder how much longer or how many more failures it will take for the democratic legitimacy premium to be squandered? Maybe it is just that we have been habituated with the idea that there is no better alternative. Habits are difficult to shake off, but it can happen. Moreover, as I have argued, on the domestic level, the Confucian hybrid regime allows freedom of expression through voting, and it is built on procedural justice. That is, my proposal tries to preserve what makes a liberal democracy function well while simultaneously trying to correct what is problematic with it. This appears to give us more hope for change.

However, since liberal democratic models have been given an almost sacred status, any perceived challenge to them often results in complete neglect and even hostile reactions. Two kinds of political environments may be more sympathetic to this kind of challenge. First, as just mentioned, it can be an environment in which a liberal democratic order is constantly in crisis. In such an environment, unfortunately, there can be "snake oil" salespeople who promote a wholesale rejection of liberal democracy or use democratic elements to suppress liberal ones (e.g., Hitler and, to a much less extent, contemporary left-wing and right-wing populists such as Hugo Chavez and Donald Trump). Second, in a nonliberal democratic order, such as an authoritarian regime, the challenge to liberal democracy may be welcomed.[11] In both kinds of environments, the critical and constructive proposals offered by a sincere reformer (such as the ones I've offered in this book) may often be distorted to support populist or authoritarian regimes that are even worse than the flawed liberal democratic regime this reformer is trying to improve. The political reformer seems to be caught between a rock and a hard place, either encountering neglect and hostility (when the democratic premium is still strong) or being listened to but misunderstood and misused when the legitimacy of liberal democracy is deeply challenged and even rejected. Indeed, there is a general political issue beneath this dilemma: How can one perform his or her political duty in an unfriendly or challenging environment, and if he or she can, how can one protect his or her integrity and the integrity of his or her political actions?[12]

11. To be clear, I find the term "authoritarian regime" deeply inadequate. Due to the poverty of political terminology, anything critical or different from the present liberal democratic regimes is often labeled "authoritarian," papering over great differences among vastly different political proposals and real-world regimes.

12. As an interesting case, we can compare the apparently contrasting and equally confusing positions of Confucius and Plato. On the surface, in the *Analects* Confucius argued for the centrality of the exemplary person's political duty to his (or her) fellow human beings and to

I don't think that I have an adequate answer to this challenge. I also don't know if my theory will ever become reality, even if I am right about its soundness and the urgency for us to find political alternatives. As a philosopher, what I can do is to offer what I consider the best possible theory. As a Confucian sympathizer, what I can do is to fulfill my duty and then to entrust myself and the human race to a heavenly destiny.

---

the state, while Socrates in various Platonic dialogues sometimes argued that the philosopher (the Platonic exemplary person) should stay away from the state, and from human affairs in general. However, in various places, Confucius suggested that one not enter or stay—let alone save—a troubled state, while Socrates himself stayed in an unjust state, apparently fulfilling his political duty to the state by accepting an unjust verdict. An attempt to explain these apparent contradictions may lead us to deeper reflections on the issue of how to reconcile a superior person's duty to the state with his or her duty to himself/herself with regard to maintaining integrity. See Bai (2010b) for details.

REFERENCES

Ackerman, Bruce, and James Fishkin. (2004). "Righting the Ship of Democracy." *Legal Affairs*, January/February, 34–39.

———. (2005). *Deliberation Day*. New Haven, CT: Yale University Press.

Alford, William P., Kenneth Winston, and William Kirby (eds.). (2011). *Prospects for the Professions in China*. London: Routledge.

Ames, Roger T., and David L. Hall (trans.). (2001). *Focusing the Familiar: A Philosophical Interpretation of the Zhongyong*. Honolulu: University of Hawi'i Press.

——— (trans.). (2003). *Daodejing*. New York: Ballantine Books.

Ames, Roger T., and Henry Rosemont Jr. (1998). *The Analects of Confucius*. New York: Random House.

Angle, Stephen. (2012). *Contemporary Confucian Political Philosophy: Toward Progressive Confucianism*. Cambridge, UK: Polity.

Arrighi, Giovanni. (2007). *Adam Smith in Beijing: Lineages of the Twenty-First Century*. London: Verso.

Bai, Tongdong 白彤东. (2005). "Does Liberal Democracy Need a Metaphysical Foundation?" 自由民主需要一个形而上学的基础吗? *Foreign Philosophy* 外国哲学 18:297–315.

———. (2008a). "A Mencian Version of Limited Democracy." *Res Publica* 14, no. 1 (March): 19–34.

———. (2008b). "Back to Confucius: A Comment on the Debate on the Confucian Idea of Consanguineous Affection." *Dao: A Journal of Comparative Philosophy* 7, no. 1 (March): 27–33.

———. (2009a). "The Price of Serving Meat: On Confucius's and Mencius's Views of Human and Animal Rights." *Asian Philosophy* 19, no. 1 (March): 85–99.

———. (2009b). "How to Rule without Taking Unnatural Actions (无为而治): A Comparative Study of the Political Philosophy of the *Laozi*." *Philosophy East and West* 59, no. 4 (October): 481–502.

———. (2009c). *Tension of Reality: Einstein, Bohr and Pauli in the EPR Debates* 实在的张力: EPR论争中的爱因斯坦, 玻尔与泡利. Beijing: Peking University Press.

———. (2010a). "Confucianism as a Moral Metaphysics or as a Political Philosophy; as an Old Mandate for a New State or as a New Mandate of an Old State?" 心性儒学还是政治儒学? 新邦旧命还是旧邦新命? *Open Times* 11:5–25.

———. (2010b). "What to Do in an Unjust State: On Confucius's and Socrates's Views on Political Duty." *Dao: A Journal of Comparative Philosophy* 9, no. 4 (December): 375–90.

Bai, Tongdong 白彤东. (2011). "Preliminary Remarks: Han Fei Zi—First Modern Political Philosopher?" *Journal of Chinese Philosophy* 38, no. 1 (March): 4–13.

———. (2012a). "Primatologists and Confucians" 灵长类动物学家与儒家. *Philosophical Researches* 哲学研究, 1:113–18.

———. (2012b). *China: The Political Philosophy of the Middle Kingdom*. London: Zed Books.

———. (2013a). "Humane Rights Override Sovereignty: A Mencian Theory of Just War" 仁权高于主权: 孟子的正义战争观. *Journal of Social Sciences* 社会科学 1:131–39.

———. (2013b). "A Confucian Version of Hybrid Regime: How Does It Work, and Why Is It Superior?" In Bell and Li 2013, 55–87.

———. (2014a). "Nietzsche, Mencius, and Compassion as a Modern Virtue" 恻隐之心的现代性本质—从尼采与孟子谈起. *World Philosophy* 世界哲学, 1:110–19.

———. (2014b). "'Classical' Chinese Thought as a Modern Political Philosophy" 作为现代政治哲学的先秦思想. *Journal of Social Sciences* 社会科学 (October): 111–21.

———. (2015a). "Ethical Issues, State Identity, and International Relations: A Confucian New *Tian Xia* Model" 现代国家认同与国际关系: 儒家的理论及其对民族国家与自由主义范式之优越性. *Historical Jurisprudence* 历史法学 10 (December): 205–42.

———. (2015b). "A Criticism of Later Rawls and a Defense of a Decent (Confucian) People." In Bruya 2015, 101–20.

———. (2015c). "Will the Idea of the Unity between Heaven and Man Solve Environmental Problems? A Chinese Philosophical Reflection on Climate Change" 天人合一能够解决环境问题么? 气候变化的政治模式反思. *Exploration and Free Views* 探索与争鸣 12:59–62.

———. (2016). "The Dark Connection between a Dark View of Human Nature and Democracy: A Criticism of Zhang Hao's Thesis" 幽暗意识与民主传统 之 幽暗: 对张灏的批评. *Journal of Social Sciences* 社会科学 10 (October): 124–32.

———. (2017). "The Middle Way in the Face of Technological Challenges" 面对技术挑战 的中庸之道. *Peking University Journal* 北京大学学报 (哲学社会科学版) 54, 2:125–30.

Barnes, J. (1984). *Complete Works of Aristotle*. Vol. 2. Princeton, NJ: Princeton University Press.

Bauer, Joanne R., and Daniel A. Bell. (1999). *The East Asian Challenge for Human Rights*. Cambridge: Cambridge University Press.

Beaney, Michael (ed.). (1997). *The Frege Reader*. Malden, MA: Blackwell.

Beitz, Charles R. (2000). "Rawls's Law of Peoples." *Ethics* 110, no. 4 (July): 669–96.

Bell, Daniel. (2006). *Beyond Liberal Democracy*. Princeton, NJ: Princeton University Press.

———. (2011). "Is Confucianism Compatible with Nationalism?" 儒家与民族主义能否相容. *Beijing Cultural Review* 文化纵横 (June): 112–18.

———. (2015). *The China Model*. Princeton, NJ: Princeton University Press.

Bell, Daniel, and Fan Ruiping. (2012). *A Confucian Constitutional Order*. Princeton, NJ: Princeton University Press.

Bell, Daniel, and Hahm Chaibong (eds.). (2003). *Confucianism for the Modern World*. Cambridge: Cambridge University Press.

Bell, Daniel, and Li Chenyang (eds.). (2013). *The East Asian Challenge for Democracy*. Cambridge: Cambridge University Press.

Benardete, Seth (trans.). (1984). *Plato's Theaetetus*. Chicago: University of Chicago Press.

Benedetto, Richard. (2005). "Who Is Smarter, Kerry or Bush?" *USA Today*. http://www .usatoday.com/news/opinion/columnist/benedetto/2005-06-10-benedetto_x.htm.

Bentham, Jeremy. (1948). *An Introduction to the Principles of Morals and Legislation*. New York: Hafner Press.

Berggruen, Nicolas, and Nathan Gardels. (2013). *Intelligent Governance for the 21st Century*. Cambridge, UK: Polity.

Berstein, Alyssa R. (2006). "A Human Right to Democracy? Legitimacy and Intervention." In Martin and Reidy 2006, 278–98.

Bloom, Allan (trans.). (1991). *The Republic of Plato*. New York: Basic Books.

Bohr, Niels. (1958). *Atomic Physics and Human Knowledge*. New York: John Wiley and Sons.

Brennan, Jason. (2012). *Ethics of Voting*. Princeton, NJ: Princeton University Press.

Brooks, David. (2008). "The Two Earthquakes." *New York Times*, January 4.

Brooks, E. Bruce, and A. Taeko Brooks. (2001). *The Original Analects*. New York: Columbia University Press.

Brown, Elizabeth A. R. (1974). "The Tyranny of a Construct: Feudalism and Historians of Medieval Europe." *American Historical Review* 79, no. 4, 1063–88.

Bruya, Brian (ed.). (2015). *The Philosophical Challenge from China*. Cambridge, MA: MIT Press.

Buchanan, Allen. (2000). "Rawls's Law of Peoples: Rules for a Vanished Westphalian World." *Ethics* 110, no. 4 (July): 697–721.

Cai, Menghan 蔡孟翰. (2017). "Political Imagination and Narration on 'Tianxia' during the Pre-Qin Period" 论天下—先秦关于 "天下" 的政治想象与论述. *Beijing Cultural Review* 文化纵横 4:60–73.

Caplan, Bryan. (2008). *The Myth of the Rational Voter: Why Democracies Choose Bad Policies*. New ed. Princeton, NJ: Princeton University Press.

Chan, Alan K. L. (1998). "A Tale of Two Commentaries: Ho-shang-kung and Wang Pi on the *Lao-tzu*." In Kohn and Lafargue 1998, 89–117.

Chan, Joseph. (1999). "A Confucian Perspective on Human Rights for Contemporary China." In Bauer and Bell 1999, 212–37.

———. (2000). "Legitimacy, Unanimity, and Perfectionism." *Philosophy & Public Affairs* 29, 1:5–42.

———. (2013a). "Political Meritocracy and Meritorious Rule: A Confucian Perspective." In Bell and Li 2013, 55–87.

———. (2013b). *Confucian Perfectionism*. Princeton, NJ: Princeton University Press.

Chan, Joseph, Doh Chull Shin, and Melissa Williams (eds.). (2017). *East Asian Perspectives on Political Legitimacy*. Cambridge: Cambridge University Press.

Chan, Sin Yee. (2003). "The Confucian Conception of Gender in the Twenty-First Century." In Bell and Chaibong 2003, 312–33.

Chan, Wing-Tsit. (1969). *A Source Book in Chinese Philosophy*. Princeton, NJ: Princeton University Press.

Chen, Guying 陈鼓应 (ed.). (1999). *Studies of Daoist Culture (Vol. 17): Special Issue on the Guo Dian Chu Slips* 道家文化研究第17辑: 郭店楚简专号. Beijing: Sanlian Shudian 三联书店.

———. (2003). *Contemporary Commentaries and Translations of the* Lao Zi 老子今注今译 (参照简帛本最新修订版). Beijing: Shangwu 商务印书馆.

Chen, Lisheng 陈立胜. (2008). *Wang Yangming's Theory of "All Things Are One"* 王阳明 "万物一体" 论. Shanghai: East China Normal University Press 华东师范大学出版社.

Chen, Qiaojian 陈乔见. (2008). "Private and Public: Autonomy and Rule of Law" 私与公: 自治 与法治. In Guo 2008, 67–119.

Chen, Shaoming 陈少明. (2012). "Between Humaneness and Righteousness" 仁义之间. *Philosophical Researches* 哲学研究 11 (2012): 32–40.

Chen, Zhiwu 陈志武. (2008). "Comments on 'On Familialism'" 关于 "论家庭主义" 的评论. *New Review of Political Economics* 新政治经济学评论 no. 4, 1:98–104.

Cheng, Chung-ying. (2004). "Dimensions of the *Dao* and Onto-Ethics in Light of the *DDJ.*" *Journal of Chinese Philosophy* 31, no. 2 (June): 143–82.

Cheng, Hao 程颢, and Cheng Yi 程颐. (1992). *Surviving Works of the Two Chengs and Additional Works of the Two Chengs* 二程遗书与二程外书. Shanghai: Shanghai Guji 上海古籍出版社.

Cheng, Shude 程树德. (1963). *Studies of the Laws of Nine Dynasties* 九朝律考. Beijing: Zhong Hua Shu Ju 中华书局.

———. (1990). *Collected Commentaries on the "Analects"* 论语集解. Beijing: Zhong Hua Shu Ju 中华书局.

Clark, Gregory. (2014). "Your Ancestors, Your Fate." *New York Times*, February 21.

Cohen, Adam. (2006). "Question for Judge Alito: What about One Person One Vote?" *New York Times*, January 3.

Creel, Herrlee G. (1970a). *The Origin of Statecraft in China*. Chicago: University of Chicago Press.

———. (1970b). *What Is Taoism?* Chicago: University of Chicago Press.

Csikszentmihalyi, Mark. (n.d.) "Disunities of Unities: A Critical Survey of Some Recent Works on the 'Unity of *Tian* and *Ren.*'" Manuscript.

Csikszentmihalyi, Mark, and Philip J. Ivanhoe (eds.). (1999). *Religious and Philosophical Aspects of the Laozi*. Albany: State University of New York Press.

Descartes, René. (1998). *Discourse on Method*. 4th ed. Translated by Donald A. Cress. Indianapolis: Hackett.

De Vos, George A. (1971). *Japan's Outcasts: The Problem of the Burakumin*. London: Minority Rights Group.

De Waal, Frans. (2006). *Primates and Philosophers: How Morality Evolved*. Princeton, NJ: Princeton University Press.

Diamond, Jared. (1999). *Gun, Germs, and Steel*. New York: W. W. Norton.

———. (2011). *Collapse: How Societies Choose to Fail or Succeed*. New York: Penguin Books.

Donnelly, Jack. (2003). *Universal Human Rights in Theory and Practice*. 2nd ed. Ithaca: Cornell University Press.

Dreben, Burton. (2003). "On Rawls and Political Liberalism." In Freeman 2003, 316–46.

Düring, Ingemar. (1957). *Aristotle in the Ancient Biographical Tradition*. Göteborg: Almqvist & Wiksell in Komm.

Eberstadt, Nicholas. (2017). "Our Miserable 21st Century." *Commentary*, February 15. https://www.commentarymagazine.com/articles/saving-conservative-judaism/.

Elliot, Mark. (2012). "Hushuo: The Northern Other and the Naming of Han Chinese." In *Critical Han Studies: The History, Representation, and Identity of China's Majority*, ed. Thomas S.

Mullaney, James Leibold, Stéphane Gros, and Eric Vanden, 173–90 and 311–18. Berkeley: California University Press.

———. (2015). "The Case of the Missing Indigene: Debate over a 'Second-Generation' Ethnic Policy." *China Journal* 73:186–213.

Elman, Benjamin. (2013). "A Society in Motion: Unexpected Consequences of Political Meritocracy in Late Imperial China, 1400–1900." In Bell and Li 2013, 203–31.

Elstein, David. (2015). *Democracy in Contemporary Confucian Philosophy*. New York: Routledge.

Fan, Ruiping 范瑞平, Daniel Bell, and Xiuping Hong 洪秀平 (eds.). (2012). *Confucian Constitutionalism and the Future of China* 儒家宪政与中国未来. Shanghai: East China Normal University Press 华东师大出版社.

Fang, Xudong 方旭东. (2011). "Why Don't Confucians Forbid the Killing of Animals?" 为何儒家不禁止杀生. *Philosophical Trends* 哲学动态 10:68–74.

Fei, Xiaotong 费孝通. (1998). *Rural China and Institutions of Birth and Child-Rearing* 乡土中国, 生育制度. Beijing: Peking University Press 北京大学出版社.

Feng, Youlan (aka "Fung, Yu-lan") 冯友兰. (1966). *A Short History of Chinese Philosophy*. New York: Free Press.

———. (1999). *A History of Modern Chinese Philosophy* 中国现代哲学史. Guangzhou: Guangdong People's Press 广东人民出版社.

———. (2000). *A History of Chinese Philosophy* 中国哲学史. Shanghai: East China Normal University Press.

———. (2001). *The Complete Sansongtang* 三松堂全集. 2nd ed. Zhengzhou: Henan People's Press 河南人民出版社.

Feyerabend, Paul. (1993). *Against Method*. 3rd ed. London: Verso.

Fleischacker, Samuel. (2004). *A Short History of Distribute Justice*. Cambridge, MA: Harvard University Press.

Fournier, Patrick, Henk van der Kolk, R. Kenneth Carty, Andre Blais, and Jonathan Rose. (2011). *When Citizens Decide: Lessons from Citizen Assemblies on Electoral Reform*. Oxford: Oxford University Press.

Freeman, Samuel (ed.). (2003). *The Cambridge Companion to Rawls*. Cambridge: Cambridge University Press.

Friedman, Milton, and Rose Friedman. (1980). *Free to Choose: A Personal Statement*. Orlando, FL: Harcourt.

Fukuyama, Francis. (1992). *The End of History and the Last Man*. New York: Avon Books.

———. (2011). *The Origins of Political Order*. New York: Farrar, Straus and Giroux.

Gan, Chunsong 干春松. (2012). *Return to the Kingly Way* 重回王道. Shanghai: East China Normal University Press 华东师范大学出版社.

Gao, You 高诱 (ed.). (1986). *Lv Shi Chun Qiu* 吕氏春秋. In *The Collected Works of Hundred Schools* 诸子集成. Shanghai: Shanghai Shudian 上海书店.

Glendon, Mary Ann. (1993). *Rights Talk: The Impoverishment of Political Discourse*. Reprint ed. New York: Free Press.

Graham, A. C. (1986). "Being in Western Philosophy Compared with Shih/Fei and Yu/Wu in Chinese Philosophy." In *Studies in Chinese Philosophy and Philosophical Literature*, by A. C.

Graham, 322–59. Singapore: Institute of East Asian Philosophies, National University of Singapore. Originally published in *Asia Major* (New Series) 8, 2 (1961).

Graham, A. C. (2001). *Chuang-Tsǔ: The Inner Chapters*. Indianapolis: Hackett.

Green, Jeffrey. (2011). *The Eyes of the People: Democracy in an Age of Spectatorship*. Oxford: Oxford University Press.

Greenhut, Steven. (2017). "It's O.K., California. Breaking Up Isn't Hard to Do." *New York Times*, April 4.

Gu, Yanwu 顾炎武. (1983). *The Collected Works of Gu Tinglin* 顾亭林诗文集. 2nd ed. Beijing: Zhonghua Shuju 中华书局.

Guo, Qiyong 郭齐勇 (ed.). (2004). *Debates on Confucian Ethics through the Mutual Concealment Case* 儒家伦理争鸣集—以"亲亲互隐"为中心. Wuhan: Hubei Education Press 湖北教育出版社.

———. (2007). "Is Confucian Ethics a 'Consanguinism'?" *Dao: A Journal of Comparative Philosophy* 6, no. 1 (March): 21–37.

——— (ed.). (2008a). *Studies of Confucian Culture, Vol. 2* 儒家文化研究第二辑. Beijing: Sanlian Shudian 三联书店.

———. (2008b). "Pre-Qin Confucians on the Issues of Private, Public, and Justice" 先秦儒家论公私与正义. In Guo 2008a, 3–49.

——— (ed.). (2011). *Critique of* "New Critique of Confucian Ethics" 儒家伦理新批判之批判. Wuhan: Wuhan University Press 武汉大学出版社.

Guo, Qiyong, and Chen, Qiaojian 陈乔见. (2009). "Confucius's and Mencius's Views on Private and Public and the Ethics of Public Affairs" 孔孟儒家的公私观与公共事务伦理. *Journal of Chinese Social Sciences* 中国社会科学 175 (January): 57–63.

Guo, Xiaodong 郭晓东. (2012). "A Confucian Theory of Ethnic Relations: From the Perspective of the Gongyang Tradition" 从春秋公羊学的夷夏之辨看儒家的民族关系理论. *Dialogue Transcultural* 跨文化对话 30:374–81.

Hagen, Kurtis. (2016). "Would Early Confucians Really Support Humanitarian Interventions?" *Philosophy East and West* 66, no. 3 (July): 818–41.

Han Fei Zi 韩非子. (1991). *Collected Commentaries on the "Han Fei Zi"* 韩非子集解. Edited by Xianshen Wang 王先慎. In *The Collected Works of the Hundred Schools* 诸子集成. Shanghai: Shanghai Shudian 上海书店.

Han, Linhe. 韩林合. (2008). "On the Issue of Interpreting Philosophical Classics" 浅论哲学经典的解释问题—以"庄子"的解释为例. In the Proceedings of the Conference of the Methodology of Comparative Philosophy 比较哲学方法论, Peking University.

Hardin, Russell. (2002). "Street-Level Epistemology and Democratic Participation." *Journal of Political Philosophy* 10, 2:212–29.

Hayward, J. (2014). "Rethinking Electoral Reform in New Zealand: The Benefits of Citizens' Assemblies." *Kōtuitui: New Zealand Journal of Social Sciences Online* 9, 1:11–19. http://dx.doi.org/10.1080/1177083X.2013.869760.

Hobbes, Thomas. (1985). *Leviathan*. Edited by C. B. MacPherson. London: Penguin Books.

Hsu, Cho-Yun. (1980). *Han Agriculture: The Formation of Early Chinese Agrarian Economy (206 B.C.–A.D. 220)*. Seattle: University of Washington Press.

Hu, Angang 胡鞍钢, and Lianhe Hu 胡联合. (2011). "Second-Generation Ethnic Policies: Promoting the Unity and Prosperity of Ethnic Groups" 第二代民族政策: 促进民族交融一

体和繁荣一体. *Xinjiang Normal University Journal* 新疆师范 大学学报 (哲学社会科学版) 32, 5 (September): 1–12.

Huang, Chun-Chieh 黄俊杰. (2008). "Modern East Asian Confucians' Reflections on the Division between the Private and the Public" 东亚近世儒者对 "公" "私" 领域分际 的思考: 从孟子与桃应的对话出发. In Huang and Jiang 2008, 85–98.

Huang, Chun-Chieh, and Yi-Huah Jiang 江宜桦 (eds.). (2008). *New Investigations of the Private and the Public Spheres: Comparative Studies between East Asia and the West* 公私领域新探: 东亚与西方观点之比较. Shanghai: East China Normal University Press 华东师范大学出版社.

Huang, Xiang 黄翔. (2016). "Philosophy of Technology Should Construct a Public Forum in the Face of Scientific Controversies" 面对科学争议, 技术哲学应搭建公 共探讨平台. *Liberation Daily* 解放日报, July 11, 2016. http://web.shobserver.com/wx/detail.do?id=23240.

Huang, Yong. (2008). "Neo-Confucian Hermeneutics at Work: CHENG Yi's Philosophical Interpretation of Analects 8.9 and 17.3." *Harvard Theological Review* 101, 2:169–201.

Hui, Victoria Tin-bor. (2005). *War and State Formation in Ancient China and Early Modern Europe*. Cambridge: Cambridge University Press.

Ing, Michael. (2017). *The Vulnerability of Integrity in Early Confucian Thought*. Oxford: Oxford University Press.

Irwin, Terence (trans.). (1985). *Aristotle: Nicomachean Ethics*. Indianapolis: Hackett.

Jacobs, Samuel P. (2013). "After Fumbled Oath, Roberts and Obama Leave Little to Chance." Reuters online, January 18. http://www.reuters.com/article/2013/01/18/us-usa -inaugration-roberts-idUSBRE90H16L20130118.

Jiang, Qing 蒋庆. (2012). *A Confucian Constitutional Order: How China's Ancient Past Can Shape Its Political Future*. Edited by Daniel A. Bell and Ruiping Fan. Princeton, NJ: Princeton University Press.

Jiao, Xun 焦循. (1986). *Meng Zi Zheng Yi* 孟子正义. In *Collected Works of the Hundred Schools* 诸子集成. Shanghai: Shanghai Shudian 上海书店.

Kang, David. (2008). *China Rising: Peace, Power, and Order in East Asia*. New York: Columbia University Press.

———. (2010). *East Asia before the West-Five Centuries of Trade and Tribute*. New York: Columbia University Press.

Kant, Immanuel. (1991). *The Metaphysics of Morals*. Translated by Mary Gregor. Cambridge: Cambridge University Press.

———. (1998). *Groundwork of the Metaphysics of Morals*. Translated by Mary Gregor. Cambridge: Cambridge University Press.

Kaplan, Robert. (1997). "Was Democracy Just a Moment?" *Atlantic Monthly* 280, 6 (December): 55–80.

Kierkegaard, Søren. (1983). *Fear and Trembling/Repetition*. Translated by Edna H. Hong and Howard V. Hong. Princeton, NJ: Princeton University Press.

Kim, Sungmoon. (2014). *Confucian Democracy in East Asia: Theory and Practice*. Cambridge: Cambridge University Press.

———. (2017). "Confucian Authority, Political Right, and Democracy." *Philosophy East and West* 67 (1): 3–14.

Kissinger, Henry. (1994). *Diplomacy*. New York: Simon & Schuster.

Kissinger, Henry. (2001). *Does America Need a Foreign Policy?* New York: Simon & Schuster.

Kohn, Livia, and Michael LaFargue (eds.). (1998). *Lao-tzu and the Tao-te-ching.* Albany: State University of New York Press.

Krieckhaus, Jonathan. (2004). "The Regime Debate Revisited: A Sensitivity Analysis of Democracy's Effects." *British Journal of Political Science* 34, 4:635–55.

———. (2006). "Democracy and Economic Growth: How Regional Context Influences Regime Effects." *British Journal of Political Science* 36, 2 (April): 317–40.

Kristof, Nicholas D. (2008). "With a Few More Brains." *New York Times,* March 30.

Kuhn, Thomas. (1959). "The Essential Tension." In *The Third (1959) University of Utah Research Conference on the Identification of Scientific Talent,* edited by C. W. Taylor, 162–74. Salt Lake City: University of Utah Press.

Landler, Mark. (2012). "In Car Country, Obama Trumpets China Trade Case." *New York Times,* September 18.

Landemore, Hélène. (2016). "Which Democracy? On Post-Representative Democracy as an Alternative Path." Paper presented at the conference "Democracy and China," National University of Singapore, December.

Larmore, Charles. (2002). "Review of *The Law of Peoples.*" *Philosophy and Phenomenological Research* 64, no. 1 (January): 241–43.

Lau, D. C. 刘殿爵 (trans.). (1963). *Tao Te Ching.* Baltimore, MD: Penguin Books.

———. (2000). *Confucius: The Analects.* First paperback ed. Hong Kong: Chinese University Press.

———. (2003). *Mencius.* Revised and bilingual ed. Hong Kong: Chinese University Press.

Levenson, Joseph R. (1968). *Confucian China and Its Modern Fate.* Berkeley: University of California Press.

Liao, Mingchun 廖明春. (2013). "New Investigations on the Mutual Concealment Chapter of the *Analects*" 论语 "父子互隐" 章新证. *Hunan University Journal* 湖南大学学报 27, no. 2 (March): 5–13.

Li, Chenyang (ed.). (2000). *The Sage and the Second Sex: Confucianism, Ethics, and Gender.* Chicago: Open Court.

Li, Feng. (2005). *Landscape and Power in Early China.* Cambridge: Cambridge University Press.

———. (2008). *Bureaucracy and the State in Early China.* Cambridge: Cambridge University Press.

Li, Ruohui 李若晖. (2016). "Criticisms of Absolutism from Ancient China" 中国古代对 于君主专制的批判. *Journal of Chinese Humanities* 5:1–11.

Li, X.-H., A. S. Tsui, X. Feng, and Y. Jia. "Achieved and Ascribed Income Inequality: A Status-Affirmation Perspective and Its Differential Implications for Employee Well-being." Manuscript.

Lilla, Mark. (2016). "The End of Identity Liberalism." *New York Times,* November 20.

Liu, Baonan 刘宝楠. (1986). *Lun Yu Zheng Yi* 论语正义. In *Collected Works of the Hundred Schools.* Shanghai: Shanghai Shudian.

Liu, Mengxi 刘梦溪 (ed.). (1996). *Chinese Contemporary Classics: The Tang Junyi Volume* 中国现代学术经典:唐君毅卷. Shijiazhuang: Hebei Education Press 河北教育出版社.

Liu, Xiaogan 刘笑敢.(1998). "Naturalness (*Tzu-jan*), the Core Value in Taoism: Its Ancient Meaning and Its Significance Today." In Kohn and Lafargue 1998, 211–28.

————. (1999). "An Inquiry into the Core Value of Laozi's Philosophy." In Csiksentmihalyi and Ivanhoe 1999, 211–37.

————. (2006). *Lao Zi Gu Jin* 老子古今. Beijing: Chinese Social Sciences Press 中国社会科学出版社.

Locke, John. (1986). *The Second Treatise on Civil Government*. Buffalo, NY: Prometheus Books.

Loewe, Michael. (2009). "Dong Zhongshu as a Consultant." *Third Series* 22, 1 (January 1): 163–82.

Lord, Carnes (trans.). (1984). *The Politics*. Chicago: University of Chicago Press.

Ma, Rong 马戎.(2004). "A New Approach to Understanding Minority Group Relations." 理解民族关系的新思路. *Journal of Peking University* 北京大学学报 no. 6 (2004): 122–33.

————. (2007). "A New Perspective in Guiding Ethnic Relations in the 21st Century." *Asian Ethnicity* 8, no. 3 (October 2007): 199–217.

————. (2010). "Does There Exist the Risk of National Break-Up in 21st-Century China?" 21世纪的中国是否存在国家分裂的风险, *Sociology of Ethnicity* 民族社会学研究 通讯 75 (November 2010): 1–35.

Macedo, Stephen. (1991). *Liberal Virtues: Citizenship, Virtue, and Community in Liberal Constitutionalism*. Oxford: Oxford University Press.

————. (2013). "Meritocratic Democracy: Learning from the American Constitution." In Bell and Li 2013, 232–58.

Mann, Michael. (2005). *The Dark Side of Democracy: Explaining Ethnic Cleansing*. Cambridge: Cambridge University Press.

Mansbridge, Jane. (1990). "On the Relation of Altruism and Self-Interest." In *Beyond Self-Interest*, ed. Jane Mansbridge, 133–46. Chicago: University of Chicago Press.

Martin, Rex, and David A. Reidy (eds.). (2006). "Introduction: Reading Rawls's *The Law of Peoples*." In Martin and Reidy 2006, 3–18.

————. (2006). *Rawls's Law of Peoples: A Realistic Utopia?* Malden, MA: Blackwell.

Metzger, Thomas A. (2005). *A Cloud across the Pacific: Essays on the Clash between Chinese and Western Political Theories*. Hong Kong: Chinese University Press.

Meyer, Michael J. (1997). "When Not to Claim Your Rights: The Abuse and the Virtuous Use of Rights." *Journal of Political Philosophy* 5, no. 2:149–62.

Mildenberger, Matto, and Anthony Leiserowitz. (2017). "Public Opinion on Climate Change: Is There an Economy-Environment Tradeoff?" *Environmental Politics*. https://www.tandfonline.com/doi/abs/10.1080/09644016.2017.1322275?journalCode=fenp20.

Mill, John Stuart. (1958). *Considerations on Representative Government*. New York: Liberal Arts Press.

————. (1985). *On Liberty*. Edited by Gertrude Himmelfarb. London: Penguin Books.

————. (2001). *Utilitarianism*. 2nd ed. Edited by George Sher. Indianapolis: Hackett.

Miller, David. (2000). *Citizenship and National Identity*. Oxford: Blackwell.

Montesquieu. (1989). *The Spirit of the Laws*. Edited and translated by Anne M. Cohler, Basia Carolyn Miller, and Harold Samuel Stone. Cambridge: Cambridge University Press.

New York Times. (2006). "Judging Samuel Alito." Editorial, January 8.

Nichols, James H. (trans.). (1998). *Plato: Gorgias*. Ithaca: Cornell University Press.

Nickel, James W. (2006). "Are Human Rights Mainly Implemented by Intervention?" In Martin and Reidy 2006, 263–77.

Nietzsche, Friedrich. (1954). *Thus Spoke Zarathustra*. Translated by Walter Kaufmann. London: Penguin Books.

———. (1994). *On the Genealogy of Morality*. Edited by Keith Ansell-Pearson. Translated by Carol Diethe. Cambridge: Cambridge University Press.

Norgaard, Kari Marie. (2011). *Living in Denial: Climate Change, Emotions and Everyday Life*. Boston, MA: MIT Press.

Olken, Benjamin A. (2008). "Direct Democracy and Local Public Goods: Evidence from a Field Experiment in Indonesia." Working Paper 14123, National Bureau of Economic Research Working Paper Series, June. http://www.nber.org/papers/w14123.

Ortega y Gasset, José. (1932). *The Revolt of the Masses*. New York: W. W. Norton.

Parfit, Derek. (1987). *Reasons and Persons*. Oxford: Oxford University Press.

Palmer, Martin. (1996). *The Book of Chuantzu*. London: Arkana, Penguin Books.

Peng, Dingqiu 彭定求 (ed.). (1960). *The Complete Collection of Tang Poems* 全唐诗. Beijing: Zhonghua Shuju 中华书局.

Perkins, Franklin. (2012). "Leibniz on the Existence of 'Philosophy' in China." Paper presented at the Philosophy Seminar Series, Department of Philosophy, National University of Singapore, September 13.

Perry, Elizabeth. (2008). "Chinese Conceptions of 'Rights': From Mencius to Mao—and Now." *Perspectives on Politics* 6, no. 1:37–50.

Pettit, Philip. (2013). "Meritocratic Representation." In Bell and Li 2013, 138–60.

Phillips, Katherine W. (2014). "How Diversity Works." *Scientific American*, October 1. https://www.scientificamerican.com/article/how-diversity-makes-us-smarter/.

Pines, Yuri. (2013). "Between Merit and Pedigree: Evolution of the Concept of 'Elevating the Worthy' in the Pre-Imperial China." In Bell and Li 2013, 161–202.

Pogge, Thomas. (1994). "An Egalitarian Law of Peoples." *Philosophy and Public Affairs* 23: 195–224.

———. (2006). "Do Rawls's Two Theories of Justice Fit Together?" In Martin and Reidy 2006, 206–25.

Pollak, Michael. (1998). *Mandarins, Jews, and Missionaries: The Jewish Experience in the Chinese Empire*. New York: Weatherhill.

Popper, Karl. (1971). *Open Society and Its Enemies*. 5th revised ed. 2 vols. Princeton, NJ: Princeton University Press.

Pye, Lucian. (1990). "China: Erratic State, Frustrated Society." *Foreign Affairs* 69, no. 4 (Fall): 56–74.

———. (1993). "How China's Nationalism was Shanghaied." *Australian Journal of Chinese Affairs*, no. 29 (January): 107–33.

Qian Mu 钱穆.(1996). *Outlines of the History of China* 国史大纲. Beijing: Shangwu Press 商务印书馆.

———. (2002). *A Biography of Confucius* 孔子传. Beijing: Sanlian Shudian 三联书店.

———. (2005a). *Successes and Failures of Traditional Chinese Politics* 中国历代政治得失. Beijing: Sanlian Shudian 三联书店.

———. (2005b). *New Discussions of the National History* 国史新论. 2nd ed. Beijing: Sanlian Shudian 三联书店.

Quine, W.V.O. (1969). *Ontological Relativity and Other Essays*. New York: Columbia University Press.

Rawls, John. (1971). *A Theory of Justice*. Cambridge, MA: Harvard University Press.

———. (1989). "The Domain of the Political and Overlapping Consensus." In Rawls 1999b, 473–96.

———. (1996). *Political Liberalism*. New York: Columbia University Press.

———. (1997). "The Idea of Public Reason Revisited." *University of Chicago Law Review* 64, no. 3:765–807.

———. (1999a). *The Law of Peoples with "The Idea of Public Reason Revisited."* Cambridge, MA: Harvard University Press.

———. (1999b). *John Rawls: Collected Papers*. Edited by Samuel Freeman. Cambridge, MA: Harvard University Press.

Regan, Tom. (1986). *Matters of Life and Death*. 2nd ed. New York: McGraw-Hill.

Renwick, Alan, and Jean-Benoit Pilet. (2016). *Faces on the Ballot: The Personalization of Electoral Systems in Europe*. Oxford: Oxford University Press.

Reynolds, Susan. (1994). *Fiefs and Vassals*. Oxford: Clarendon Press.

Ross, David (trans.). (1925). *Aristotle: The Nicomachean Ethics*. Oxford: Oxford University Press.

Rousseau, Jean-Jacques. (1964). *The First and Second Discourses*. Translated by Roger D. and Judith R. Masters. New York: St. Martin's Press.

———. (1978). *On the Social Contract with Geneva Manuscript and Political Economy*. Edited by Roger D. Masters and translated by Judith R. Masters. New York: St. Martin's Press.

Sagar, Rahul. (2016). "Are Charter Cities Legitimate?" *Journal of Political Philosophy* 24, no. 4:509–29.

Sanderovitch, Sharon. (2007). "Is There a Bug in the Confucian Program of Harmony?" Unpublished manuscript.

Schwartz, Benjamin. (1985). *The World of Thought in Ancient China*. Cambridge, MA: Belknap Press of Harvard University Press.

Shapiro, Sidney (ed. and trans.). (1984). *Jews in Old China, Studies by Chinese Scholars*. New York: Hippocrene Books.

Sheng, Hong 盛洪. (2008). "On Familialism [*sic*]" 论家庭主义. *New Review of Political Economics* 新政治经济学评论 4, no. 1:72–97.

———. (2010). "'Families Having Been Doing Charitable Things Will Be Particularly Blessed': On the Historical Dimension of Confucian Constitutionalism" 积善之家, 必有余庆: 论儒家宪政原则的历史维度. In Fan et al. 2012, 42–54.

Shi, Weimin 史伟民. "Ethics of Autonomy and Its Problems" 自律伦理学及其问题 Manuscript.

Shin, Doh Chull. (2013). "How East Asians View Meritocracy: A Confucian Perspective." In Bell and Li 2013, 259–87.

Shue, Henry. (1980). *Basic Rights*. Princeton, NJ: Princeton University Press.

Sima, Qian 司马迁. (1981). *Shi Ji* 史记. In *Twenty-Five Historical Records* 二十五史. Shanghai: Shanghai Guji 上海古籍.

Singer, Peter. (1972). "Famine, Affluence, and Morality." *Philosophy and Public Affairs* 1, no. 3 (Spring): 229–43.

Singer, Peter. (1986). "Animals and the Value of Life." In Regan 1986, 338–80.

Sivanathan, N., and N. C. Pettit. (2010). "Protecting the Self through Consumption: Status Goods as Affirmational Commodities." *Journal of Experimental Social Psychology* 46:564–70.

Slingerland, Edward (trans.). (2006). *Confucius: The Essential Analects; Selected Passages with Commentary*. Indianapolis: Hackett.

Solnick, S. J., and D. Hemenway. (1998). "Is More Always Better? A Survey on Positional Concerns." *Journal of Economic Behavior and Organization* 37 (3): 373–83.

Strauss, Leo. (1983). *Studies in Platonic Political Philosophy*. Chicago: University of Chicago Press.

Sun Xiangchen 孙向晨. (2014a). "Being towards Death and Endless Coming into Being" 向死而生与生生不息—中国文化传统的生存论结构. *Religion and Philosophy* 宗教与哲学 3:223–35.

———. (2014b). "Nation-State, Civilized State, and the Idea of Tian Xia" 民族国家, 文明 国家与天下意识. *Exploration and Free Views* 探索与争鸣, September, 64–71.

Tamir, Yael. (1993). *Liberal Nationalism*. Princeton, NJ: Princeton University Press.

Tan, Kok-chor. (1998). "Liberal Toleration in Rawls's Law of Peoples." *Ethics* 108, no. 2 (January): 276–95.

———. (2006). "The Problem of Decent People." In Martin and Reidy 2006, 76–94.

Tang, Qingwei 唐清威. (2014). "Mencius's and Xun Zi's Theories of Just War" 孟荀的 义战理论: 从孟子"吊民伐罪"和荀子"禁暴除害"谈起. Master's thesis, Fudan University.

Tang, Wenming 唐文明. (2010). "The Yi-Xia Distinction and the Issue of Legitimacy in the Construction of the Modern Chinese State" 夷夏之辨与现代中国国家建构 中的正当性问题. In *Present Danger: Cultural Politics and the Future of China* 近忧: 文化政治与中国的未来 by Tang 2010, 3–40. Shanghai: East China Norma University Press 华东师范大学出版社.

———. (2011). "Confucianism to Save Nationalism" 从儒家拯救民族主义. *Beijing Cultural Review* 文化纵横 (October): 103–5.

Taylor, Charles. (1999). "Conditions for an Unforced Consensus on Human Rights." In Bauer and Bell 1999, 124–46.

Tian, Ye 田野. (2015). "Tian Xia System vs. International System." Conference Presentation, Conference on Chinese Perspectives on International Order, School of International Relations and Public Administration, Fudan University, December 2015.

Tilly, Charles. (1998). "Westphalia and China." Keynote address, Conference on "Westphalia and Beyond," Enschede, Netherlands, July. http://www.ibrarian.net/navon/paper/CIAO_DATE__6_99.pdf?paperid=1215872.

Tiwald, Justin. (2008). "A Right of Rebellion in the *Mengzi*?" *Dao: A Journal of Comparative Philosophy* 3:269–82.

———. (2013). "Confucian Rights as a 'Fallback Apparatus'" "作为备用机制的儒家权利. *Academic Monthly* 学术月刊 45 (11): 41–49.

Treisman, Daniel. (2000). "The Causes of Corruption: A Cross-National Study." *Journal of Public Economics* 76, no. 3:399–457.

Van Norden, Bryan (ed.). (2002a). *Confucius and the "Analects": New Essays*. Oxford: Oxford University Press.

———. (2002b). "Unweaving the 'One Thread' of *Analects* 4:15." In Van Norden 2002a, 216–36.

Waldron, Jeremy. (1992). "Superseding Historical Injustice." *Ethics* 103:4–28.

Walker, Richard. (1953). *The Multi-State System of Ancient China*. Westport, CT: Greenwood Press.

Waltz, Kenneth. (1979). *Theory of International Politics*. Reading, MA: Addison-Wesley.

Wang, Bi 王弼. (1991). *The Wang Bi Commentary of Lao Zi's Dao De Jing* 老子道德经:王弼注. In *Collected Works of the Hundred Schools*. Shanghai: Shanghai Shudian 上海书店.

Wang, Guoyu 王国豫. (2016). "The Necessity of Institutionalization of the Ethics of Technology" 技术伦理必须机制化. *Social Sciences* 社会科学报 no. 1523 (August 25): 5.

Wang, Huaiyu. (2011). "Piety and Individuality through a Convoluted Path of Rightness." *Asian Philosophy* 21, no. 4:395–418.

Wang, Ka 王卡 (ed.). (1993). *The He Shang Gong Version of Lao Zi's Dao De Jing* 老子 道德经河上公章句. Beijing: Zhonghua Shuju 中华书局.

Wang, Robin R. (ed.). (2003). *Images of Women in Chinese Thought and Culture*. Indianapolis: Hackett.

Wang, Su 王肃 (ed.). (1990). *Sayings of Confucius's School* 孔子家语. Shanghai: Shanghai Guji 上海古籍.

Wang, Yangming 王阳明. (1992). *The Complete Works of Wang Yangming* 王阳明全集. Shanghai: Shanghai Guji 上海古籍.

Warren, Mark E., and Hilary Pearse (eds.). (2008). *Designing Deliberative Democracy: The British Columbia Citizens' Assembly*. Cambridge: Cambridge University Press.

Watson, Burton (trans.). (1964). *Han Fei Tzu: Basic Writings*. New York: Columbia University Press.

West, Thomas G., and Grace Starry West. (1984). *Four Texts on Socrates*. Ithaca, NY: Cornell University Press.

Winston, Kenneth. (2011). "Advisors to Rulers: Serving the State and the Way." In Alford et al. (eds.) 2011, 225–54.

Wilkinson, Steven I. (2005). *Votes and Violence: Electoral Competition and Ethnic Riots in India*. Cambridge: Cambridge University Press.

Wong, Bin. (1997). *China Transformed: Historical Change and the Limits of European Experience*. Ithaca, NY: Cornell University Press.

Wrangham, Richard. (2004). "Killer Species." *Daedalus*, Fall 2004, 25–35.

Xu, Xin. (2003). *The Jews of Kaifeng, China*. Jersey City: KTAV.

Yang, Bojun 杨伯峻. (1960). *Translations and Commentaries of the "Mencius"* 孟子译注. Beijing: Zhonghua Shuju 中华书局.

———. (1980). *Translations and Commentaries of the "Analects"* 论语译注. 2nd ed. Beijing: Zhonghua Shuju 中华书局.

Yang, Zhiyi 杨治宜. "A Beautiful House on Quicksand: Liu Yazi and the Cultural Nationalism of Nanshe" 流沙上的绮楼: 柳亚子与南社的文化民族主义. Manuscript.

Young, Michael. (1958). *The Rise of Meritocracy*. London: Thames and Hudson.

Yu, Ying-shih 余英时. (2004). *The Historical World of Zhu Xi* 朱熹的历史世界. Beijing: Sanlian Shudian 三联书店.

Zakaria, Fareed. (2003). *The Future of Freedom: Illiberal Democracy at Home and Abroad.* New York: W. W. Norton.

Zeng, Zhenyu 曾振宇. (2013). *The Conceptual System of the World of Thought* 思想世界的概念系统. Beijing: People's Press 人民出版社.

Zhang, Hao (aka Chang, Hao 张灏). (2010). *The Dark Consciousness and Democratic Tradition* 幽暗意识与民主传统. 2nd ed. Beijing: Xin Xing Press 新星出版社.

Zhang, Taiyan 章太炎. (1986). *The Complete Works of Zhang Taiyan.* Vol. 6 章太炎全集(六). Shanghai: Shanghai People's Press 上海人民出版社.

Zhang, Zai 张载. (1978). *The Collected Works of Zhang Zai* 张载集. Beijing: Zhonghua Shuju 中华书局.

Zhao, Tingyang 赵汀阳. (2007a). "One's Own and Not One's Own: An Unsolved Problem in Confucianism" 身与身外: 儒家的一个未决问题. *Renmin University Journal* 中国人民大学学报, no. 1:15–21.

———. (2007b). "The Ethical Turn of Confucian Politics" 儒家政治的伦理学转向. *Social Sciences in China* 中国社会科学(内刊版) no. 4:146–51.

Zheng, Jiadong 郑家栋. (2001). "The Issue of 'Legitimacy' of 'Chinese Philosophy.'" "中国哲学"的 "合法性" 问题. Originally in *Shiji Zhongguo* 世纪中国. http://www.confucius2000.com/poetry/zgzxdhfxwt.htm.

———. (2004). "The Modern Predicament of Writing 'the History of Chinese Philosophy' and the Tradition of Chinese Thought." 中国哲学史 写作与中国思想传统的现代困境. *Renmin University Journal* 中国人民大学学报, no. 3:2–11.

Zhou, Lian 周濂. (2007). "Political Society, Pluralistic Community, and the Life of Happiness." 政治社会, 多元共同体与幸福生活. Proceedings of the 12th Annual Meeting of Chinese Phenomenology Society at Zhejiang University 浙江大学"第12届中国现象学年会"发表论文.

———. (2008a). "The Most Desirable and the Most Relevant: How to Do Political Philosophy in the Contemporary Context." 最可欲的与最相关的——今日语境下 如何做政治哲学. In *Thought* 思想, 8:237–53. Taiwan: Lianjing Press 联经出版社.

———. (2008b). "What Do We Owe Each Other? On the Theoretical Limit of Moral Philosophy." 我们彼此亏欠什么: 兼论道德哲学的理论限度. *World Philosophy* 世界哲学, no. 2 (March): 3–13.

———. (2011). "The 'Thinness' of Liberal Nationalism and the 'Weakness' of Confucian Nationalism." 自由民族主义之'薄'与儒家民族主义之'弱'. *Beijing Cultural Review* 文化纵横 (October): 97–102.

Zhu, Xi 朱熹. (1985). *Collected Commentaries on the "Mencius"* 孟子章句集注. In *Four Books and Five Canons* 四书五经. 2nd ed. Beijing: Zhongguo Shudian 中国书店.

———. (2001). *Inquiries on the Four Books* 四书或问. Shanghai: Shanghai Guji 上海古籍.

INDEX

Ackerman, Bruce, and James Fishkin, 56, 56n11; Deliberation Day proposed by, 62

Ames, Roger T., and Henry Rosemont Jr., 266

Analects: aphoristic and brief style of, 11, 146; on the continuity between the public and the private, 141; educability distinguished from equality in, 33; familial love related to moral expansion in, 127; inadequate resolution of conflicts in, 147, 147n13; mutual concealment case discussed in book **13.18**, 128n27, 141–45, 142n4, 150, 152; on service to the people as a priority, 36–37, 289–90n12; and the threat from the private to the public, 165; wisdom equated with serving the good of the people (humanity, ren [仁]) in, 161n30; and *zheng ming* (正名) "making the name right," 46, 127

— books of: **1.2**, 127; **1.9**, 131; **2.3**, 144; **2.4**, 16n20; **3.3**, 112; **3.7**, 269; **3.19**, 128n27; **4.18**, 144; **6.21**, 46; **6.30**, 136; **7.7**, 33, 269; **7.14**, 269; **7.27**, 269; **8.9**, 46; **8.14**, 46, 265–66; **9.14**, 7; **10.9**, 269; **10.17**, 269; **12.5**, 127; **12.9**, 36; **12.11**, 46, 127, 128n27; **13.3**, 46, 112; **13.15**, 265; **13.16**, 179; **13.18**, 128n27, 141–45, 142n4, 150, 152; **13.24**, 47; **14.7**, 265; **14.21**, 236n28; **14.26**, 46, 266; **14.34**, 11, 277n35; **15.28**, 36n6, 40n16, 46–47; **16.1**, 179, 215, 216, 265; **17.2**, 46; **17.3**, 46; **17.5**, 215; **17.21**, 11, 66, 111; **18.06**, 115

Angle, Stephen, 14n17, 17n21, 19n23, 170, 279n36; on the compatibility of liberal democracy and Confucianism, 243–44

argumentation sketches: advantages of, 11–12; and elucidation and systematization efforts, 16–19, 16n20; and the problem of speaking about the unspeakable, 12; and the scattered and unsystematic appearance of traditional Chinese philosophical writing, 9–12, 12n15

Aristotle, 126n23; ethical system of, 117–18, 117n10; his notion of democracy compared with the Confucian hybrid regime, 100, 100n24

Arrighi, Giovanni, 196–97

Arrow, Kenneth, 65

Beetham, David, 51n24

Bell, Daniel, 53n2, 54, 55n9, 66, 74n34, 79n40, 84n1, 210n49, 245, 279n36; on the compatibility of liberal democracy and Confucianism, 243; on the ideal Confucian unified world, 238; on ideas of a just war in the *Analects* and in the *Mencius*, 214n1; on *ke ju* (科举, public service examinations) for selecting representatives, 73–74, 74n32; model of the Confucian ideal regime proposed by, 82n45; on the symbolic ritual of free and fair competitive elections, 85–86

Bentham, Jeremy, 34, 271–72

Berthrong, John, 122n19

Bloom, Allan, 155, 156

Bohr, Niels, 248

Book of Odes (诗经), xii, 5–6

British Columbia, 91–92

Brooks, David, 37

Neo-Confucianism; overseas New
Confucians
Confucius: and the chaotic times he lived
in, 147–48, 217, 266; criticism of Guanzhong (管仲) and Duke Huan of Qi
(齐桓公) by, 147n13; feudalism during
his lifetime, 217, 236n28, 266; on his character at different ages, 16n20; ideas of animal treatment compared with Mencius's,
269–71; and Pre-Qin notions of equality,
33; Xun Zi and Mencius compared with,
33–34n1. See also *Analects*
continuum and harmony model. *See* private
and public relations—continuum and
harmony model of
cosmopolitan models: and communism,
204–5; the Confucian new tian xia model
compared with, xvi, xviii, 191, 201–3, 206;
and the nation-state, 192–93; and the no-
identity model, 198–99, 201, 203; and notions that human rights override sovereignty, 2, 203–4, 230; and the thin-
identity model, 198–200
Creel, Herrlee G., 27
criminal deeds, and Mencius on the need
for economic stability, 36, 36n7
criteria of the just war of liberation. *See* justification of wars of invasion; Mencius's
criteria of the just war of liberation

Descartes, René, on language and reason as
distinct features of human beings, 271
De Waal, Frans, 114n5, 246n5
Dong Zhongshu (董仲舒), 126–27n25, 178
Donnelly, Jack, 193
Downs, Anthony, 65
Dreben, Burton, xix, 28–29n38, 107–8n41

education: Confucian advocacy of education for all, 33–35, 47–50, 125n22, 187, 282;
and the Confucian hybrid regime, 84–85,
89; and the participation of informed citizens in contemporary democracies, 58,
60–62, 68–69, 70, 256; and the produc-

tion of white-collar professionals with
narrow specializations, 46, 63. See also
jun zi (君子, Confucian exemplary persons); *ke ju* (科举) system; sixth fact of
democracy (capacity to make sound
judgment on political matters)
electoral reforms, 91–92
Elliot, Mark, 211n50, 211–12n52
Elman, Benjamin, 74, 76n37, 86n4
Elstein, David, 56n11, 89n9, 102n27, 103n28,
109n42
ethnic problems: burka ban in France, 211;
and the distinction between civilized
(*xia* [夏]) and barbaric (*yi* [夷]), 7, 7n8,
180–84; ethnic conflicts and separatist
movements in China, 198, 207–13; and
the inadequacy of the democratic model,
52, 52–53n2; the nation-state model as a
root cause of, 1–2, 193–94, 207–8; the tian
xia model of state identity as a solution
to, xvi–xvii, 180–81, 213; Tibetan and Uighur problems in China, 198, 207–11; and
violence in newly democratized countries, 1, 55–56
exemplary persons. See *jun zi* (君子, Confucian exemplary persons)

facts of modern democracy. *See* Rawls,
John: facts of democratic society; sixth
fact of democracy
Fang Xudong (方旭东), 237n29, 237n31
Fei Xiaotong (费孝通), 123, 125n22
Feng Youlan (aka Fung, Yu-lan [冯友兰]):
distinction between faithful reading (照
着讲) and continuous reading (接着讲)
introduced by, 5–6; and the elucidation
and systematization approach to Chinese
classics, 17; philosophy defined as systematic reflection by, 10n12; and reconstruction of argumentation as an approach to Chinese classics, 17; on the
scattered and unsystematic appearance
of traditional Chinese philosophical
writing, 12n15, 13

liberal democracy: and arguments against perfectionism, 169–70; as the end of history in terms of political models, 26, 28, 52; institutions to assure its success proposed by Rawls, 61–62. *See also* one person, one vote; United States
— and Confucianism: compatibility with, 244–45; Confucian criticism of its defense of state neutrality, 169, 170–71; and Rawls's later philosophy, xiii, xix; and the tian xia (天下) model's ideal of universal but unequal care, xviii. *See also* Chan, Joseph: on the compatibility of liberal democracy and Confucianism

Lin Mingzhao (林明照), 28n38

Liu Qing (刘擎), 206nn41–42

Liu Wei (刘玮), 117n9, 117n11, 157n26

Lo Ping Cheung, 231n18

Locke, John, 39, 41, 43n18

Loy, Hui-chieh, 139n1, 159n28

Macedo, Stephen, 94, 98

Mann, Michael, 53n2

Mansbridge, Jane, 77n39; on state coercions, 262, 262n19

Mao Zedong and Maoism: and attitudes toward Chinese thought and traditional institutions, 6, 123–24, 279; ethnic conflicts and separatist movements in China traced to his policies, 208; hostility of Maoist Leftists to Confucian conservatives, 253–54; and people's interest or the "common good" under the communist regime, 167; and the upheaval of traditional Chinese society, 123–24

masses, the: education of (*see* education); terms used for, 39, 39–40n16. *See also* mass participation

mass participation: as a check on abuse by the aristocracy, 88; and the Confucian hybrid regime, 85–86, 90, 90n12; and Confucius's warning that the masses are uneducable, 46; and the need for education, 48–49; psychological satisfaction of, 85–86, 85–86n4

May Fourth movements, 142, 241, 256

Mencius: and the adaptability of his theories to a "modern" world, 32; bond for the society of strangers developed by, 123–25; championing of Yao and Shun by, 33–34, 33–34n1, 38, 144–46, 146–47n11, 178; and the concept of compassion, 33, 112–15, 112n4, 114n5; Confucius's writing style compared with, 147–48; and Duke Wen of Teng, 221–22, 221n7; "five hegemons" (*wu ba* [五霸]) condemned by, 69n26; and government for the people, 39–41, 44–46; ideals of, compared with Confucius and Xun Zi's, 33–34n1; ideas of animal treatment compared with Confucius's, 269–71; and King Hui of the state of Wei, 218–19; and King Xuan of the state of Qi, 40, 122, 136, 219, 224, 226, 270; and the original goodness of human beings, 114n6; on the social and political costs of egalitarianism, 104, 104n29
— on basic moral virtues: and care-based neofeudal order, 134–35; and compassion, 112–13; and education, 49; and the role of government, 34–36, 35n4, 267–68; and social relations, 35; and stable ownership of property, 34–36, 126

Mencius's criteria of the just war of liberation: and the connection between humane governance and the strength of the state, 217–23; and patriotism, 179, 226–29, 229n16, 235–36; and the Responsibility to Protect (R2P), 232–34, 236; thick vs. thin criteria for, 237–38

Mencius: Chen Liang as an interlocutor with Mencius in, 103, 181; on the difference between a sage and a common person, 33; familial love related to moral expansion in, 127; on graded and hierarchical care (爱有差等), 133–34; on humane governance and moral persuasion, 280; on humane governance and patriotism, 178–79; and justification of wars of invasion (*see* Mencius's criteria of the just war of liberation); on Shun's steadfast

A NOTE ON THE TYPE

This book has been composed in Arno, an Old-style serif typeface in the
classic Venetian tradition, designed by Robert Slimbach at Adobe.